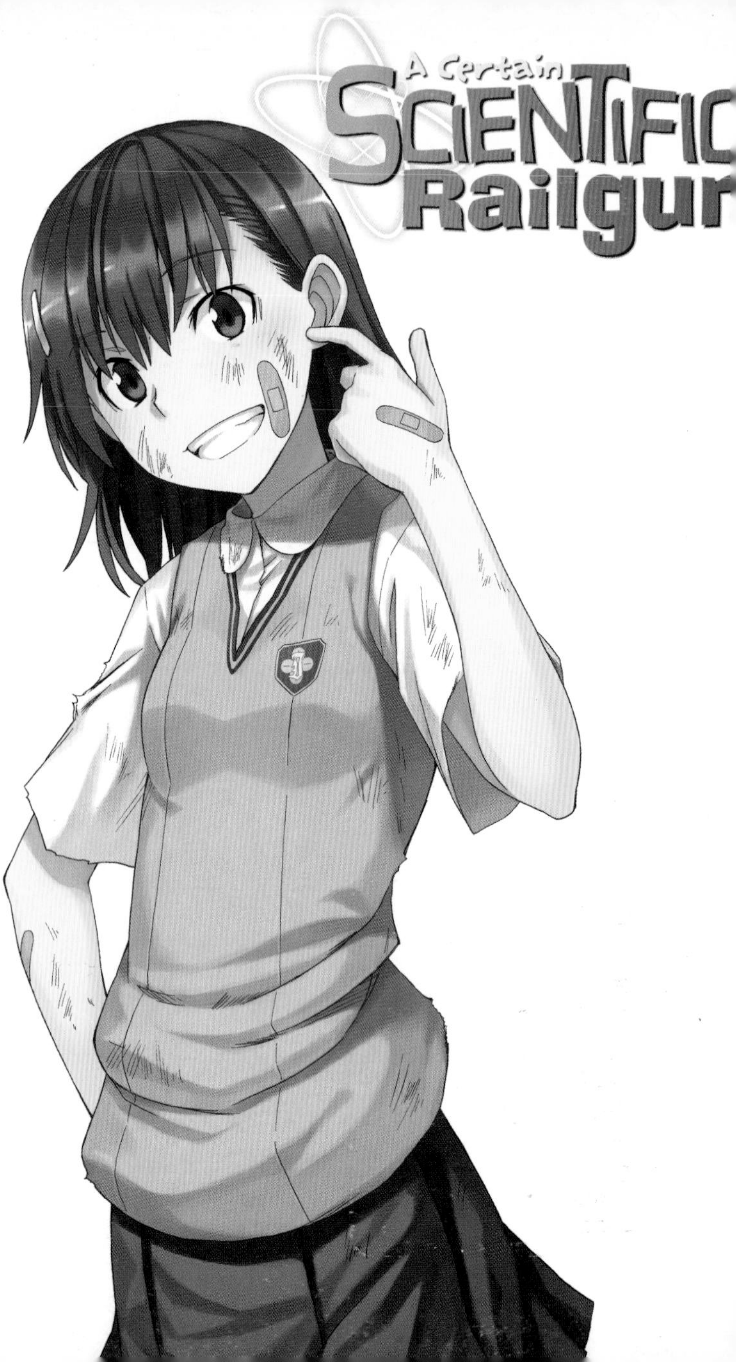
A Certain
SCIENTIFIC
Railgu

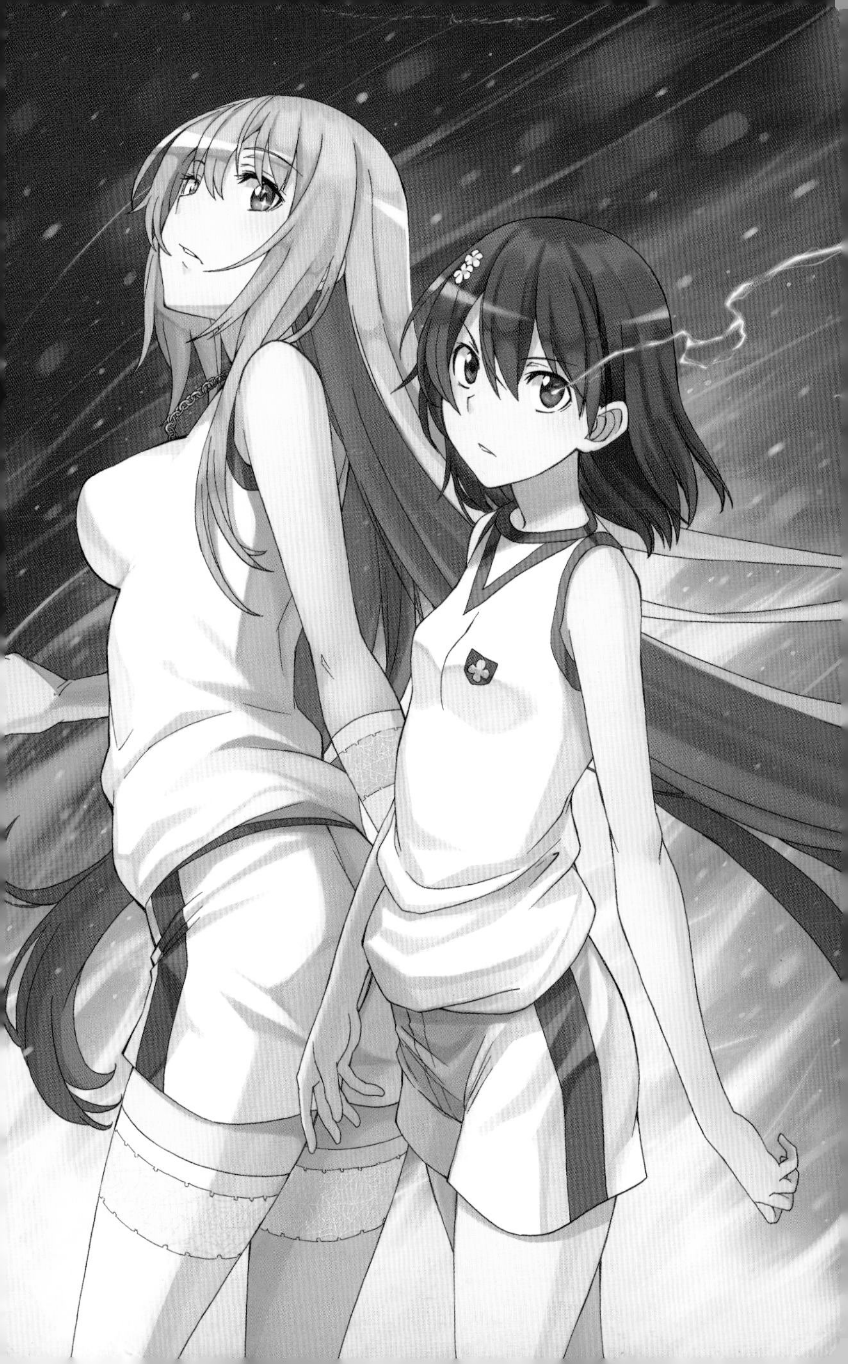

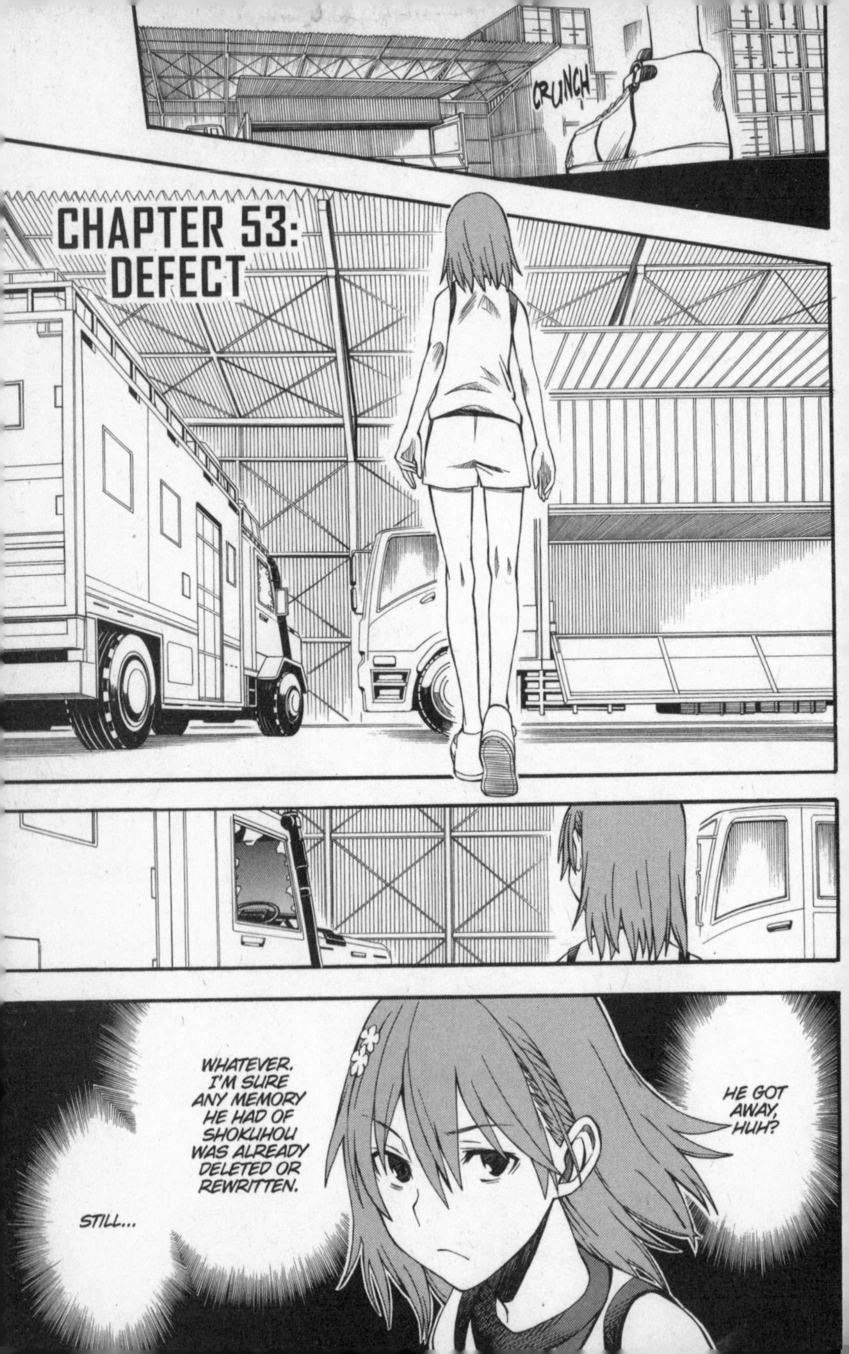
CRUNCH
CHAPTER 53: DEFECT
HE GOT AWAY, HUH?
WHATEVER. I'M SURE ANY MEMORY HE HAD OF SHOKUHOU WAS ALREADY DELETED OR REWRITTEN.
STILL...

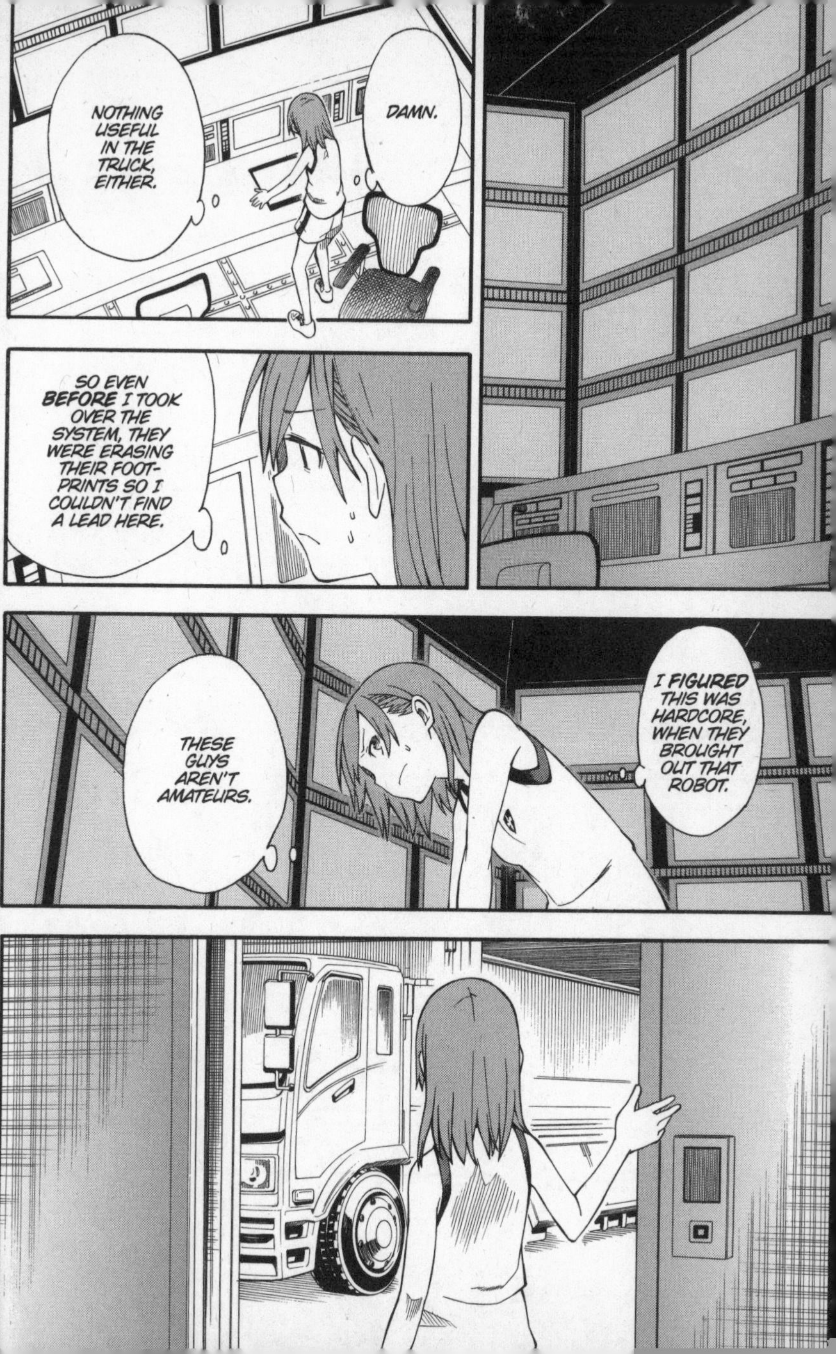
DAMN.
NOTHING USEFUL IN THE TRUCK, EITHER.
SO EVEN BEFORE I TOOK OVER THE SYSTEM, THEY WERE ERASING THEIR FOOT-PRINTS SO I COULDN'T FIND A LEAD HERE.
I FIGURED THIS WAS HARDCORE, WHEN THEY BROUGHT OUT THAT ROBOT.
THESE GUYS AREN'T AMATEURS.

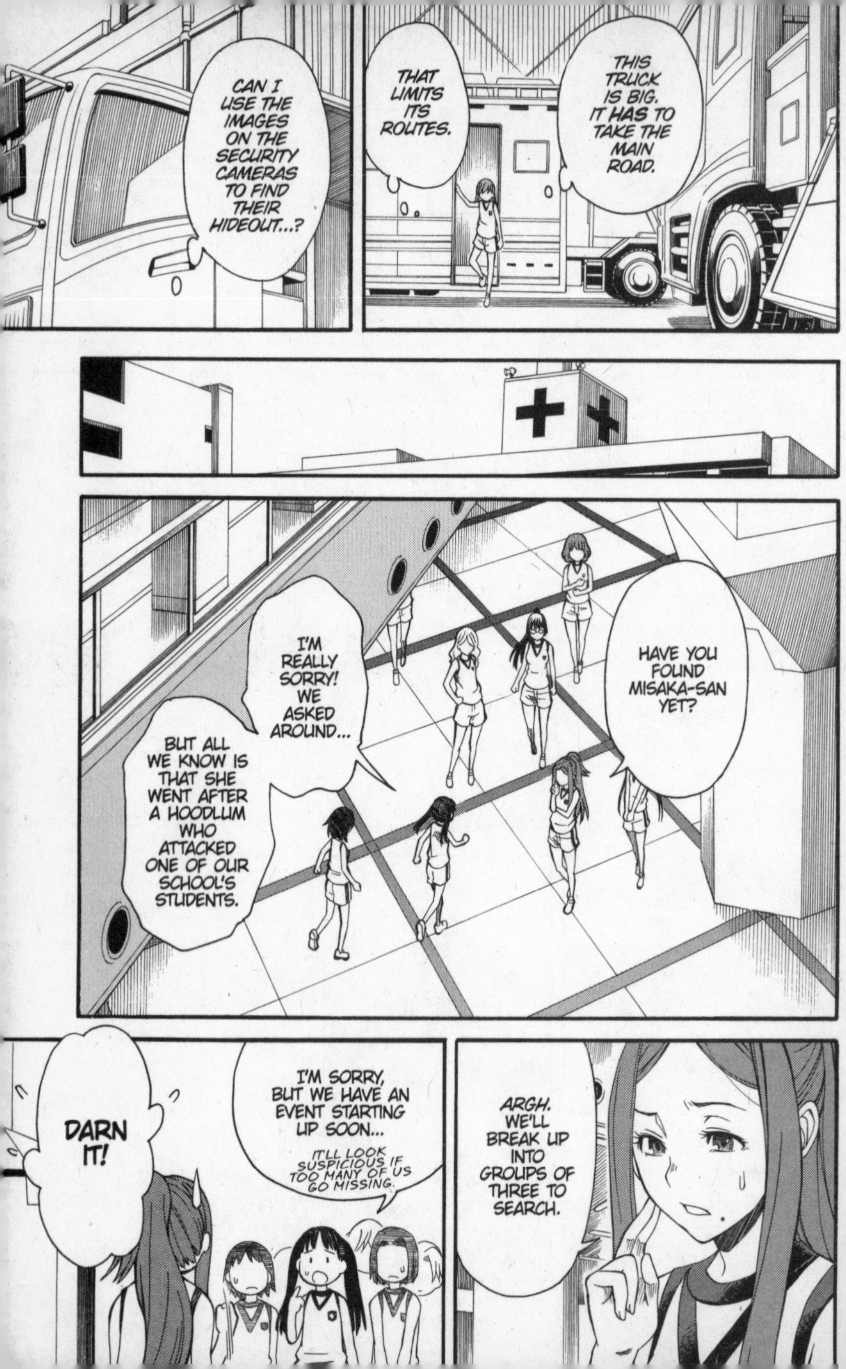
THIS TRUCK IS BIG. IT HAS TO TAKE THE MAIN ROAD.
THAT LIMITS ITS ROUTES.
CAN I USE THE IMAGES ON THE SECURITY CAMERAS TO FIND THEIR HIDEOUT...?
HAVE YOU FOUND MISAKA-SAN YET?
I'M REALLY SORRY! WE ASKED AROUND...
BUT ALL WE KNOW IS THAT SHE WENT AFTER A HOODLUM WHO ATTACKED ONE OF OUR SCHOOL'S STUDENTS.
ARGH. WE'LL BREAK UP INTO GROUPS OF THREE TO SEARCH.
I'M SORRY, BUT WE HAVE AN EVENT STARTING UP SOON...
IT'LL LOOK SUSPICIOUS IF TOO MANY OF US GO MISSING.
DARN IT!

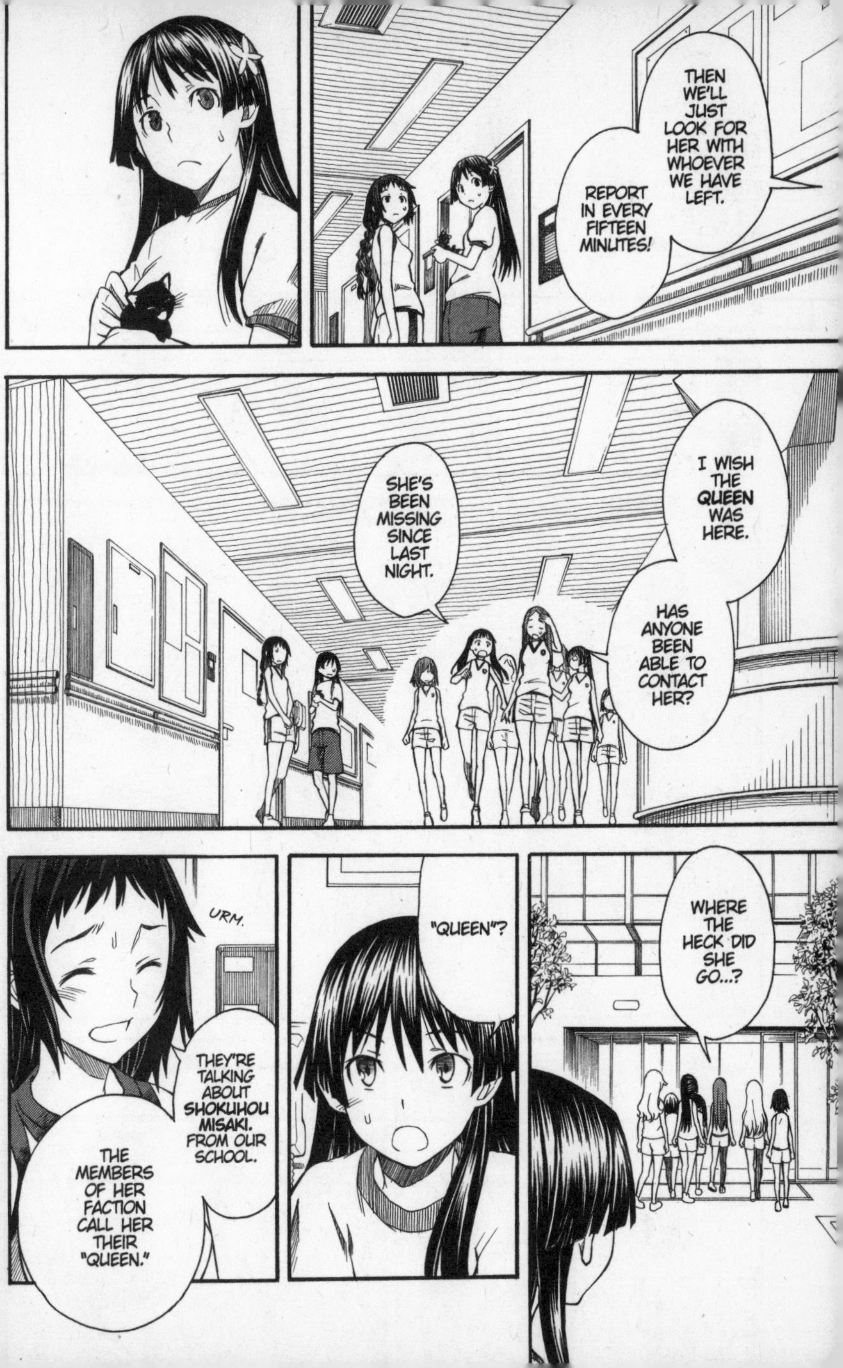
THEN WE'LL JUST LOOK FOR HER WITH WHOEVER WE HAVE LEFT.
REPORT IN EVERY FIFTEEN MINUTES!
I WISH THE QUEEN WAS HERE.
HAS ANYONE BEEN ABLE TO CONTACT HER?
SHE'S BEEN MISSING SINCE LAST NIGHT.
WHERE THE HECK DID SHE GO...?
"QUEEN"?
URM.
THEY'RE TALKING ABOUT SHOKUHOU MISAKI. FROM OUR SCHOOL.
THE MEMBERS OF HER FACTION CALL HER THEIR "QUEEN."

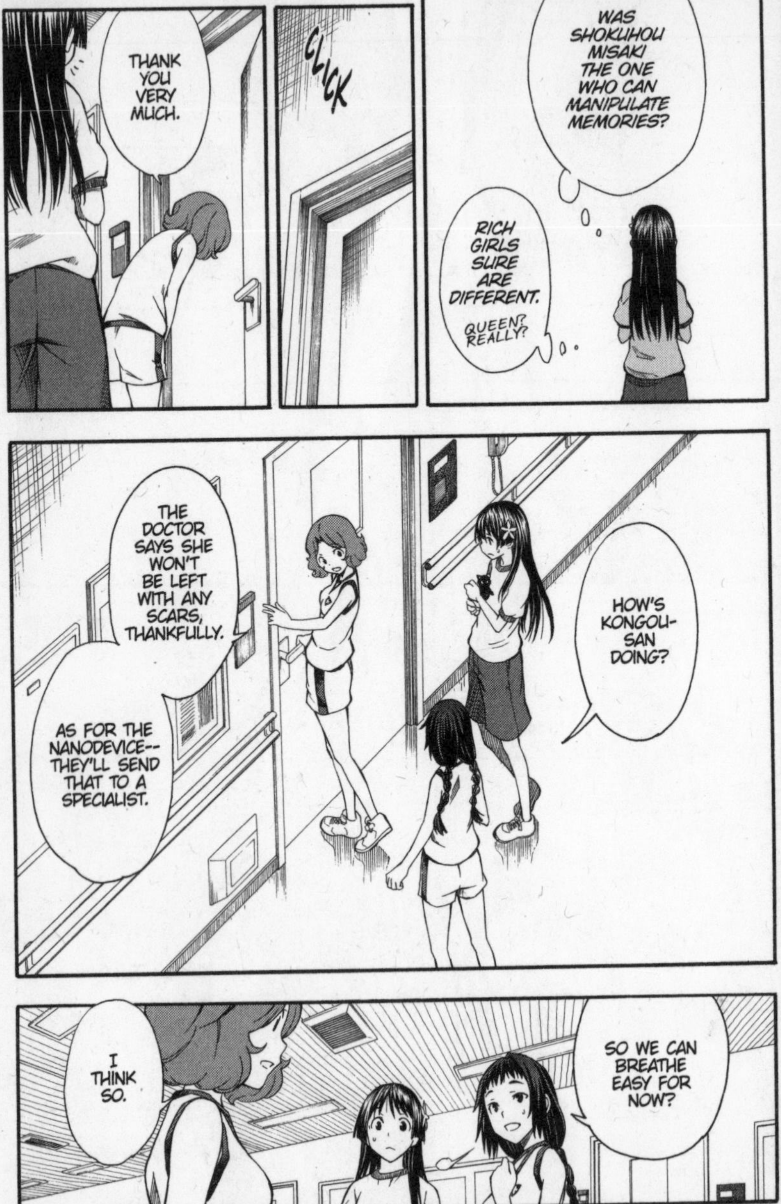
WAS SHOKUHOU MISAKI THE ONE WHO CAN MANIPULATE MEMORIES?
RICH GIRLS SURE ARE DIFFERENT.
QUEEN? REALLY?
CLICK
THANK YOU VERY MUCH.
HOW'S KONGOU-SAN DOING?
THE DOCTOR SAYS SHE WON'T BE LEFT WITH ANY SCARS, THANKFULLY.
AS FOR THE NANODEVICE-- THEY'LL SEND THAT TO A SPECIALIST.
SO WE CAN BREATHE EASY FOR NOW?
I THINK SO.

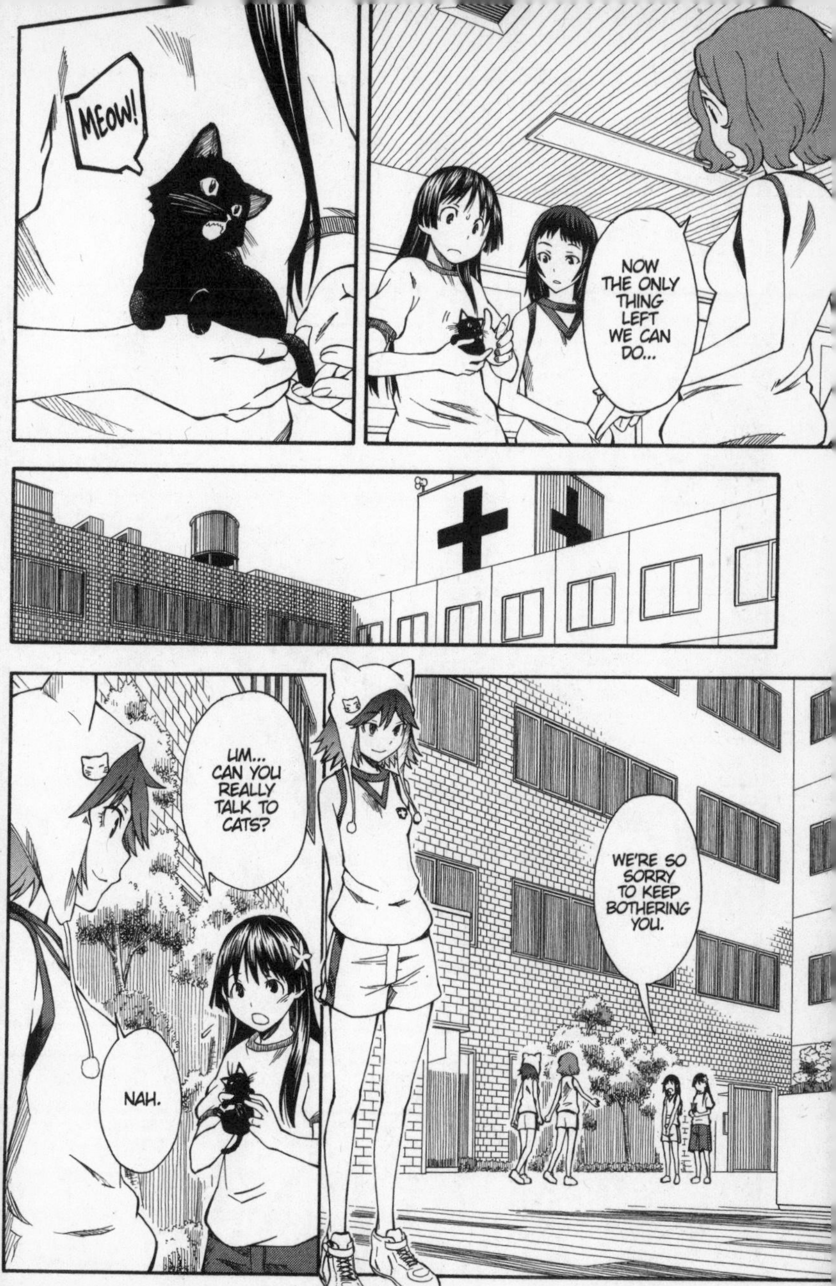
NOW THE ONLY THING LEFT WE CAN DO...
MEOW!
WE'RE SO SORRY TO KEEP BOTHERING YOU.
UM... CAN YOU REALLY TALK TO CATS?
NAH.

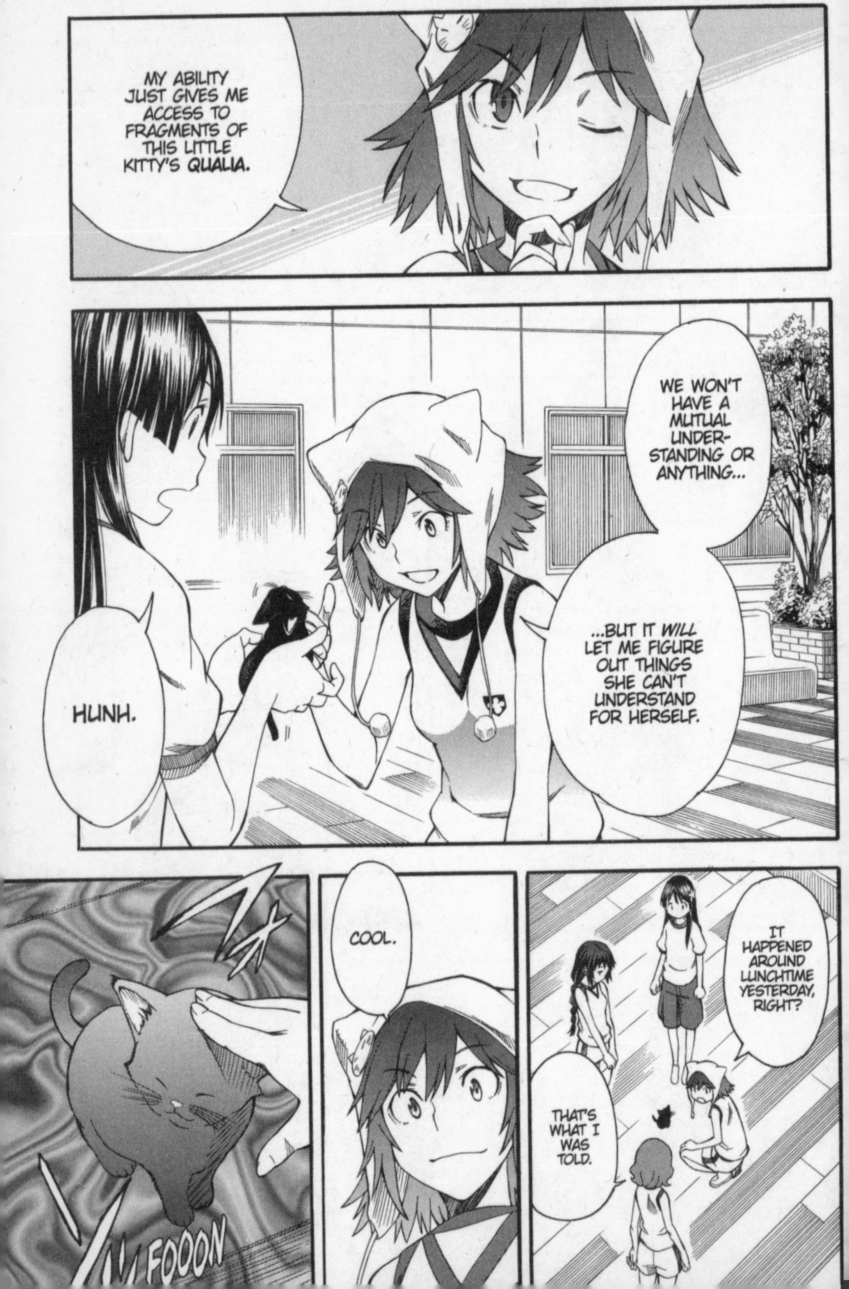
MY ABILITY JUST GIVES ME ACCESS TO FRAGMENTS OF THIS LITTLE KITTY'S QUALIA.
WE WON'T HAVE A MUTUAL UNDER-STANDING OR ANYTHING...
...BUT IT WILL LET ME FIGURE OUT THINGS SHE CAN'T UNDERSTAND FOR HERSELF.
HUNH.
FOOON
COOL.
IT HAPPENED AROUND LUNCHTIME YESTERDAY, RIGHT?
THAT'S WHAT I WAS TOLD.

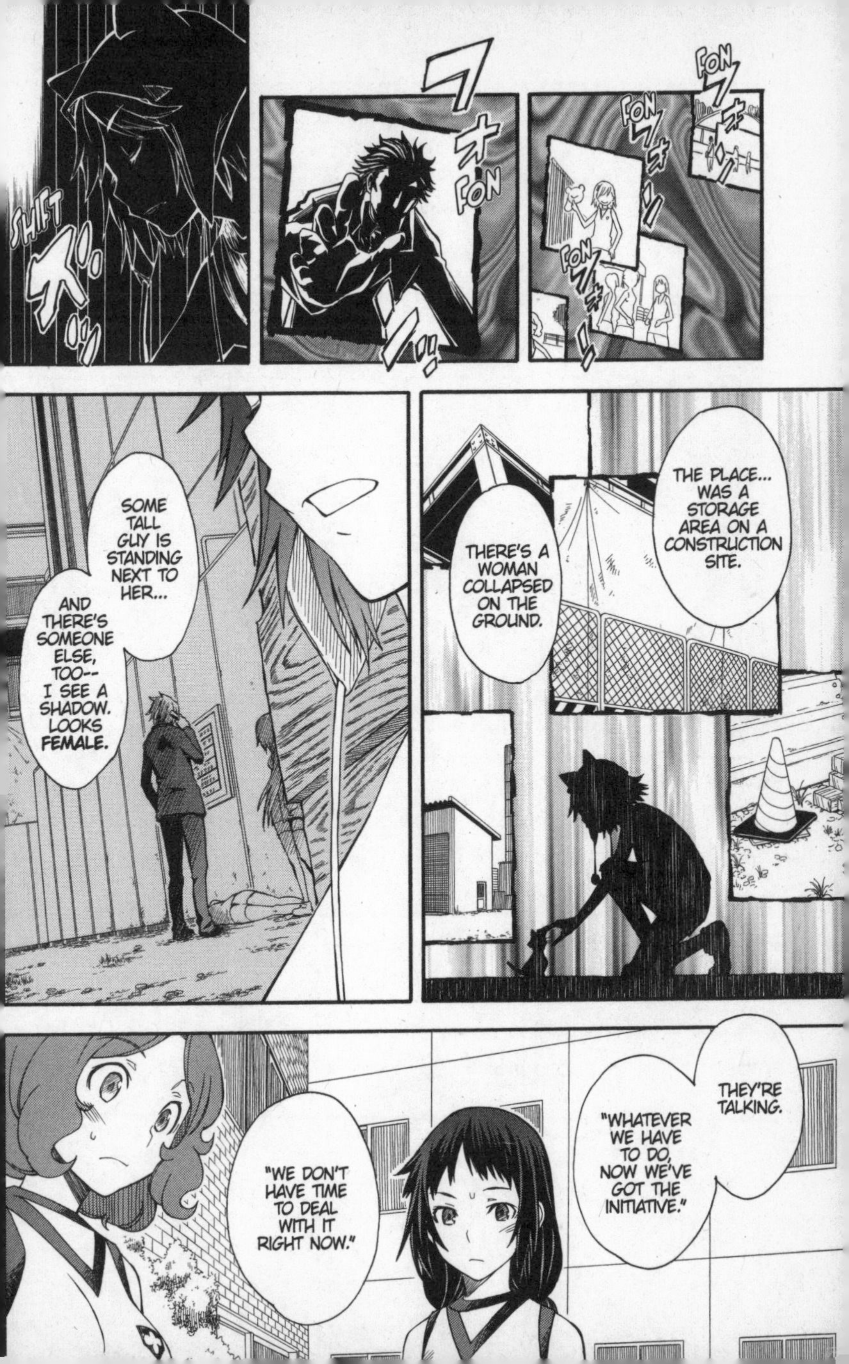
FON
FON
FON
FON
SHIFT
THE PLACE... WAS A STORAGE AREA ON A CONSTRUCTION SITE.
THERE'S A WOMAN COLLAPSED ON THE GROUND.
SOME TALL GUY IS STANDING NEXT TO HER...
AND THERE'S SOMEONE ELSE, TOO-- I SEE A SHADOW. LOOKS FEMALE.
THEY'RE TALKING.
"WHATEVER WE HAVE TO DO, NOW WE'VE GOT THE INITIATIVE."
"WE DON'T HAVE TIME TO DEAL WITH IT RIGHT NOW."

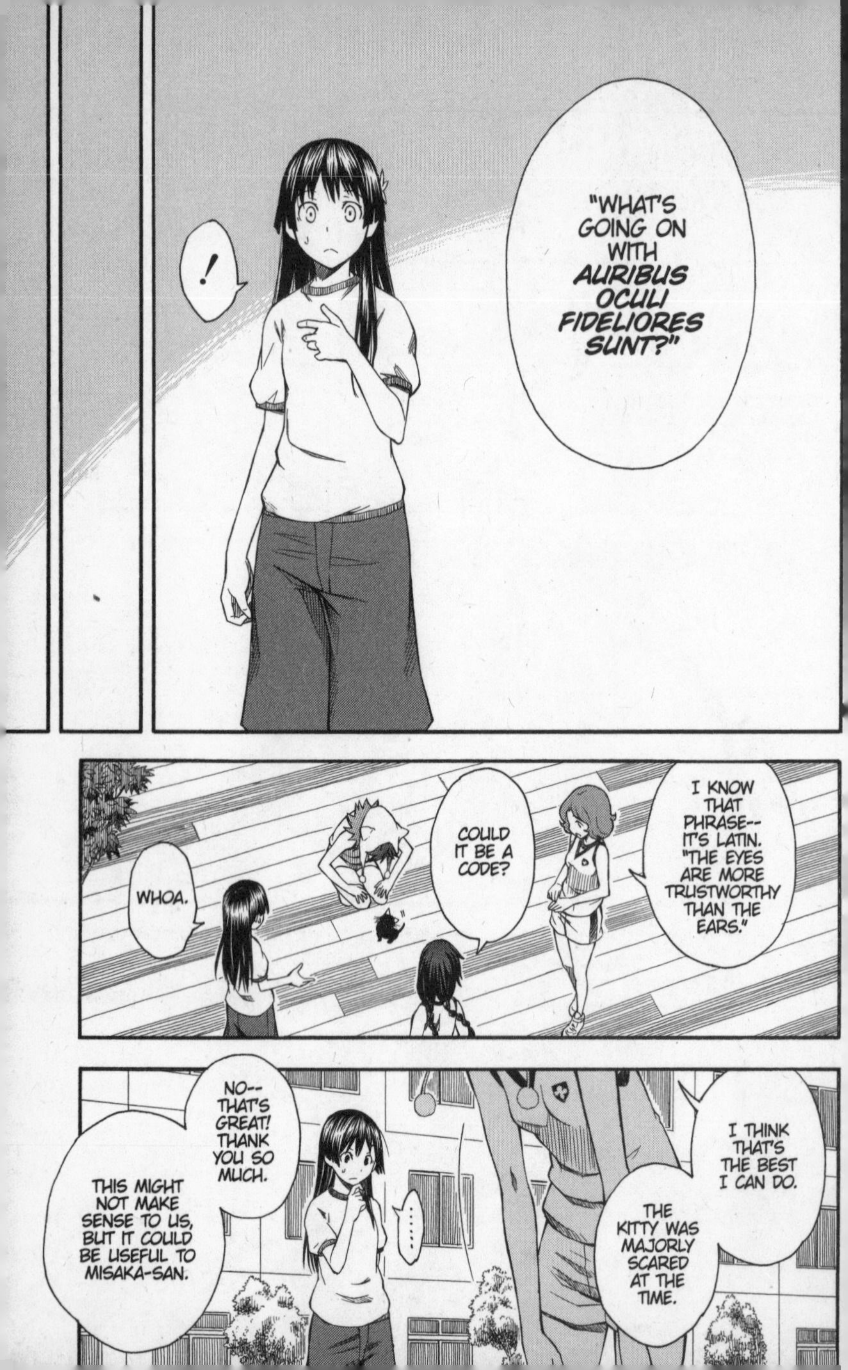
"WHAT'S GOING ON WITH AURIBUS OCULI FIDELIORES SUNT?"
!
I KNOW THAT PHRASE-- IT'S LATIN. "THE EYES ARE MORE TRUSTWORTHY THAN THE EARS."
COULD IT BE A CODE?
WHOA.
I THINK THAT'S THE BEST I CAN DO.
THE KITTY WAS MAJORLY SCARED AT THE TIME.
......
NO-- THAT'S GREAT! THANK YOU SO MUCH.
THIS MIGHT NOT MAKE SENSE TO US, BUT IT COULD BE USEFUL TO MISAKA-SAN.

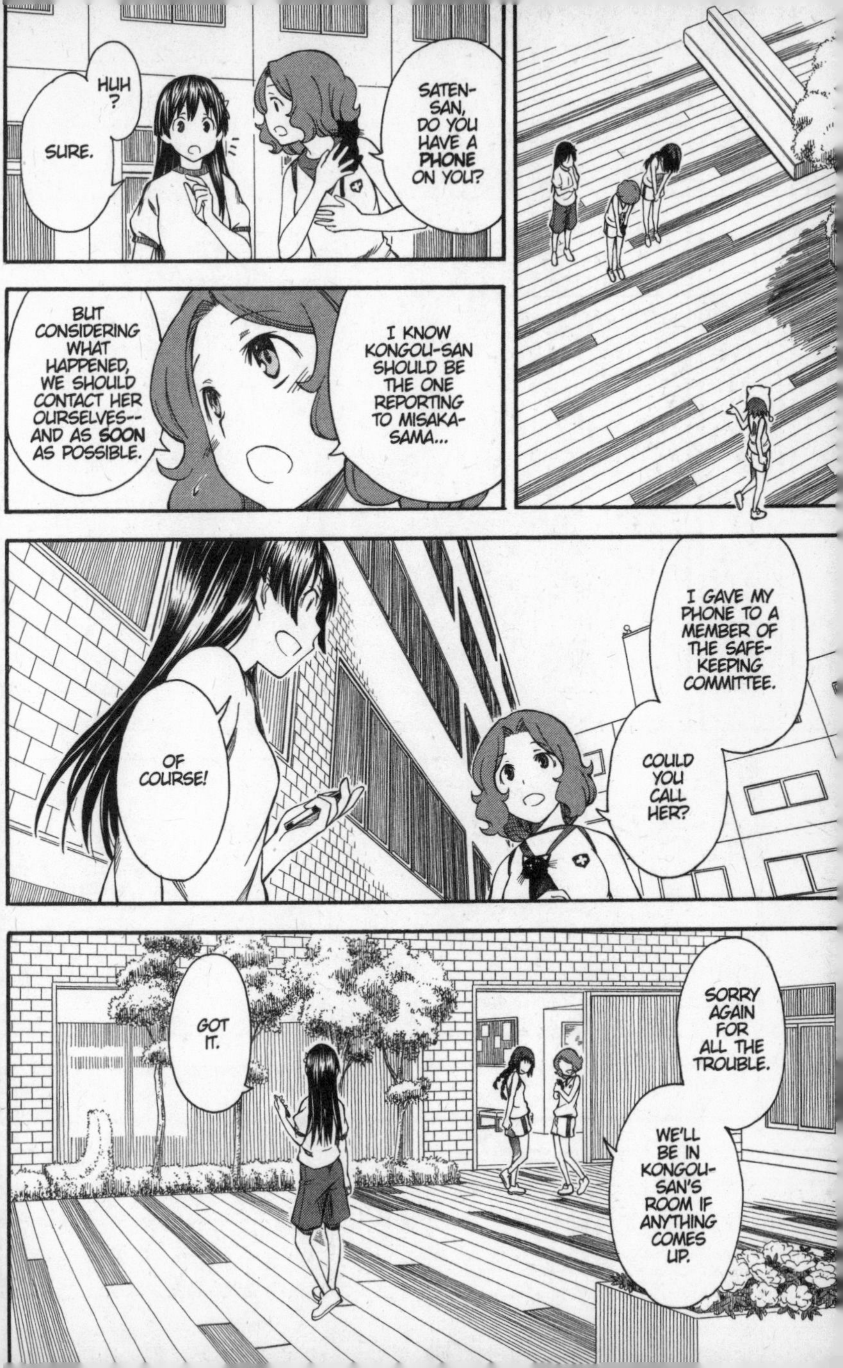
SATEN-SAN, DO YOU HAVE A PHONE ON YOU?
HUH? SURE.
I KNOW KONGOU-SAN SHOULD BE THE ONE REPORTING TO MISAKA-SAMA...
BUT CONSIDERING WHAT HAPPENED, WE SHOULD CONTACT HER OURSELVES--AND AS SOON AS POSSIBLE.
I GAVE MY PHONE TO A MEMBER OF THE SAFE-KEEPING COMMITTEE.
COULD YOU CALL HER?
OF COURSE!
SORRY AGAIN FOR ALL THE TROUBLE.
WE'LL BE IN KONGOU-SAN'S ROOM IF ANYTHING COMES UP.
GOT IT.

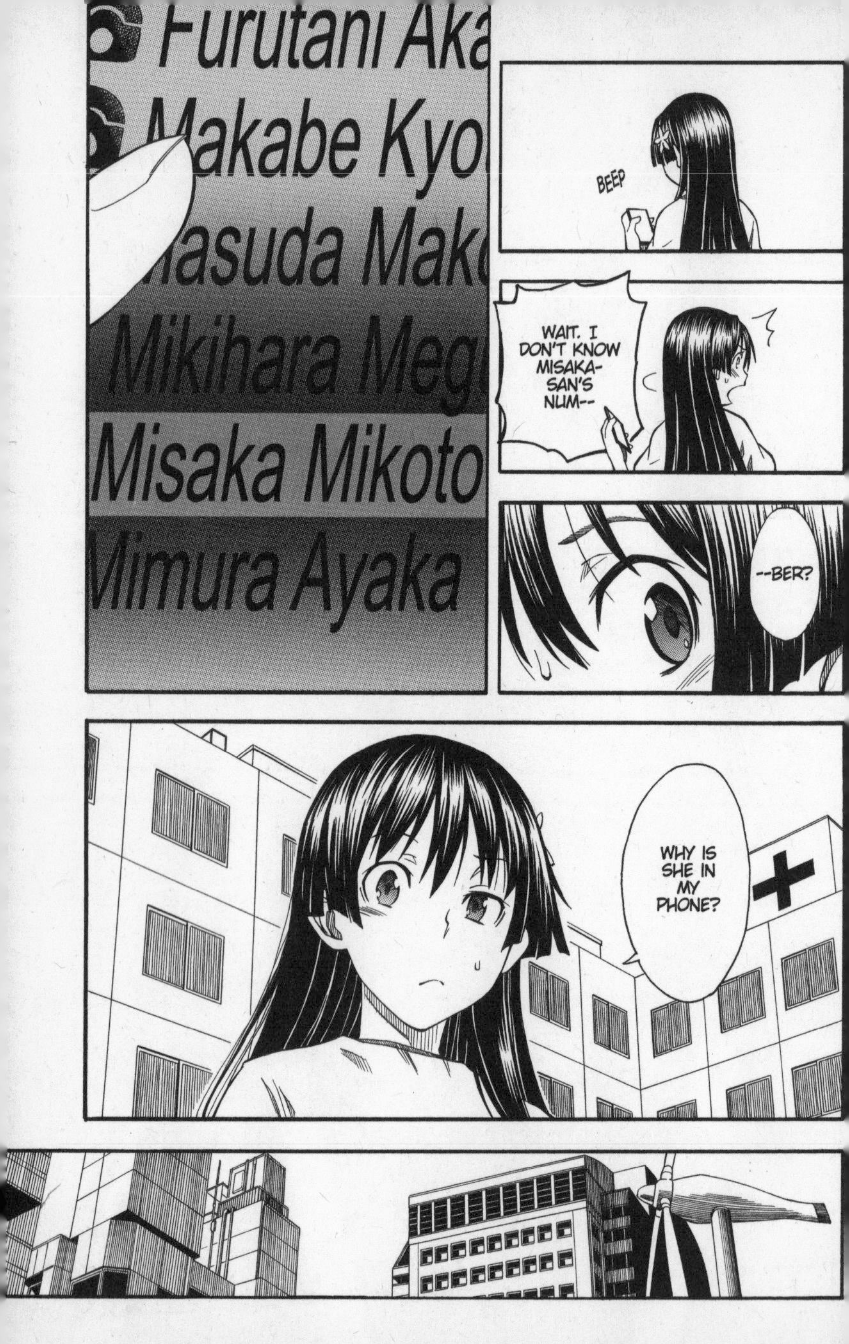
BEEP
WAIT. I DON'T KNOW MISAKA-SAN'S NUM--
--BER?
Furutani Aka
Makabe Kyo
Masuda Mak
Mikihara Meg
Misaka Mikoto
Mimura Ayaka
WHY IS SHE IN MY PHONE?

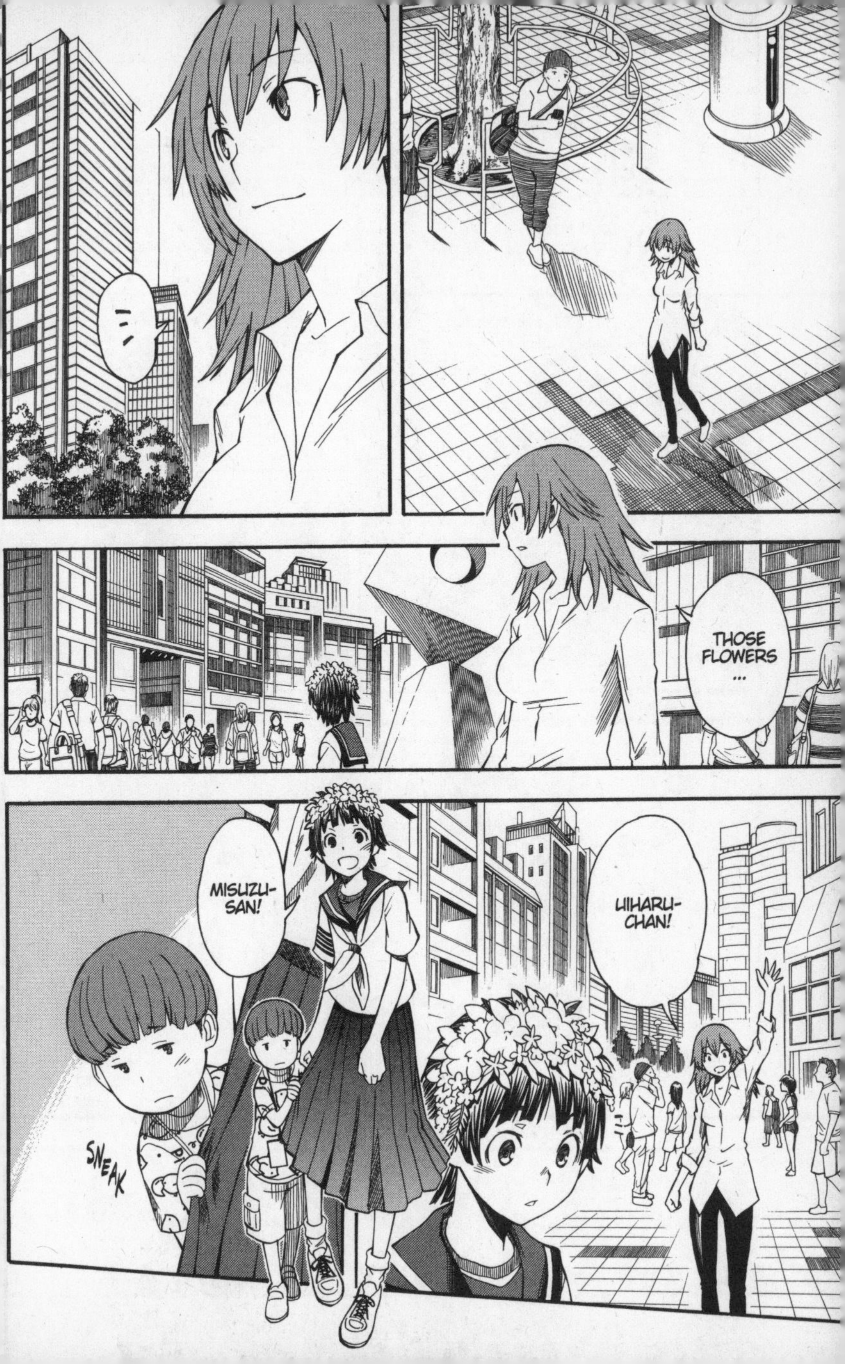
…
THOSE FLOWERS …
UIHARU-CHAN!
MISUZU-SAN!
SNEAK

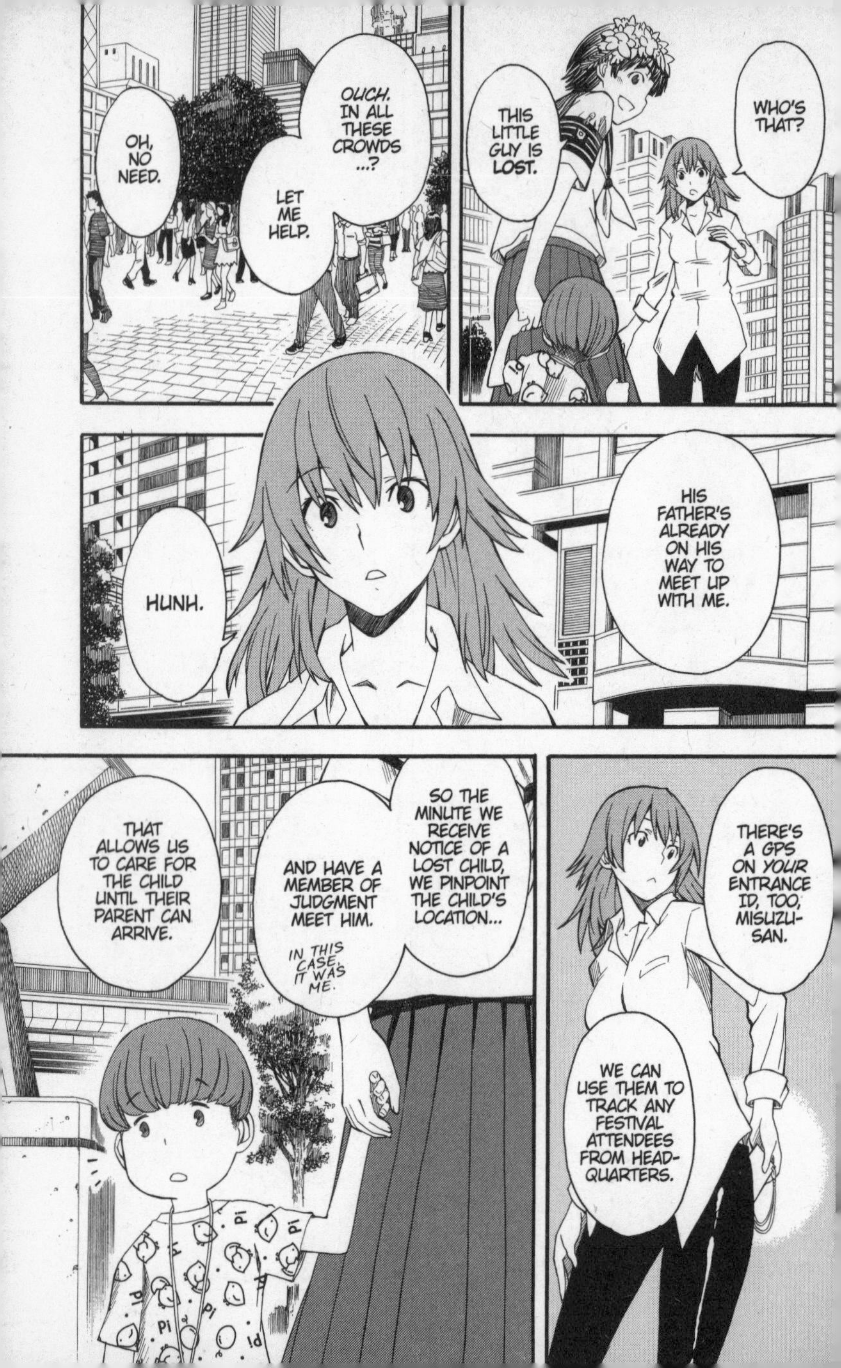
WHO'S THAT?
THIS LITTLE GUY IS LOST.
OUCH. IN ALL THESE CROWDS ...?
LET ME HELP.
OH, NO NEED.
HIS FATHER'S ALREADY ON HIS WAY TO MEET UP WITH ME.
HUNH.
THERE'S A GPS ON *YOUR* ENTRANCE ID, TOO, MISUZU-SAN.
WE CAN USE THEM TO TRACK ANY FESTIVAL ATTENDEES FROM HEAD-QUARTERS.
SO THE MINUTE WE RECEIVE NOTICE OF A LOST CHILD, WE PINPOINT THE CHILD'S LOCATION...
AND HAVE A MEMBER OF JUDGMENT MEET HIM.
IN THIS CASE, IT WAS ME.
THAT ALLOWS US TO CARE FOR THE CHILD UNTIL THEIR PARENT CAN ARRIVE.

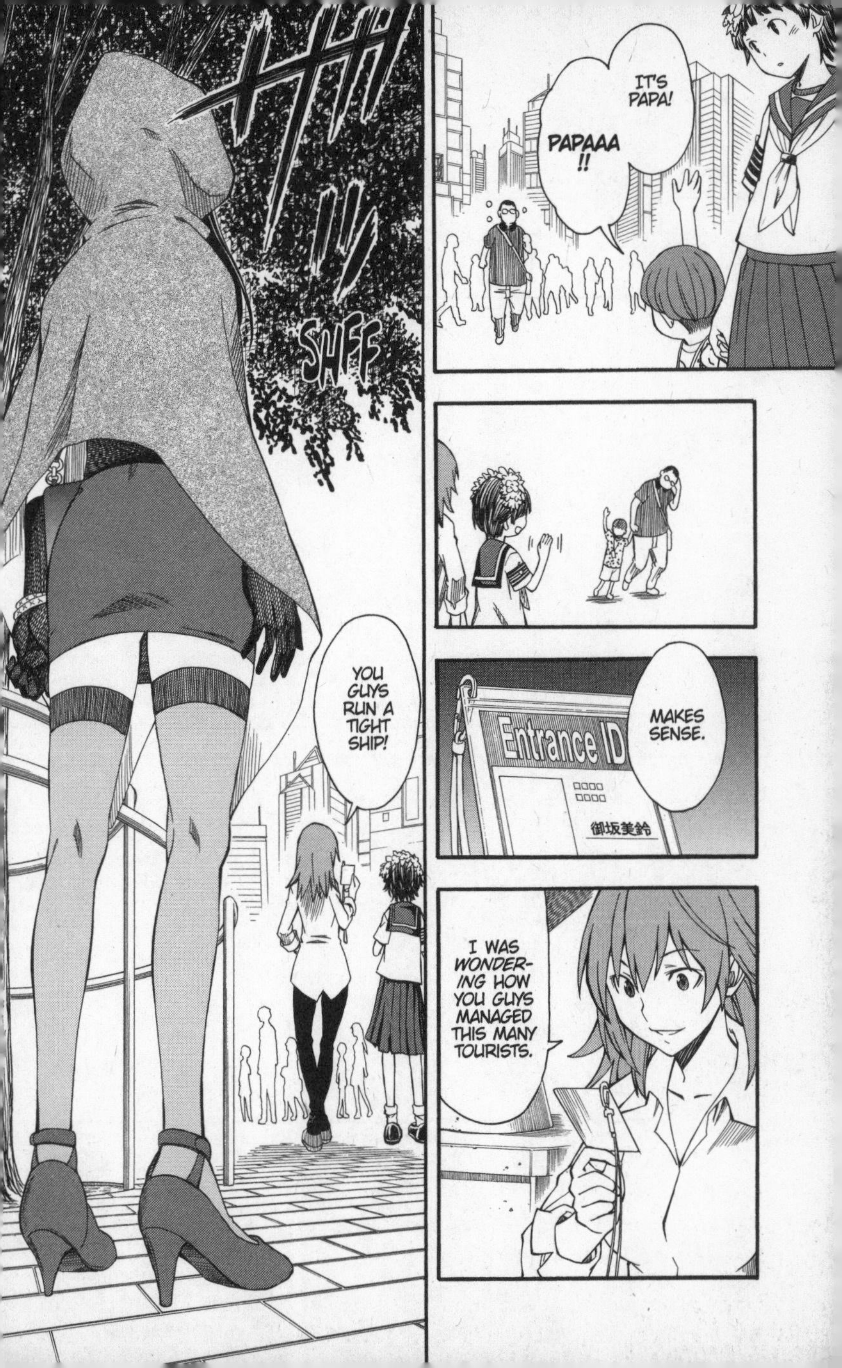
IT'S PAPA!
PAPAAA!!
Entrance ID
御坂美鈴
MAKES SENSE.
I WAS WONDERING HOW YOU GUYS MANAGED THIS MANY TOURISTS.
SHFF
YOU GUYS RUN A TIGHT SHIP!

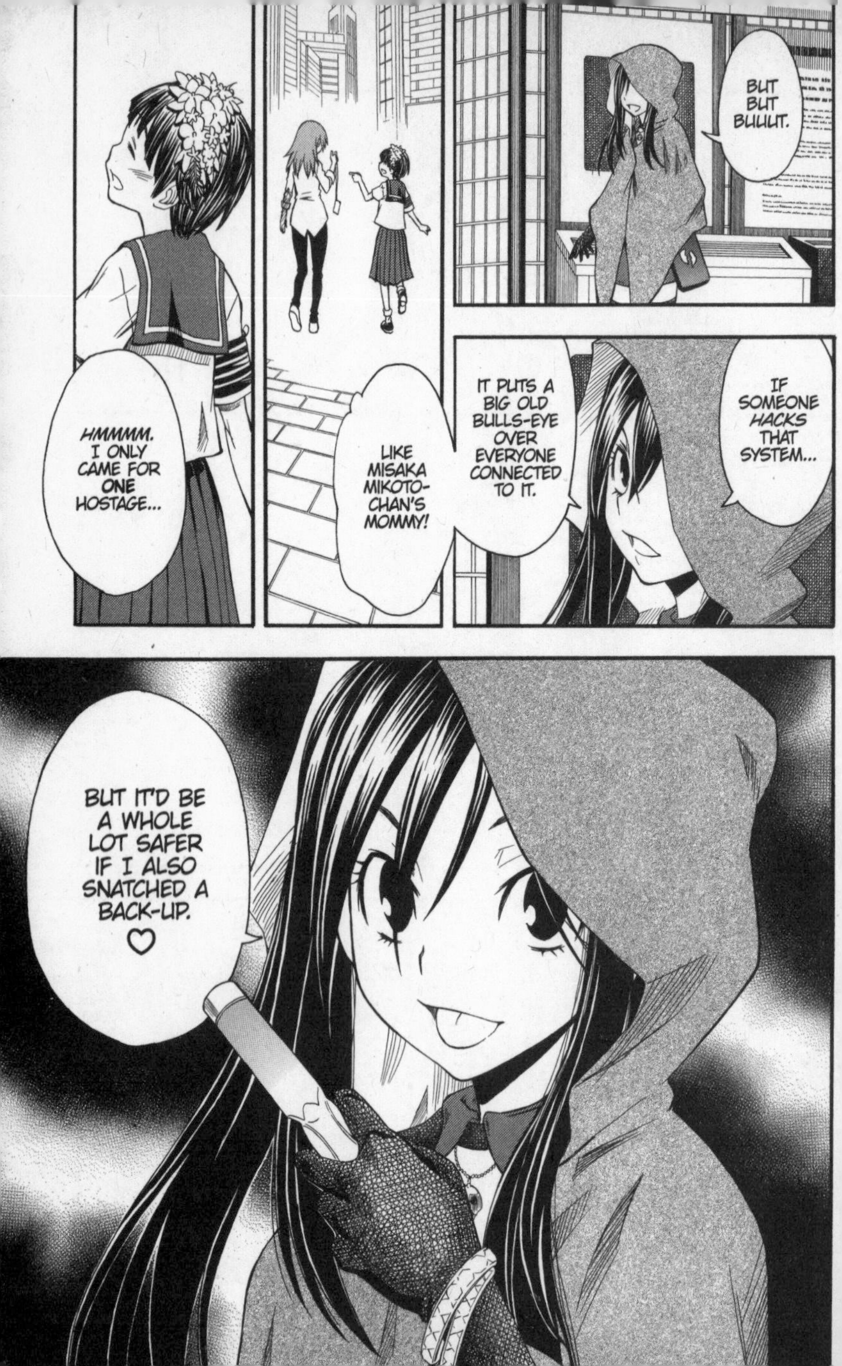
BUT BUT BUUUT.
IF SOMEONE HACKS THAT SYSTEM...
IT PUTS A BIG OLD BULLS-EYE OVER EVERYONE CONNECTED TO IT.
LIKE MISAKA MIKOTO-CHAN'S MOMMY!
HMMMM. I ONLY CAME FOR ONE HOSTAGE...
BUT IT'D BE A WHOLE LOT SAFER IF I ALSO SNATCHED A BACK-UP. ♡

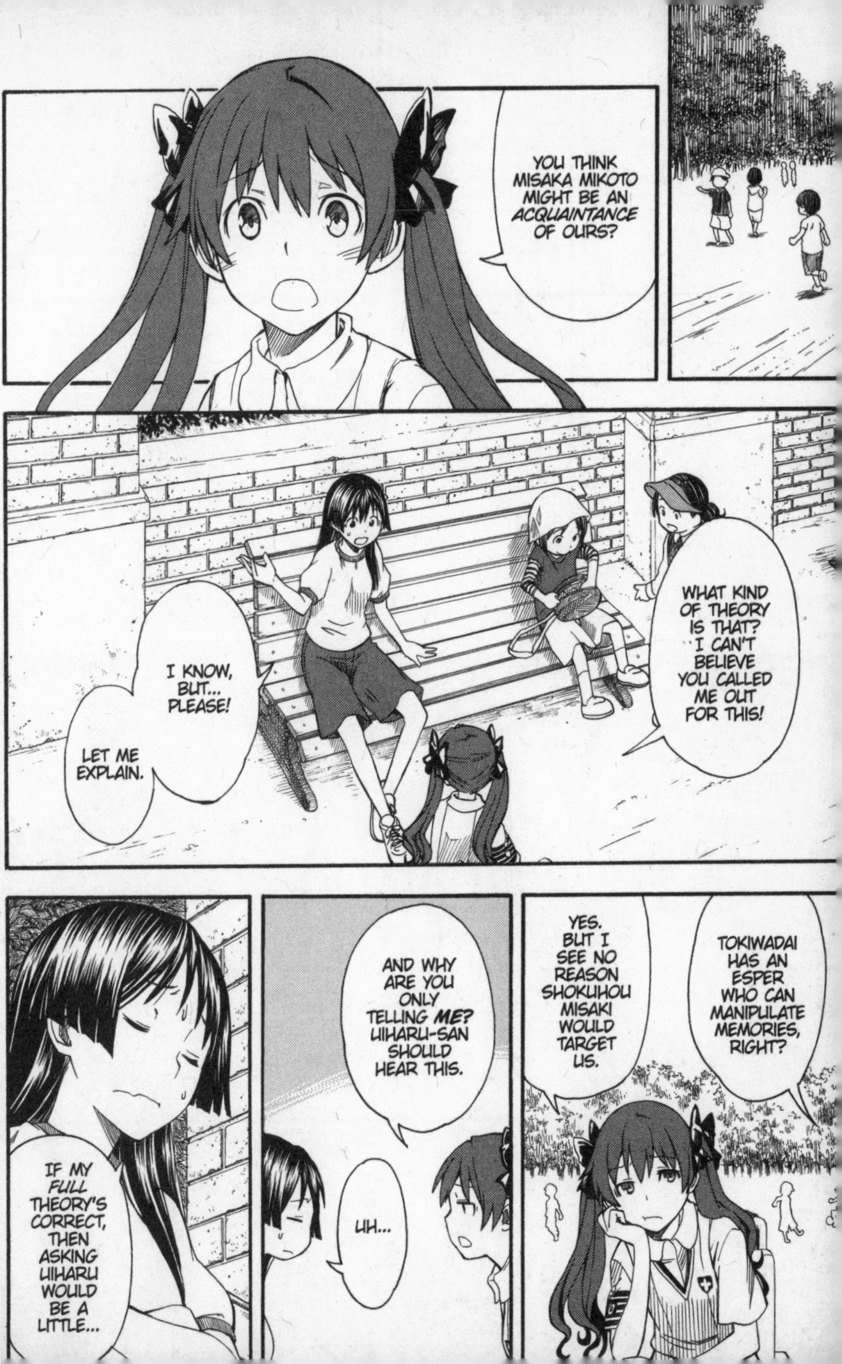

YOU THINK MISAKA MIKOTO MIGHT BE AN ACQUAINTANCE OF OURS?
WHAT KIND OF THEORY IS THAT? I CAN'T BELIEVE YOU CALLED ME OUT FOR THIS!
I KNOW, BUT... PLEASE!
LET ME EXPLAIN.
TOKIWADAI HAS AN ESPER WHO CAN MANIPULATE MEMORIES, RIGHT?
YES. BUT I SEE NO REASON SHOKUHOU MISAKI WOULD TARGET US.
AND WHY ARE YOU ONLY TELLING ME? UIHARU-SAN SHOULD HEAR THIS.
UH...
IF MY FULL THEORY'S CORRECT, THEN ASKING UIHARU WOULD BE A LITTLE...

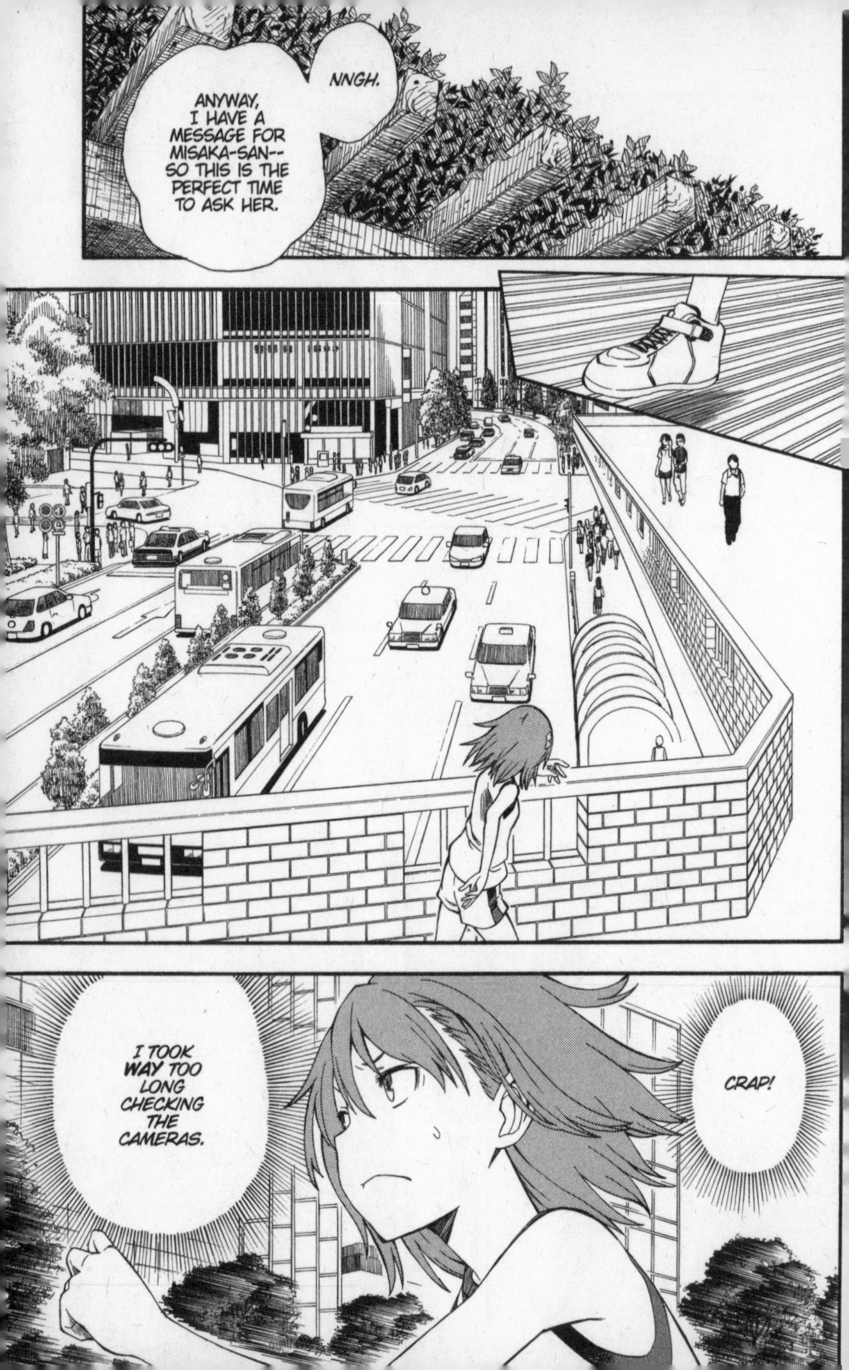
NNGH.
ANYWAY, I HAVE A MESSAGE FOR MISAKA-SAN-- SO THIS IS THE PERFECT TIME TO ASK HER.
CRAP!
I TOOK WAY TOO LONG CHECKING THE CAMERAS.

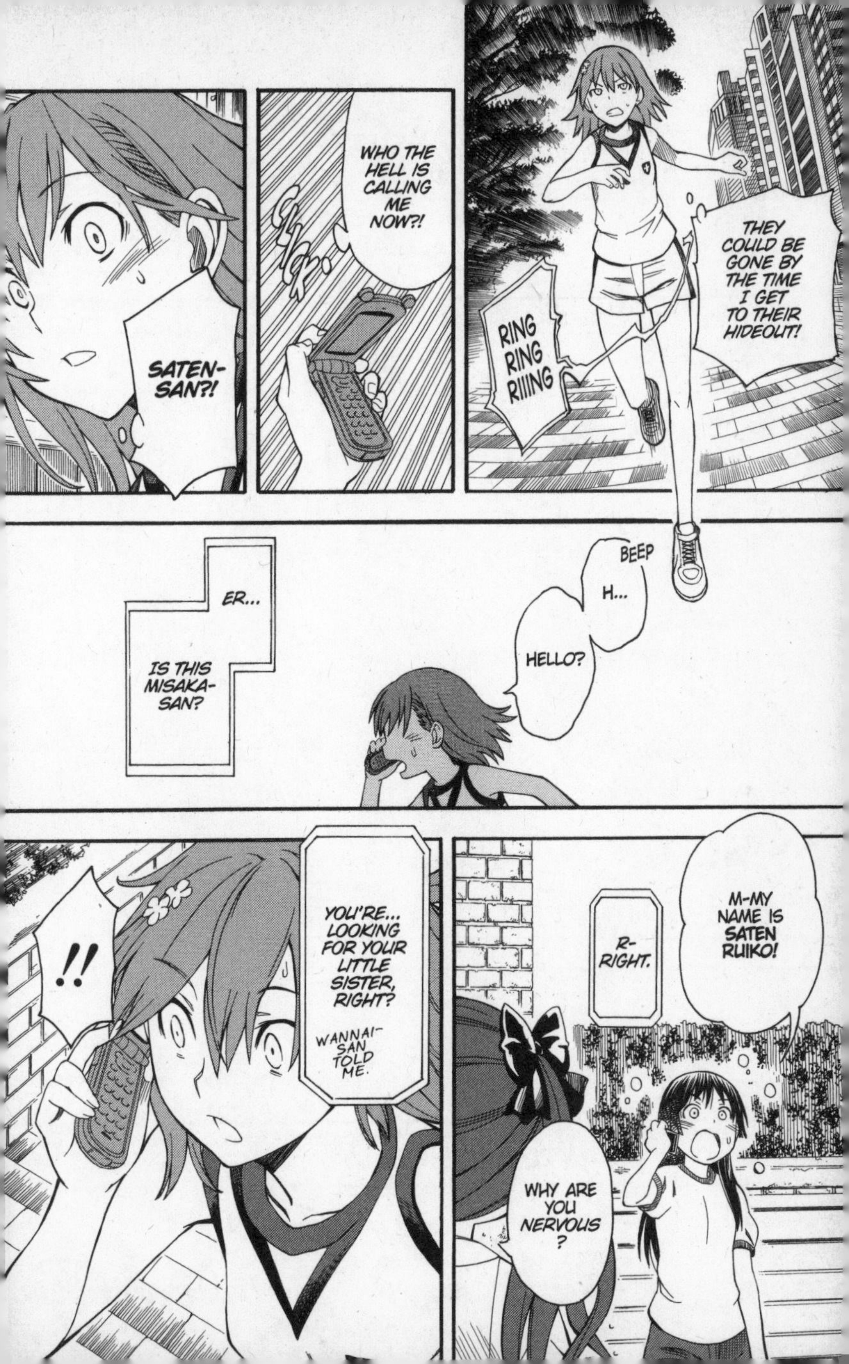
THEY COULD BE GONE BY THE TIME I GET TO THEIR HIDEOUT!
RING RING RIIING
WHO THE HELL IS CALLING ME NOW?!
SATEN-SAN?!
BEEP
H...
HELLO?
ER...
IS THIS MISAKA-SAN?
M-MY NAME IS SATEN RUIKO!
R-RIGHT.
WHY ARE YOU NERVOUS?
YOU'RE... LOOKING FOR YOUR LITTLE SISTER, RIGHT?
WANNAI-SAN TOLD ME.
!!

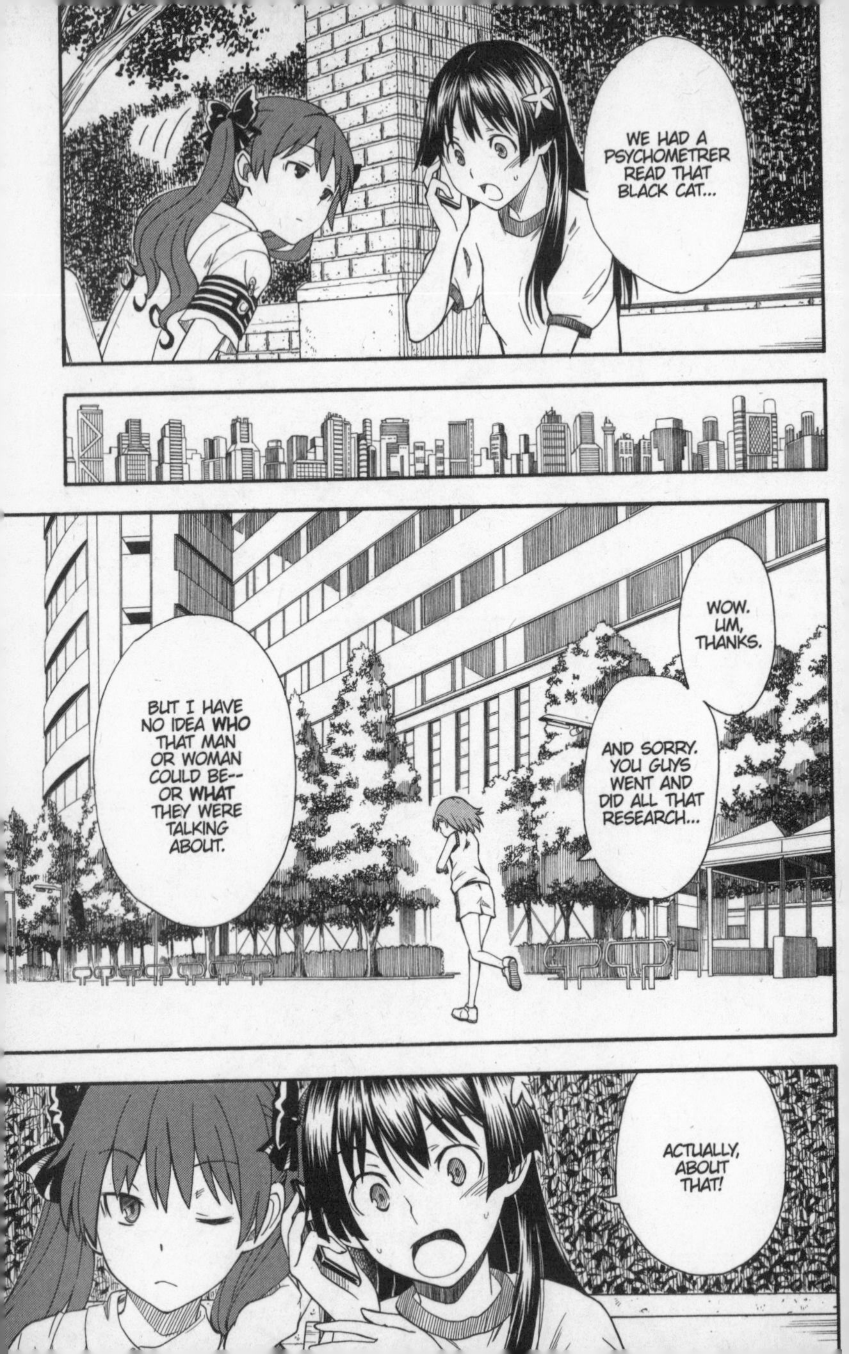

WE HAD A PSYCHOMETRER READ THAT BLACK CAT...
BUT I HAVE NO IDEA **WHO** THAT MAN OR WOMAN COULD BE-- OR **WHAT** THEY WERE TALKING ABOUT.
WOW. UM, THANKS.
AND SORRY. YOU GUYS WENT AND DID ALL THAT RESEARCH...
ACTUALLY, ABOUT THAT!

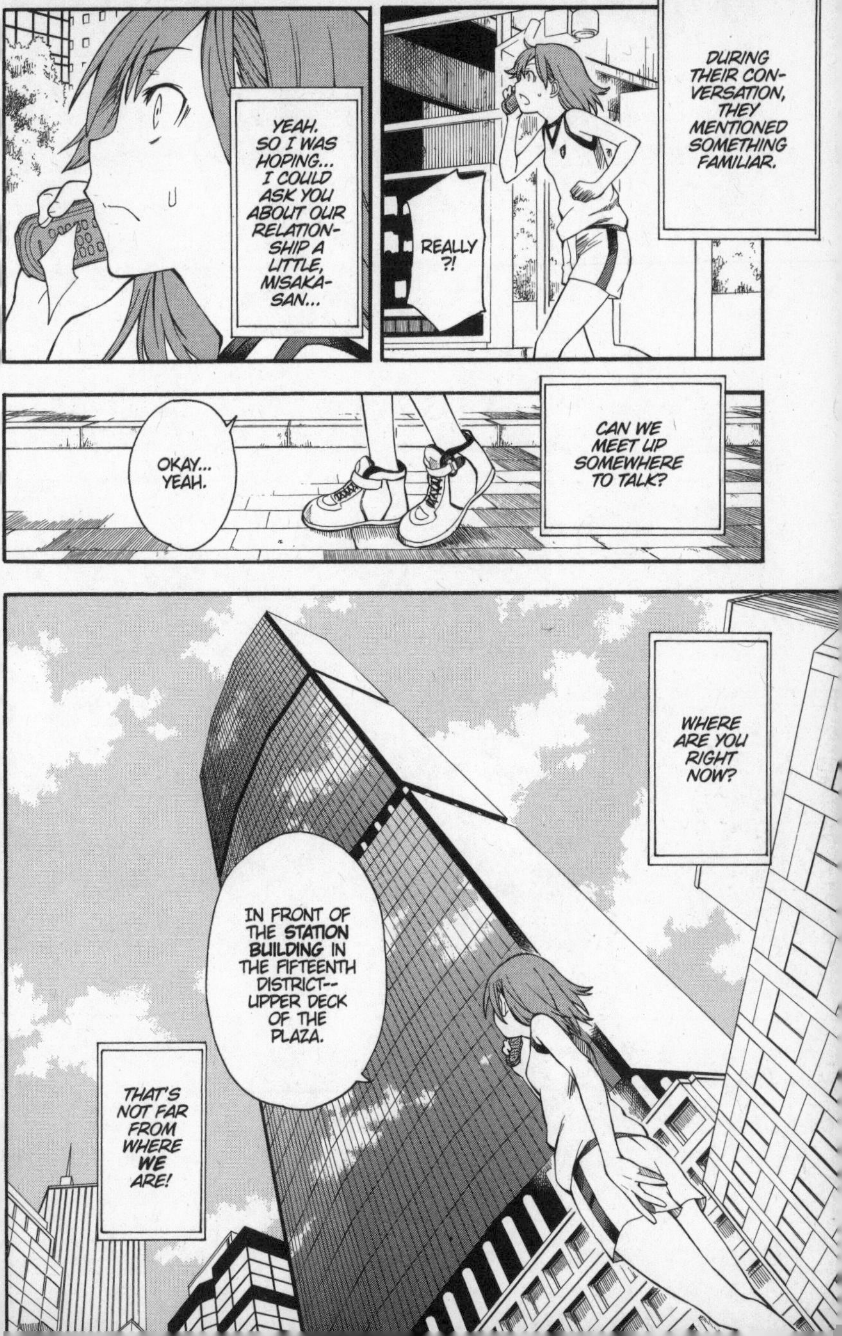
DURING THEIR CON- VERSATION, THEY MENTIONED SOMETHING FAMILIAR.
REALLY ?!
YEAH. SO I WAS HOPING... I COULD ASK YOU ABOUT OUR RELATION- SHIP A LITTLE, MISAKA- SAN...
CAN WE MEET UP SOMEWHERE TO TALK?
OKAY... YEAH.
WHERE ARE YOU RIGHT NOW?
IN FRONT OF THE STATION BUILDING IN THE FIFTEENTH DISTRICT-- UPPER DECK OF THE PLAZA.
THAT'S NOT FAR FROM WHERE WE ARE!

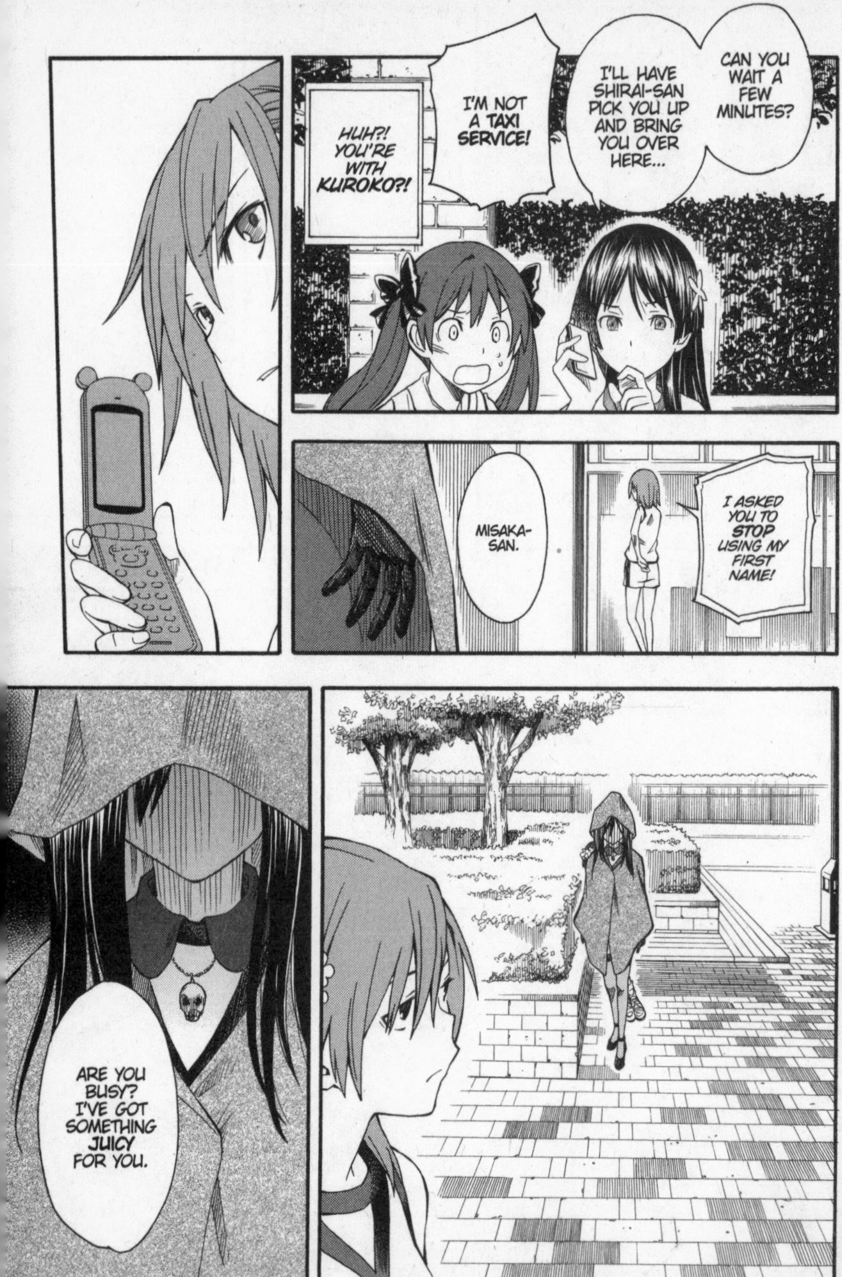
CAN YOU WAIT A FEW MINUTES?
I'LL HAVE SHIRAI-SAN PICK YOU UP AND BRING YOU OVER HERE...
I'M NOT A TAXI SERVICE!
HUH?! YOU'RE WITH KUROKO?!
I ASKED YOU TO STOP USING MY FIRST NAME!
MISAKA-SAN.
ARE YOU BUSY? I'VE GOT SOMETHING JUICY FOR YOU.

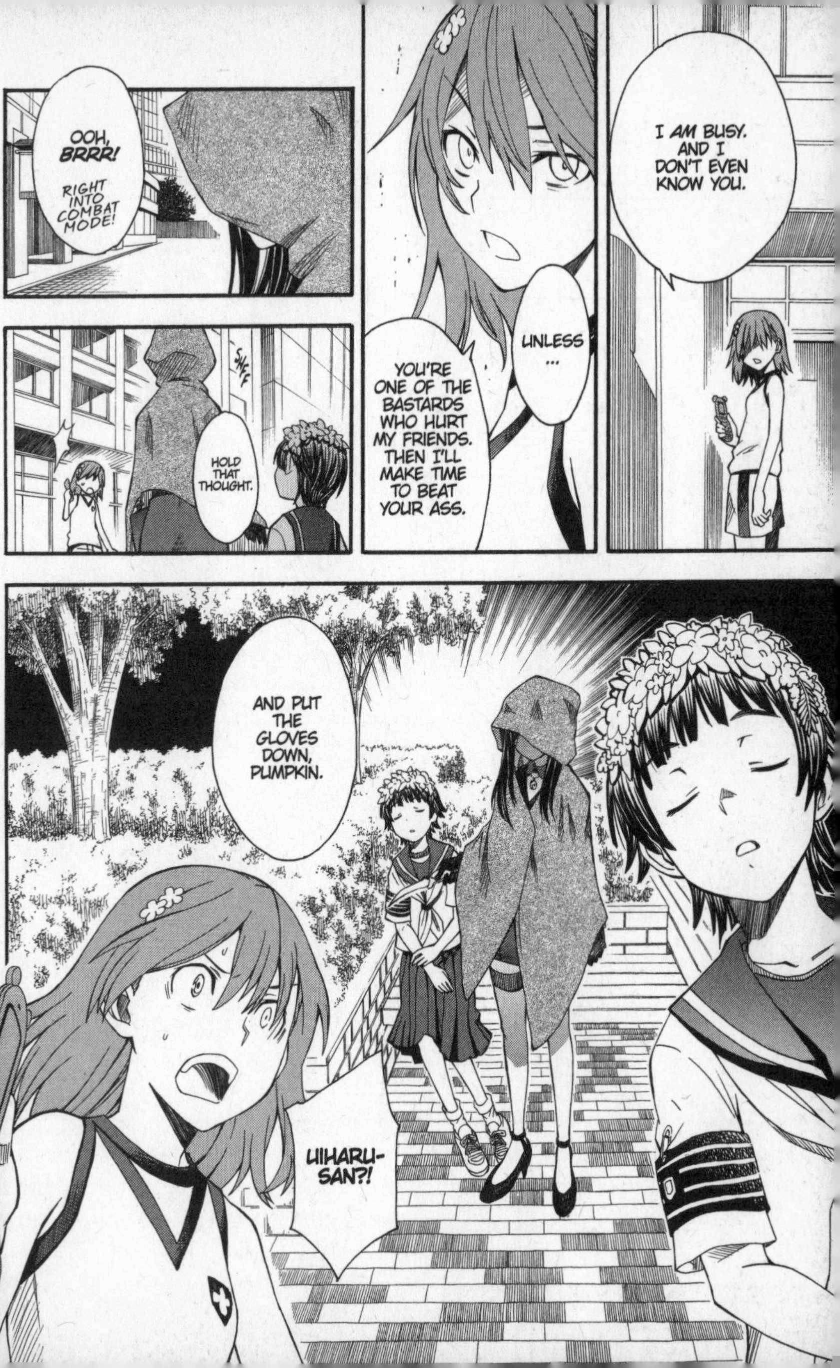
I AM BUSY. AND I DON'T EVEN KNOW YOU.
UNLESS ...
YOU'RE ONE OF THE BASTARDS WHO HURT MY FRIENDS. THEN I'LL MAKE TIME TO BEAT YOUR ASS.
OOH, BRRR!
RIGHT INTO COMBAT MODE!
SHFF
HOLD THAT THOUGHT.
AND PUT THE GLOVES DOWN, PUMPKIN.
UIHARU-SAN?!

A Certain SCIENTIFIC Railgun

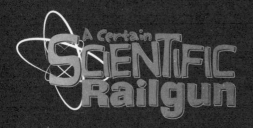

とある魔術の禁書目録外伝
とある科学の
超電磁砲
レールガン

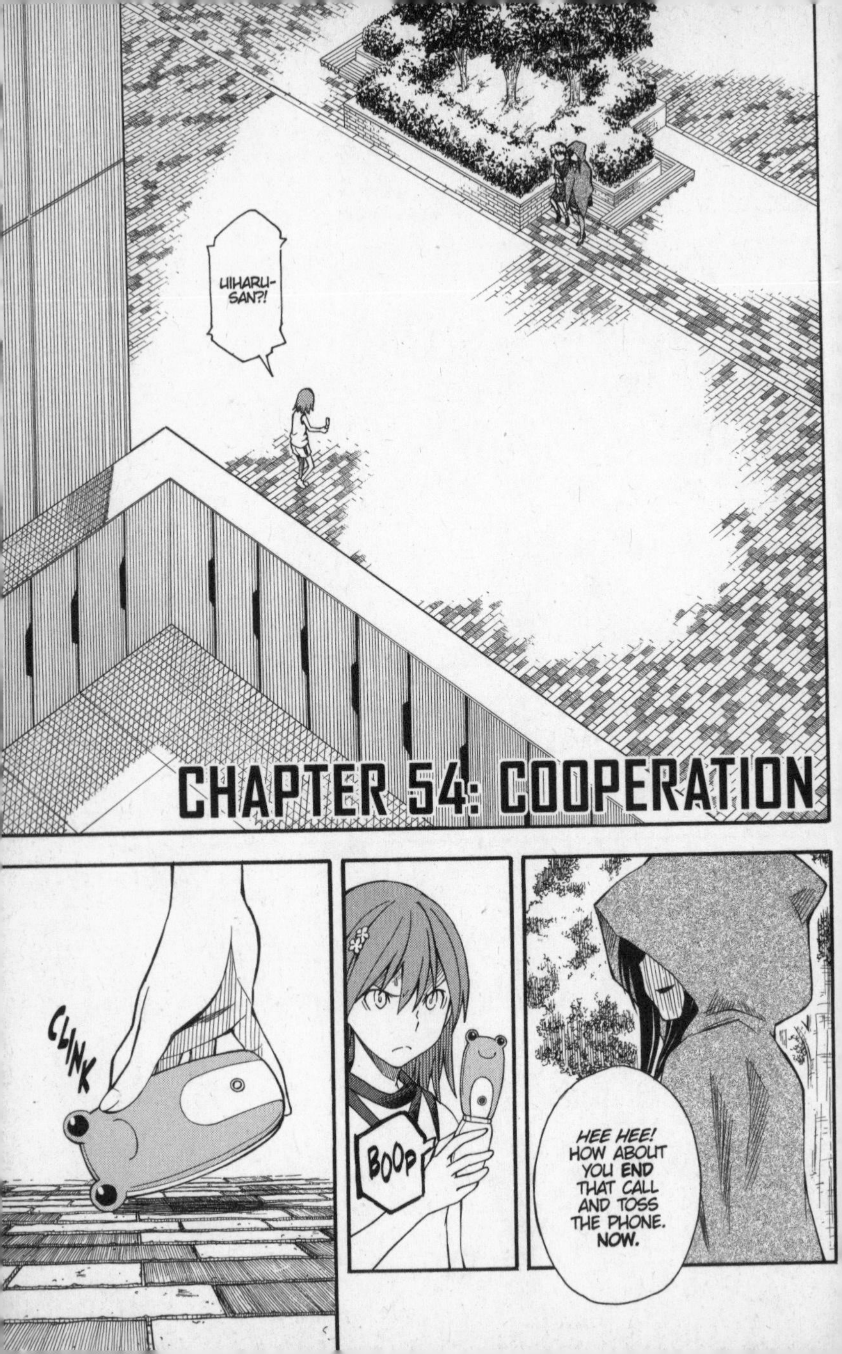
UIHARU-SAN?!
CHAPTER 54: COOPERATION
HEE HEE! HOW ABOUT YOU END THAT CALL AND TOSS THE PHONE. NOW.
BOOP
CLINK

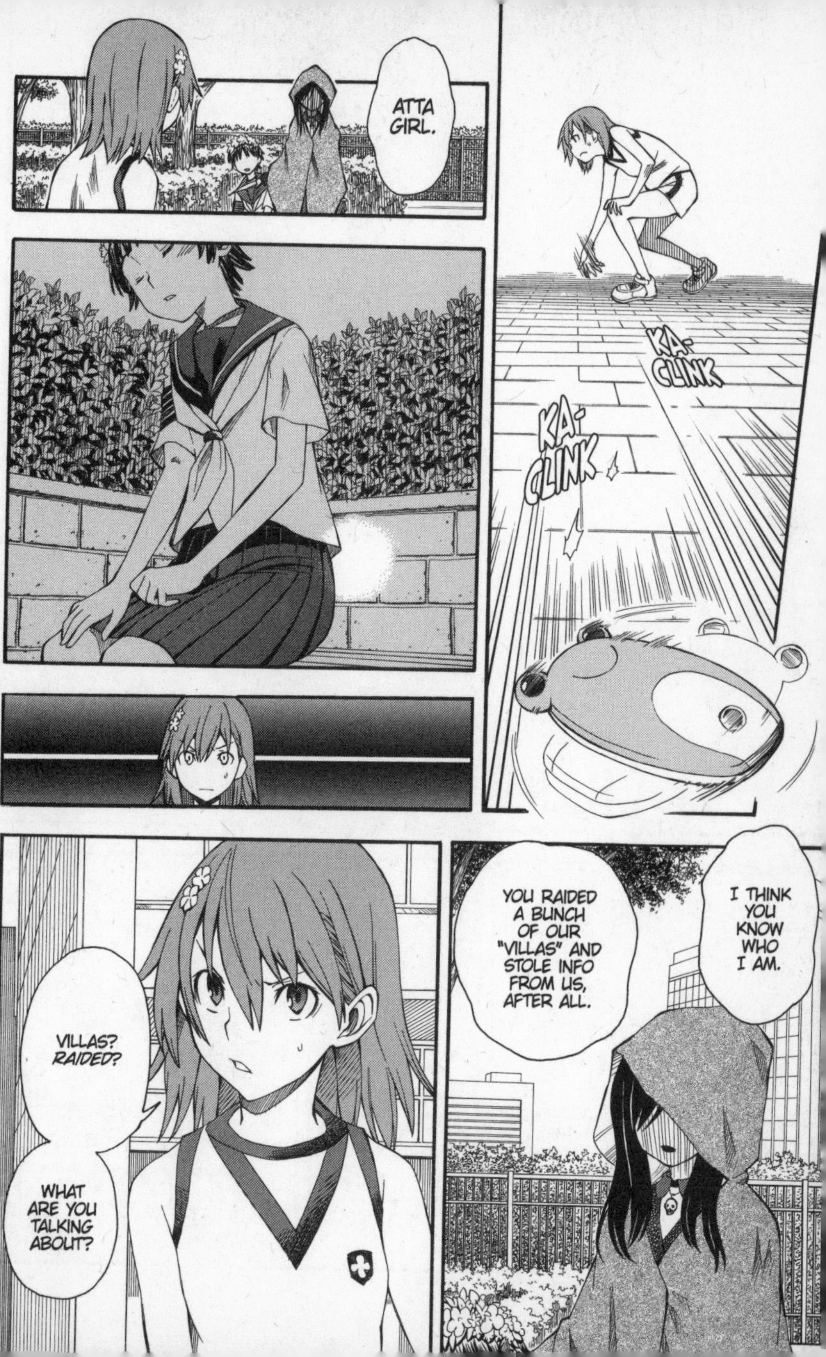
KA-CLINK
KA-CLINK
ATTA GIRL.
I THINK YOU KNOW WHO I AM.
YOU RAIDED A BUNCH OF OUR "VILLAS" AND STOLE INFO FROM US, AFTER ALL.
VILLAS? RAIDED?
WHAT ARE YOU TALKING ABOUT?

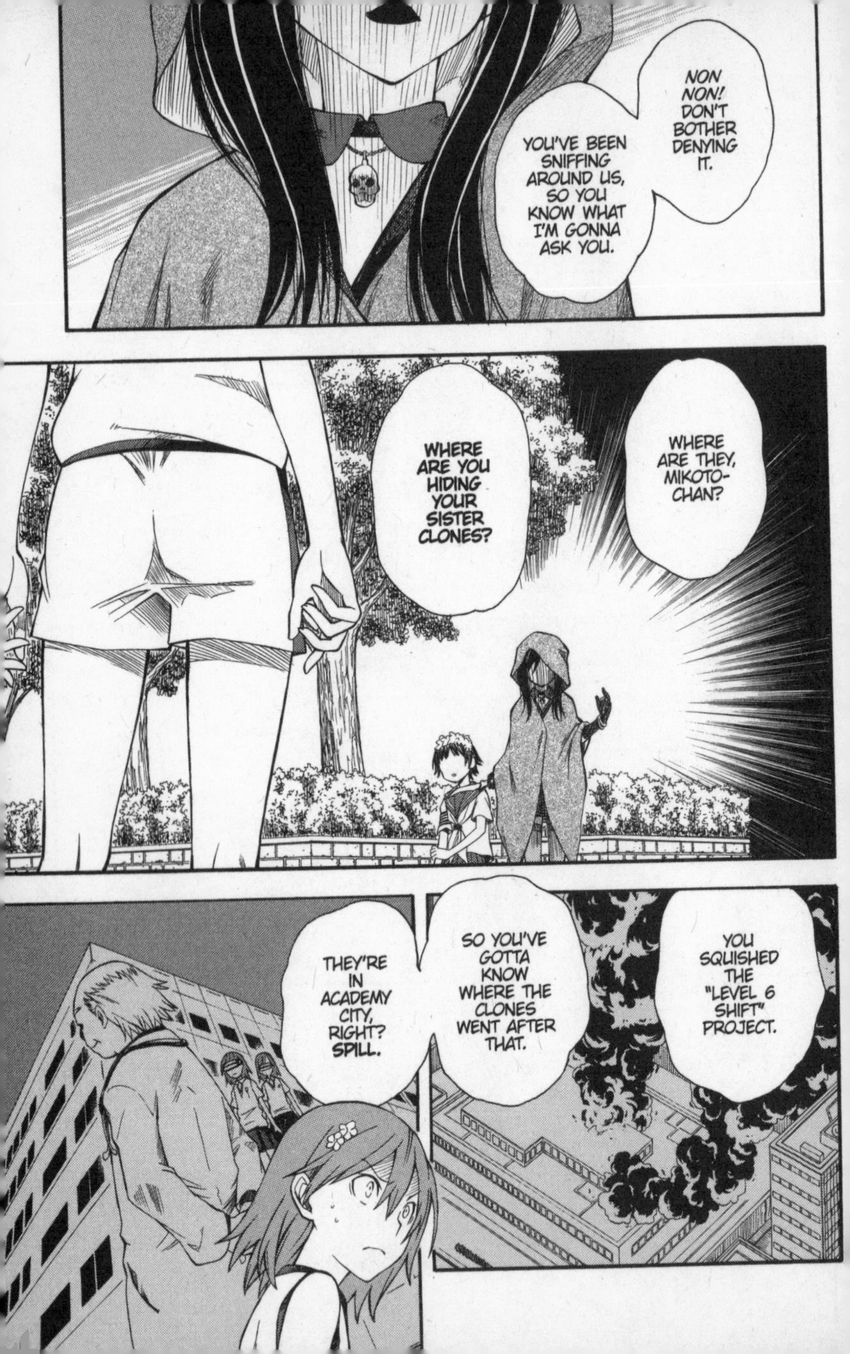
NON NON! DON'T BOTHER DENYING IT.
YOU'VE BEEN SNIFFING AROUND US, SO YOU KNOW WHAT I'M GONNA ASK YOU.
WHERE ARE THEY, MIKOTO-CHAN?
WHERE ARE YOU HIDING YOUR SISTER CLONES?
YOU SQUISHED THE "LEVEL 6 SHIFT" PROJECT.
SO YOU'VE GOTTA KNOW WHERE THE CLONES WENT AFTER THAT.
THEY'RE IN ACADEMY CITY, RIGHT? SPILL.

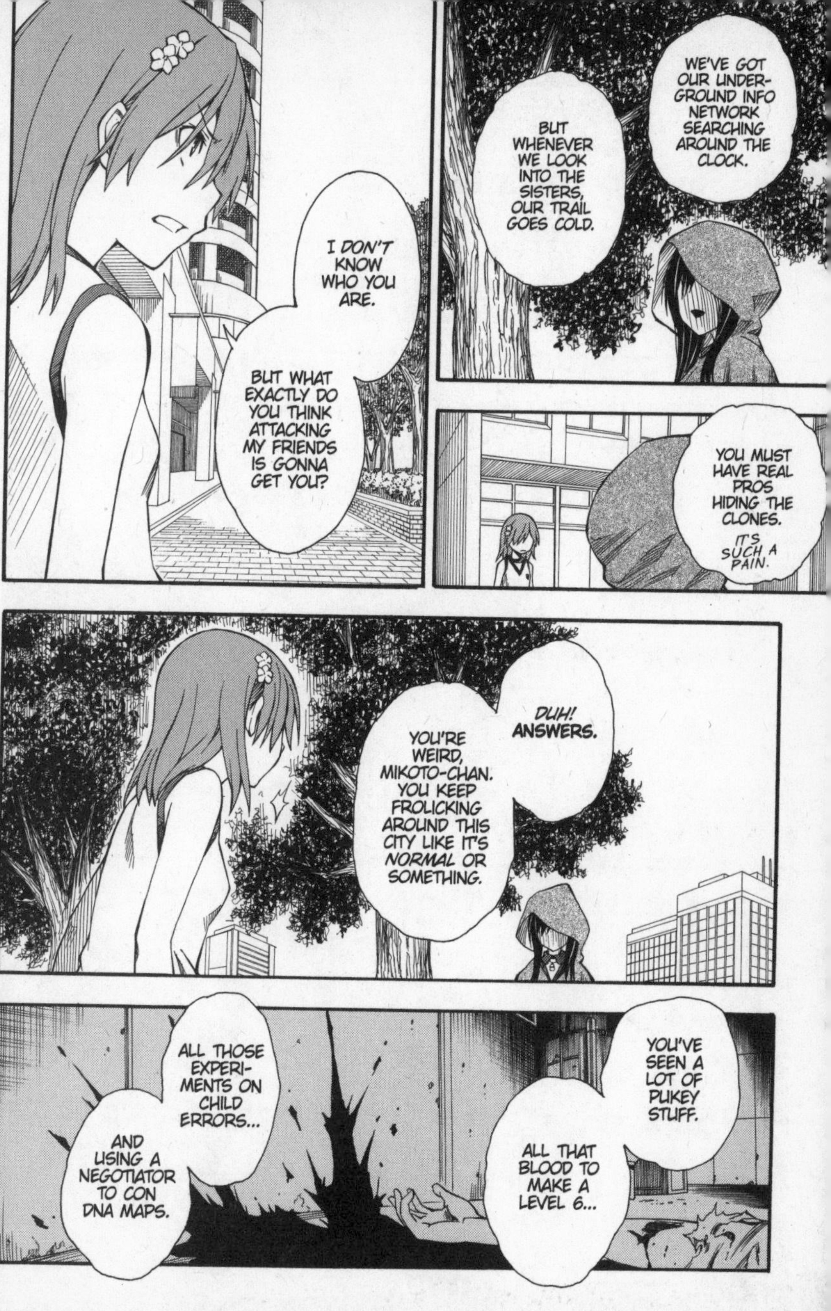
WE'VE GOT OUR UNDER-GROUND INFO NETWORK SEARCHING AROUND THE CLOCK.
BUT WHENEVER WE LOOK INTO THE SISTERS, OUR TRAIL GOES COLD.
YOU MUST HAVE REAL PROS HIDING THE CLONES.
IT'S SUCH A PAIN.
I *DON'T* KNOW WHO YOU ARE.
BUT WHAT EXACTLY DO YOU THINK ATTACKING MY FRIENDS IS GONNA GET YOU?
DUH! **ANSWERS.**
YOU'RE WEIRD, MIKOTO-CHAN. YOU KEEP FROLICKING AROUND THIS CITY LIKE IT'S *NORMAL* OR SOMETHING.
YOU'VE SEEN A LOT OF PUKEY STUFF.
ALL THAT BLOOD TO MAKE A LEVEL 6...
ALL THOSE EXPERI-MENTS ON CHILD ERRORS...
AND USING A NEGOTIATOR TO CON DNA MAPS.

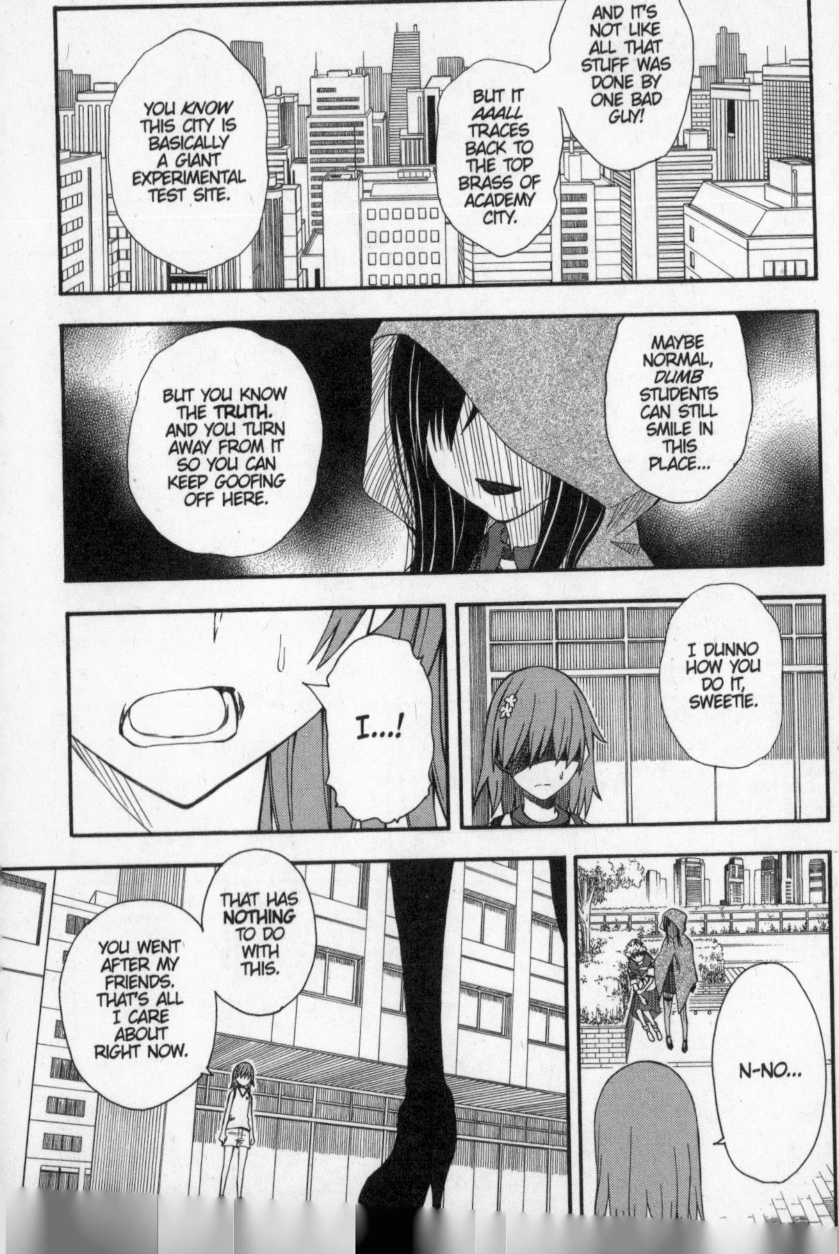

AND IT'S NOT LIKE ALL THAT STUFF WAS DONE BY ONE BAD GUY!
BUT IT *AAALL* TRACES BACK TO THE TOP BRASS OF ACADEMY CITY.
YOU *KNOW* THIS CITY IS BASICALLY A GIANT EXPERIMENTAL TEST SITE.
MAYBE NORMAL, *DUMB* STUDENTS CAN STILL SMILE IN THIS PLACE...
BUT YOU KNOW THE TRUTH. AND YOU TURN AWAY FROM IT SO YOU CAN KEEP GOOFING OFF HERE.
I DUNNO HOW YOU DO IT, SWEETIE.
I...!
N-NO...
THAT HAS NOTHING TO DO WITH THIS.
YOU WENT AFTER MY FRIENDS. THAT'S ALL I CARE ABOUT RIGHT NOW.

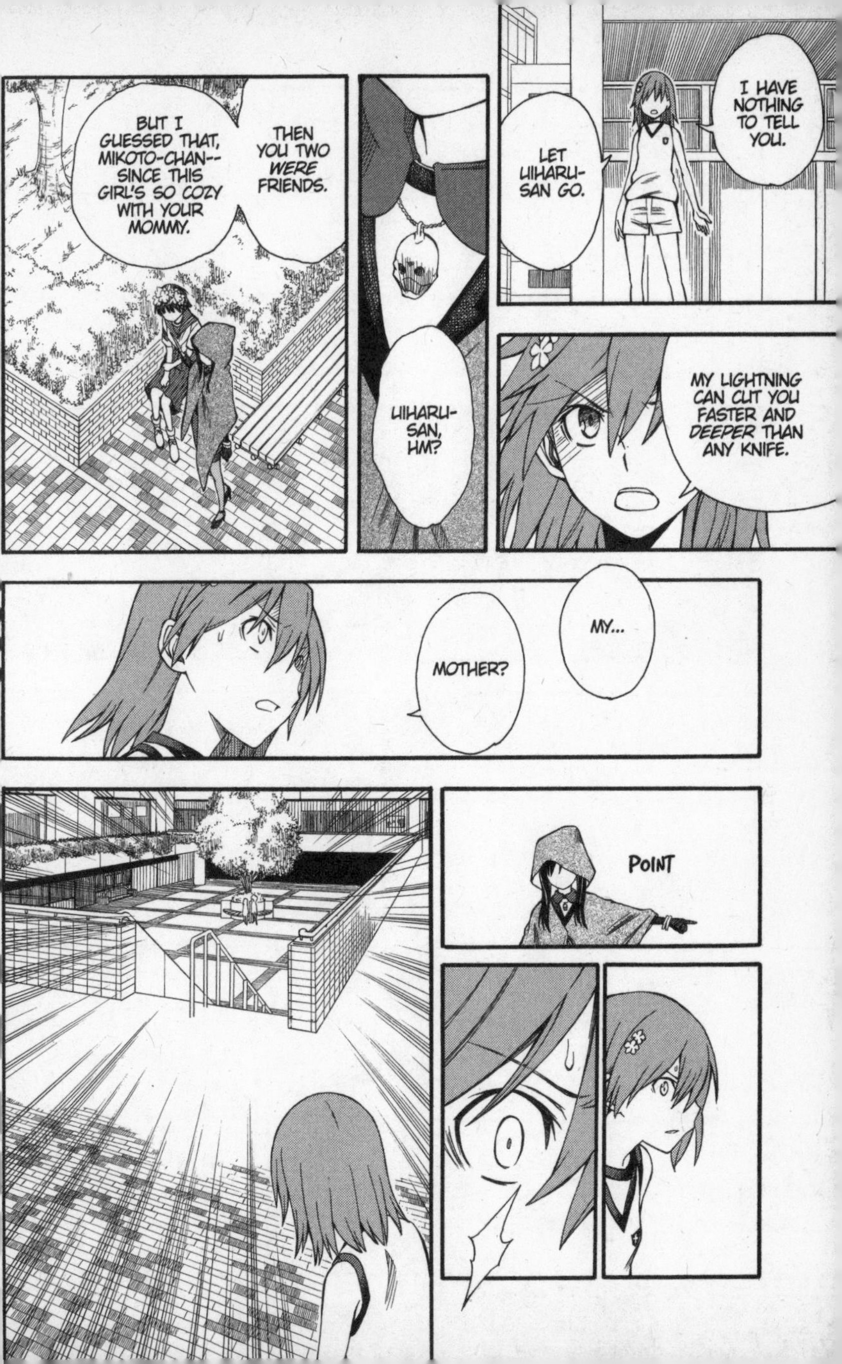
I HAVE NOTHING TO TELL YOU.
LET UIHARU-SAN GO.
MY LIGHTNING CAN CUT YOU FASTER AND DEEPER THAN ANY KNIFE.
UIHARU-SAN, HM?
THEN YOU TWO *WERE* FRIENDS.
BUT I GUESSED THAT, MIKOTO-CHAN-- SINCE THIS GIRL'S SO COZY WITH YOUR MOMMY.
MY...
MOTHER?
POINT

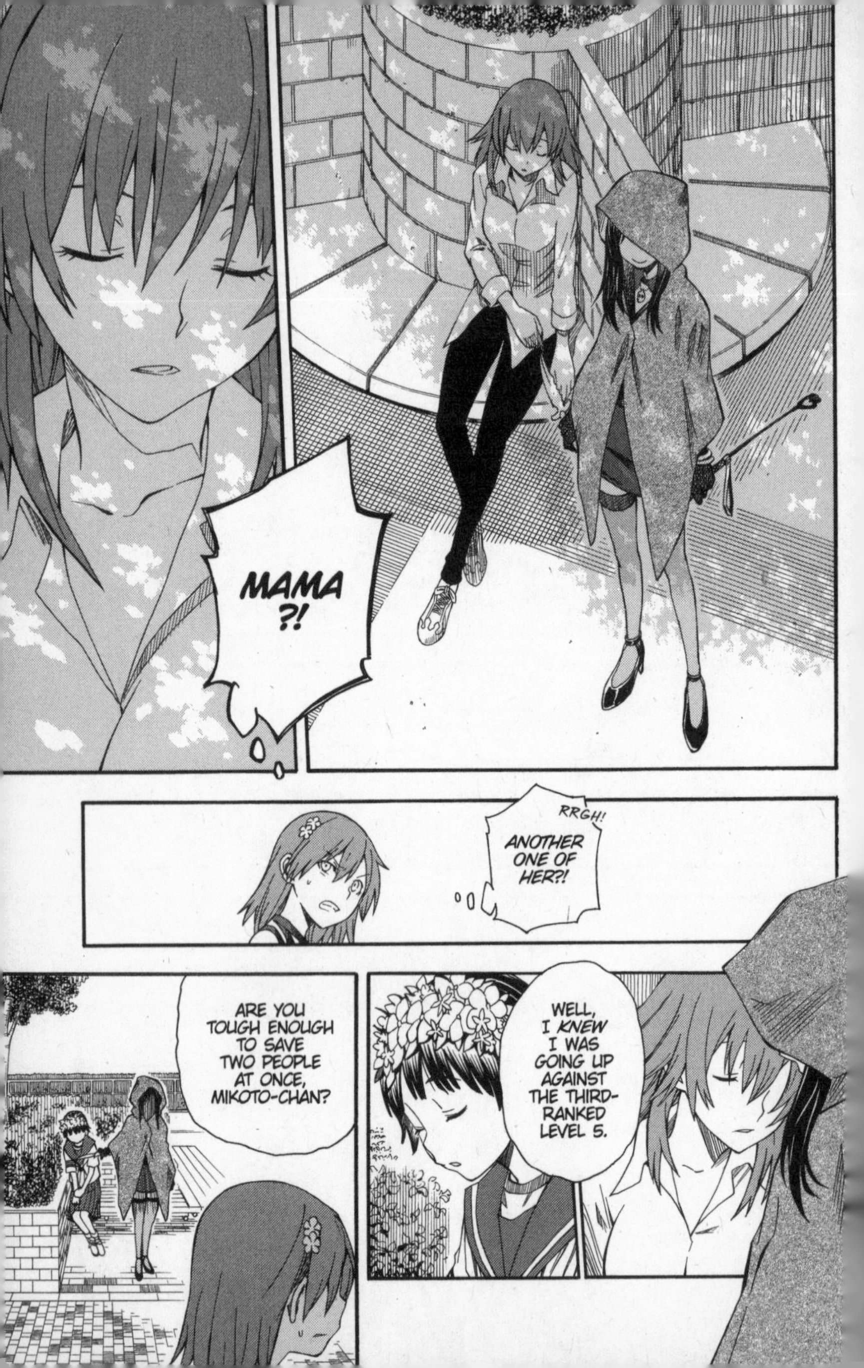
MAMA ?!
RRGH!
ANOTHER ONE OF HER?!
WELL, I KNEW I WAS GOING UP AGAINST THE THIRD-RANKED LEVEL 5.
ARE YOU TOUGH ENOUGH TO SAVE TWO PEOPLE AT ONCE, MIKOTO-CHAN?

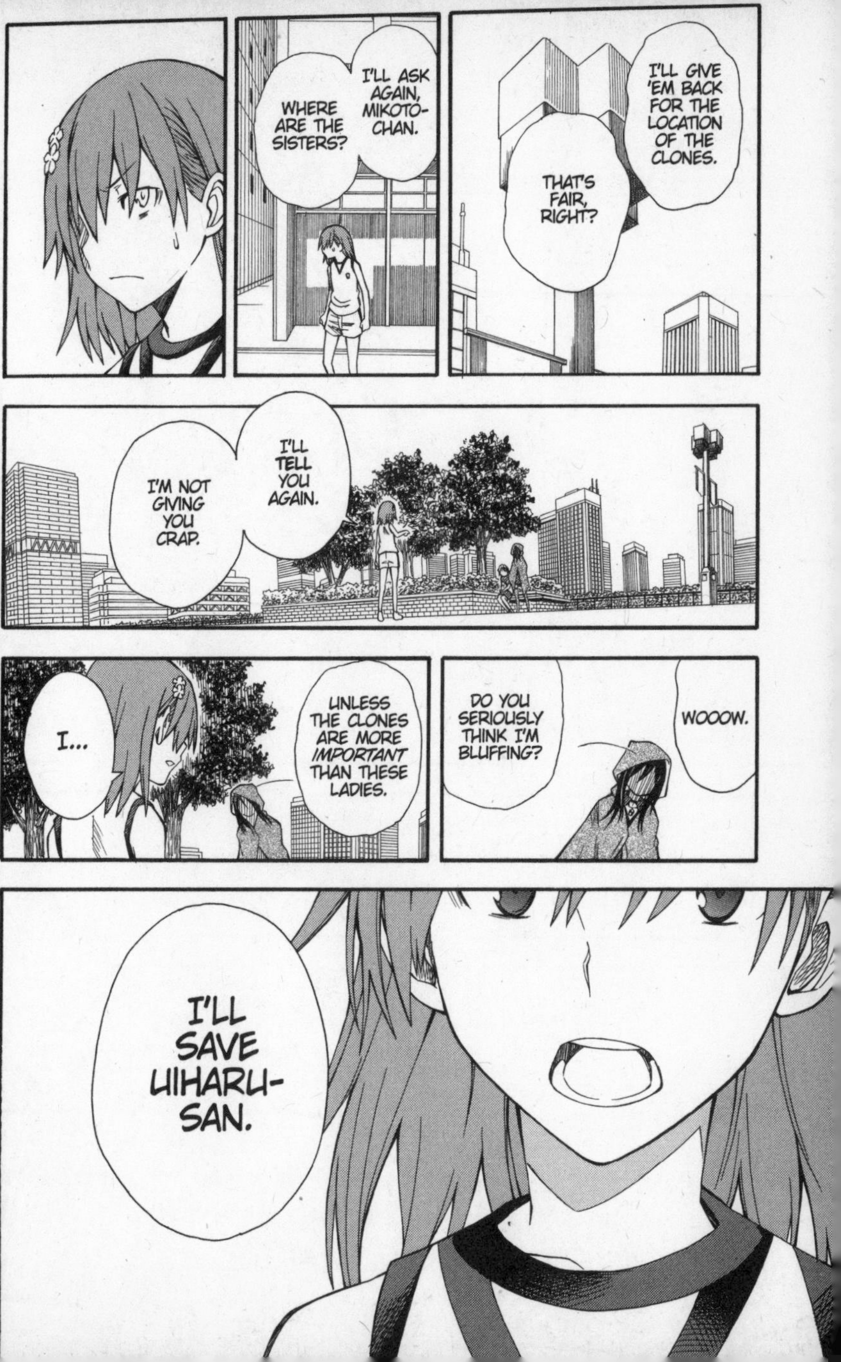
I'LL GIVE 'EM BACK FOR THE LOCATION OF THE CLONES.
THAT'S FAIR, RIGHT?
I'LL ASK AGAIN, MIKOTO-CHAN.
WHERE ARE THE SISTERS?
I'LL TELL YOU AGAIN.
I'M NOT GIVING YOU CRAP.
WOOOW.
DO YOU SERIOUSLY THINK I'M BLUFFING?
UNLESS THE CLONES ARE MORE *IMPORTANT* THAN THESE LADIES.
I...
I'LL SAVE UIHARU-SAN.

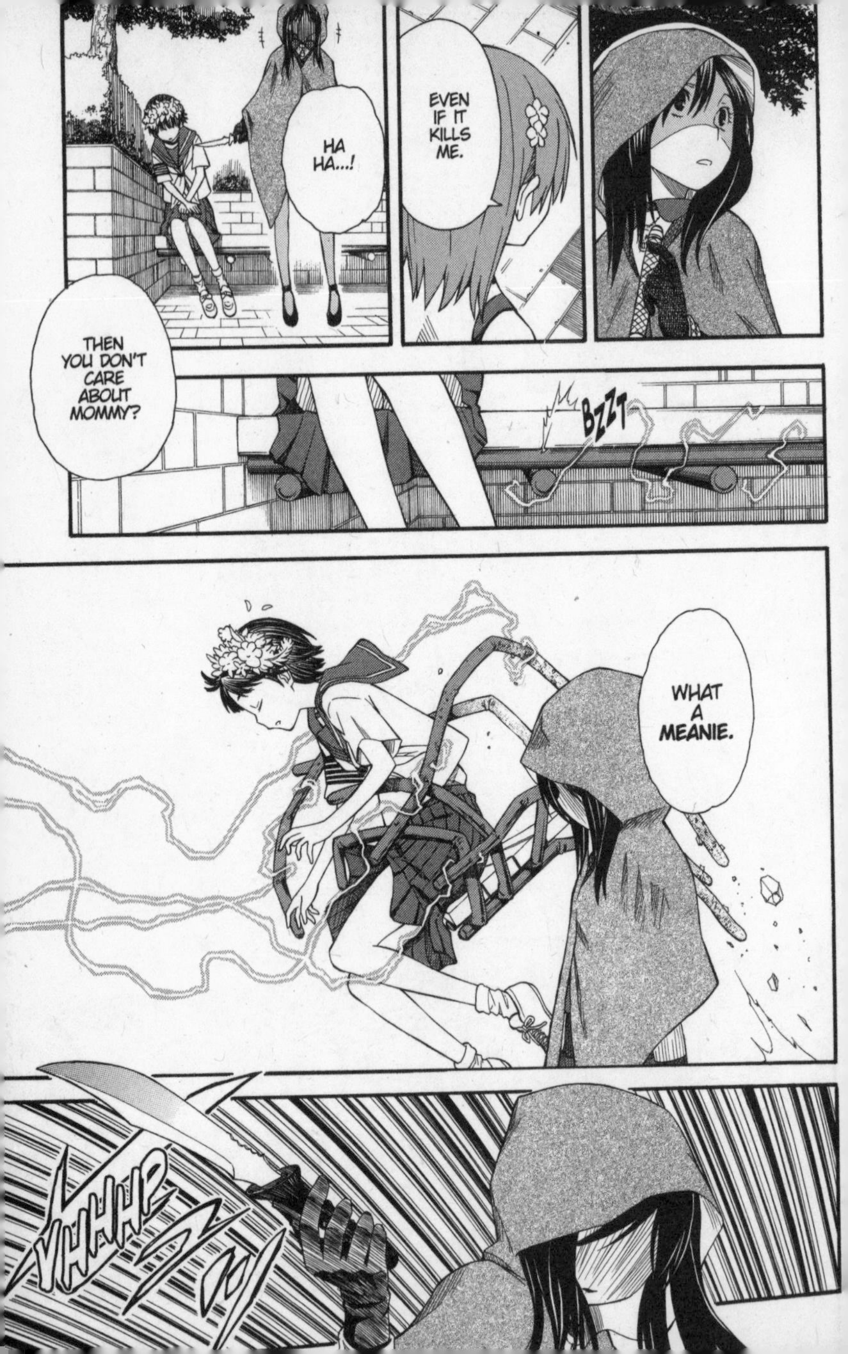
EVEN IF IT KILLS ME.
HA HA...!
THEN YOU DON'T CARE ABOUT MOMMY?
BZZT
WHAT A MEANIE.

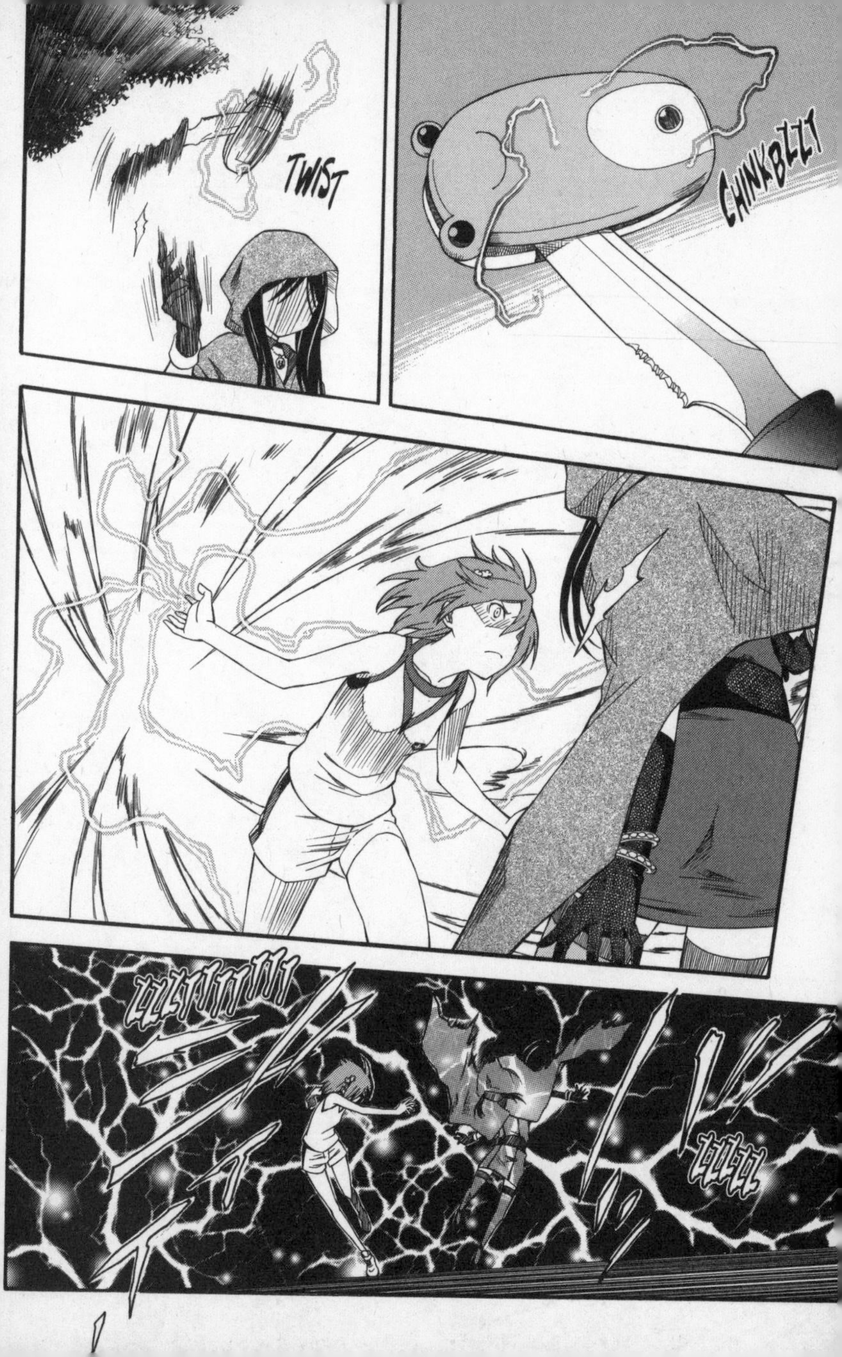
CHINKBZZT
TWIST
ZZZZTTTTTTTT
ZZZZZ

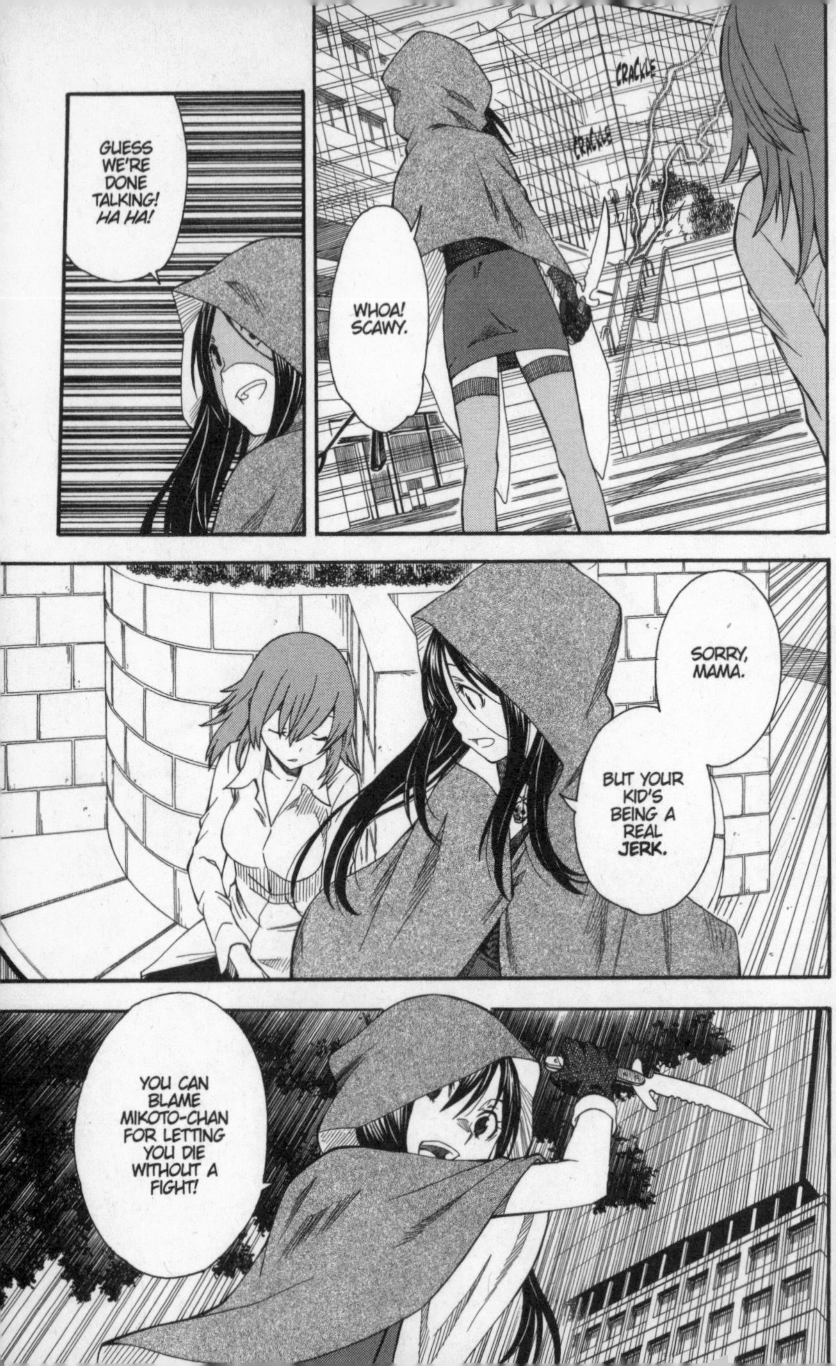
CRACKLE
CRACKLE
WHOA! SCAWY.
GUESS WE'RE DONE TALKING! HA HA!
SORRY, MAMA.
BUT YOUR KID'S BEING A REAL JERK.
YOU CAN BLAME MIKOTO-CHAN FOR LETTING YOU DIE WITHOUT A FIGHT!

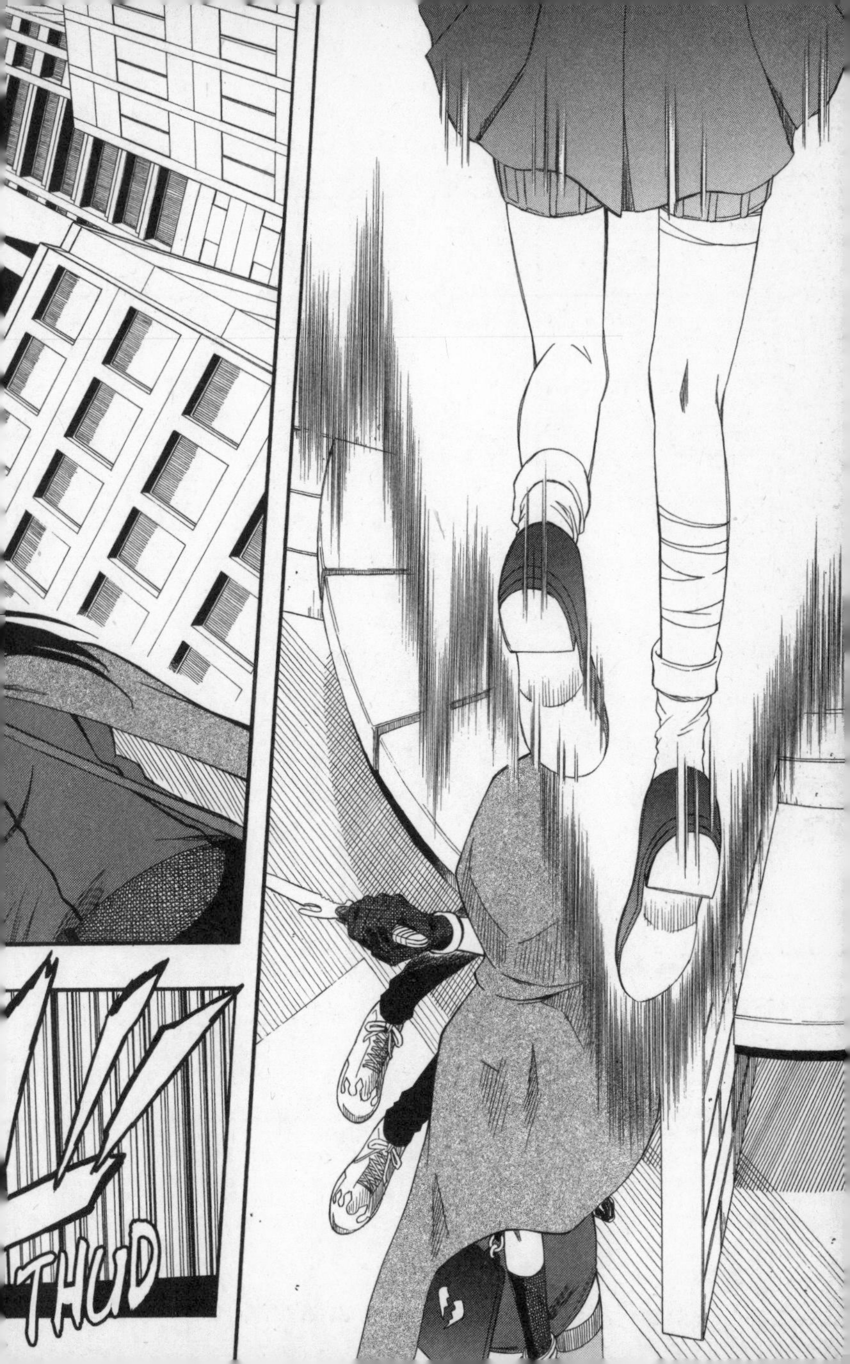
THUD

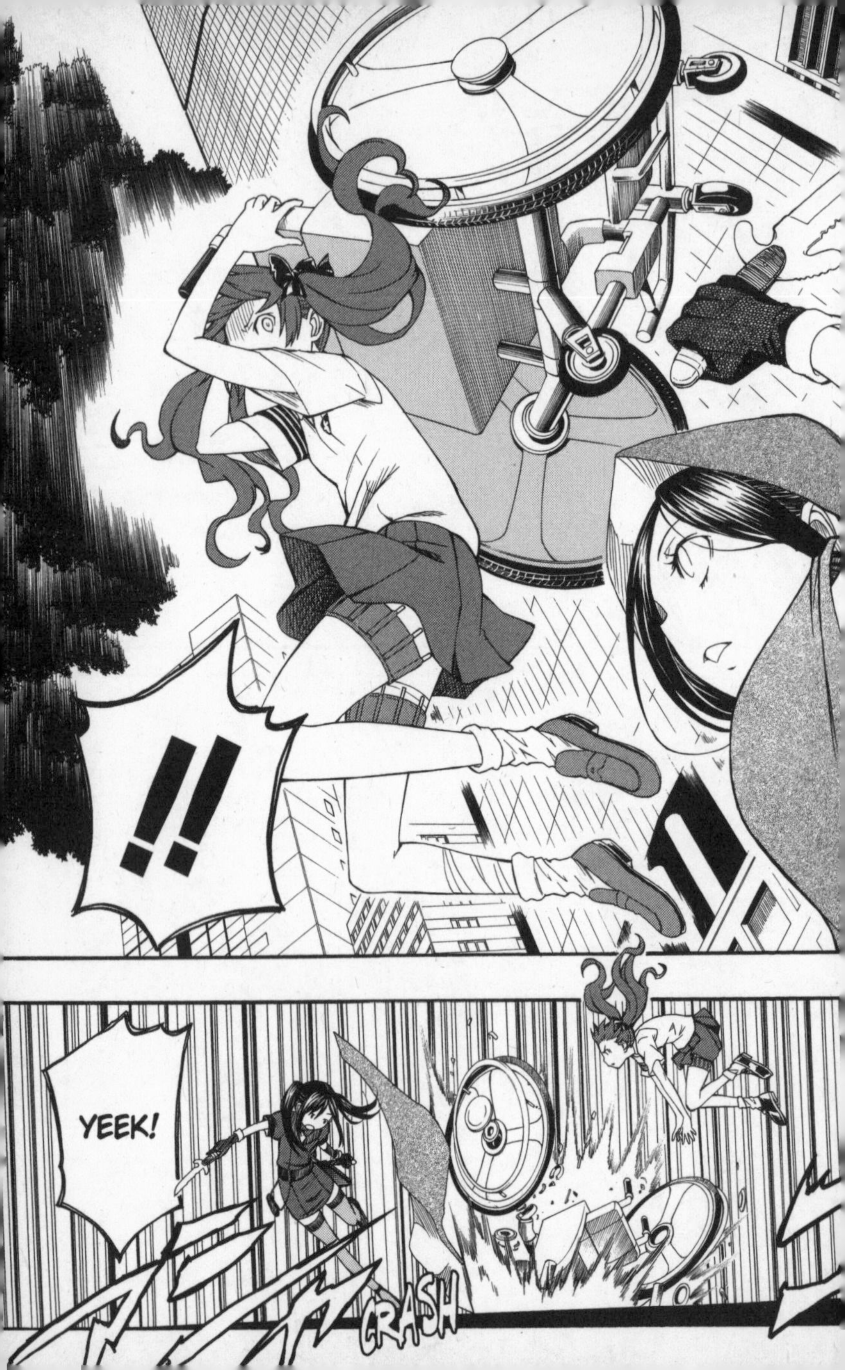
!!
YEEK!
CRASH

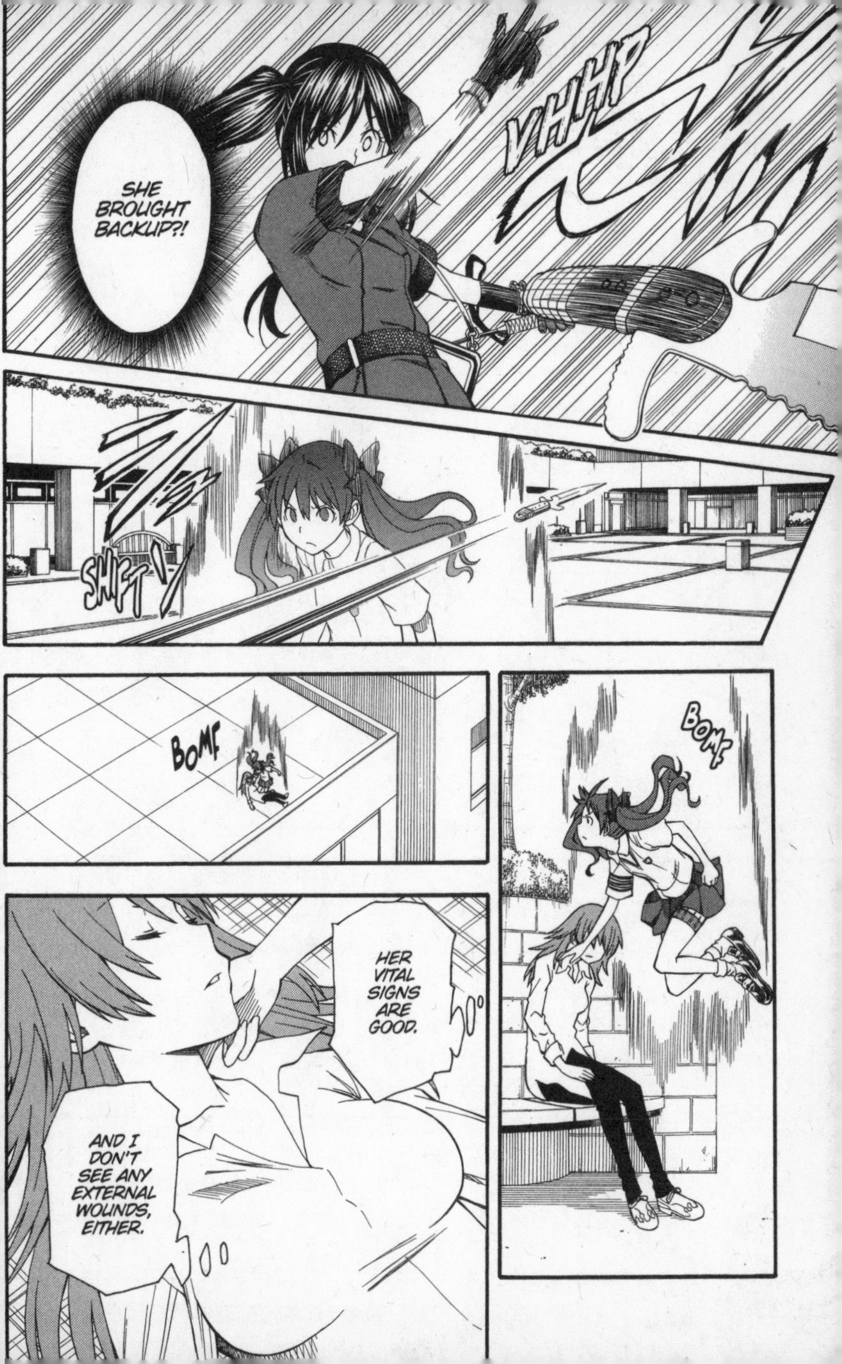
VHHP
SHE BROUGHT BACKUP?!
SHIFT
BOMF
BOMF
HER VITAL SIGNS ARE GOOD.
AND I DON'T SEE ANY EXTERNAL WOUNDS, EITHER.

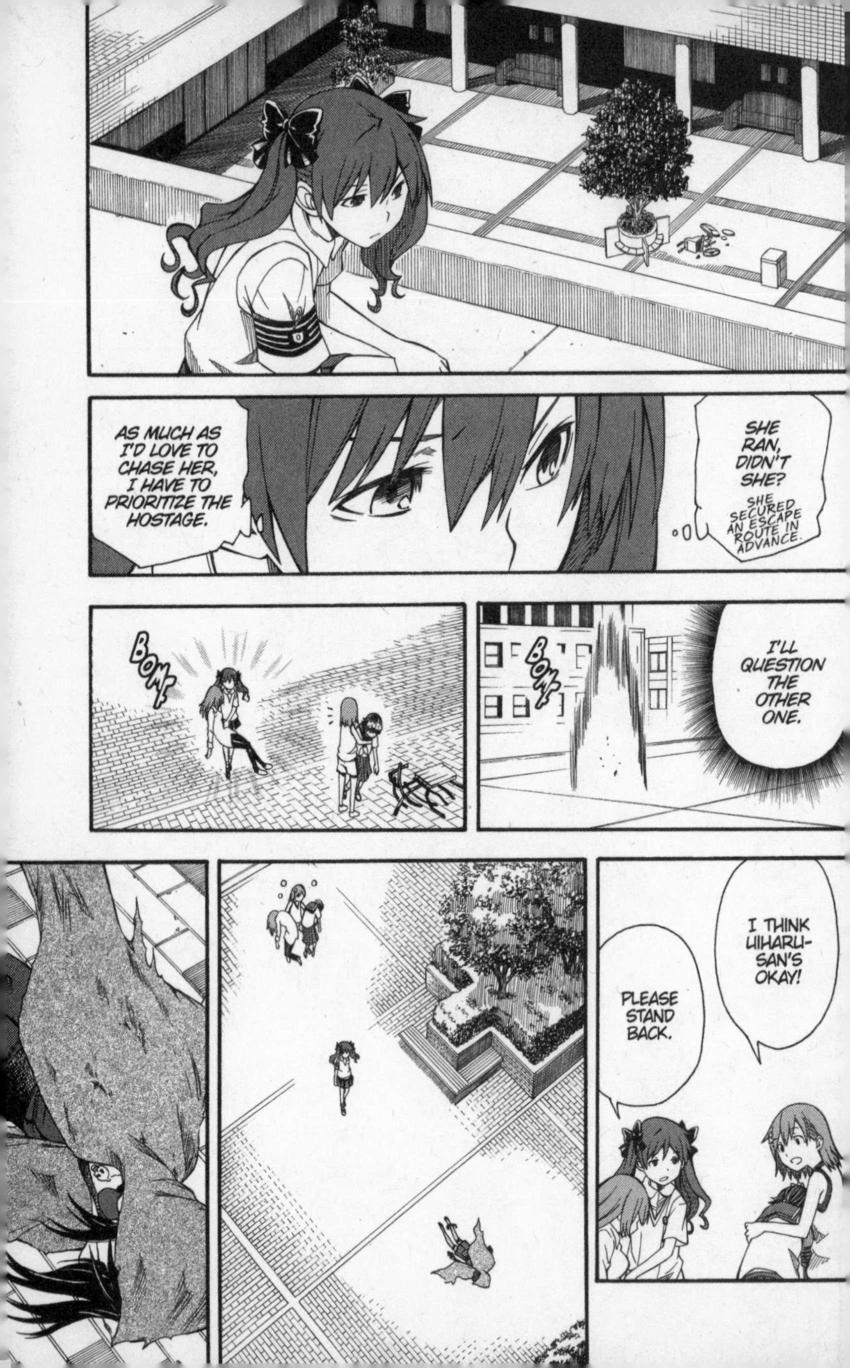
SHE RAN, DIDN'T SHE?
SHE SECURED AN ESCAPE ROUTE IN ADVANCE.
AS MUCH AS I'D LOVE TO CHASE HER, I HAVE TO PRIORITIZE THE HOSTAGE.
I'LL QUESTION THE OTHER ONE.
BOMF
BOMF
I THINK UIHARU-SAN'S OKAY!
PLEASE STAND BACK.

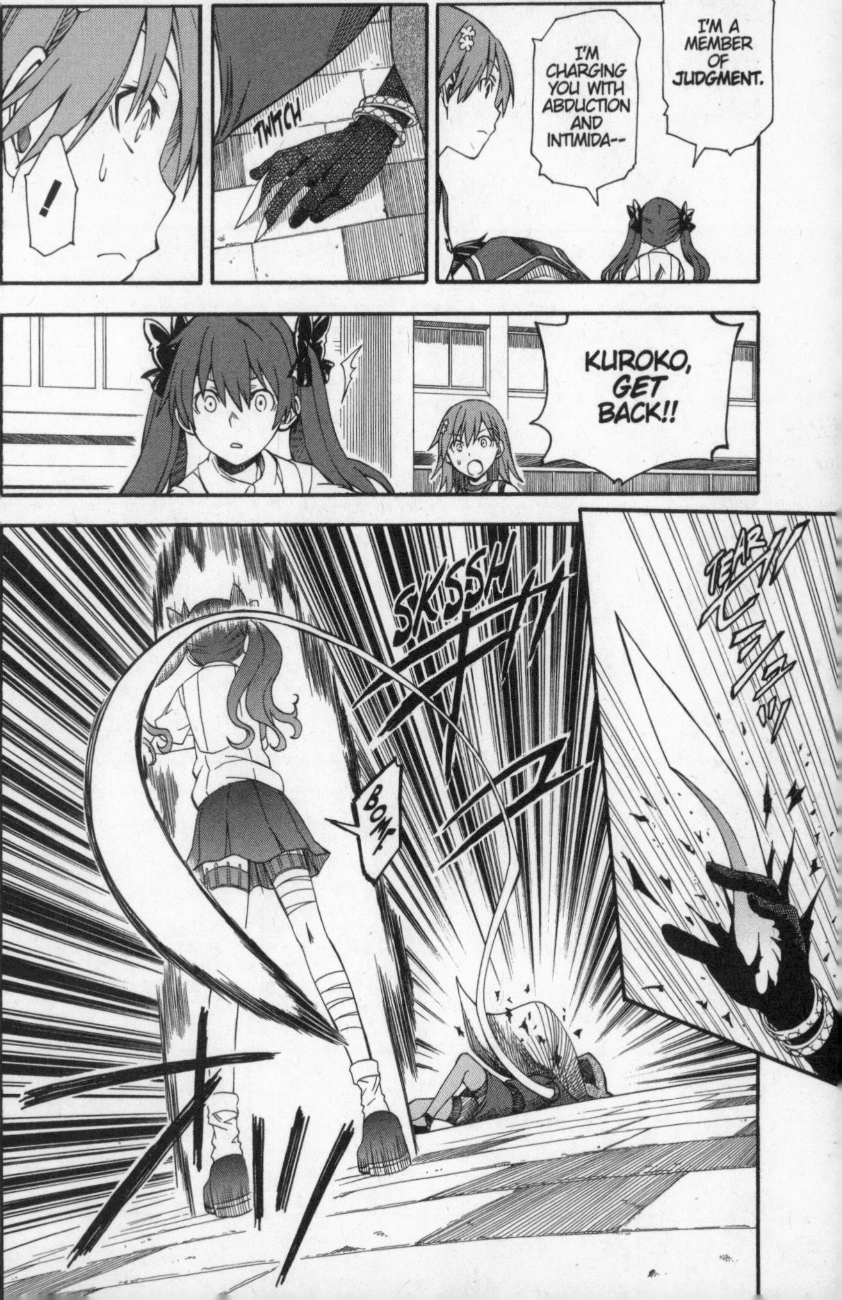
I'M A MEMBER OF JUDGMENT.
I'M CHARGING YOU WITH ABDUCTION AND INTIMIDA--
TWITCH
!
KUROKO, GET BACK!!
TEAR
SKSSH
BOM

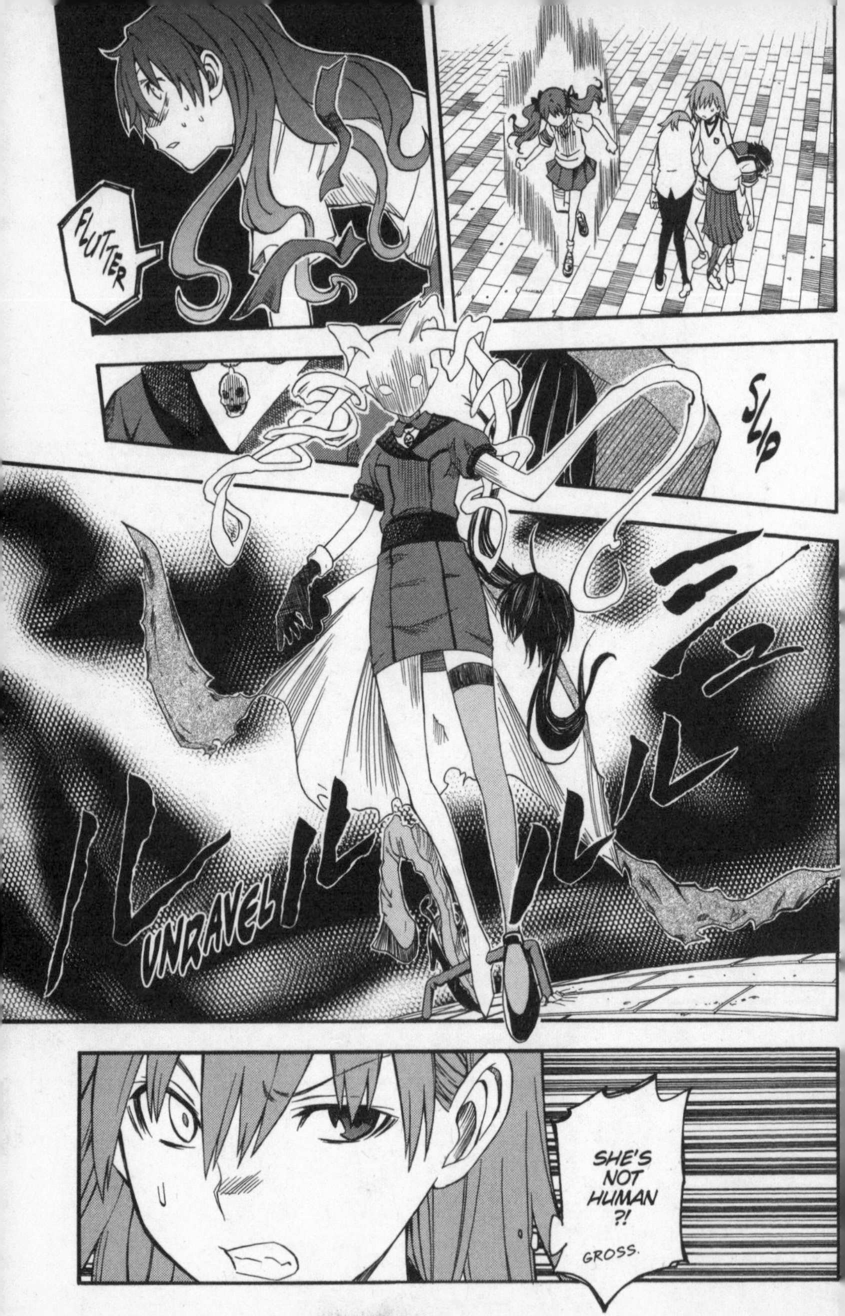
FLUTTER
SLIP
UNRAVEL
SHE'S NOT HUMAN ?!
GROSS.

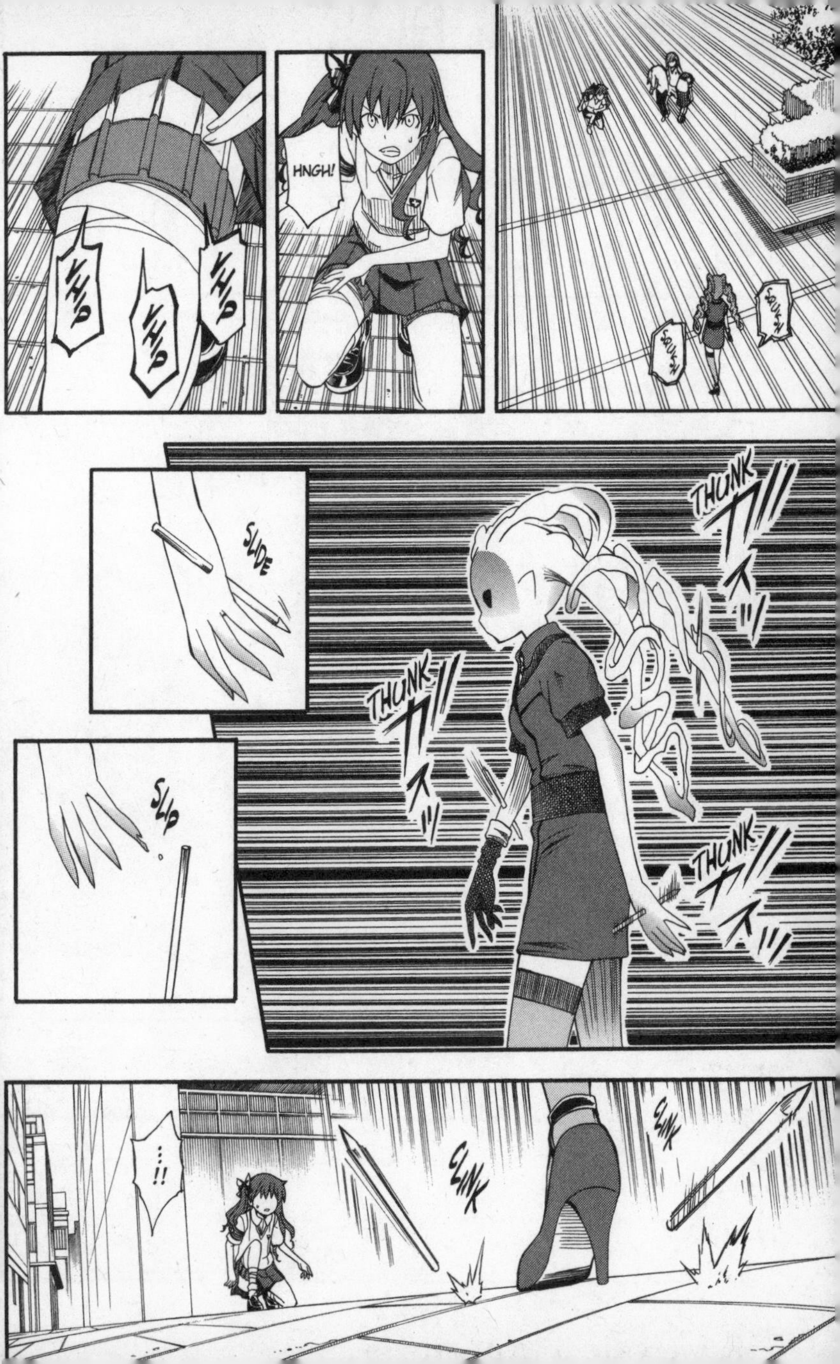
SQUISH
SQUISH
HNGH!
WHIP
WHIP
WHIP
THUNK
THUNK
THUNK
SLIDE
SLIP
CLINK
CLINK
...!!

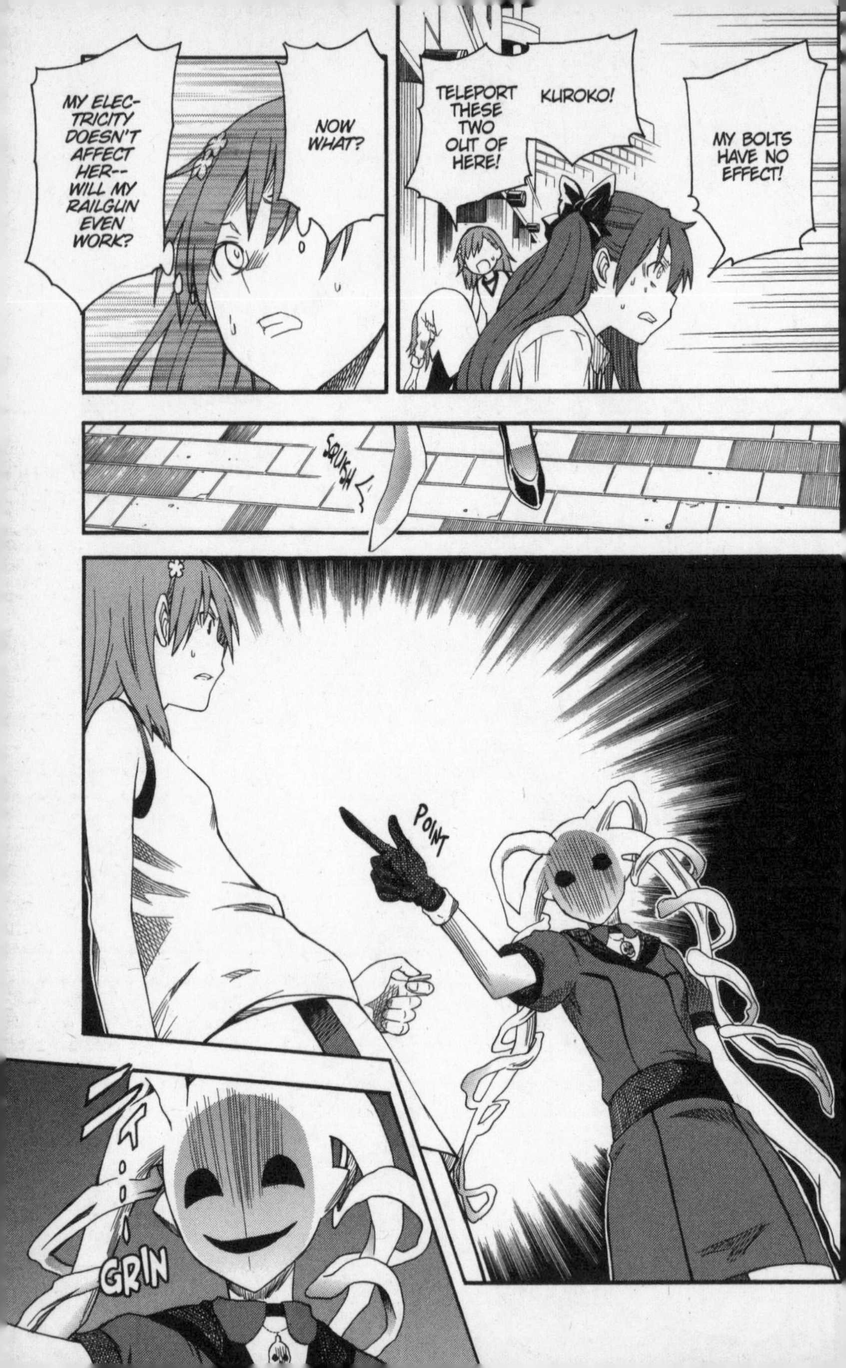
MY BOLTS HAVE NO EFFECT!
KUROKO!
TELEPORT THESE TWO OUT OF HERE!
NOW WHAT?
MY ELEC-TRICITY DOESN'T AFFECT HER-- WILL MY RAILGUN EVEN WORK?
SQUISH
POINT
GRIN

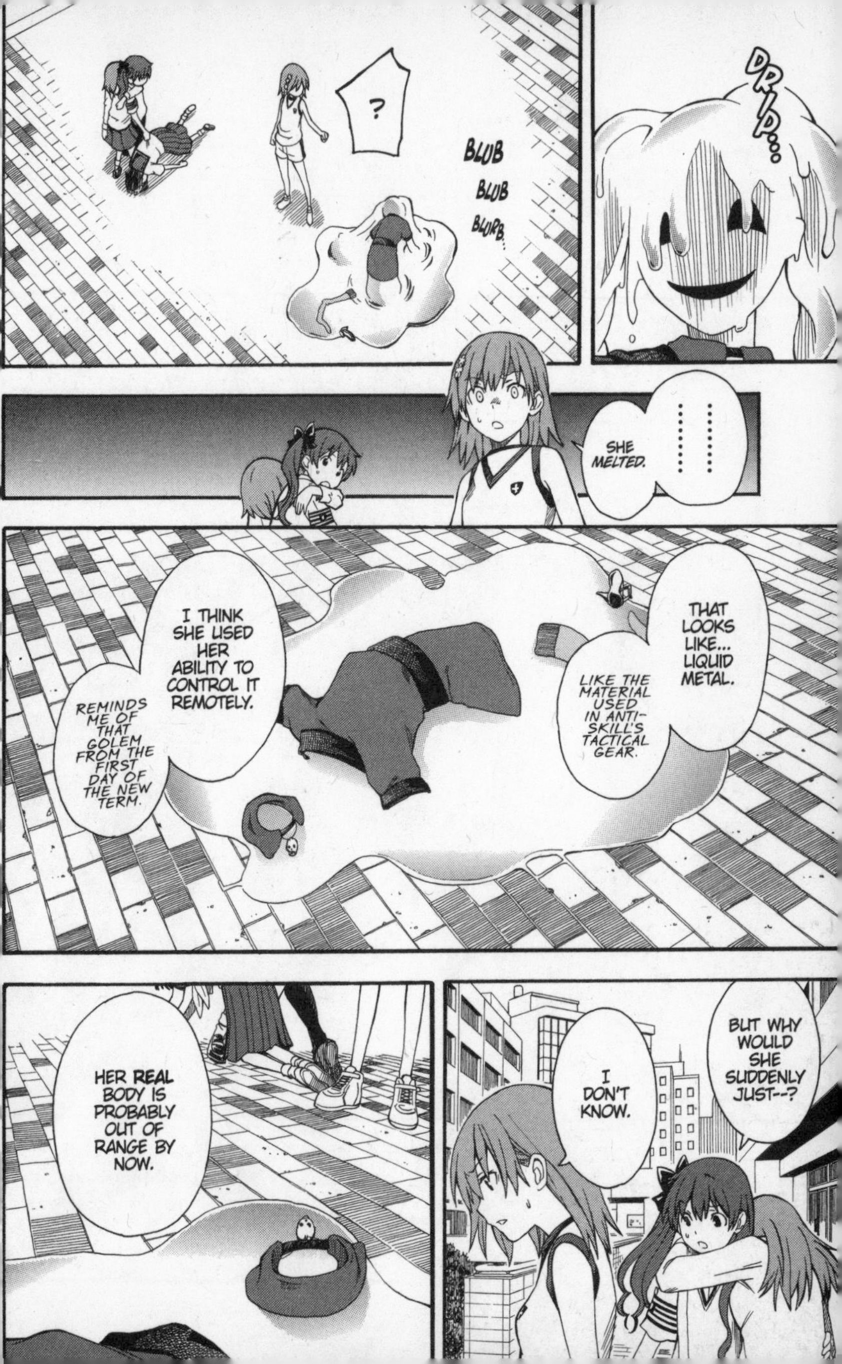
DRIP...
?
BLUB
BLUB
BLURB...
......
SHE MELTED.
THAT LOOKS LIKE... LIQUID METAL.
LIKE THE MATERIAL USED IN ANTI-SKILL'S TACTICAL GEAR.
I THINK SHE USED HER ABILITY TO CONTROL IT REMOTELY.
REMINDS ME OF THAT GOLEM FROM THE FIRST DAY OF THE NEW TERM.
BUT WHY WOULD SHE SUDDENLY JUST--?
I DON'T KNOW.
HER REAL BODY IS PROBABLY OUT OF RANGE BY NOW.

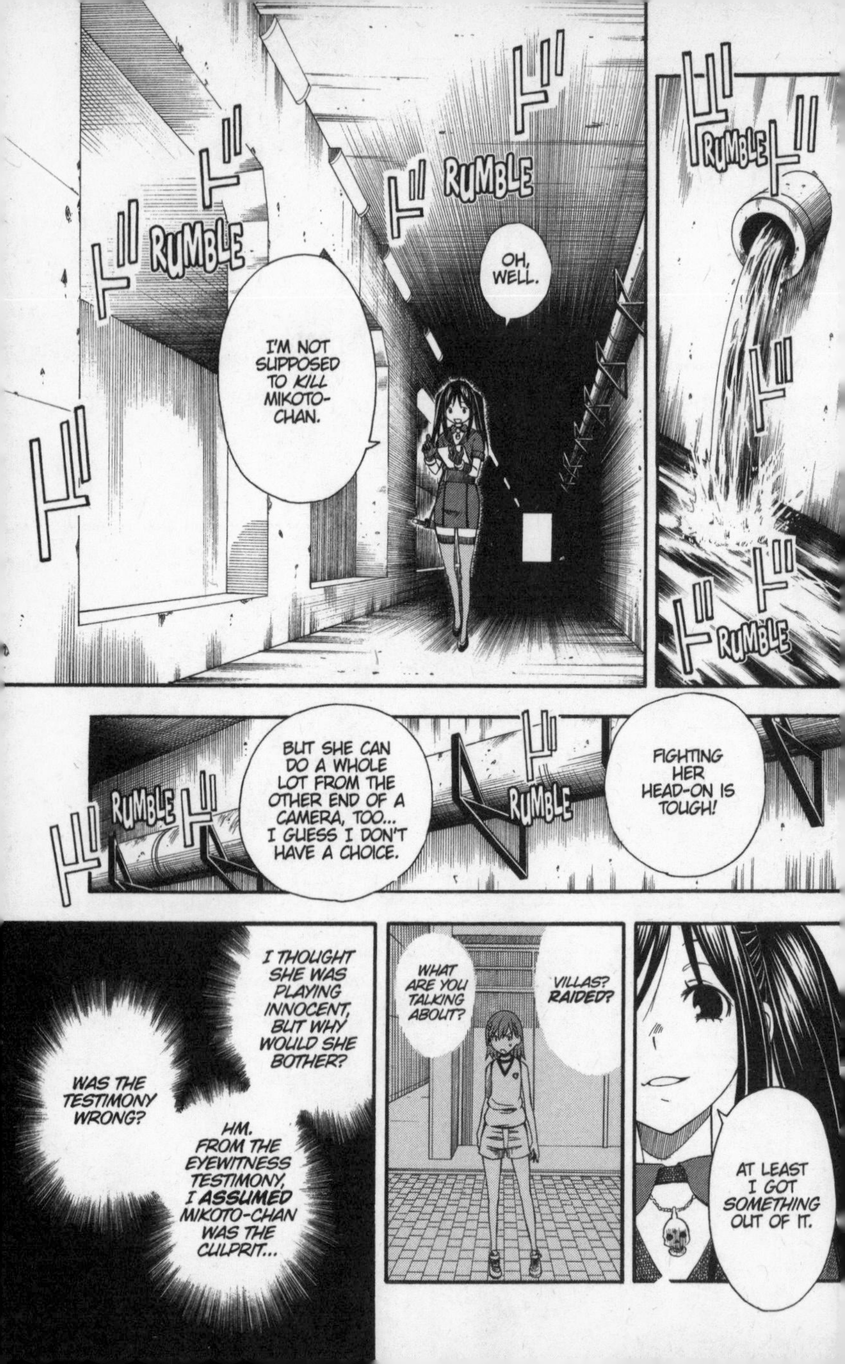

RUMBLE
RUMBLE
RUMBLE
RUMBLE
OH, WELL.
I'M NOT SUPPOSED TO *KILL* MIKOTO-CHAN.
FIGHTING HER HEAD-ON IS TOUGH!
RUMBLE
BUT SHE CAN DO A WHOLE LOT FROM THE OTHER END OF A CAMERA, TOO... I GUESS I DON'T HAVE A CHOICE.
RUMBLE
AT LEAST I GOT SOMETHING OUT OF IT.
VILLAS? RAIDED?
WHAT ARE YOU TALKING ABOUT?
HM. FROM THE EYEWITNESS TESTIMONY, I **ASSUMED** MIKOTO-CHAN WAS THE CULPRIT...
I THOUGHT SHE WAS PLAYING INNOCENT, BUT WHY WOULD SHE BOTHER?
WAS THE TESTIMONY WRONG?

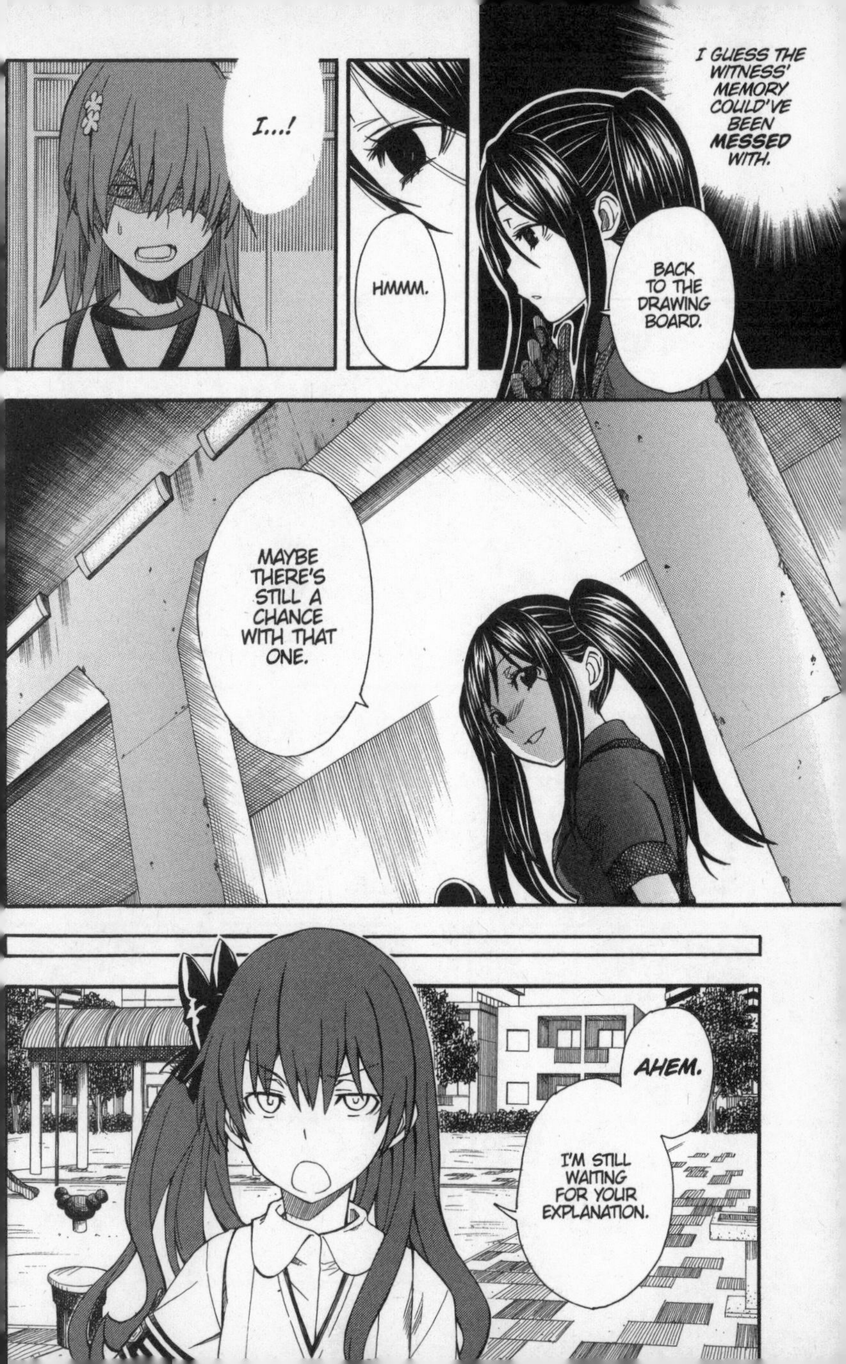
I GUESS THE WITNESS' MEMORY COULD'VE BEEN MESSED WITH.
BACK TO THE DRAWING BOARD.
HMMM.
I...!
MAYBE THERE'S STILL A CHANCE WITH THAT ONE.
AHEM.
I'M STILL WAITING FOR YOUR EXPLANATION.

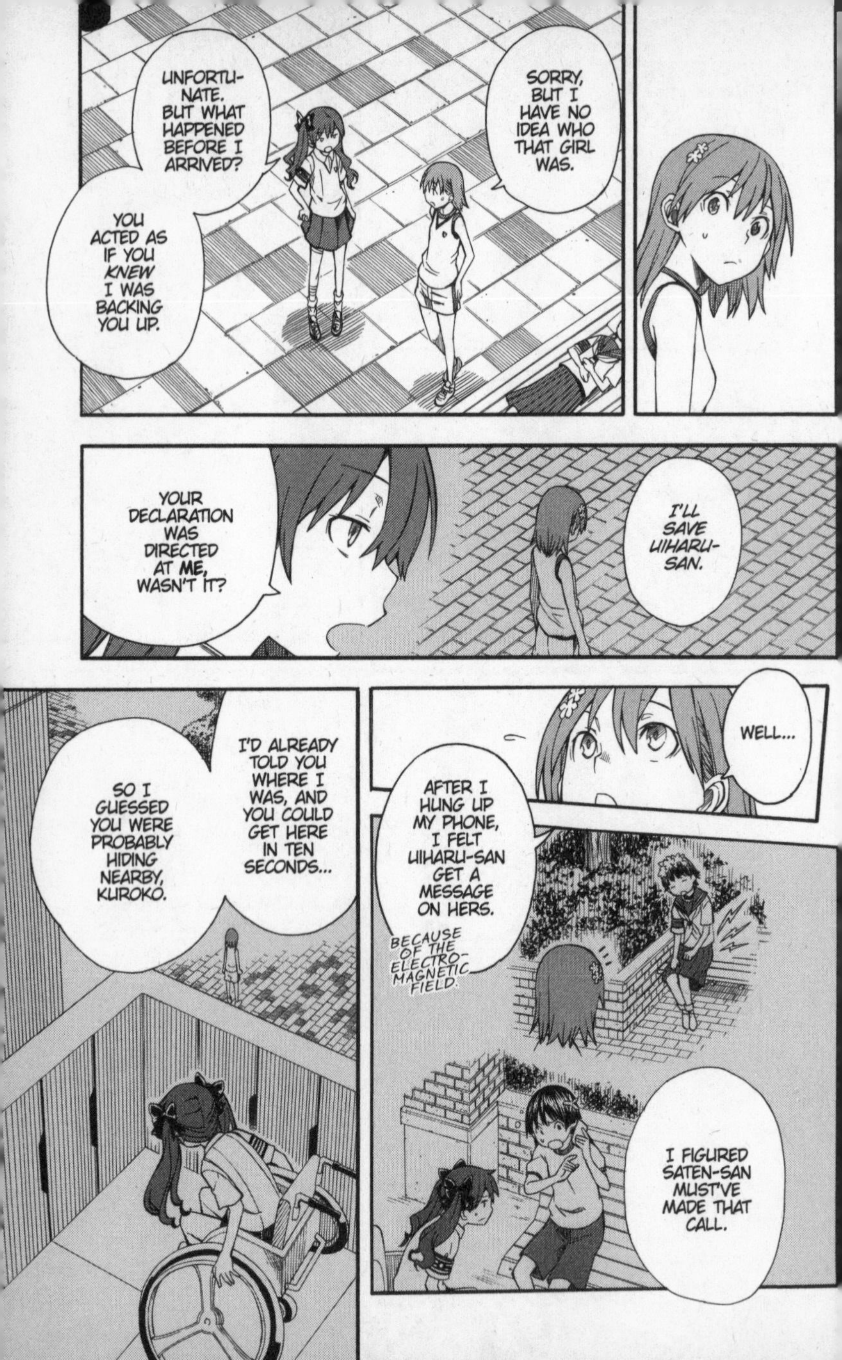
SORRY, BUT I HAVE NO IDEA WHO THAT GIRL WAS.
UNFORTUNATE. BUT WHAT HAPPENED BEFORE I ARRIVED?
YOU ACTED AS IF YOU *KNEW* I WAS BACKING YOU UP.
I'LL SAVE UIHARU-SAN.
YOUR DECLARATION WAS DIRECTED AT ME, WASN'T IT?
WELL...
AFTER I HUNG UP MY PHONE, I FELT UIHARU-SAN GET A MESSAGE ON HERS.
BECAUSE OF THE ELECTRO-MAGNETIC FIELD.
I FIGURED SATEN-SAN MUST'VE MADE THAT CALL.
I'D ALREADY TOLD YOU WHERE I WAS, AND YOU COULD GET HERE IN TEN SECONDS...
SO I GUESSED YOU WERE PROBABLY HIDING NEARBY, KUROKO.

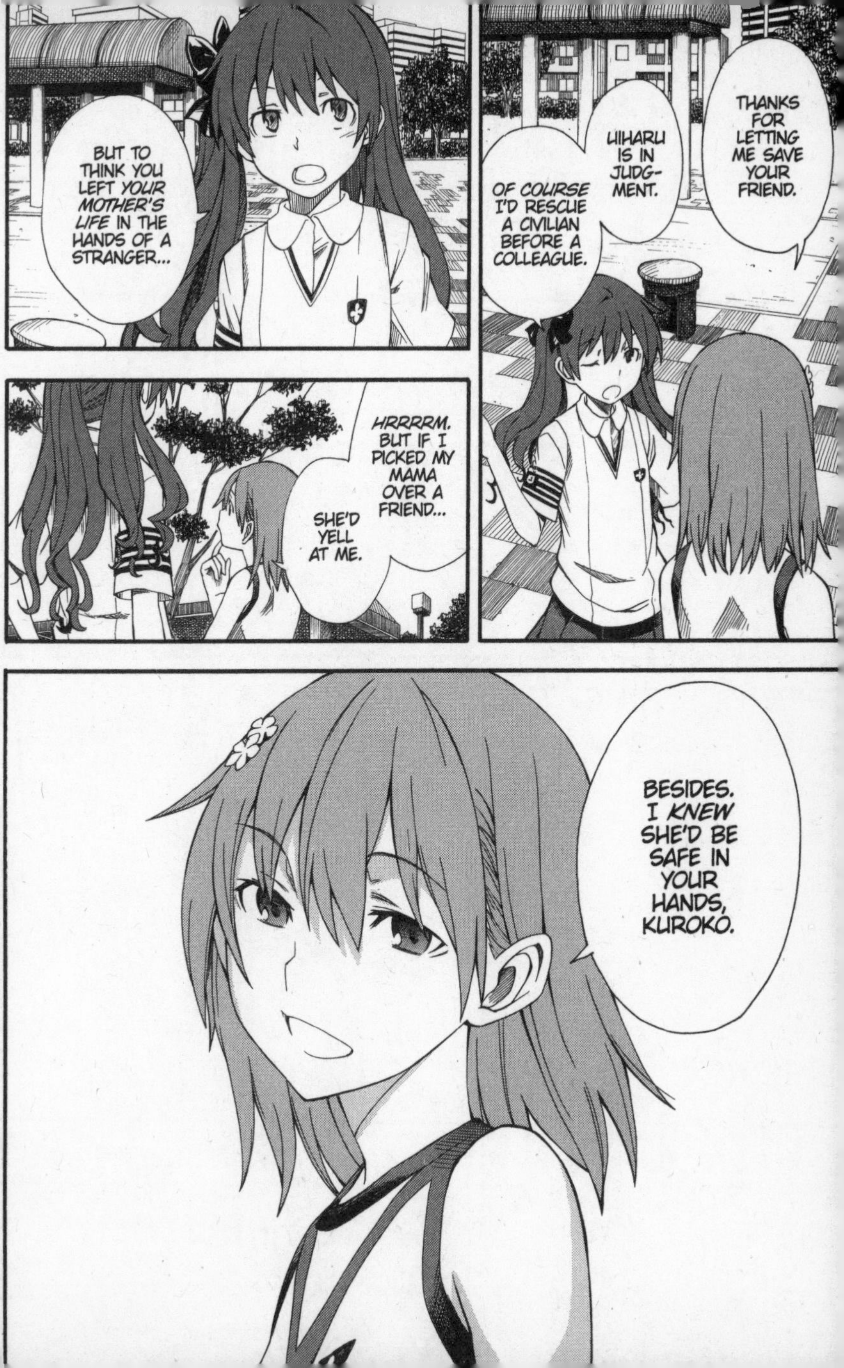
THANKS FOR LETTING ME SAVE YOUR FRIEND.
UIHARU IS IN JUDGMENT.
OF COURSE I'D RESCUE A CIVILIAN BEFORE A COLLEAGUE.
BUT TO THINK YOU LEFT *YOUR MOTHER'S LIFE* IN THE HANDS OF A STRANGER...
HRRRRM. BUT IF I PICKED MY MAMA OVER A FRIEND...
SHE'D YELL AT ME.
BESIDES. I *KNEW* SHE'D BE SAFE IN YOUR HANDS, KUROKO.

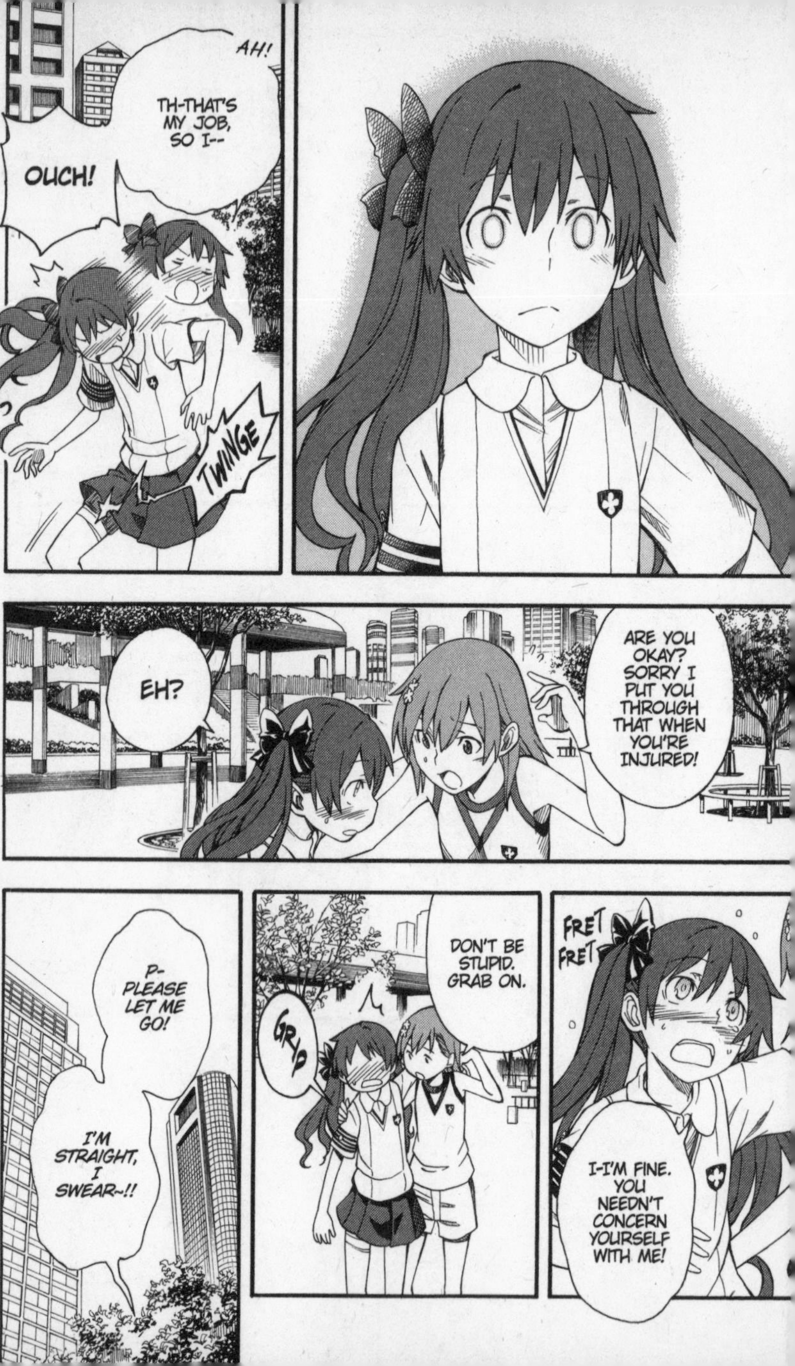
AH!
TH-THAT'S MY JOB, SO I--
OUCH!
TWINGE
ARE YOU OKAY? SORRY I PUT YOU THROUGH THAT WHEN YOU'RE INJURED!
EH?
FRET FRET
I-I'M FINE. YOU NEEDN'T CONCERN YOURSELF WITH ME!
DON'T BE STUPID. GRAB ON.
GRIP
P-PLEASE LET ME GO!
I'M STRAIGHT, I SWEAR~!!

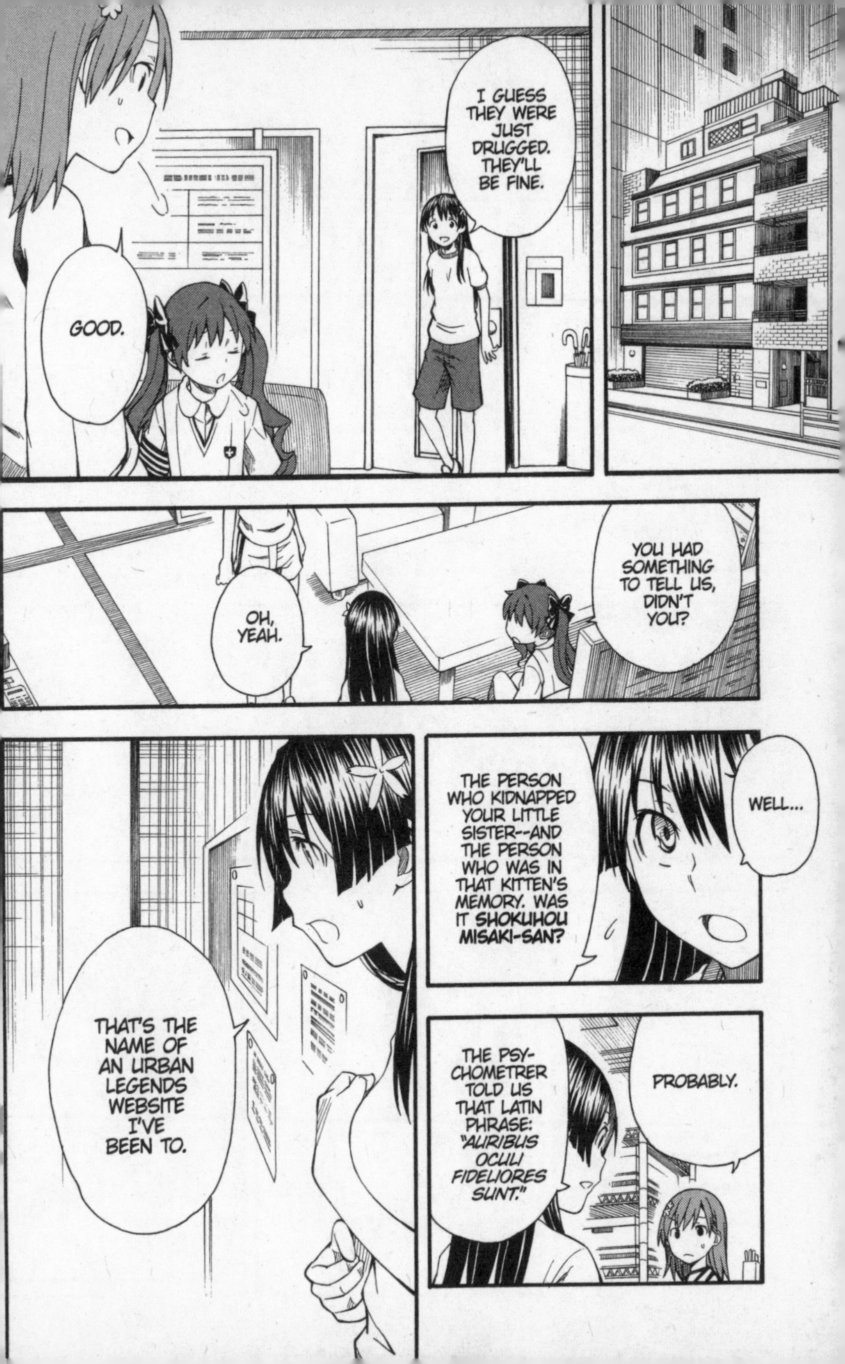
I GUESS THEY WERE JUST DRUGGED. THEY'LL BE FINE.
GOOD.
YOU HAD SOMETHING TO TELL US, DIDN'T YOU?
OH, YEAH.
WELL...
THE PERSON WHO KIDNAPPED YOUR LITTLE SISTER--AND THE PERSON WHO WAS IN THAT KITTEN'S MEMORY. WAS IT SHOKUHOU MISAKI-SAN?
PROBABLY.
THE PSY-CHOMETRER TOLD US THAT LATIN PHRASE: "AURIBUS OCULI FIDELIORES SUNT."
THAT'S THE NAME OF AN URBAN LEGENDS WEBSITE I'VE BEEN TO.

AN URBAN LEGENDS WEBSITE? WHY WOULD SHOKUHOU MISAKI CARE ABOUT THAT?

IT'S NOT JUST A RUMOR HUB.

THEY ACTUALLY HAVE A TEAM OF INVESTIGATORS WHO GO OUT TO VERIFY THINGS.

A LITTLE PAST LUNCH YESTERDAY, RIGHT AFTER YOUR SISTER WAS KIDNAPPED...

I WAS LOOKING FOR THE SHADOW METAL AND UIHARU TRIED TO GET BACK ON THE SITE.

BUT SHE COULDN'T FIND IT.

BUT I JUST FOUND A MOUNTAIN OF SIMILAR PAGES.

Bestiaria Latin Proverbs: Dulcis in
...sunt, omnes tamen usui... Ma
...ctra • Haec manus inimica ty
• Auriculas asini Mida rex h

Bestiaria Latin Proverbs: Quo alt
...sunt, omnes tamen usui... M
...ctra • Haec manus inimica
nt • Auriculas asini Mida rex

Bestiaria Latina: Audio Latin Proverbs: E verb
Manus digiti coaequales non sunt, omnes tamen usui... M
corporis, digiti chordarum plectra • Haec manus inimic
Auribus oculi fideliores sunt • Auriculas asini Mida r
E verbis fatuos, ex aure ...

Bestiaria Latina: Audio Latin Proverbs: Pari
And spills the upper boulders in the sun, ... Manus op
digiti chordarum plectra • Haec manus inimica tyran
fideliores sunt • Auriculas asini Mida rex habet • E
ex aure tenemus ...

Bestiaria Latina: Audio Latin Proverbs: An
Manus digiti coaequales non sunt, omnes tamen us
corporis, digiti chordarum plectra • Haec manus in
Auribus oculi fideliores sunt • Auriculas asini Mi
E verbis fatuos, ex aure ...

Bestiaria Latina: Audio Latin Proverbs: N
Manus digiti coaequales non sunt, omnes tamen
corporis, digiti chordarum plectra • Haec manus
oculi fideliores sunt • Auriculas asini

?!

AND JUST NOW, I SEARCHED FOR IT AGAIN...

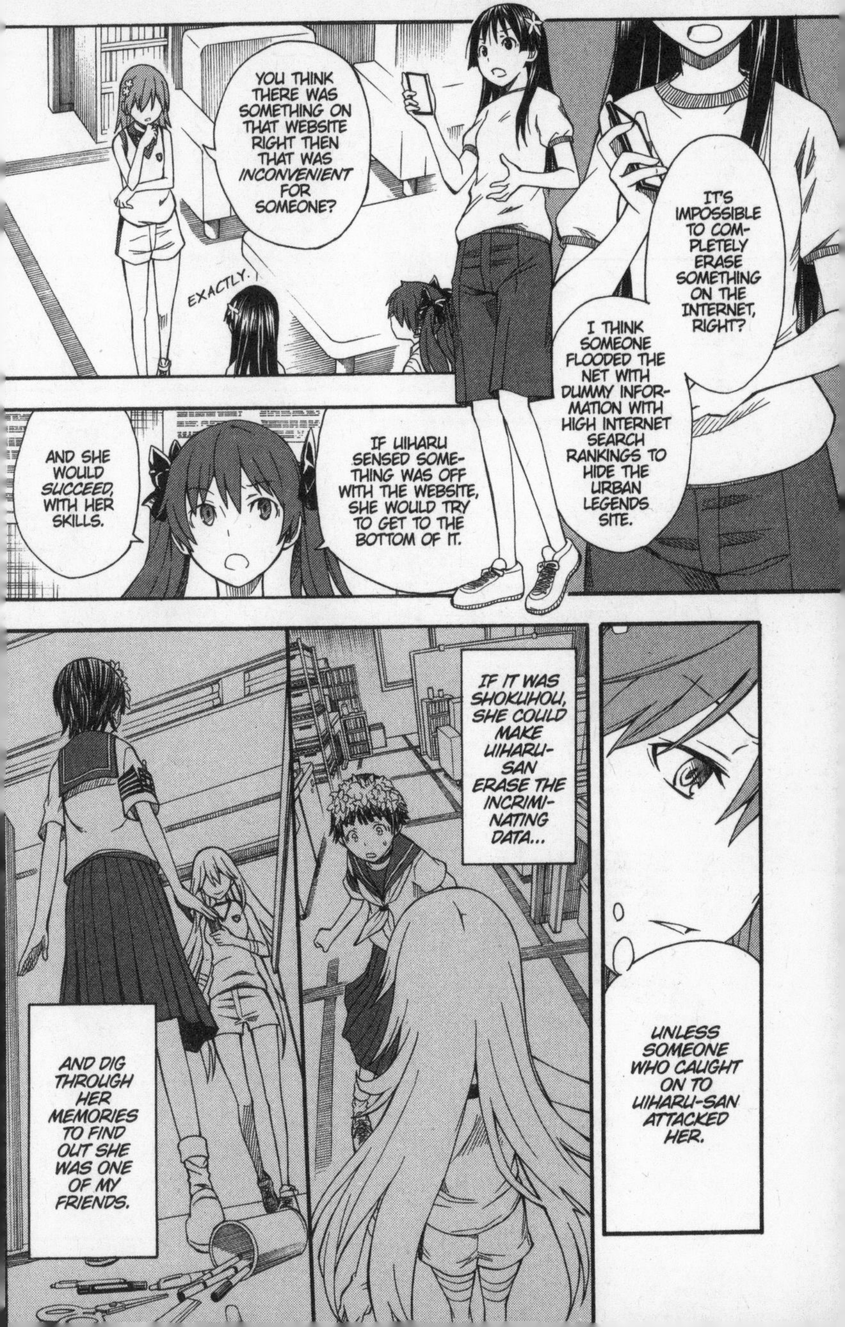
IT'S IMPOSSIBLE TO COMPLETELY ERASE SOMETHING ON THE INTERNET, RIGHT?
I THINK SOMEONE FLOODED THE NET WITH DUMMY INFORMATION WITH HIGH INTERNET SEARCH RANKINGS TO HIDE THE URBAN LEGENDS SITE.
YOU THINK THERE WAS SOMETHING ON THAT WEBSITE RIGHT THEN THAT WAS INCONVENIENT FOR SOMEONE?
EXACTLY.
IF UIHARU SENSED SOMETHING WAS OFF WITH THE WEBSITE, SHE WOULD TRY TO GET TO THE BOTTOM OF IT.
AND SHE WOULD SUCCEED, WITH HER SKILLS.
UNLESS SOMEONE WHO CAUGHT ON TO UIHARU-SAN ATTACKED HER.
IF IT WAS SHOKUHOU, SHE COULD MAKE UIHARU-SAN ERASE THE INCRIMINATING DATA...
AND DIG THROUGH HER MEMORIES TO FIND OUT SHE WAS ONE OF MY FRIENDS.

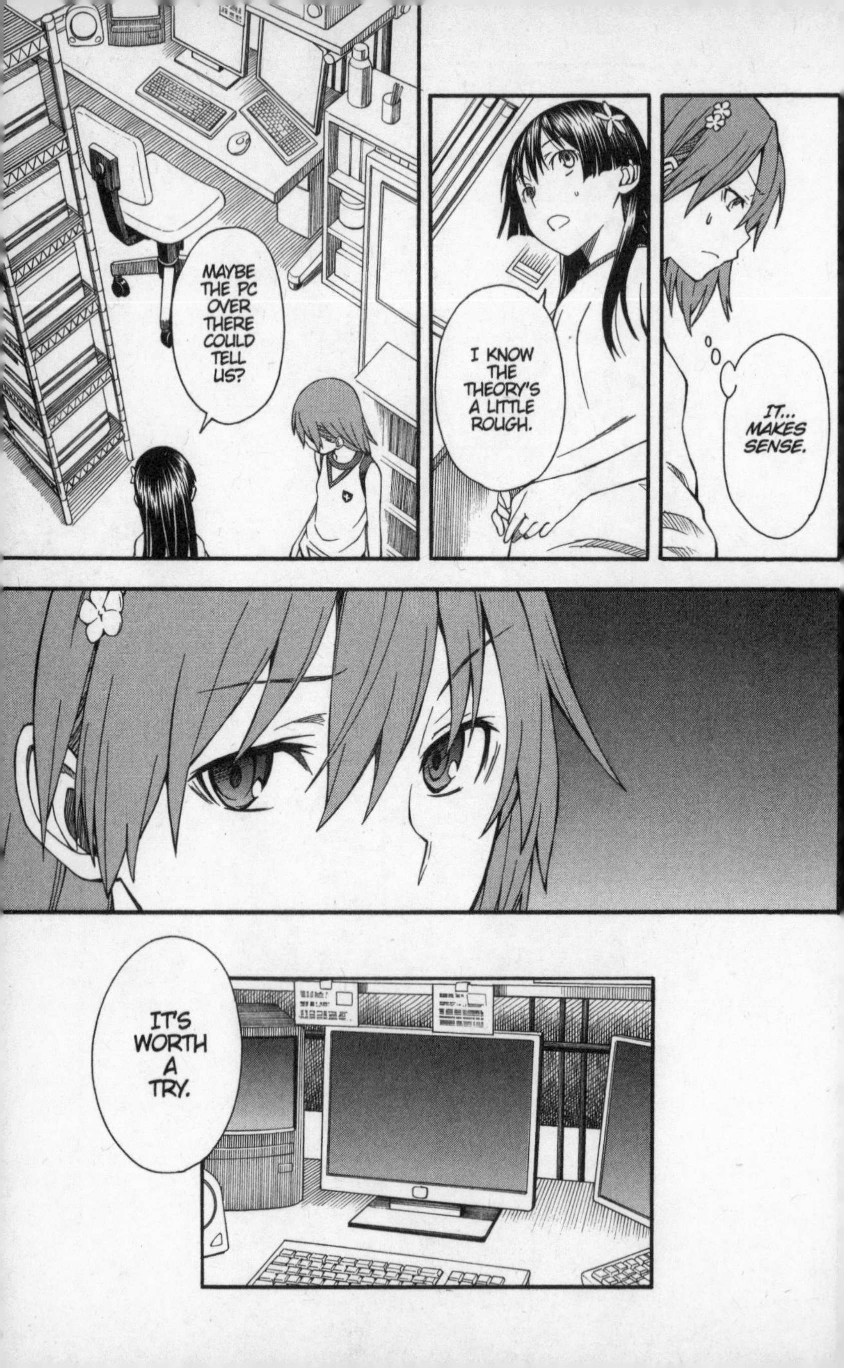
IT... MAKES SENSE.
I KNOW THE THEORY'S A LITTLE ROUGH.
MAYBE THE PC OVER THERE COULD TELL US?
IT'S WORTH A TRY.

A Certain SCIENTIFIC Railgun

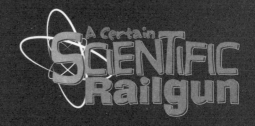

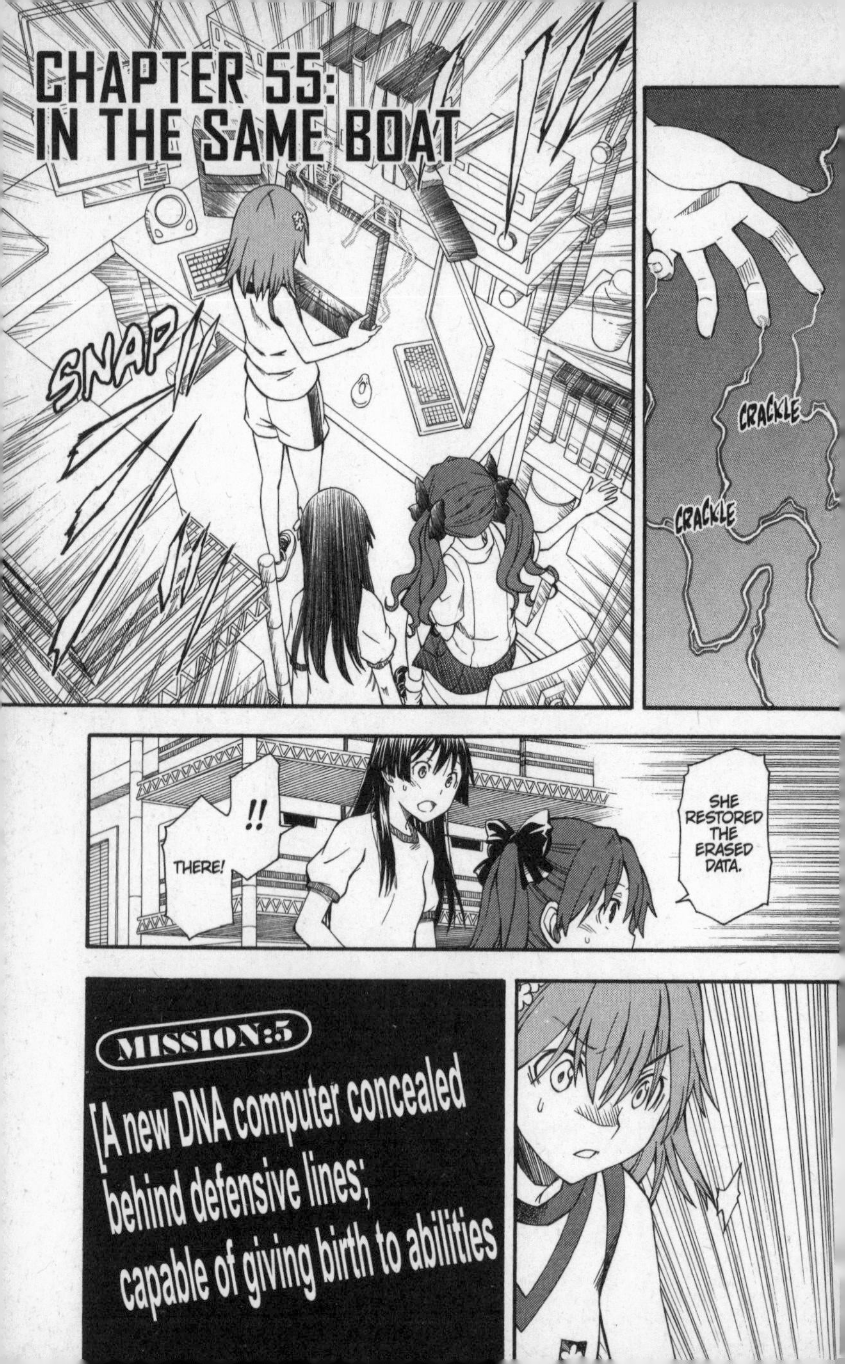
CHAPTER 55:
IN THE SAME BOAT
CRACKLE
CRACKLE
SNAP
SHE RESTORED THE ERASED DATA.
!!
THERE!
MISSION:5
[A new DNA computer concealed behind defensive lines; capable of giving birth to abilities

We investigated a rumor of a DNA computer that could "give birth to abilities." After clearing a number of concealed constructs, we stumbled upon a secret research facility in the Seventh School District,

After getting past numerous defenses masquerading as soundproof walls, you'll never believe what we saw!

A number of alleged researchers (male) guided Miss S to the building in question. Miss S is the fifth-ranked psychic enrolled at Tokiwadai Middle School.

SHOKUHOU!

I KNEW IT.

UH... HRM.

THAT BUILDING LOOKS LIKE A JUDGMENT BRANCH. THE ONLY PLACE I CAN THINK OF IN THE SECOND DISTRICT THAT LOOKS LIKE THAT...

HUH?!

LOOK AT THE PHOTOS. ANY IDEA WHERE THAT COULD BE?

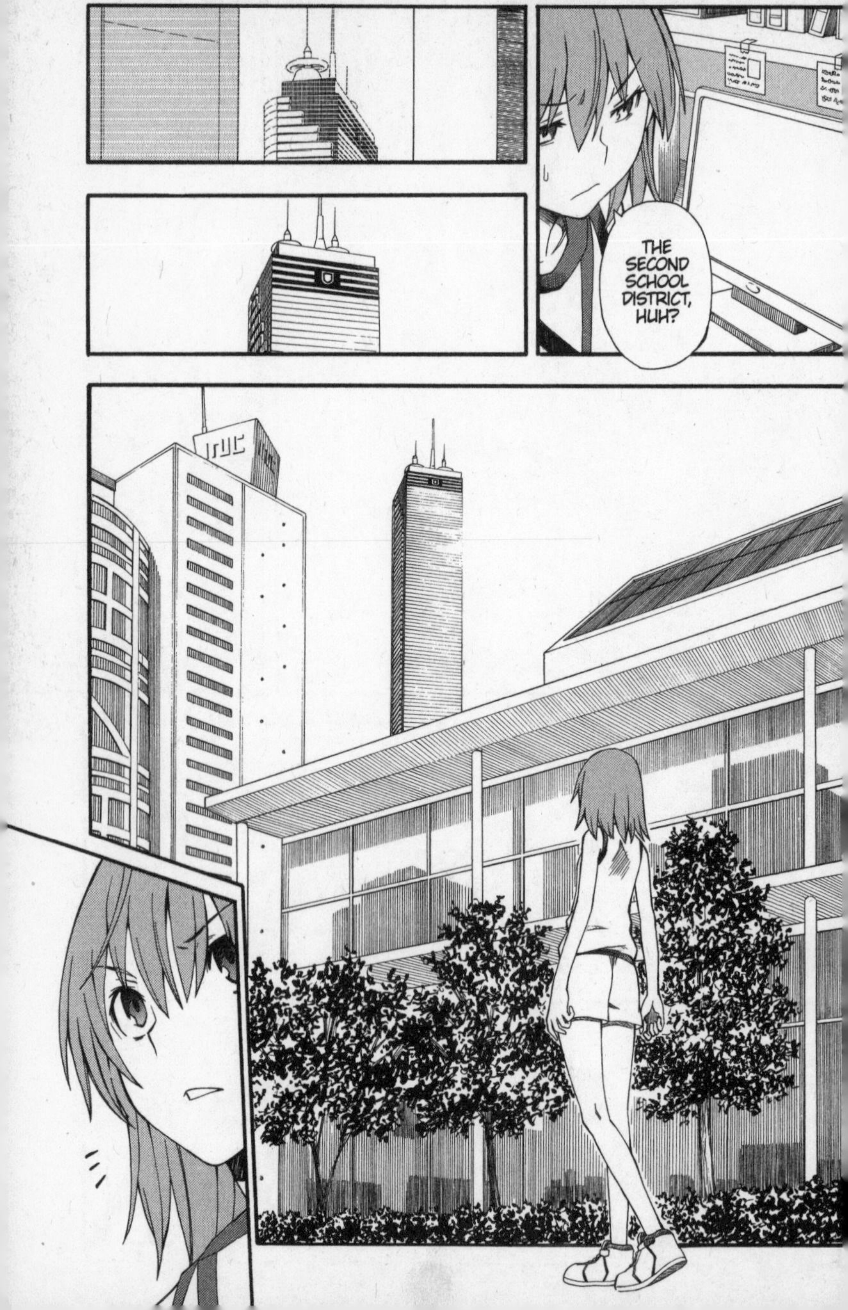
THE SECOND SCHOOL DISTRICT, HUH?

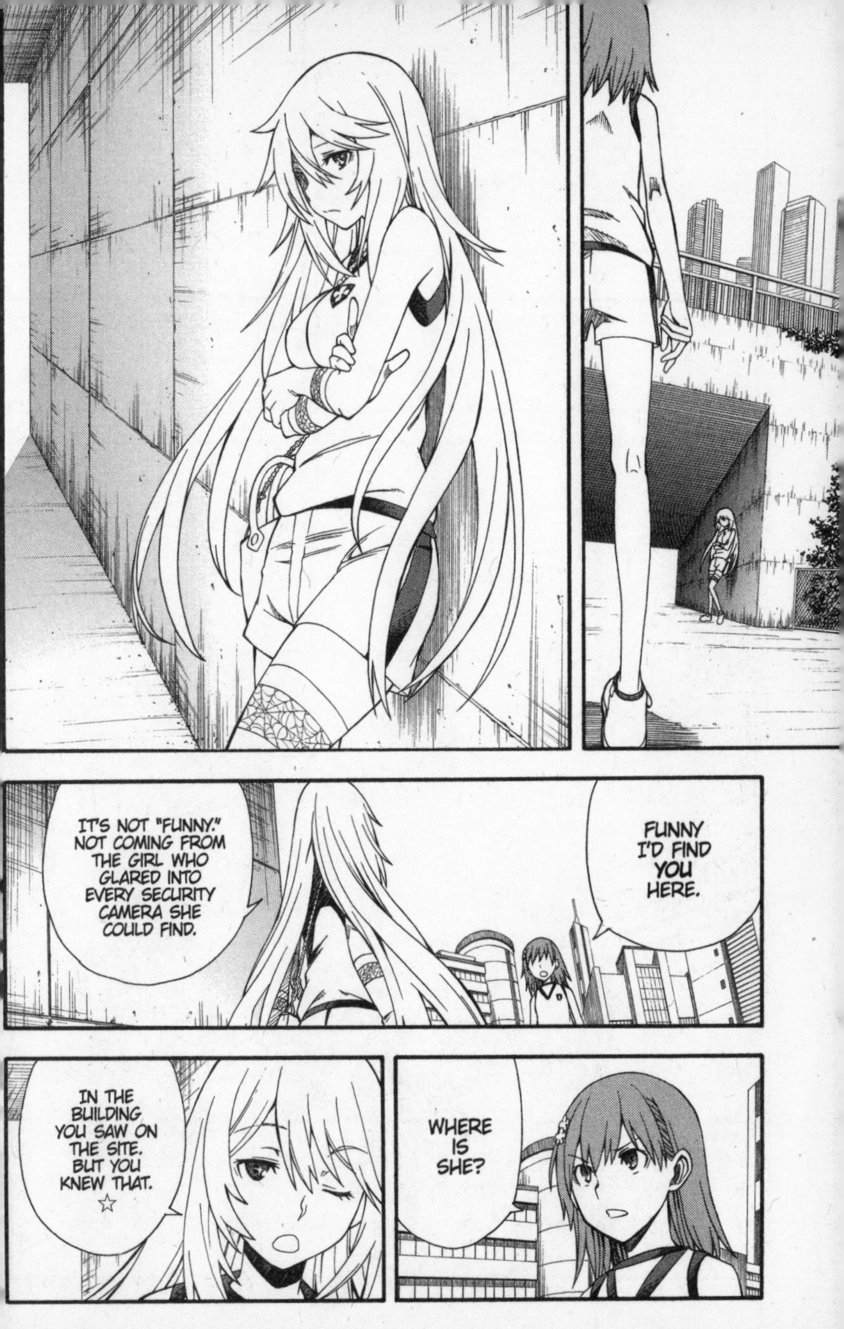
FUNNY I'D FIND YOU HERE.
IT'S NOT "FUNNY." NOT COMING FROM THE GIRL WHO GLARED INTO EVERY SECURITY CAMERA SHE COULD FIND.
WHERE IS SHE?
IN THE BUILDING YOU SAW ON THE SITE. BUT YOU KNEW THAT. ☆

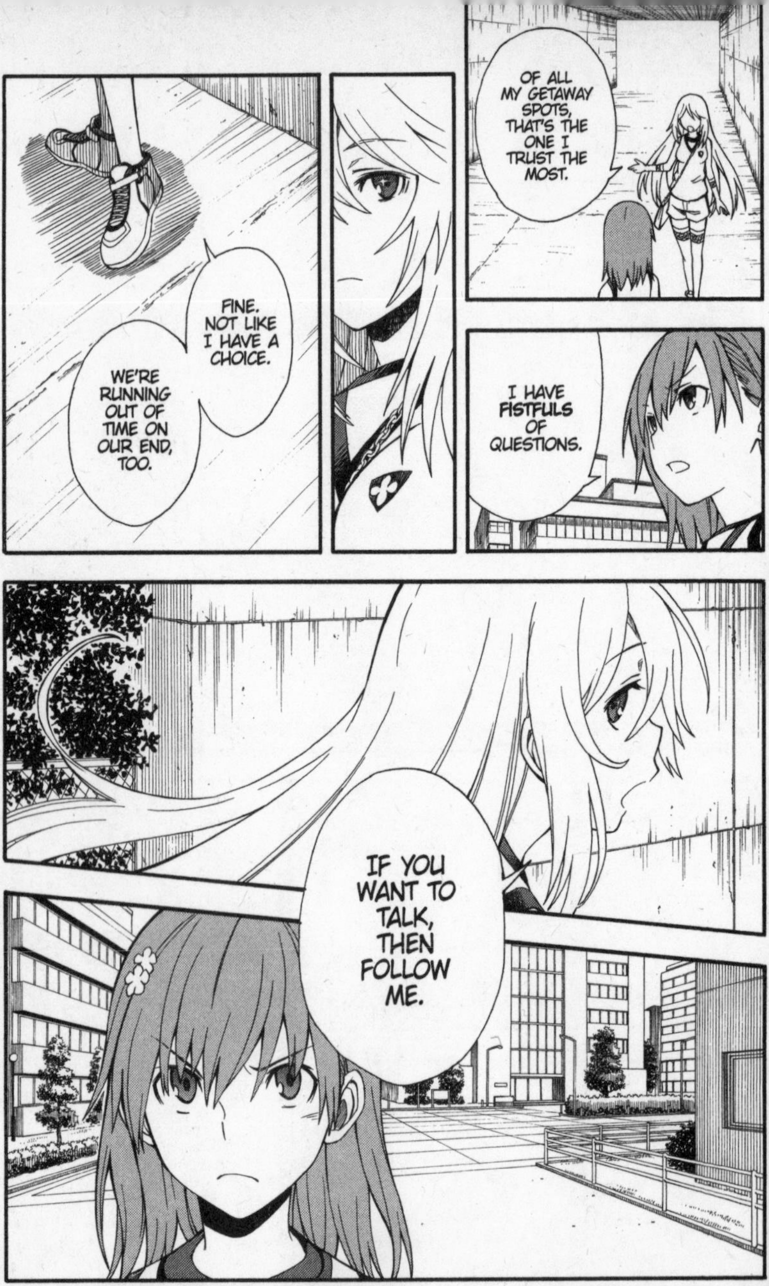
OF ALL MY GETAWAY SPOTS, THAT'S THE ONE I TRUST THE MOST.
I HAVE FISTFULS OF QUESTIONS.
FINE. NOT LIKE I HAVE A CHOICE.
WE'RE RUNNING OUT OF TIME ON OUR END, TOO.
IF YOU WANT TO TALK, THEN FOLLOW ME.

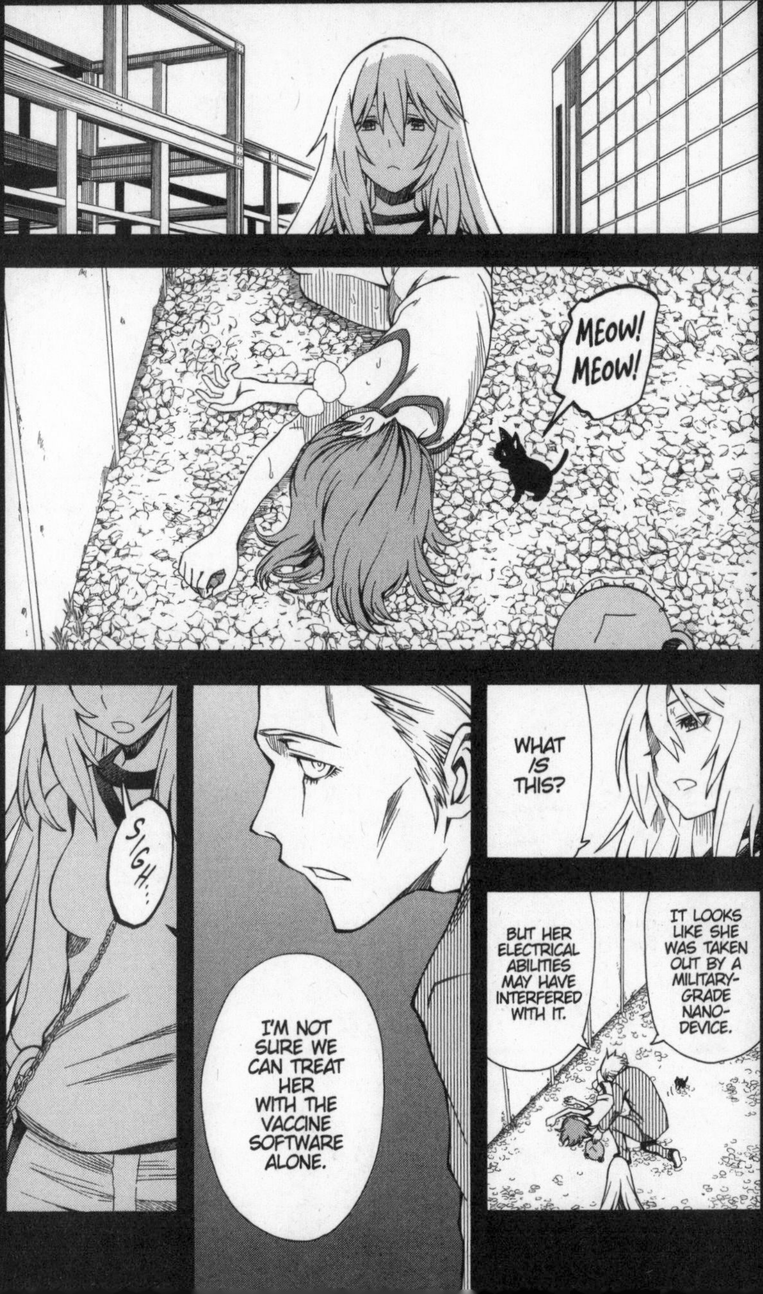
MEOW! MEOW!
WHAT IS THIS?
IT LOOKS LIKE SHE WAS TAKEN OUT BY A MILITARY-GRADE NANO-DEVICE.
BUT HER ELECTRICAL ABILITIES MAY HAVE INTERFERED WITH IT.
I'M NOT SURE WE CAN TREAT HER WITH THE VACCINE SOFTWARE ALONE.
SIGH...

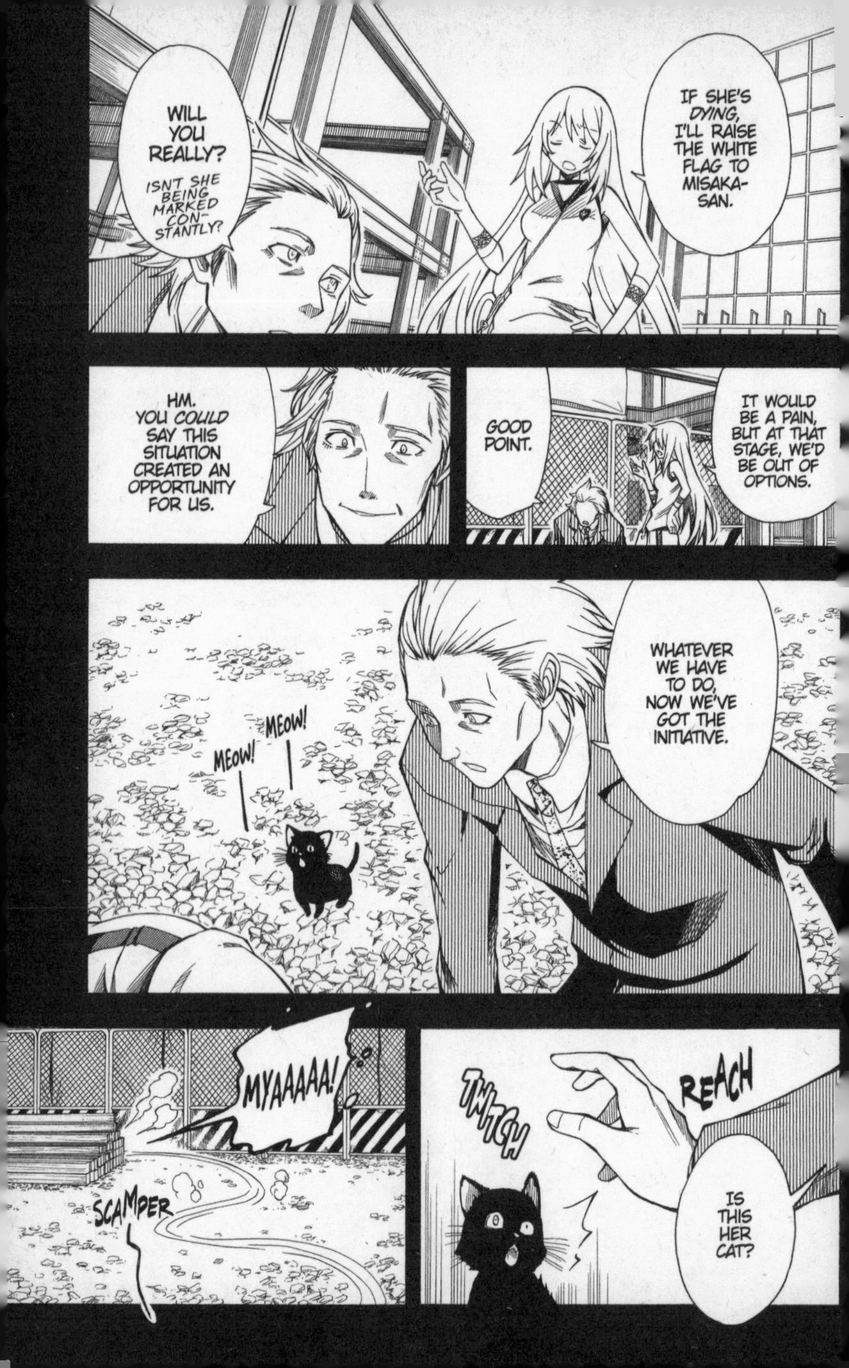
IF SHE'S DYING, I'LL RAISE THE WHITE FLAG TO MISAKA-SAN.
WILL YOU REALLY?
ISN'T SHE BEING MARKED CONSTANTLY?
IT WOULD BE A PAIN, BUT AT THAT STAGE, WE'D BE OUT OF OPTIONS.
GOOD POINT.
HM. YOU COULD SAY THIS SITUATION CREATED AN OPPORTUNITY FOR US.
WHATEVER WE HAVE TO DO, NOW WE'VE GOT THE INITIATIVE.
MEOW!
MEOW!
REACH
TWITCH
IS THIS HER CAT?
MYAAAAA!
SCAMPER

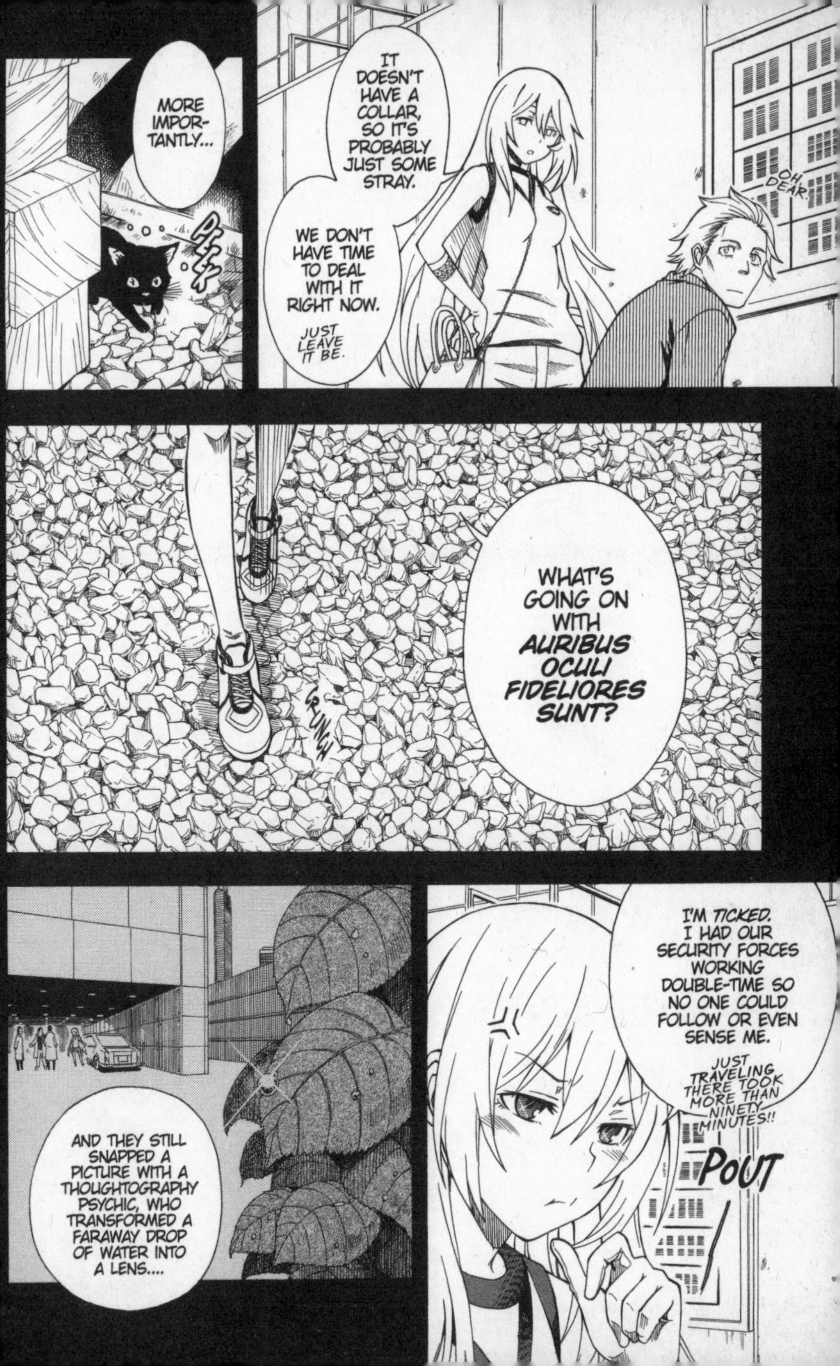
IT DOESN'T HAVE A COLLAR, SO IT'S PROBABLY JUST SOME STRAY.
WE DON'T HAVE TIME TO DEAL WITH IT RIGHT NOW.
JUST LEAVE IT BE.
OH, DEAR.
MORE IMPORTANTLY...
PEEK
WHAT'S GOING ON WITH *AURIBUS OCULI FIDELIORES SUNT?*
CRUNCH
I'M *TICKED.* I HAD OUR SECURITY FORCES WORKING DOUBLE-TIME SO NO ONE COULD FOLLOW OR EVEN SENSE ME.
JUST TRAVELING THERE TOOK MORE THAN NINETY MINUTES!!
POUT
AND THEY STILL SNAPPED A PICTURE WITH A THOUGHTOGRAPHY PSYCHIC, WHO TRANSFORMED A FARAWAY DROP OF WATER INTO A LENS....

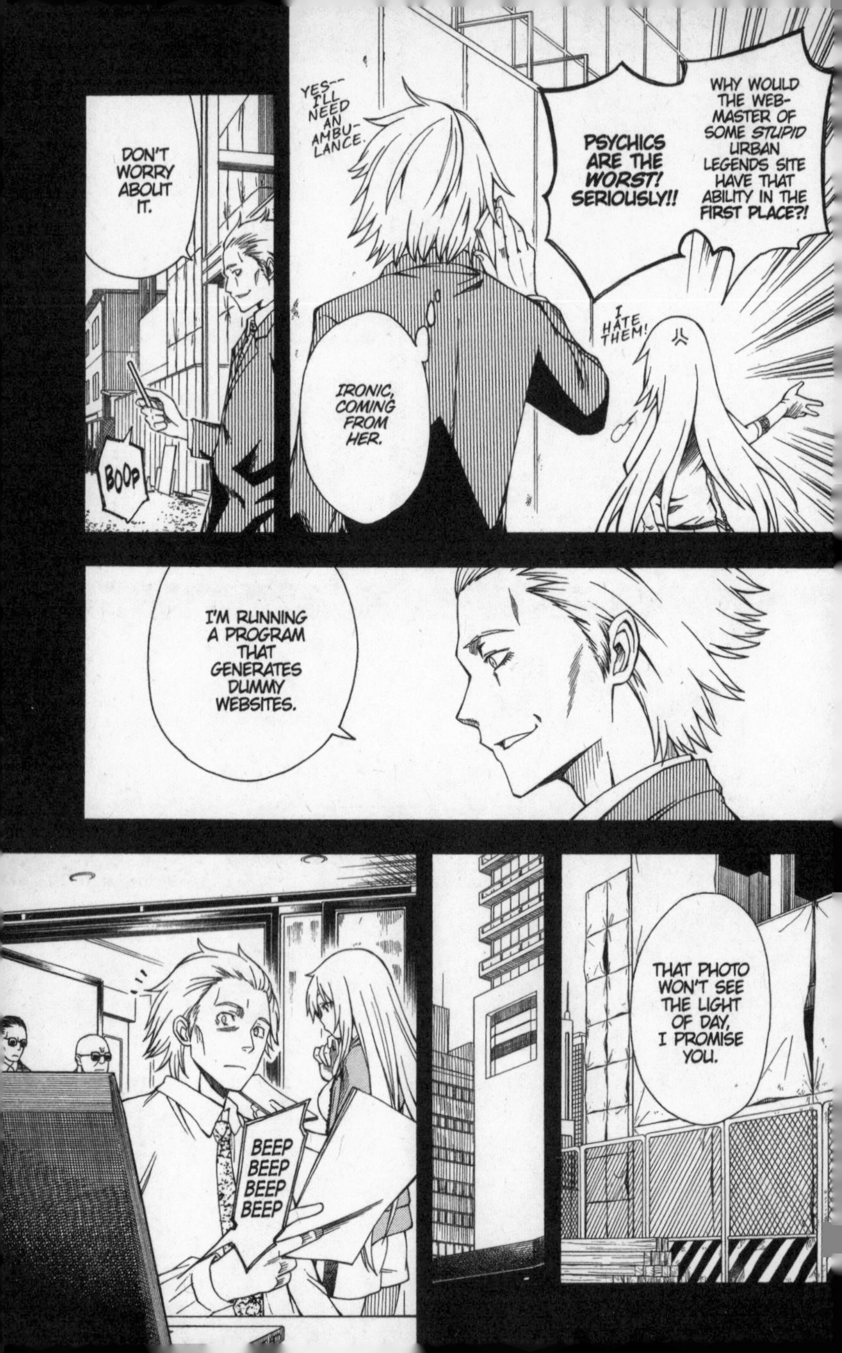
WHY WOULD THE WEB-MASTER OF SOME *STUPID* URBAN LEGENDS SITE HAVE THAT ABILITY IN THE FIRST PLACE?!
PSYCHICS ARE THE *WORST!* SERIOUSLY!!
I HATE THEM!
YES-- I'LL NEED AN AMBU-LANCE.
IRONIC, COMING FROM HER.
DON'T WORRY ABOUT IT.
BOOP
I'M RUNNING A PROGRAM THAT GENERATES DUMMY WEBSITES.
THAT PHOTO WON'T SEE THE LIGHT OF DAY, I PROMISE YOU.
BEEP BEEP BEEP BEEP

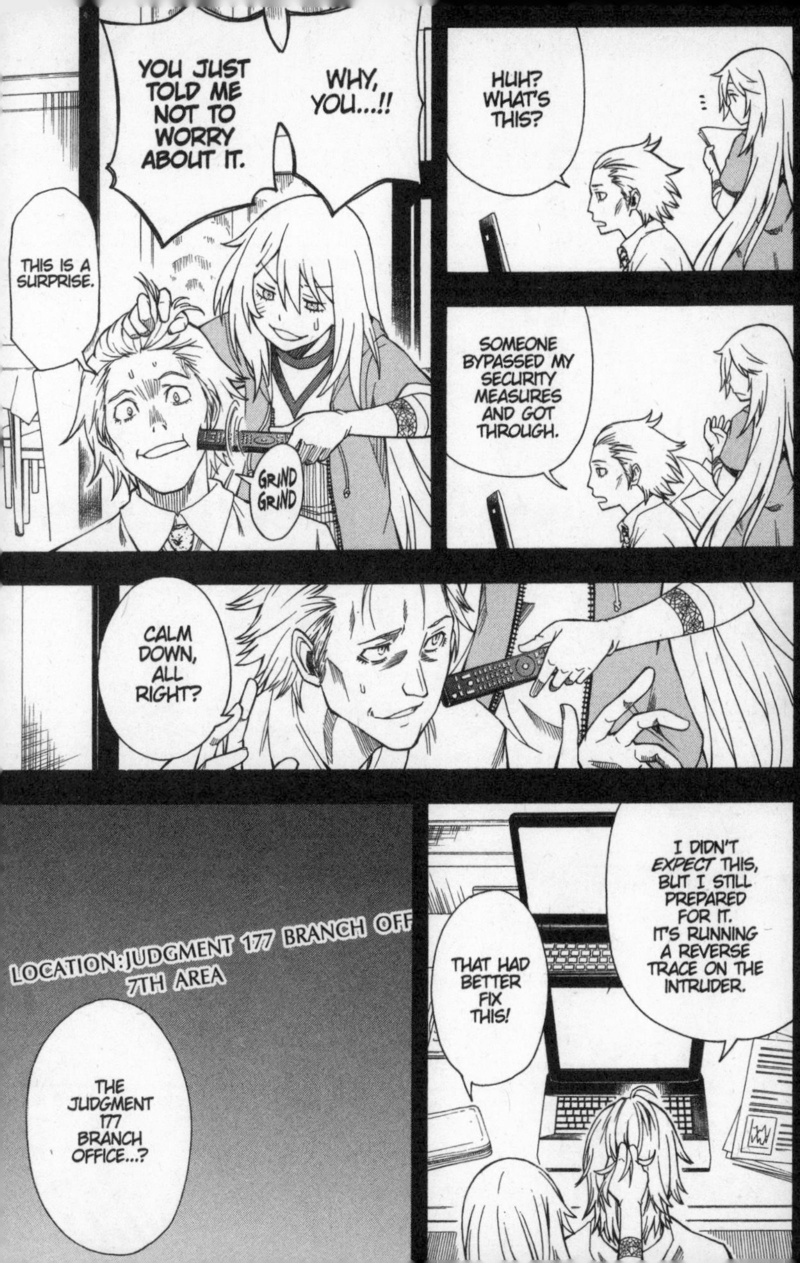
HUH? WHAT'S THIS?
SOMEONE BYPASSED MY SECURITY MEASURES AND GOT THROUGH.
WHY, YOU...!!
YOU JUST TOLD ME NOT TO WORRY ABOUT IT.
THIS IS A SURPRISE.
GRIND GRIND
CALM DOWN, ALL RIGHT?
I DIDN'T *EXPECT* THIS, BUT I STILL PREPARED FOR IT. IT'S RUNNING A REVERSE TRACE ON THE INTRUDER.
THAT HAD BETTER FIX THIS!
LOCATION:JUDGMENT 177 BRANCH OFF
7TH AREA
THE JUDGMENT 177 BRANCH OFFICE...?

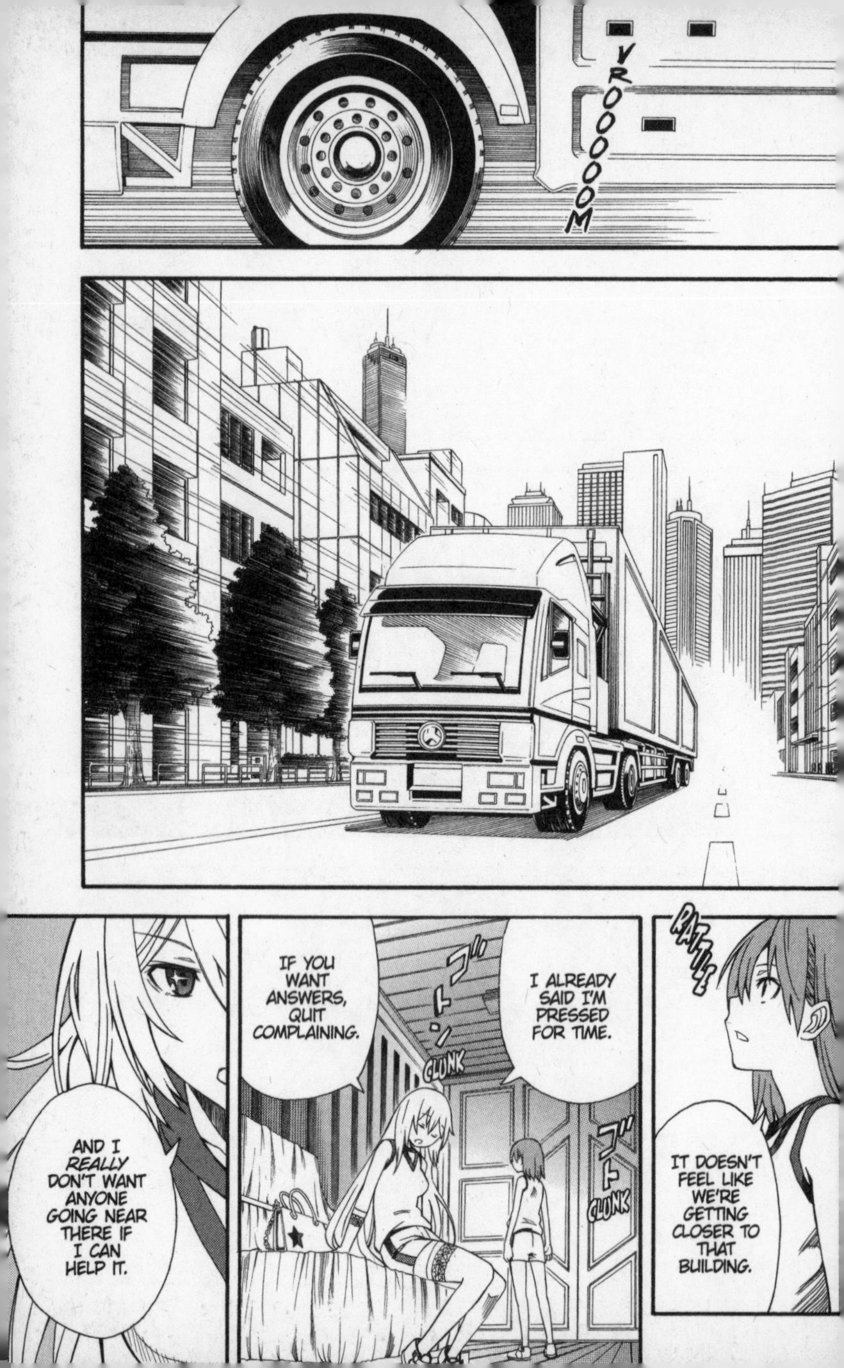
VROOOOOOOM
RATTLE
IT DOESN'T FEEL LIKE WE'RE GETTING CLOSER TO THAT BUILDING.
I ALREADY SAID I'M PRESSED FOR TIME.
CLUNK
CLUNK
IF YOU WANT ANSWERS, QUIT COMPLAINING.
AND I REALLY DON'T WANT ANYONE GOING NEAR THERE IF I CAN HELP IT.

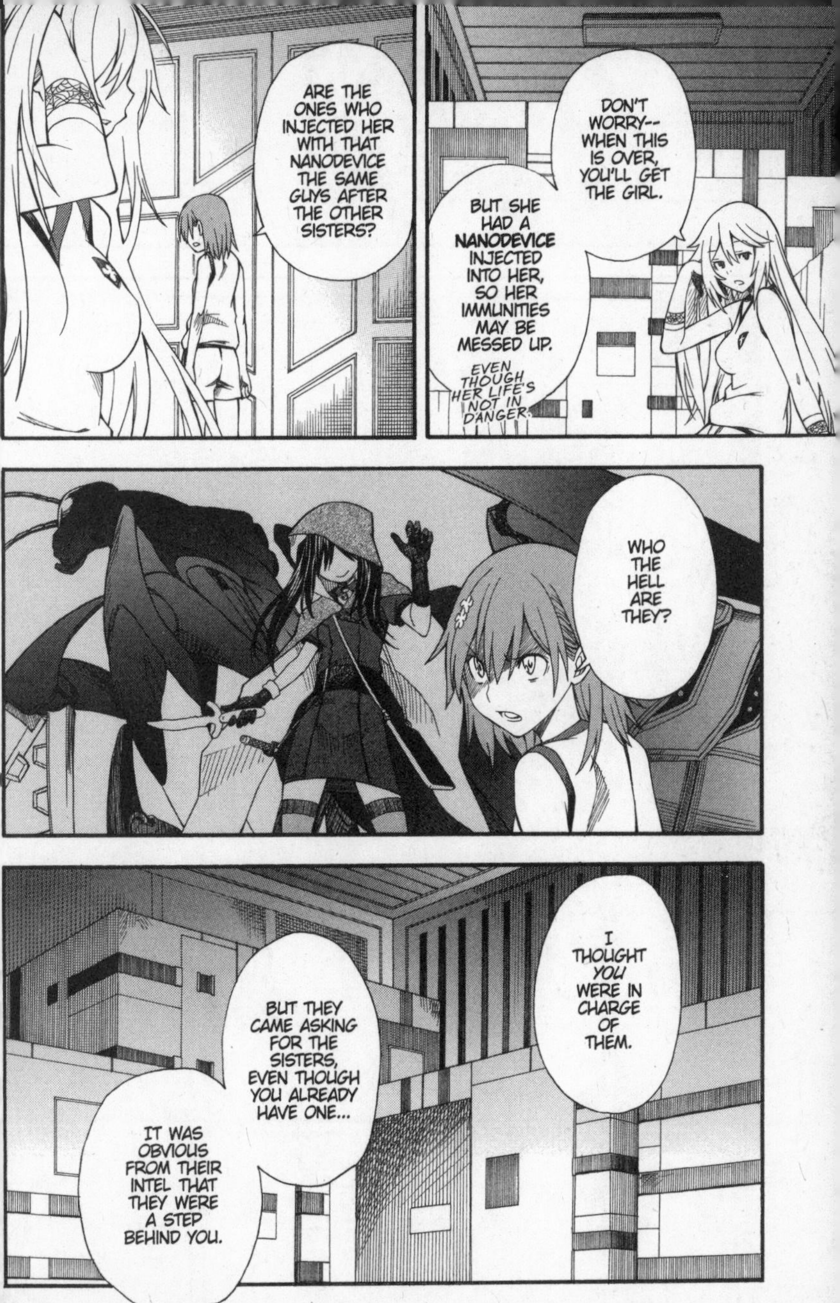
DON'T WORRY-- WHEN THIS IS OVER, YOU'LL GET THE GIRL.
BUT SHE HAD A **NANODEVICE** INJECTED INTO HER, SO HER IMMUNITIES MAY BE MESSED UP.
EVEN THOUGH HER LIFE'S NOT IN DANGER.
ARE THE ONES WHO INJECTED HER WITH THAT NANODEVICE THE SAME GUYS AFTER THE OTHER SISTERS?
WHO THE HELL ARE THEY?
I THOUGHT *YOU* WERE IN CHARGE OF THEM.
BUT THEY CAME ASKING FOR THE SISTERS, EVEN THOUGH YOU ALREADY HAVE ONE...
IT WAS OBVIOUS FROM THEIR INTEL THAT THEY WERE A STEP BEHIND YOU.

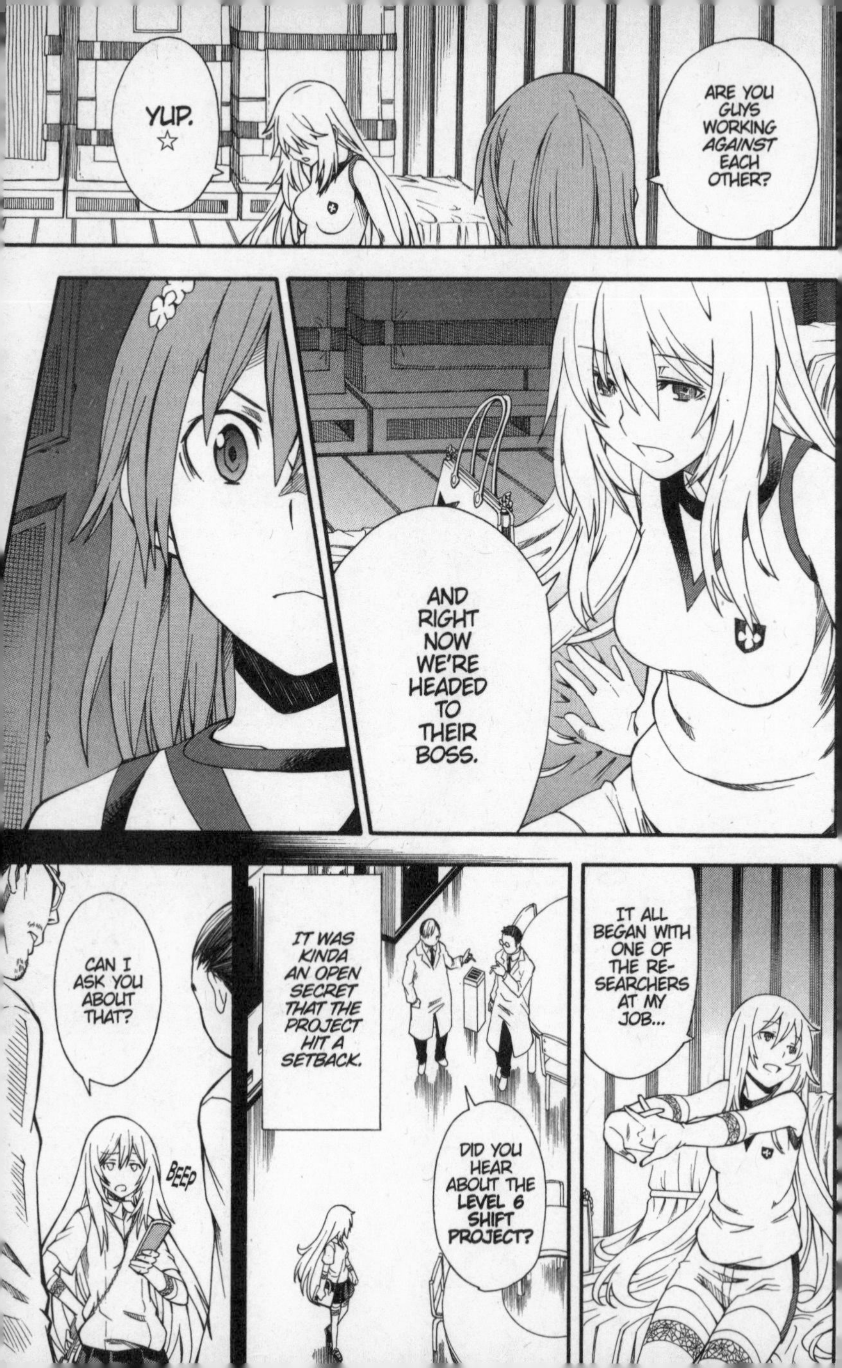
ARE YOU GUYS WORKING AGAINST EACH OTHER?
YUP. ☆
AND RIGHT NOW WE'RE HEADED TO THEIR BOSS.
IT ALL BEGAN WITH ONE OF THE RE-SEARCHERS AT MY JOB...
IT WAS KINDA AN OPEN SECRET THAT THE PROJECT HIT A SETBACK.
DID YOU HEAR ABOUT THE LEVEL 6 SHIFT PROJECT?
CAN I ASK YOU ABOUT THAT?
BEEP

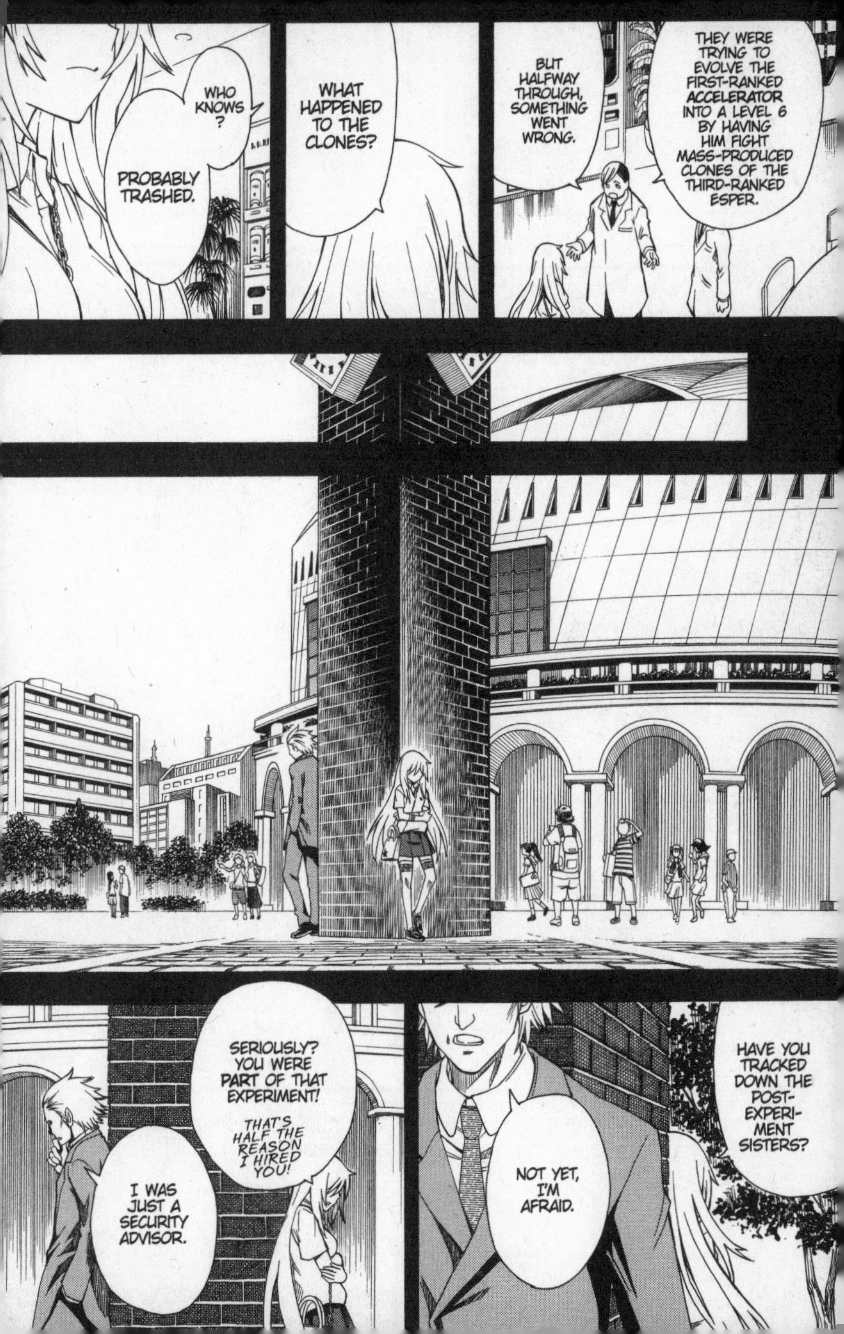
THEY WERE TRYING TO EVOLVE THE FIRST-RANKED ACCELERATOR INTO A LEVEL 6 BY HAVING HIM FIGHT MASS-PRODUCED CLONES OF THE THIRD-RANKED ESPER.
BUT HALFWAY THROUGH, SOMETHING WENT WRONG.
WHAT HAPPENED TO THE CLONES?
WHO KNOWS?
PROBABLY TRASHED.
HAVE YOU TRACKED DOWN THE POST-EXPERIMENT SISTERS?
NOT YET, I'M AFRAID.
SERIOUSLY? YOU WERE PART OF THAT EXPERIMENT!
THAT'S HALF THE REASON I HIRED YOU!
I WAS JUST A SECURITY ADVISOR.

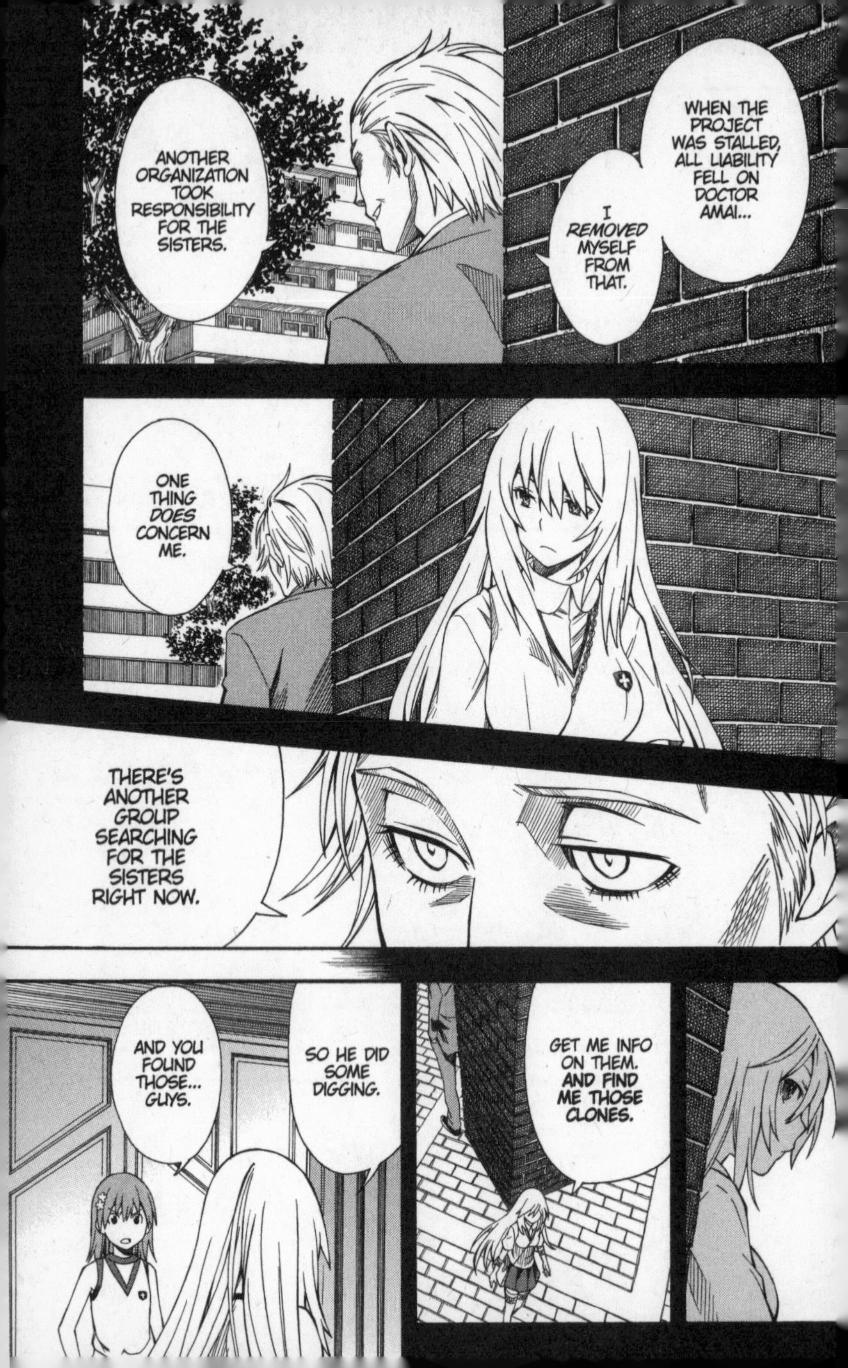
WHEN THE PROJECT WAS STALLED, ALL LIABILITY FELL ON DOCTOR AMAI...
I *REMOVED* MYSELF FROM THAT.
ANOTHER ORGANIZATION TOOK RESPONSIBILITY FOR THE SISTERS.
ONE THING *DOES* CONCERN ME.
THERE'S ANOTHER GROUP SEARCHING FOR THE SISTERS RIGHT NOW.
GET ME INFO ON THEM. AND FIND ME THOSE CLONES.
SO HE DID SOME DIGGING.
AND YOU FOUND THOSE... GUYS.

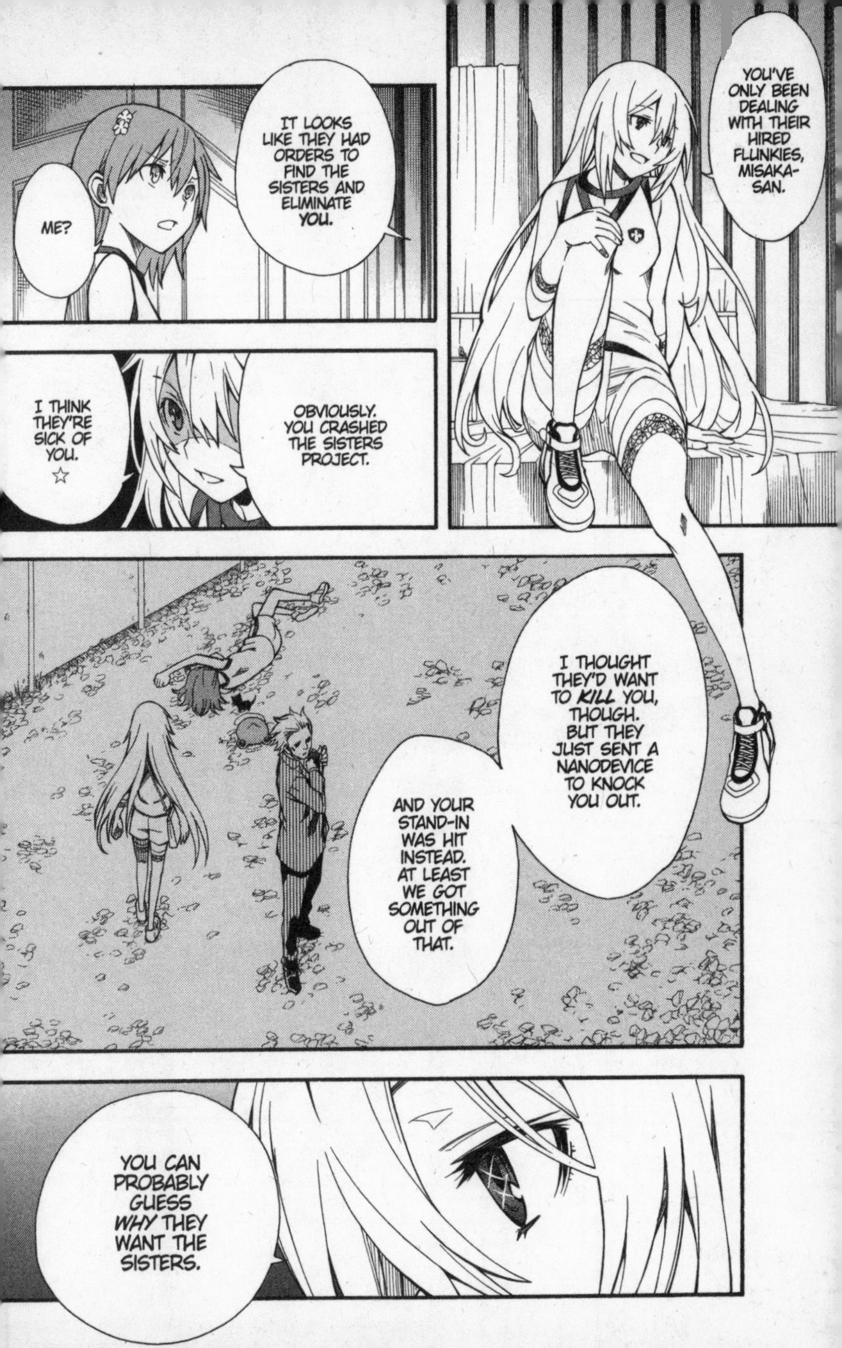
YOU'VE ONLY BEEN DEALING WITH THEIR HIRED FLUNKIES, MISAKA-SAN.
IT LOOKS LIKE THEY HAD ORDERS TO FIND THE SISTERS AND ELIMINATE *YOU.*
ME?
OBVIOUSLY. YOU CRASHED THE SISTERS PROJECT.
I THINK THEY'RE SICK OF YOU. ☆
I THOUGHT THEY'D WANT TO ***KILL*** YOU, THOUGH. BUT THEY JUST SENT A NANODEVICE TO KNOCK YOU OUT.
AND YOUR STAND-IN WAS HIT INSTEAD. AT LEAST WE GOT SOMETHING OUT OF THAT.
YOU CAN PROBABLY GUESS *WHY* THEY WANT THE SISTERS.

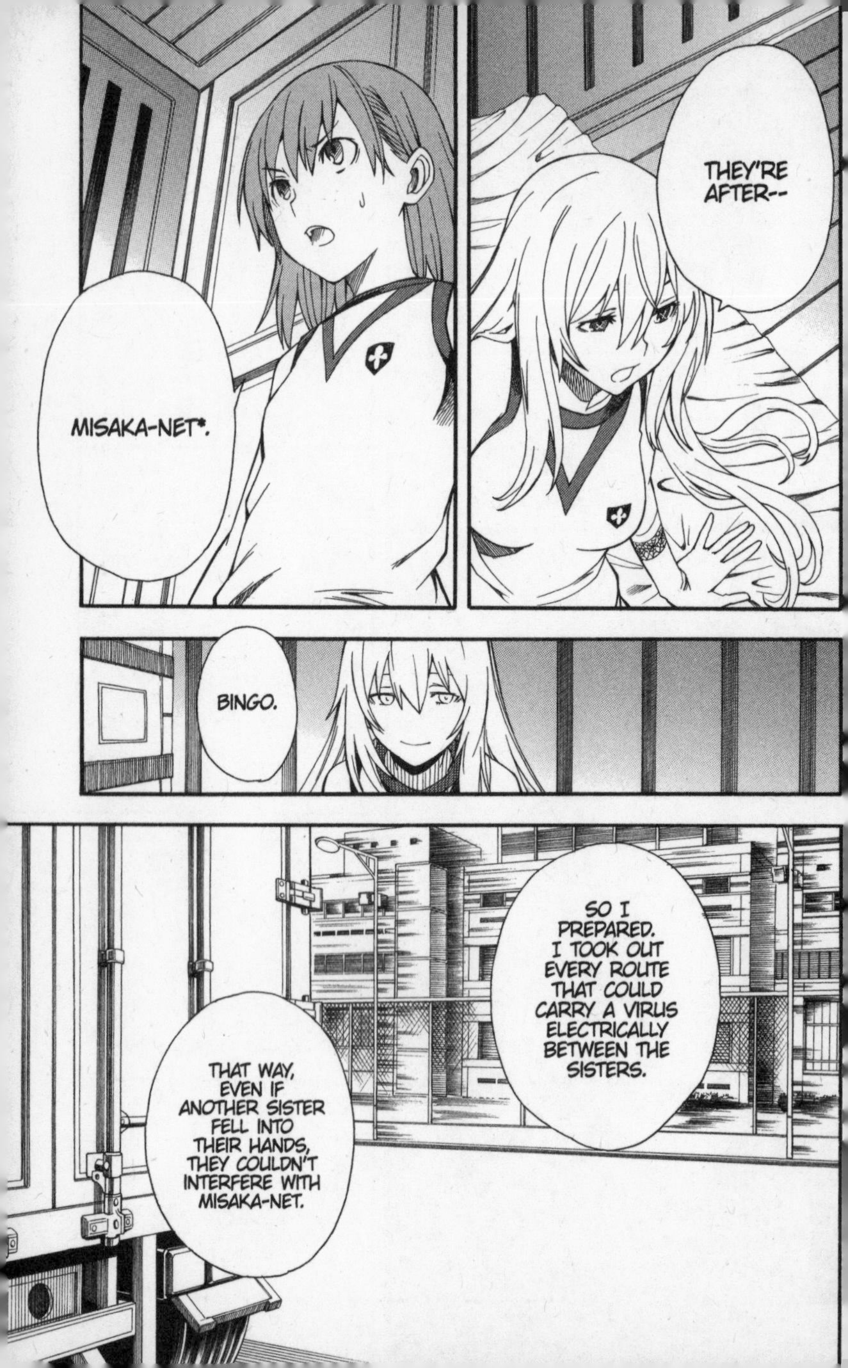
THEY'RE AFTER--
MISAKA-NET*.
BINGO.
SO I PREPARED. I TOOK OUT EVERY ROUTE THAT COULD CARRY A VIRUS ELECTRICALLY BETWEEN THE SISTERS.
THAT WAY, EVEN IF ANOTHER SISTER FELL INTO THEIR HANDS, THEY COULDN'T INTERFERE WITH MISAKA-NET.

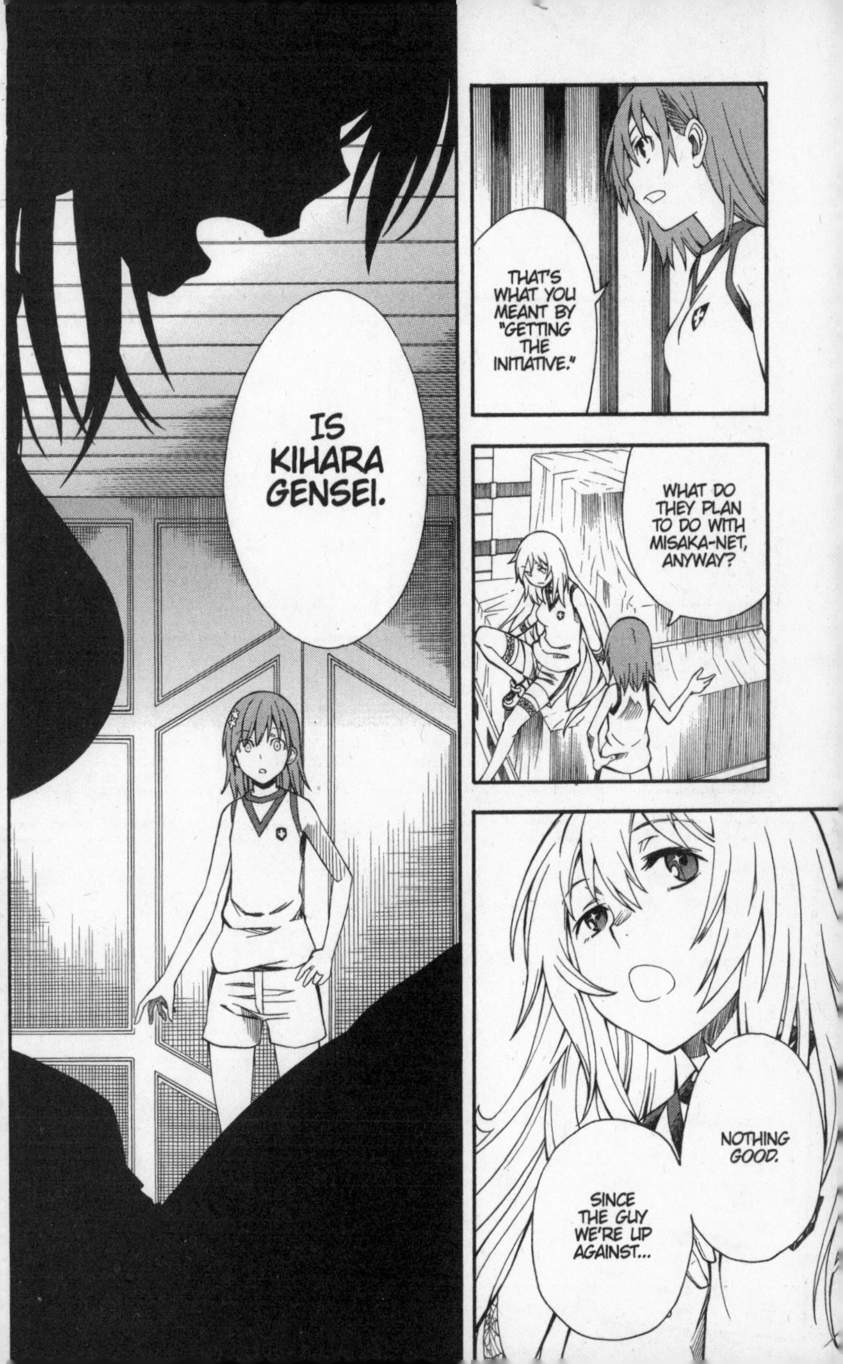
THAT'S WHAT YOU MEANT BY "GETTING THE INITIATIVE."
WHAT DO THEY PLAN TO DO WITH MISAKA-NET, ANYWAY?
NOTHING GOOD.
SINCE THE GUY WE'RE UP AGAINST...
IS KIHARA GENSEI.

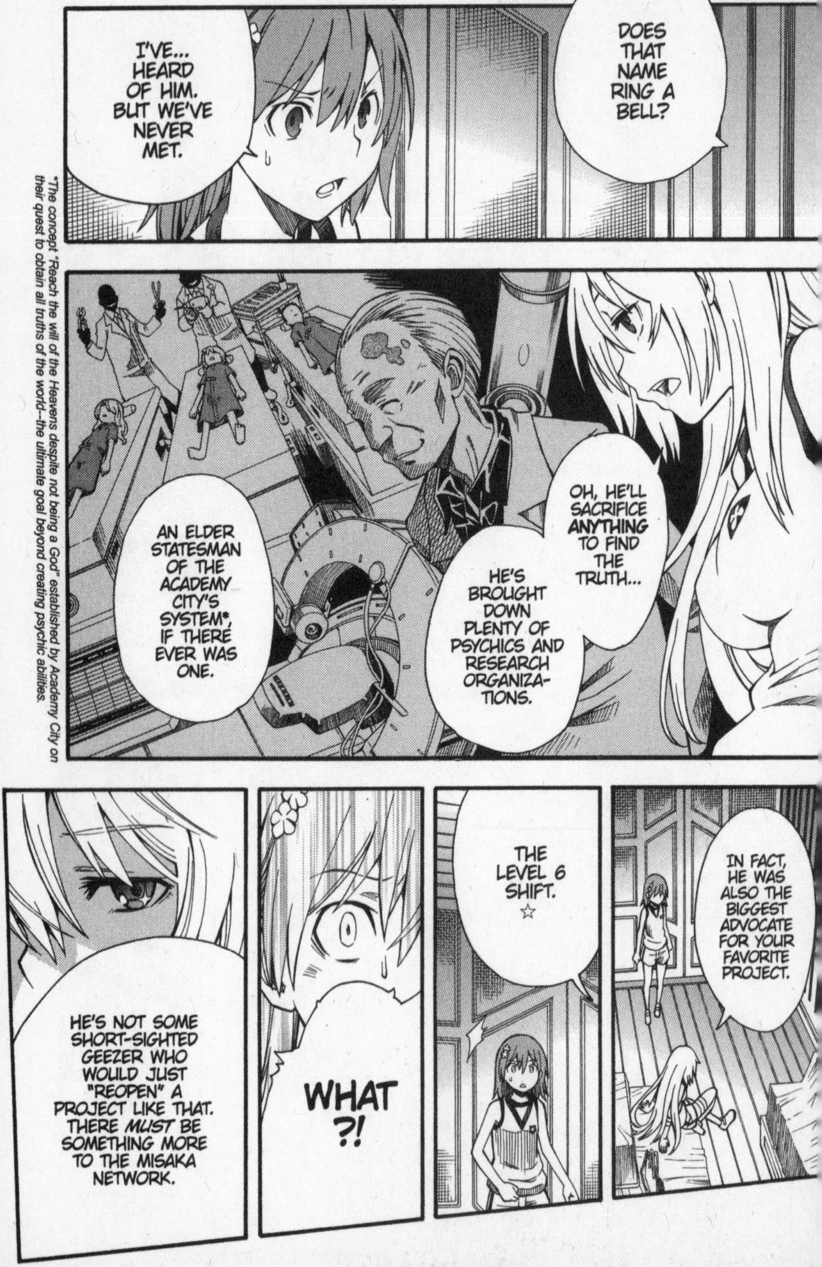

DOES THAT NAME RING A BELL?
I'VE... HEARD OF HIM. BUT WE'VE NEVER MET.
OH, HE'LL SACRIFICE **ANYTHING** TO FIND THE TRUTH...
HE'S BROUGHT DOWN PLENTY OF PSYCHICS AND RESEARCH ORGANIZA-TIONS.
AN ELDER STATESMAN OF THE ACADEMY CITY'S SYSTEM*, IF THERE EVER WAS ONE.
IN FACT, HE WAS ALSO THE BIGGEST ADVOCATE FOR YOUR FAVORITE PROJECT.
THE LEVEL 6 SHIFT. ☆
WHAT ?!
HE'S NOT SOME SHORT-SIGHTED GEEZER WHO WOULD JUST "REOPEN" A PROJECT LIKE THAT. THERE *MUST* BE SOMETHING MORE TO THE MISAKA NETWORK.

*The concept "Reach the will of the Heavens despite not being a God" established by Academy City on their quest to obtain all truths of the world--the ultimate goal beyond creating psychic abilities.

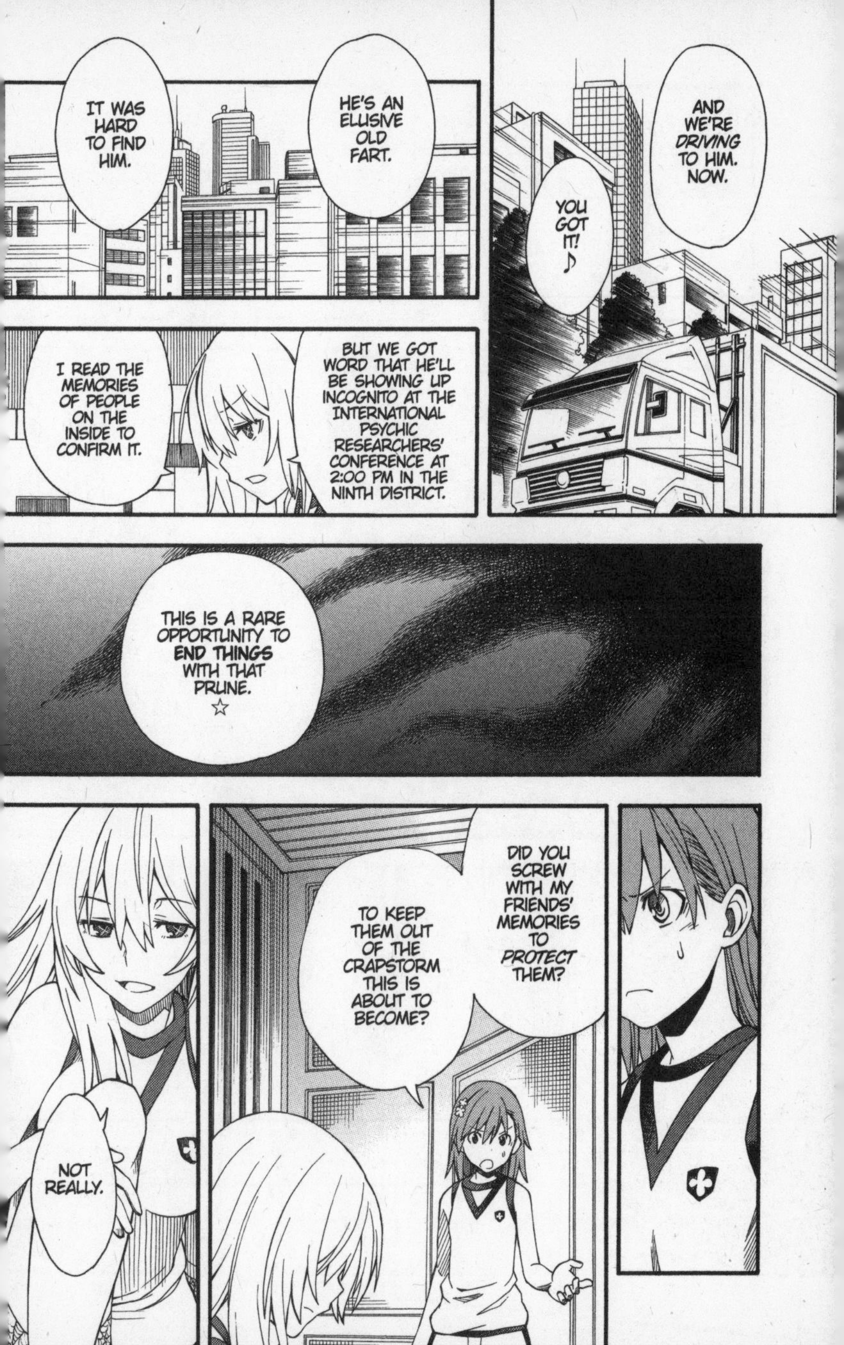
HE'S AN ELUSIVE OLD FART.
IT WAS HARD TO FIND HIM.
BUT WE GOT WORD THAT HE'LL BE SHOWING UP INCOGNITO AT THE INTERNATIONAL PSYCHIC RESEARCHERS' CONFERENCE AT 2:00 PM IN THE NINTH DISTRICT.
I READ THE MEMORIES OF PEOPLE ON THE INSIDE TO CONFIRM IT.
AND WE'RE *DRIVING* TO HIM. NOW.
YOU GOT IT! ♪
THIS IS A RARE OPPORTUNITY TO **END THINGS** WITH THAT PRUNE. ☆
DID YOU SCREW WITH MY FRIENDS' MEMORIES TO *PROTECT* THEM?
TO KEEP THEM OUT OF THE CRAPSTORM THIS IS ABOUT TO BECOME?
NOT REALLY.

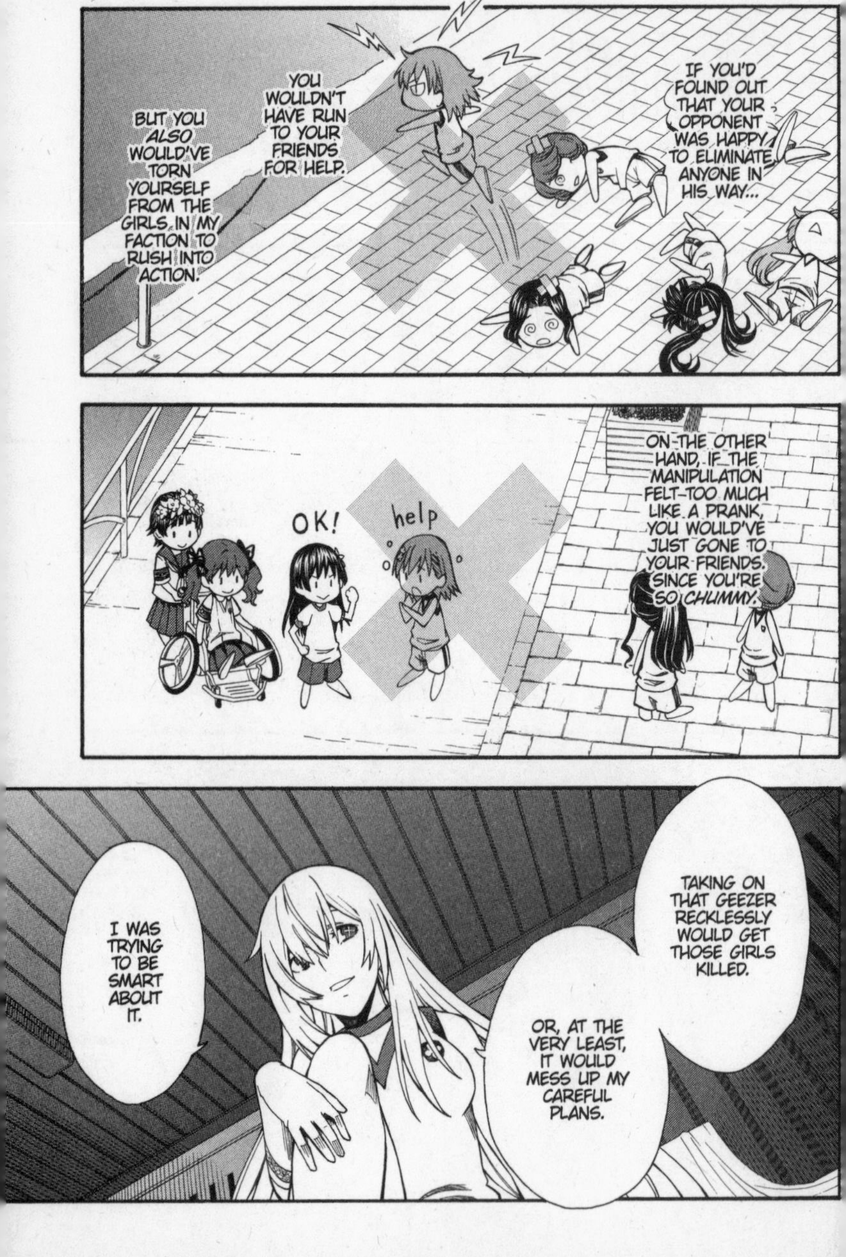
IF YOU'D FOUND OUT THAT YOUR OPPONENT WAS HAPPY TO ELIMINATE ANYONE IN HIS WAY...
YOU WOULDN'T HAVE RUN TO YOUR FRIENDS FOR HELP.
BUT YOU *ALSO* WOULD'VE TORN YOURSELF FROM THE GIRLS IN MY FACTION TO RUSH INTO ACTION.
ON THE OTHER HAND, IF THE MANIPULATION FELT TOO MUCH LIKE A PRANK, YOU WOULD'VE JUST GONE TO YOUR FRIENDS. SINCE YOU'RE SO *CHUMMY*.
help
OK!
TAKING ON THAT GEEZER RECKLESSLY WOULD GET THOSE GIRLS KILLED.
OR, AT THE VERY LEAST, IT WOULD MESS UP MY CAREFUL PLANS.
I WAS TRYING TO BE SMART ABOUT IT.

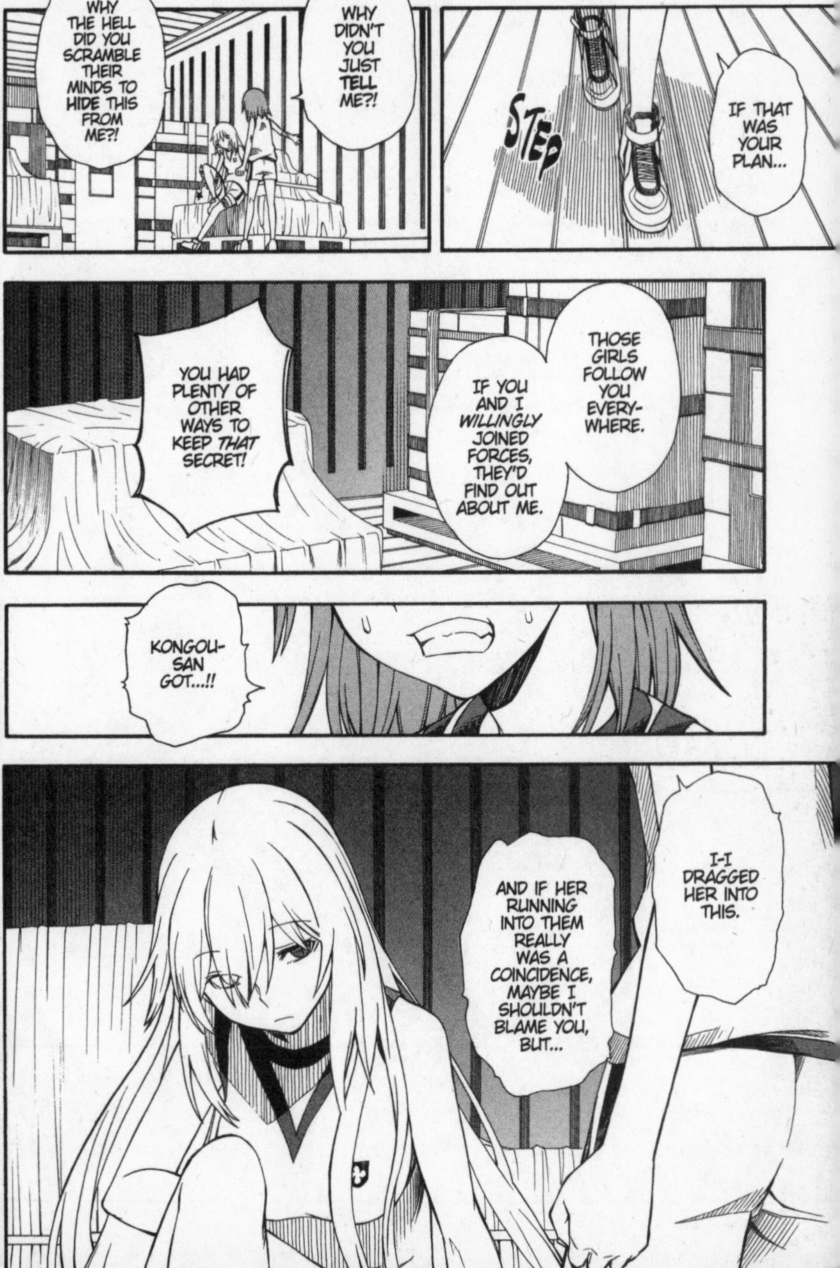
STEP
IF THAT WAS YOUR PLAN...
WHY DIDN'T YOU JUST TELL ME?!
WHY THE HELL DID YOU SCRAMBLE THEIR MINDS TO HIDE THIS FROM ME?!
THOSE GIRLS FOLLOW YOU EVERY-WHERE.
IF YOU AND I WILLINGLY JOINED FORCES, THEY'D FIND OUT ABOUT ME.
YOU HAD PLENTY OF OTHER WAYS TO KEEP THAT SECRET!
KONGOU-SAN GOT...!!
I-I DRAGGED HER INTO THIS.
AND IF HER RUNNING INTO THEM REALLY WAS A COINCIDENCE, MAYBE I SHOULDN'T BLAME YOU, BUT...

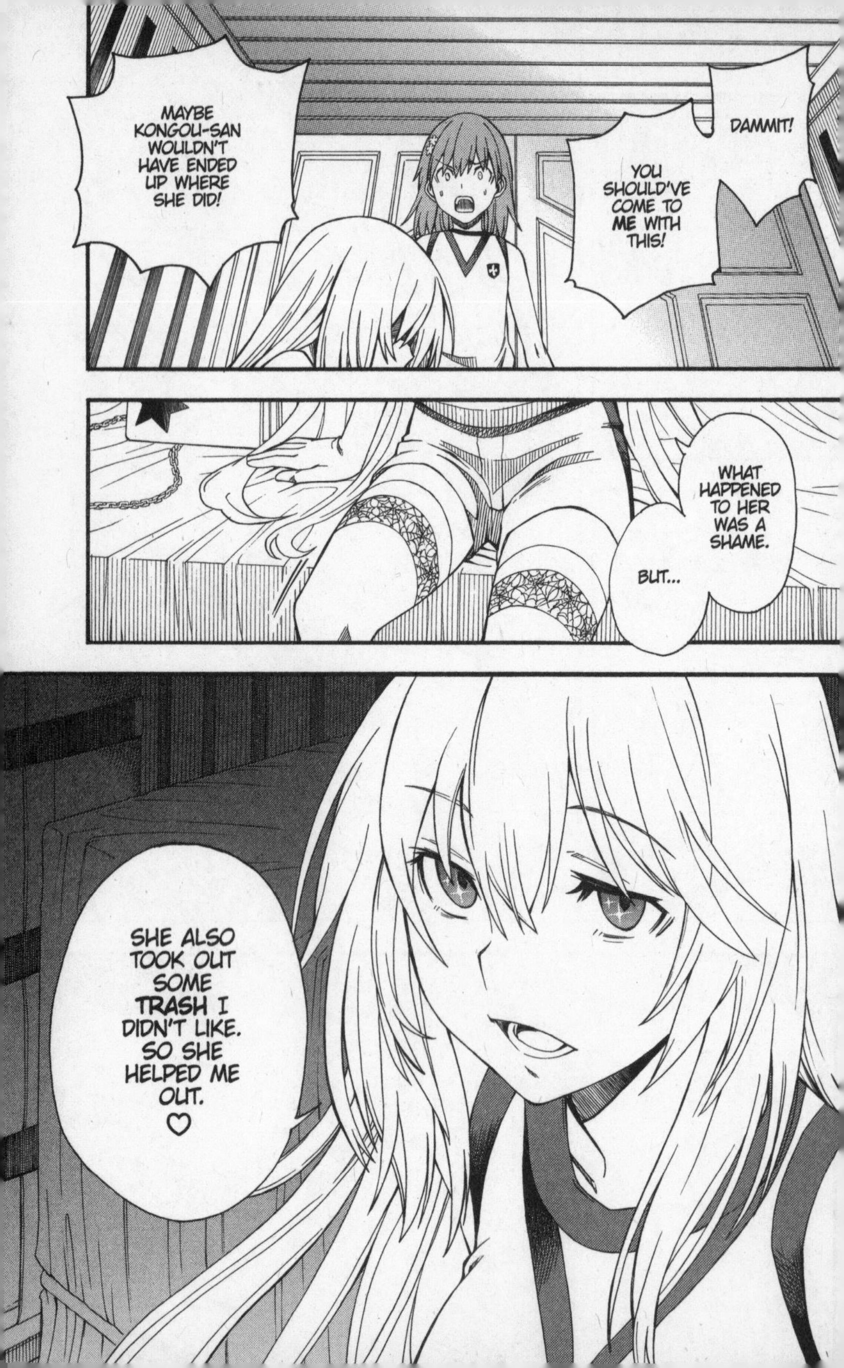
DAMMIT!
YOU SHOULD'VE COME TO ME WITH THIS!
MAYBE KONGOU-SAN WOULDN'T HAVE ENDED UP WHERE SHE DID!
WHAT HAPPENED TO HER WAS A SHAME.
BUT...
SHE ALSO TOOK OUT SOME TRASH I DIDN'T LIKE. SO SHE HELPED ME OUT. ♡

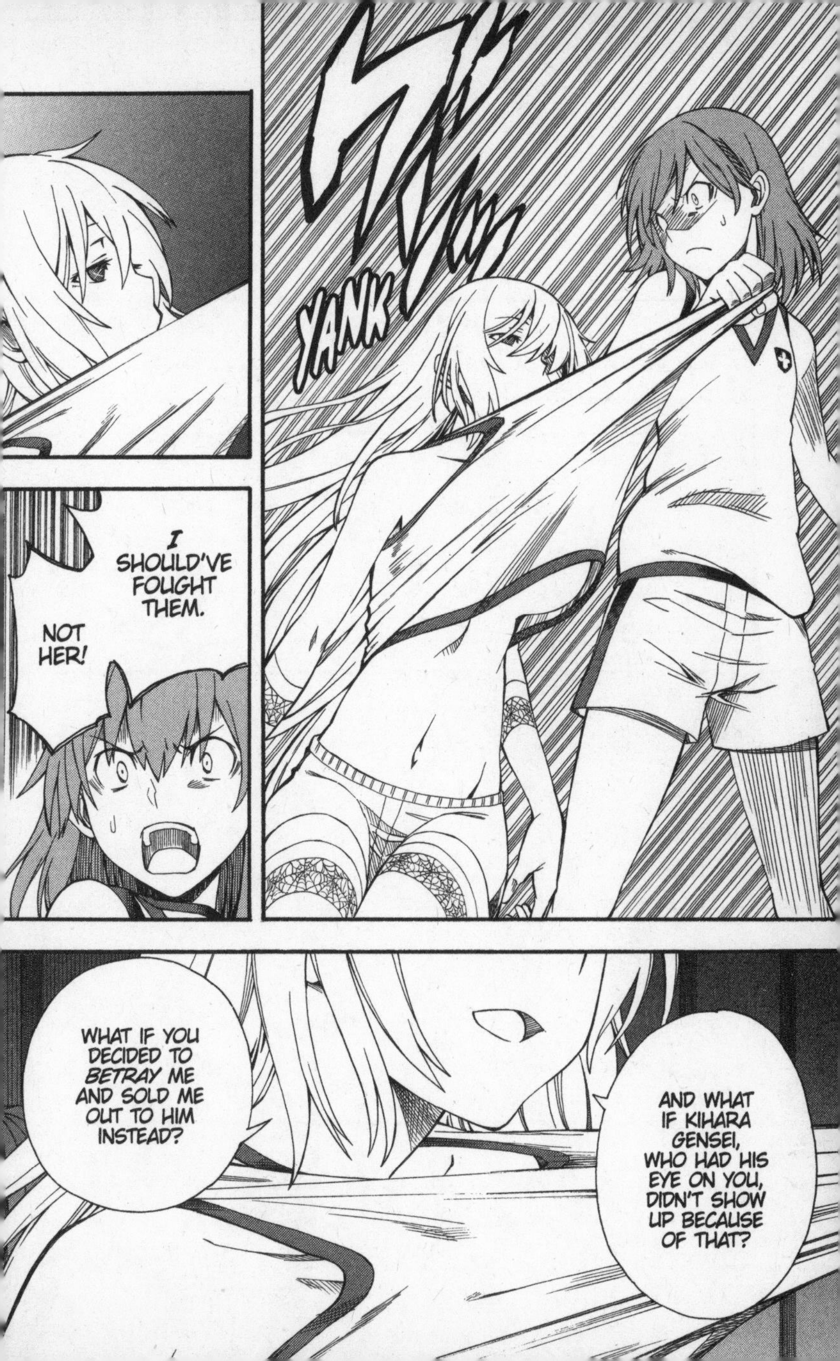
YANK
I SHOULD'VE FOUGHT THEM.
NOT HER!
AND WHAT IF KIHARA GENSEI, WHO HAD HIS EYE ON YOU, DIDN'T SHOW UP BECAUSE OF THAT?
WHAT IF YOU DECIDED TO *BETRAY* ME AND SOLD ME OUT TO HIM INSTEAD?

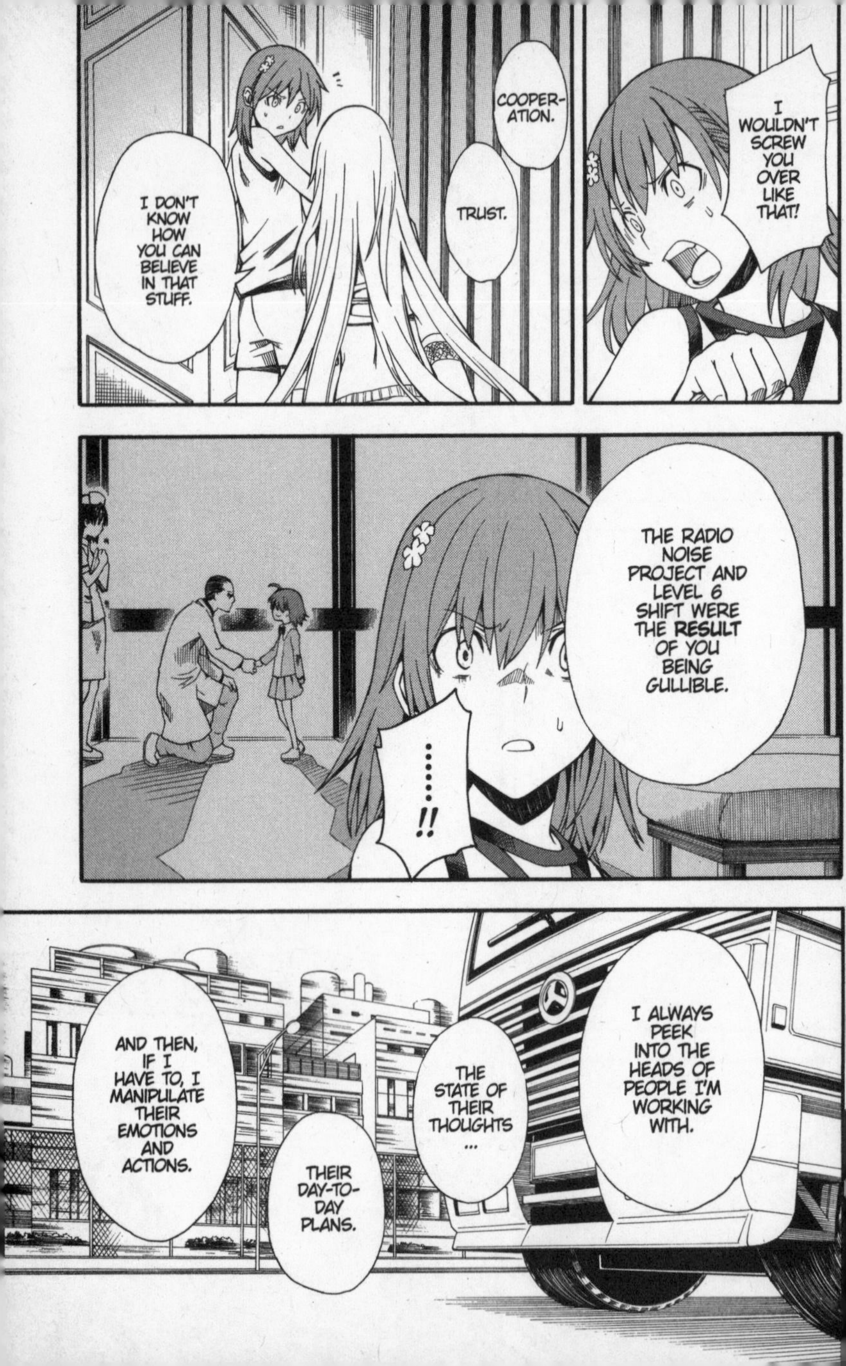
I WOULDN'T SCREW YOU OVER LIKE THAT!
COOPERATION.
TRUST.
I DON'T KNOW HOW YOU CAN BELIEVE IN THAT STUFF.
THE RADIO NOISE PROJECT AND LEVEL 6 SHIFT WERE THE **RESULT** OF YOU BEING GULLIBLE.
......!!
I ALWAYS PEEK INTO THE HEADS OF PEOPLE I'M WORKING WITH.
THE STATE OF THEIR THOUGHTS...
THEIR DAY-TO-DAY PLANS.
AND THEN, IF I HAVE TO, I MANIPULATE THEIR EMOTIONS AND ACTIONS.

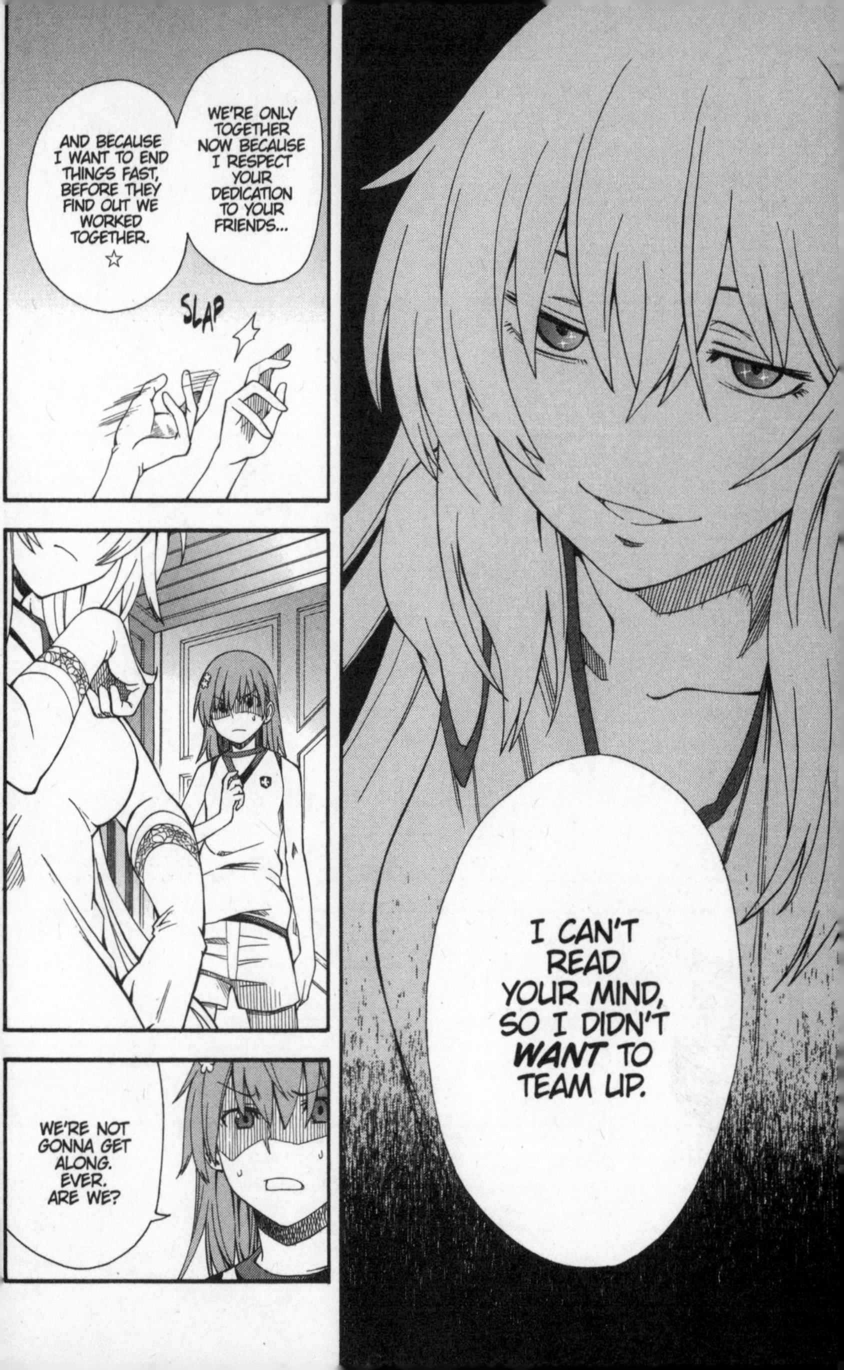
I CAN'T READ YOUR MIND, SO I DIDN'T *WANT* TO TEAM UP.
WE'RE ONLY TOGETHER NOW BECAUSE I RESPECT YOUR DEDICATION TO YOUR FRIENDS...
AND BECAUSE I WANT TO END THINGS FAST, BEFORE THEY FIND OUT WE WORKED TOGETHER. ☆
SLAP
WE'RE NOT GONNA GET ALONG. EVER. ARE WE?

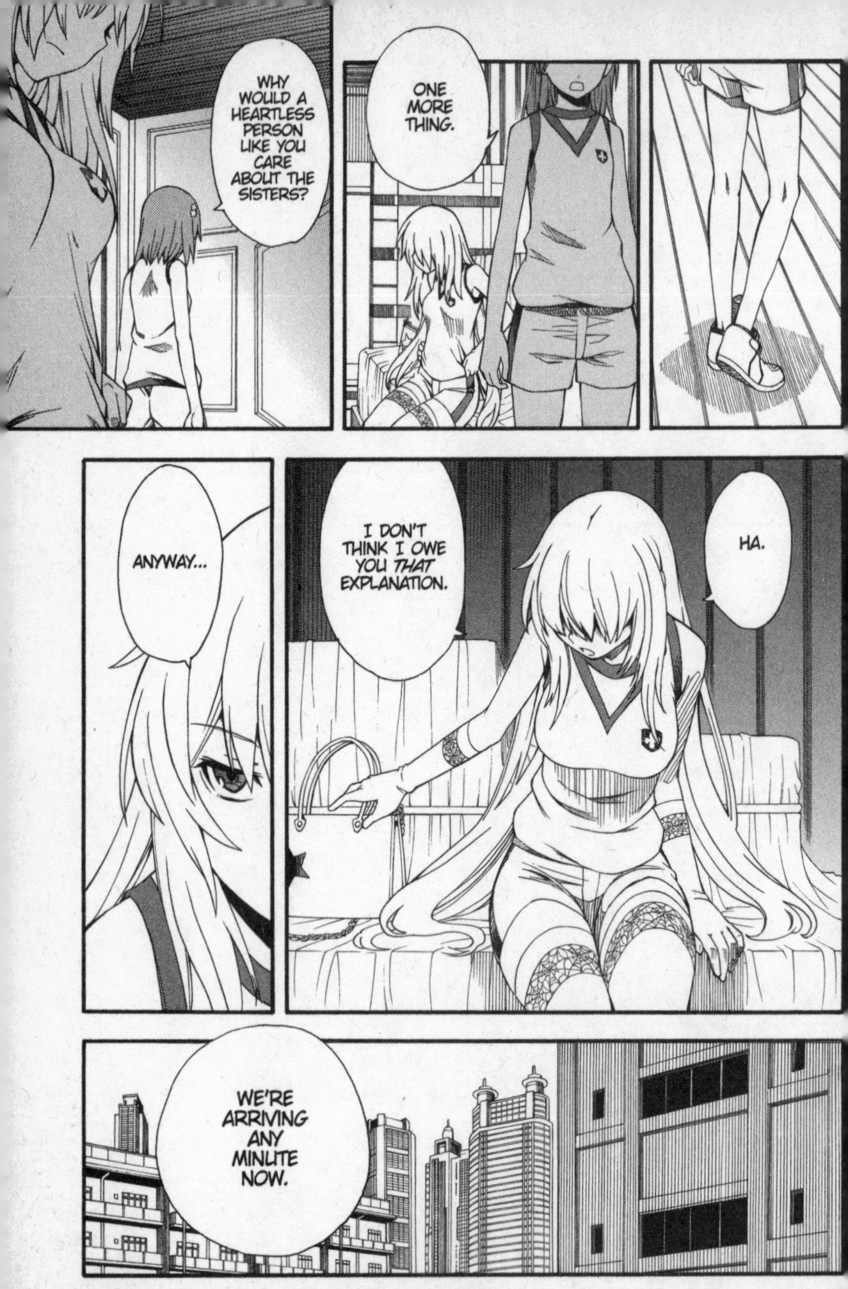
ONE MORE THING.
WHY WOULD A HEARTLESS PERSON LIKE YOU CARE ABOUT THE SISTERS?
HA.
I DON'T THINK I OWE YOU *THAT* EXPLANATION.
ANYWAY...
WE'RE ARRIVING ANY MINUTE NOW.

A Certain
SCIENTIFIC
Railgun

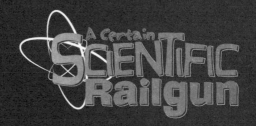

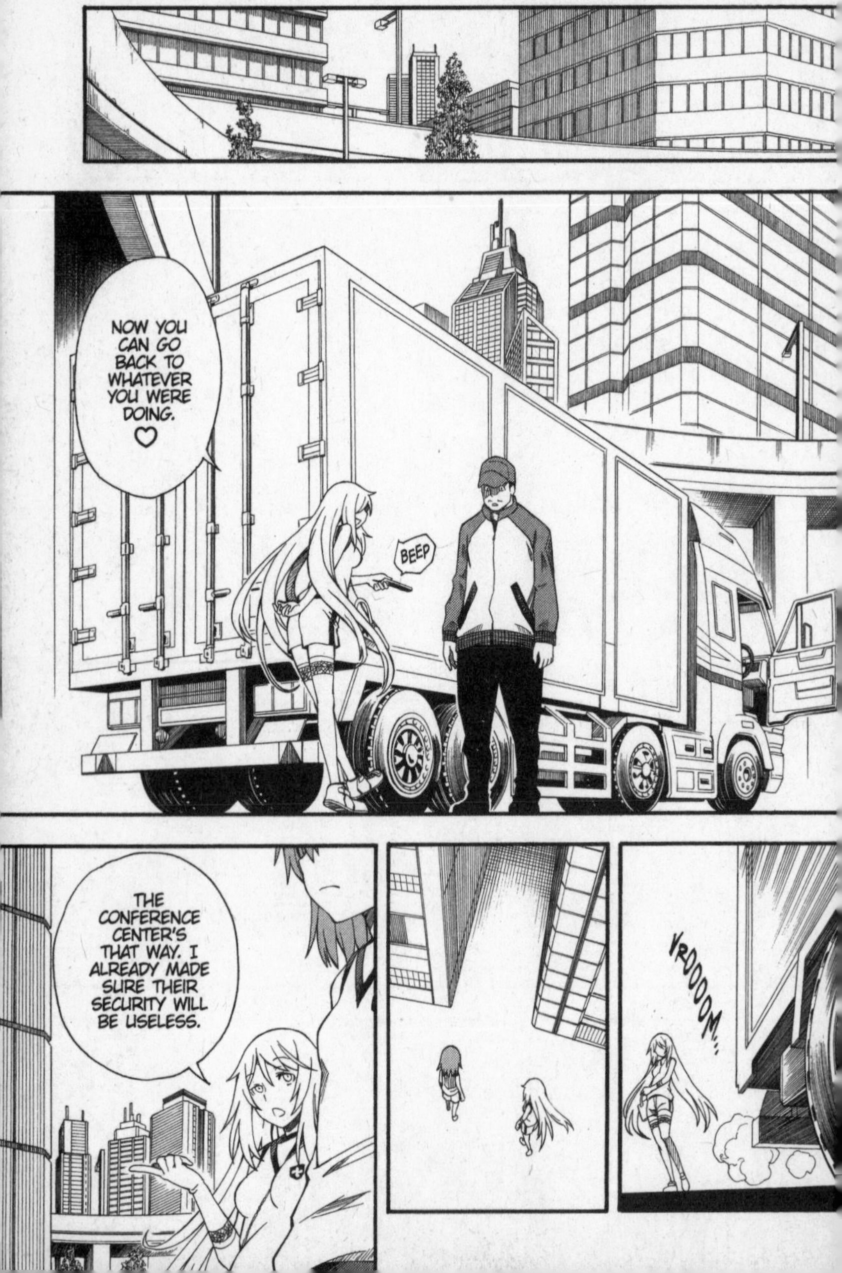
NOW YOU CAN GO BACK TO WHATEVER YOU WERE DOING. ♡
BEEP
THE CONFERENCE CENTER'S THAT WAY. I ALREADY MADE SURE THEIR SECURITY WILL BE USELESS.
VROOOOOM...

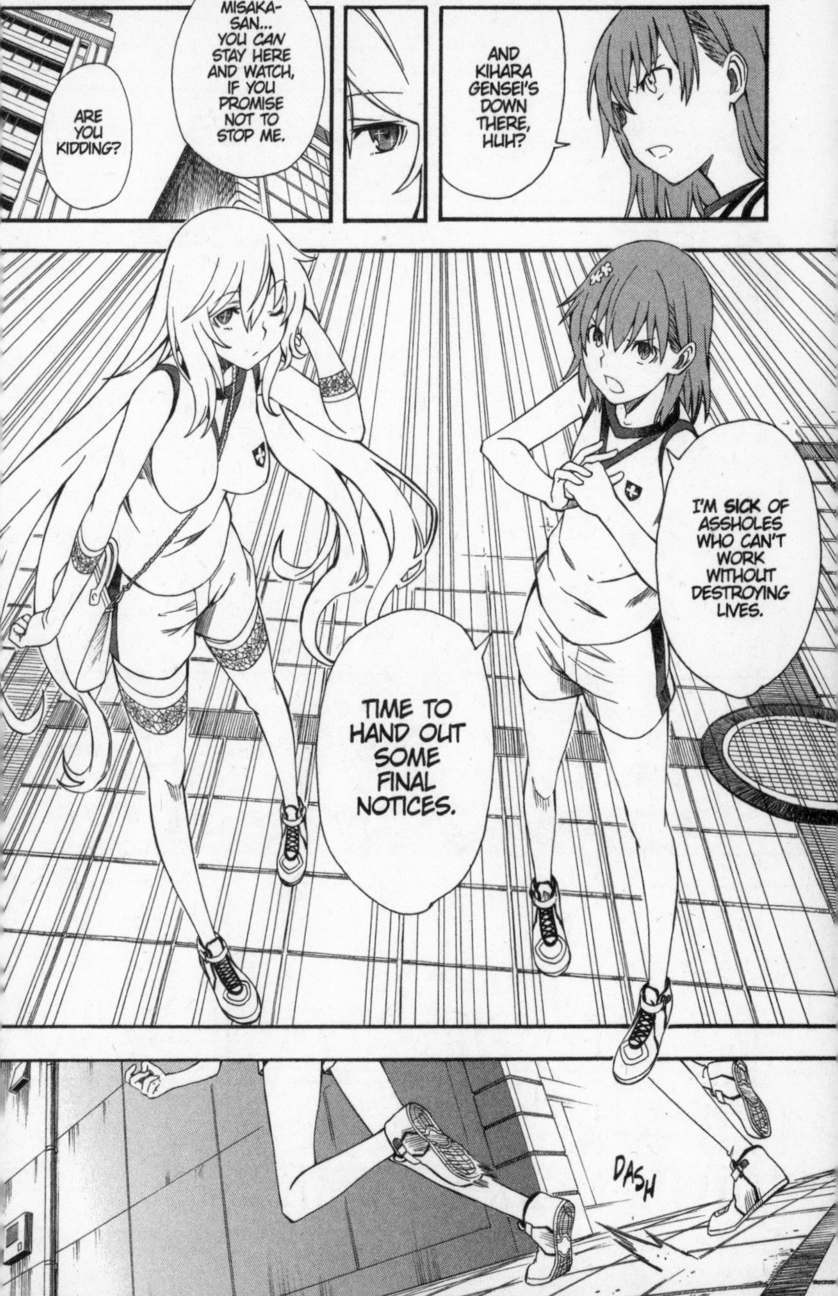
AND KIHARA GENSEI'S DOWN THERE, HUH?
MISAKA-SAN... YOU CAN STAY HERE AND WATCH, IF YOU PROMISE NOT TO STOP ME.
ARE YOU KIDDING?
I'M SICK OF ASSHOLES WHO CAN'T WORK WITHOUT DESTROYING LIVES.
TIME TO HAND OUT SOME FINAL NOTICES.
DASH

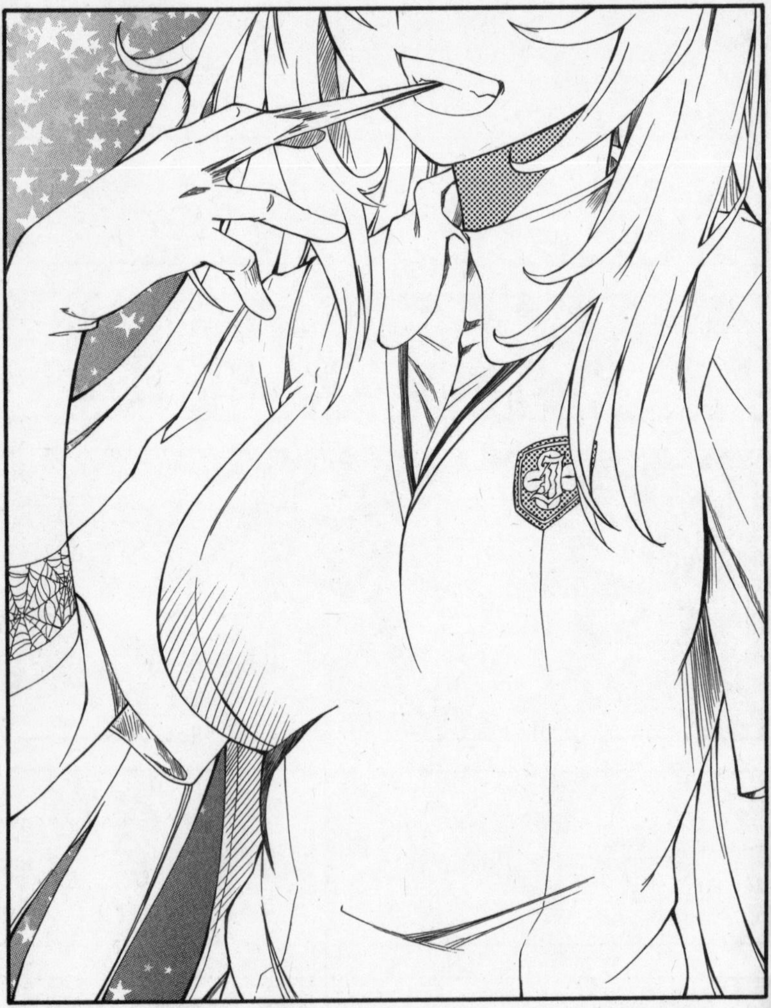

CHAPTER 56: DIVIDING AND ADVANCING

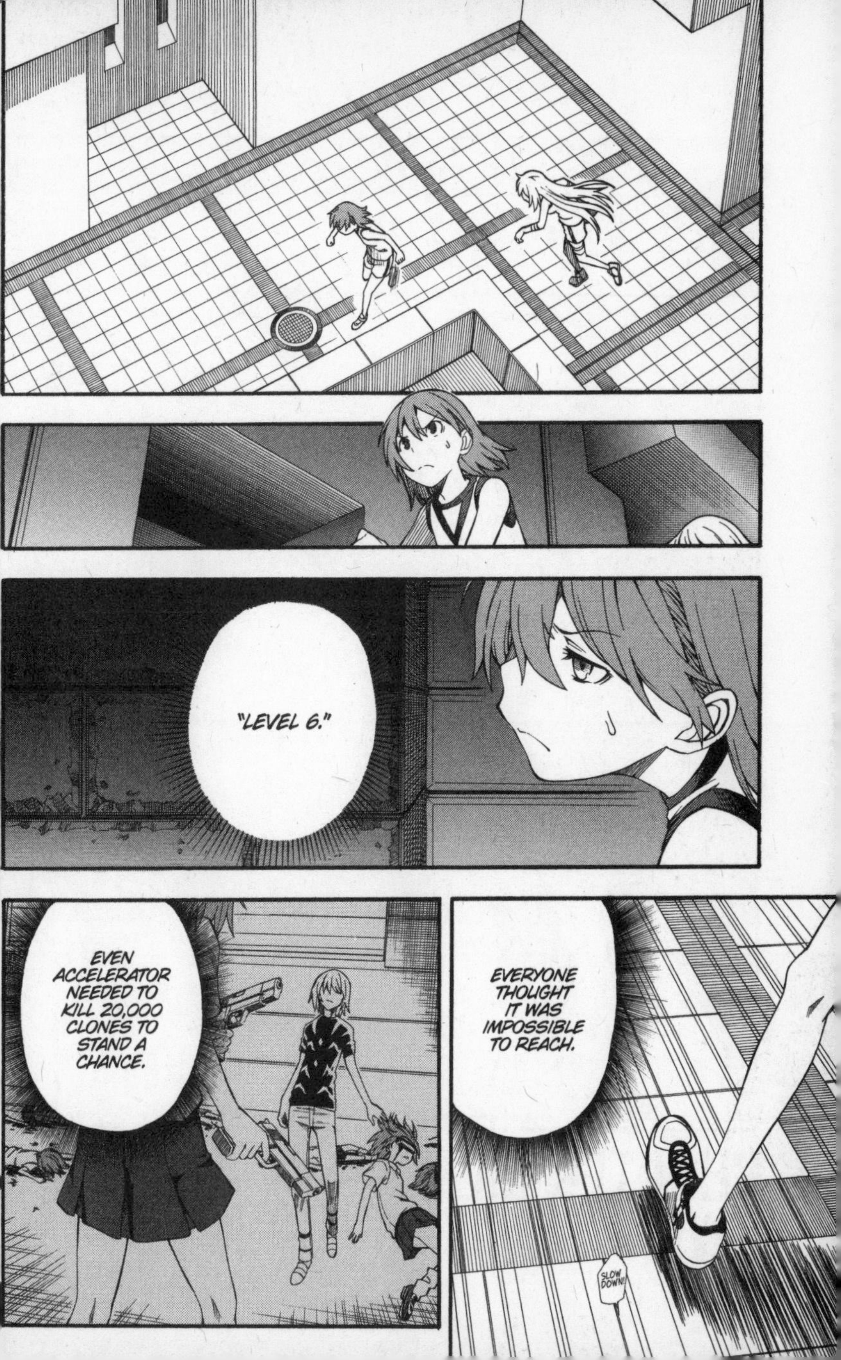
"LEVEL 6."
EVERYONE THOUGHT IT WAS IMPOSSIBLE TO REACH.
SLOW DOWN!
EVEN ACCELERATOR NEEDED TO KILL 20,000 CLONES TO STAND A CHANCE.

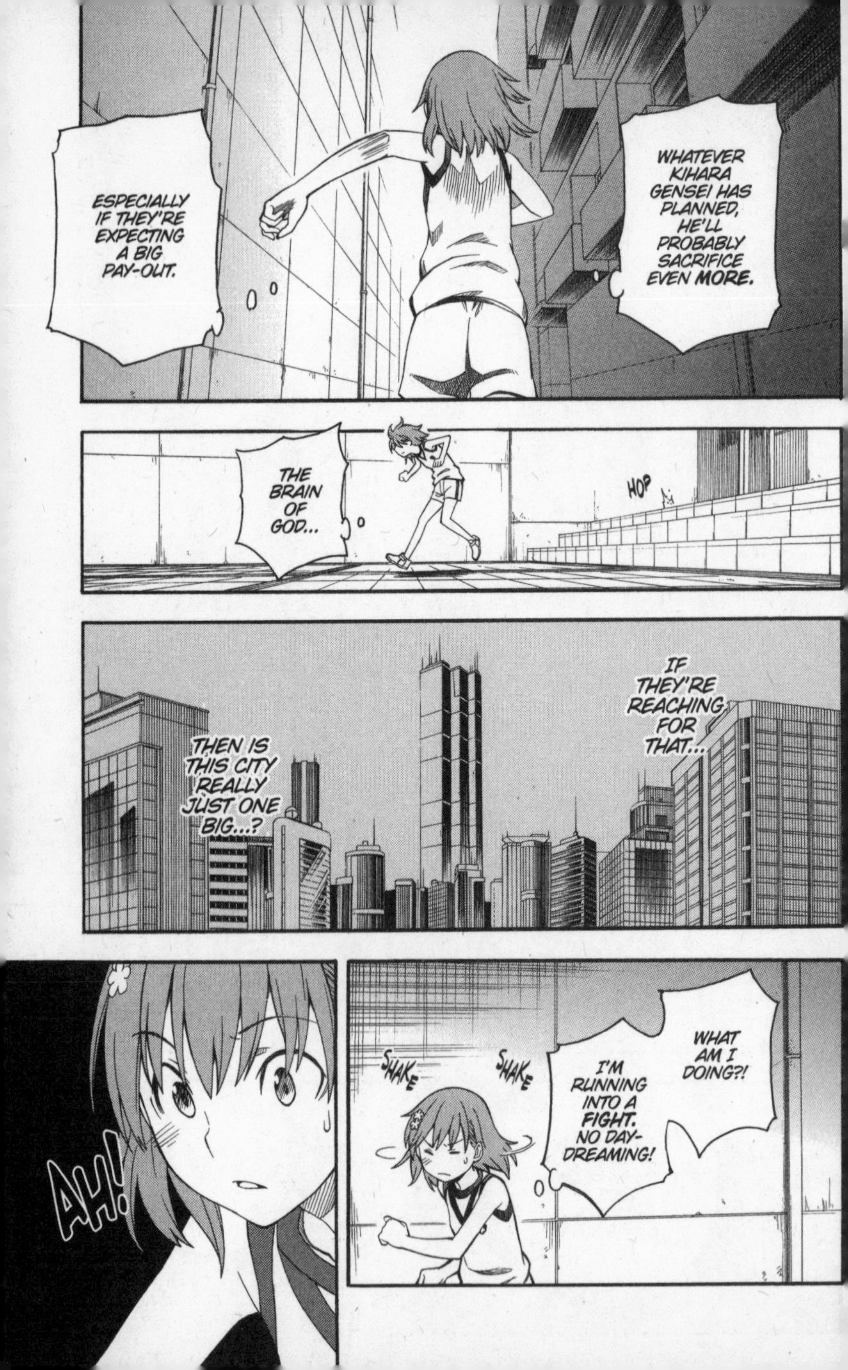
WHATEVER KIHARA GENSEI HAS PLANNED, HE'LL PROBABLY SACRIFICE EVEN MORE.
ESPECIALLY IF THEY'RE EXPECTING A BIG PAY-OUT.
HOP
THE BRAIN OF GOD...
IF THEY'RE REACHING FOR THAT...
THEN IS THIS CITY REALLY JUST ONE BIG...?
WHAT AM I DOING?!
I'M RUNNING INTO A FIGHT. NO DAY-DREAMING!
SHAKE
SHAKE
AH!

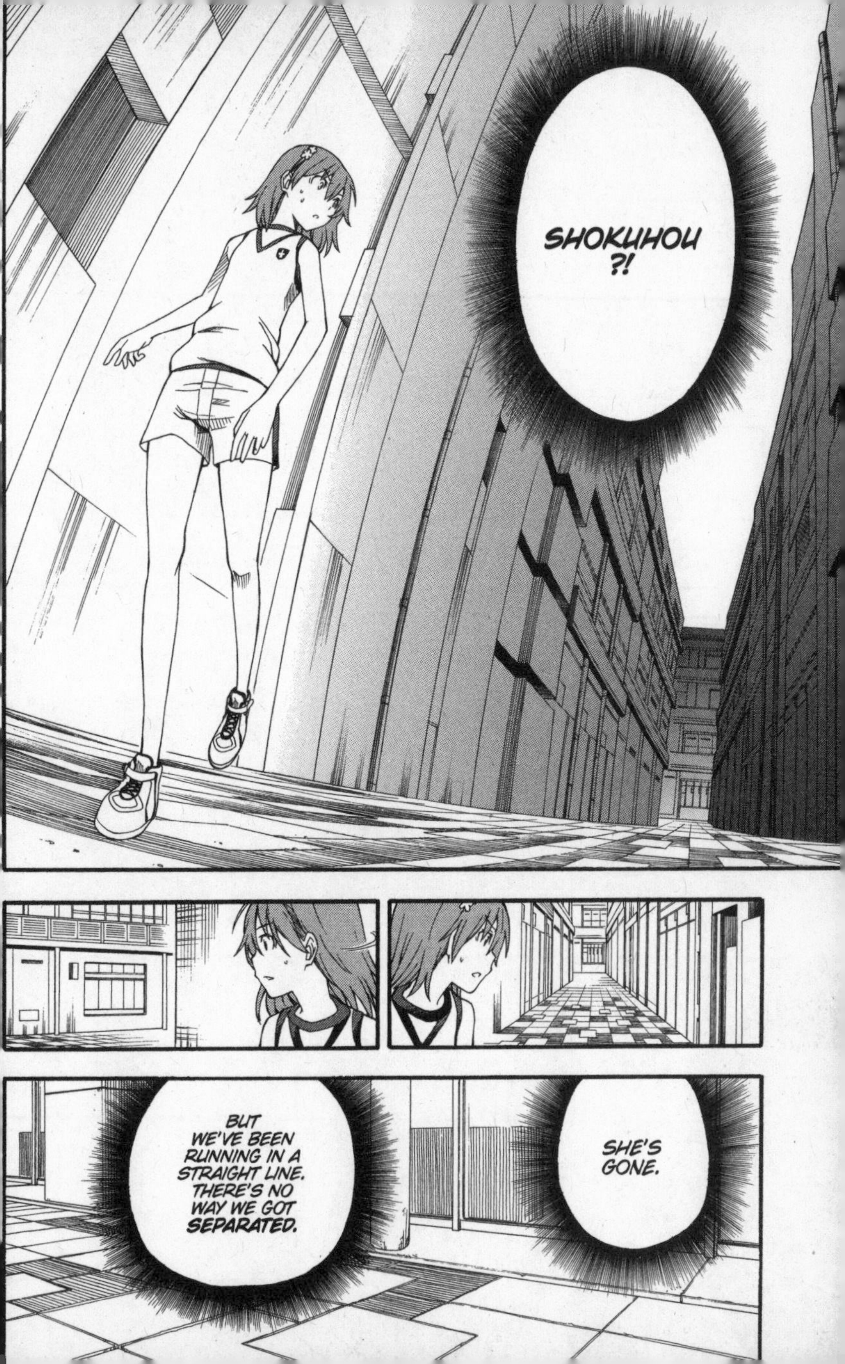
SHOKUHOU ?!
SHE'S GONE.
BUT WE'VE BEEN RUNNING IN A STRAIGHT LINE. THERE'S NO WAY WE GOT SEPARATED.

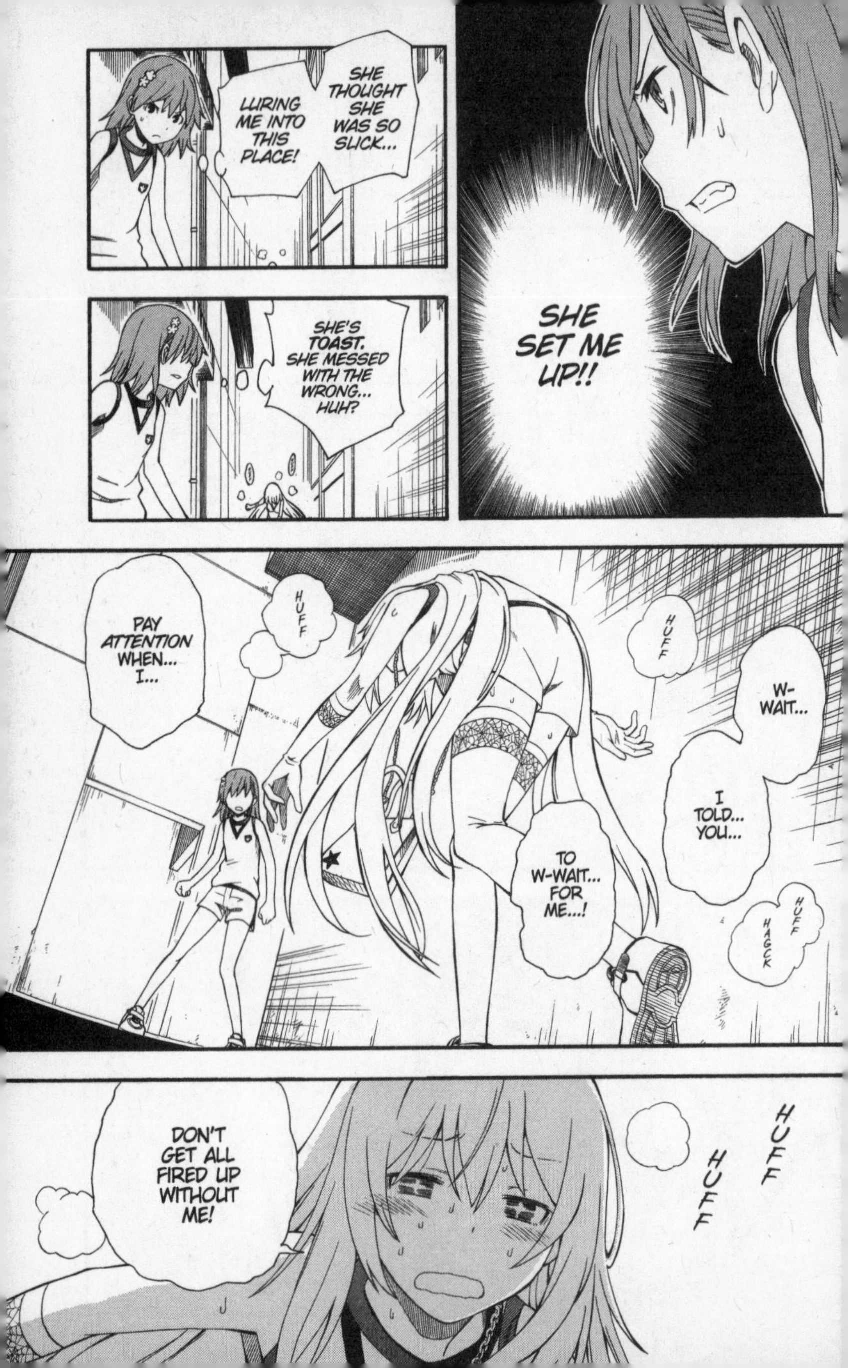
SHE SET ME UP!!
SHE THOUGHT SHE WAS SO SLICK...
LURING ME INTO THIS PLACE!
SHE'S TOAST. SHE MESSED WITH THE WRONG... HUH?
HUFF
W-WAIT...
I TOLD... YOU...
HUFF HAGCK
TO W-WAIT... FOR ME...!
HUFF
PAY ATTENTION WHEN... I...
HUFF HUFF
DON'T GET ALL FIRED UP WITHOUT ME!

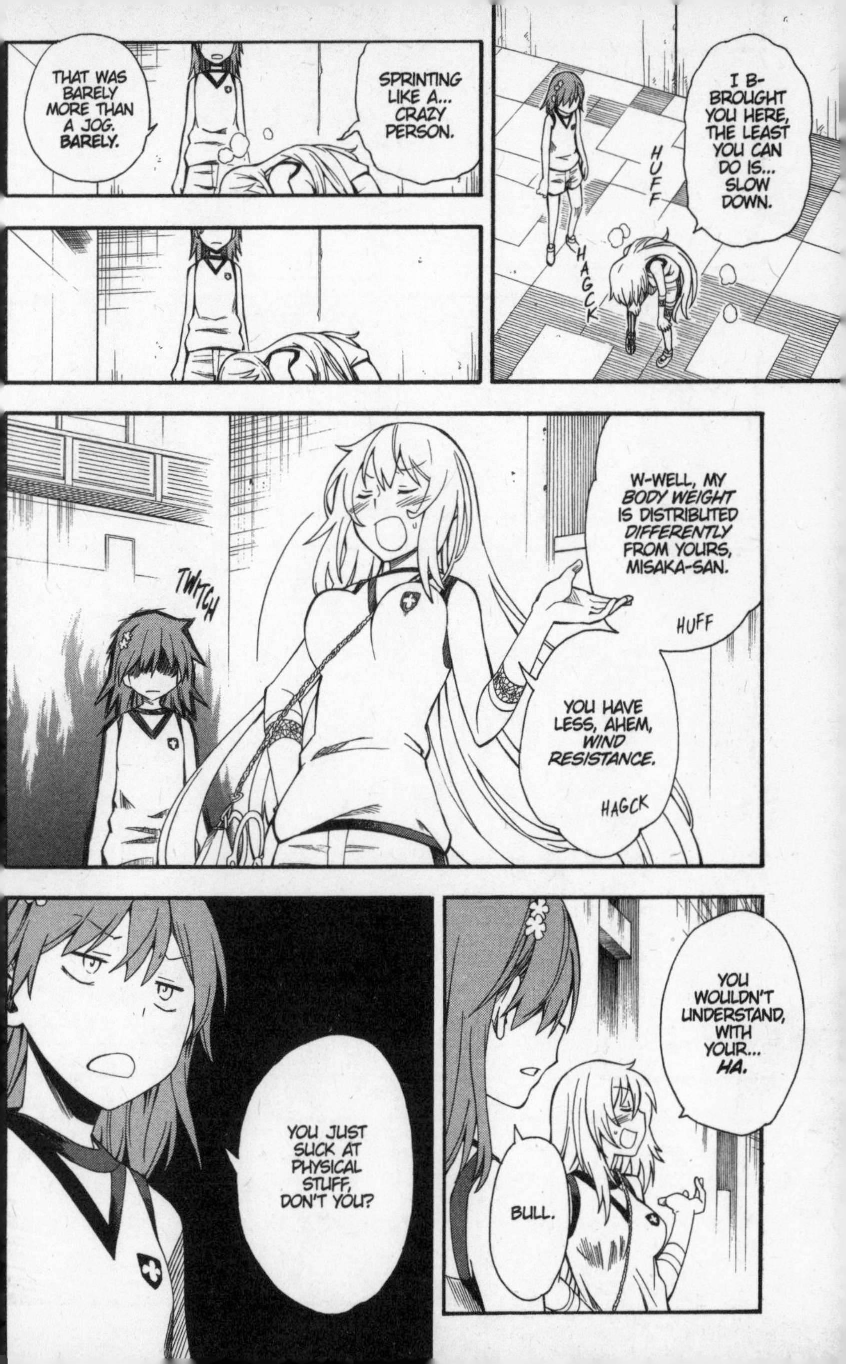
I B-BROUGHT YOU HERE, THE LEAST YOU CAN DO IS... SLOW DOWN.
HUFF
HAGCK
SPRINTING LIKE A... CRAZY PERSON.
THAT WAS BARELY MORE THAN A JOG. BARELY.
W-WELL, MY *BODY WEIGHT* IS DISTRIBUTED *DIFFERENTLY* FROM YOURS, MISAKA-SAN.
HUFF
YOU HAVE LESS, AHEM, *WIND RESISTANCE.*
HAGCK
TWITCH
YOU WOULDN'T UNDERSTAND, WITH YOUR... ***HA.***
BULL.
YOU JUST SUCK AT PHYSICAL STUFF, DON'T YOU?

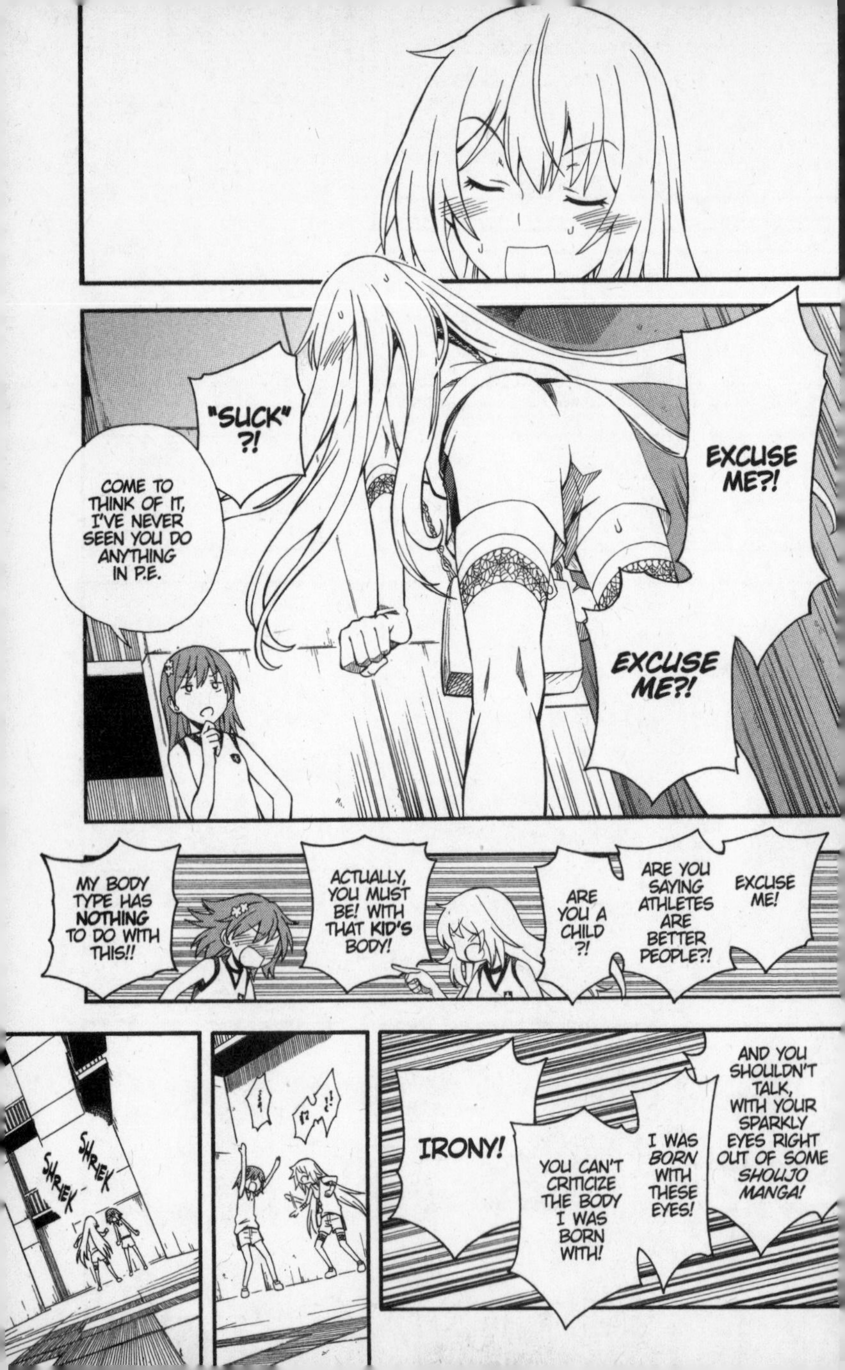
EXCUSE ME?!
EXCUSE ME?!
"SUCK"?!
COME TO THINK OF IT, I'VE NEVER SEEN YOU DO ANYTHING IN P.E.
EXCUSE ME!
ARE YOU SAYING ATHLETES ARE BETTER PEOPLE?!
ARE YOU A CHILD?!
ACTUALLY, YOU MUST BE! WITH THAT KID'S BODY!
MY BODY TYPE HAS NOTHING TO DO WITH THIS!!
AND YOU SHOULDN'T TALK, WITH YOUR SPARKLY EYES RIGHT OUT OF SOME *SHOUJO MANGA!*
I WAS *BORN* WITH THESE EYES!
YOU CAN'T CRITICIZE THE BODY I WAS BORN WITH!
IRONY!
SHRIEK
SHRIEK

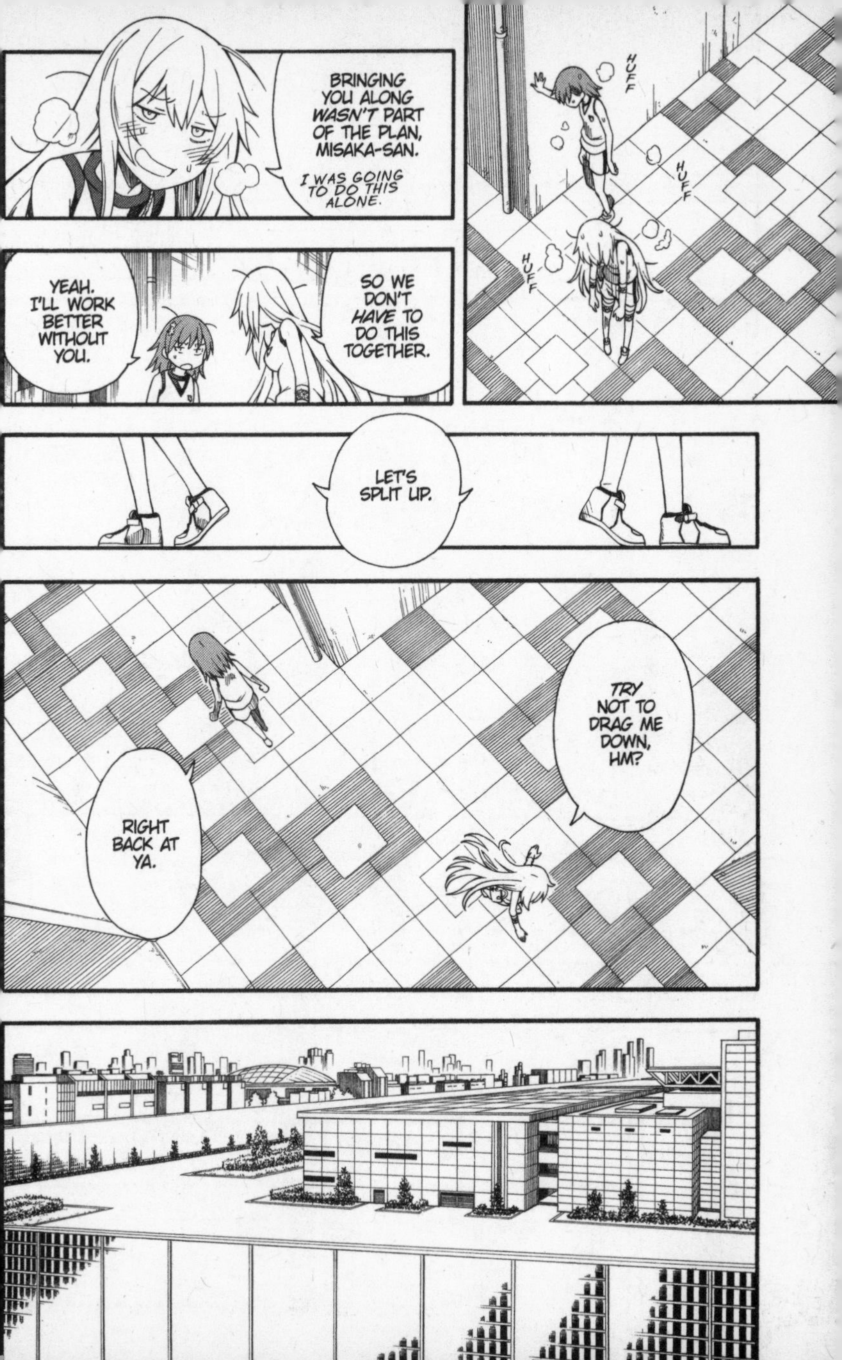
HUFF
HUFF
HUFF
BRINGING YOU ALONG *WASN'T* PART OF THE PLAN, MISAKA-SAN.
I WAS GOING TO DO THIS ALONE.
SO WE DON'T *HAVE* TO DO THIS TOGETHER.
YEAH. I'LL WORK BETTER WITHOUT YOU.
LET'S SPLIT UP.
TRY NOT TO DRAG ME DOWN, HM?
RIGHT BACK AT YA.

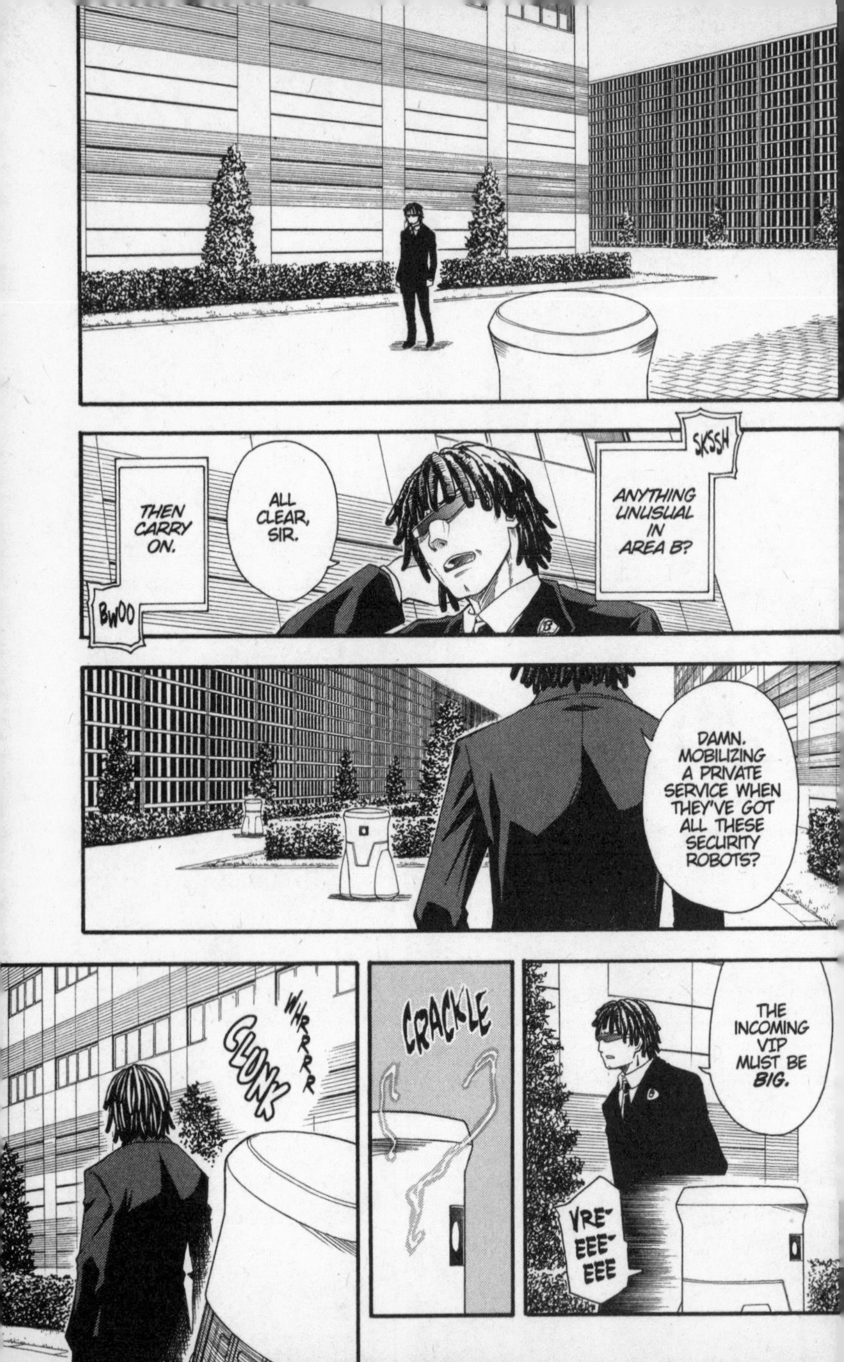
SKSSH
ANYTHING UNUSUAL IN AREA B?
ALL CLEAR, SIR.
THEN CARRY ON.
BWOO
DAMN. MOBILIZING A PRIVATE SERVICE WHEN THEY'VE GOT ALL THESE SECURITY ROBOTS?
THE INCOMING VIP MUST BE BIG.
VRE-EEE-EEE
CRACKLE
WHRRRR
CLONK

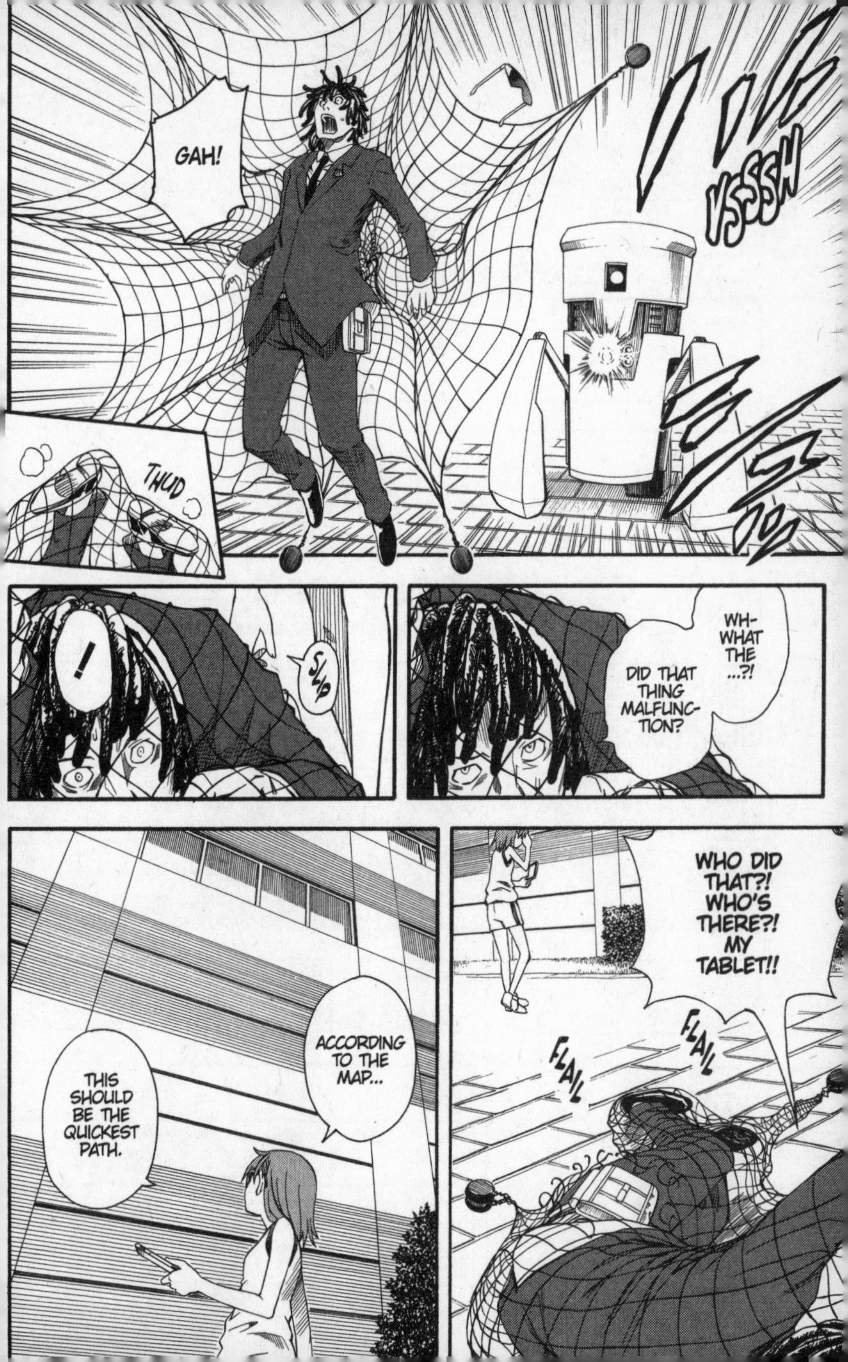
VSSSH
GAH!
THUD
!
SLIP
WH- WHAT THE ...?!
DID THAT THING MALFUNCTION?
WHO DID THAT?! WHO'S THERE?! MY TABLET!!
FLAIL
FLAIL
ACCORDING TO THE MAP...
THIS SHOULD BE THE QUICKEST PATH.

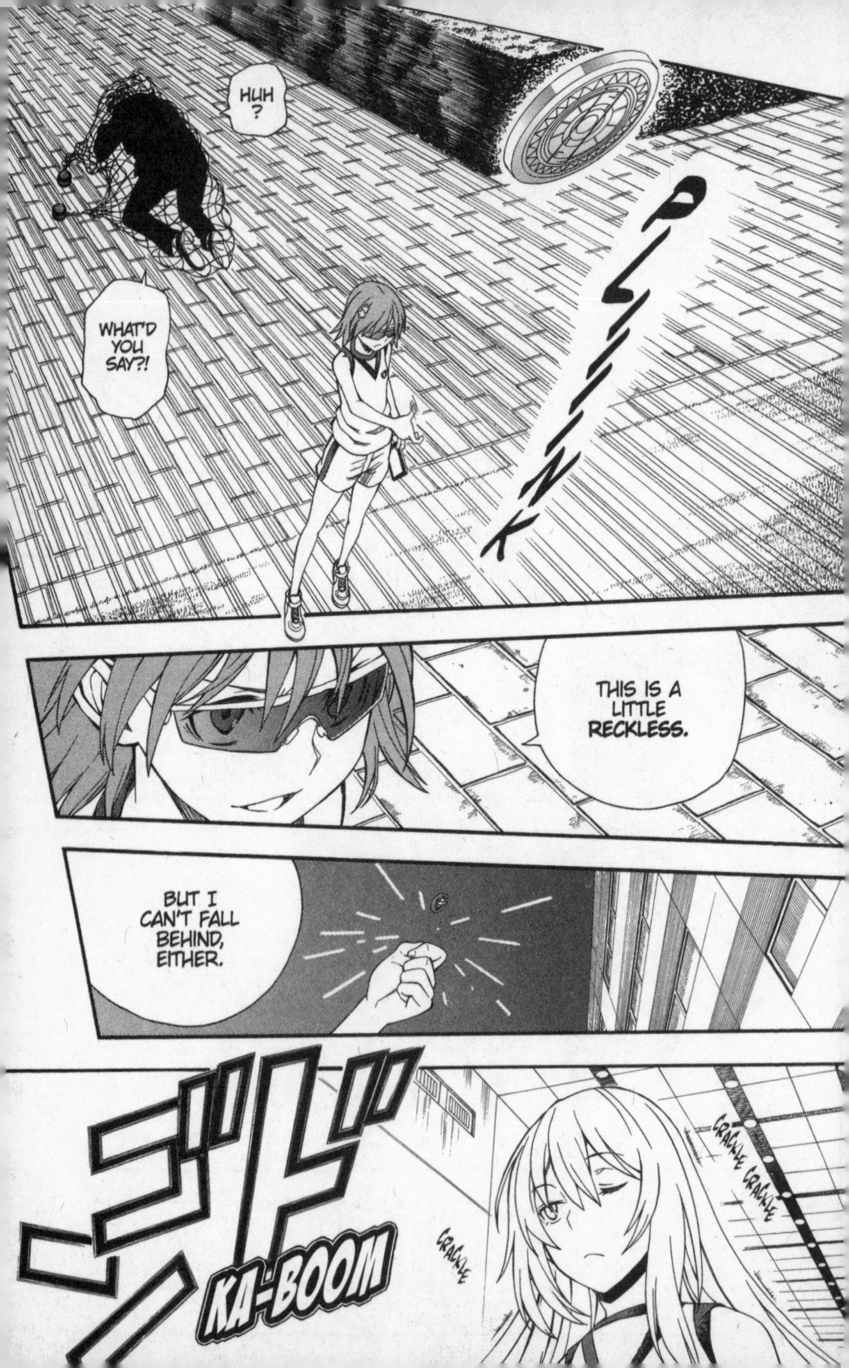

HUH?
WHAT'D YOU SAY?!
PLIIINK
THIS IS A LITTLE RECKLESS.
BUT I CAN'T FALL BEHIND, EITHER.
KA-BOOM
CRACKLE
CRACKLE CRACKLE

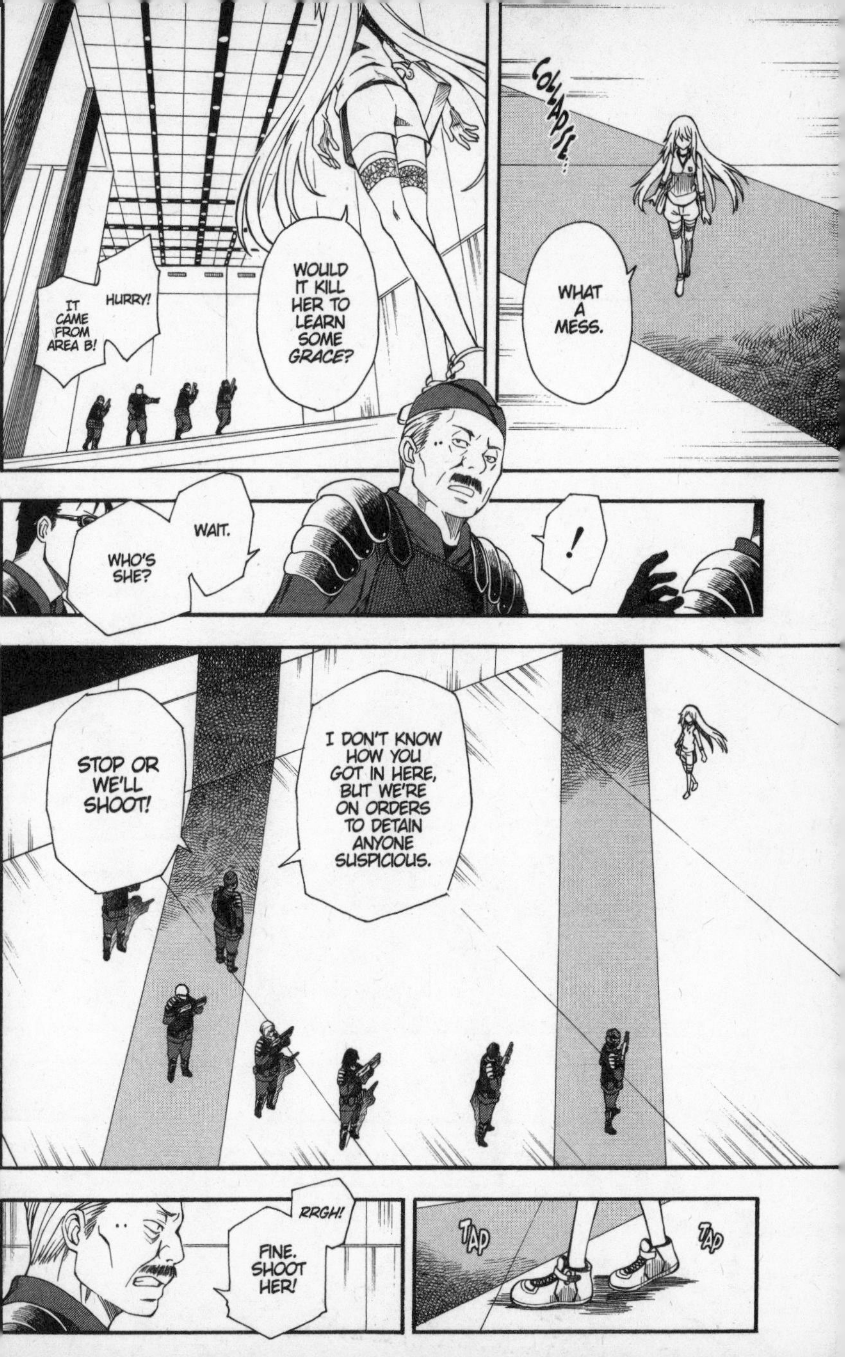
IT CAME FROM AREA B!
HURRY!
WOULD IT KILL HER TO LEARN SOME GRACE?
COLLAPSE...
WHAT A MESS.
WAIT.
WHO'S SHE?
!
STOP OR WE'LL SHOOT!
I DON'T KNOW HOW YOU GOT IN HERE, BUT WE'RE ON ORDERS TO DETAIN ANYONE SUSPICIOUS.
...
RRGH!
FINE. SHOOT HER!
TAP
TAP

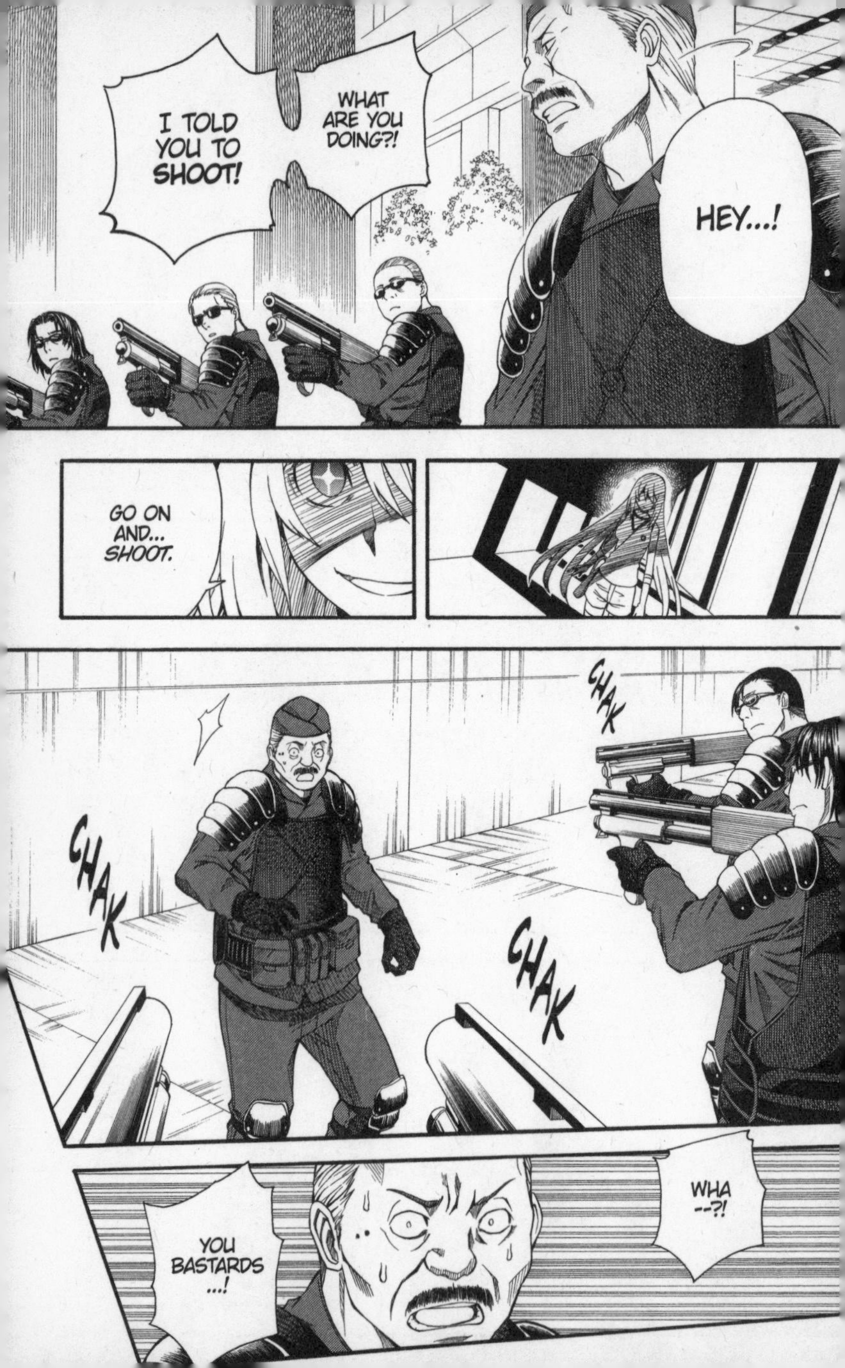
HEY...!
WHAT ARE YOU DOING?!
I TOLD YOU TO SHOOT!
GO ON AND... SHOOT.
CHAK
CHAK
CHAK
WHA --?!
YOU BASTARDS ...!

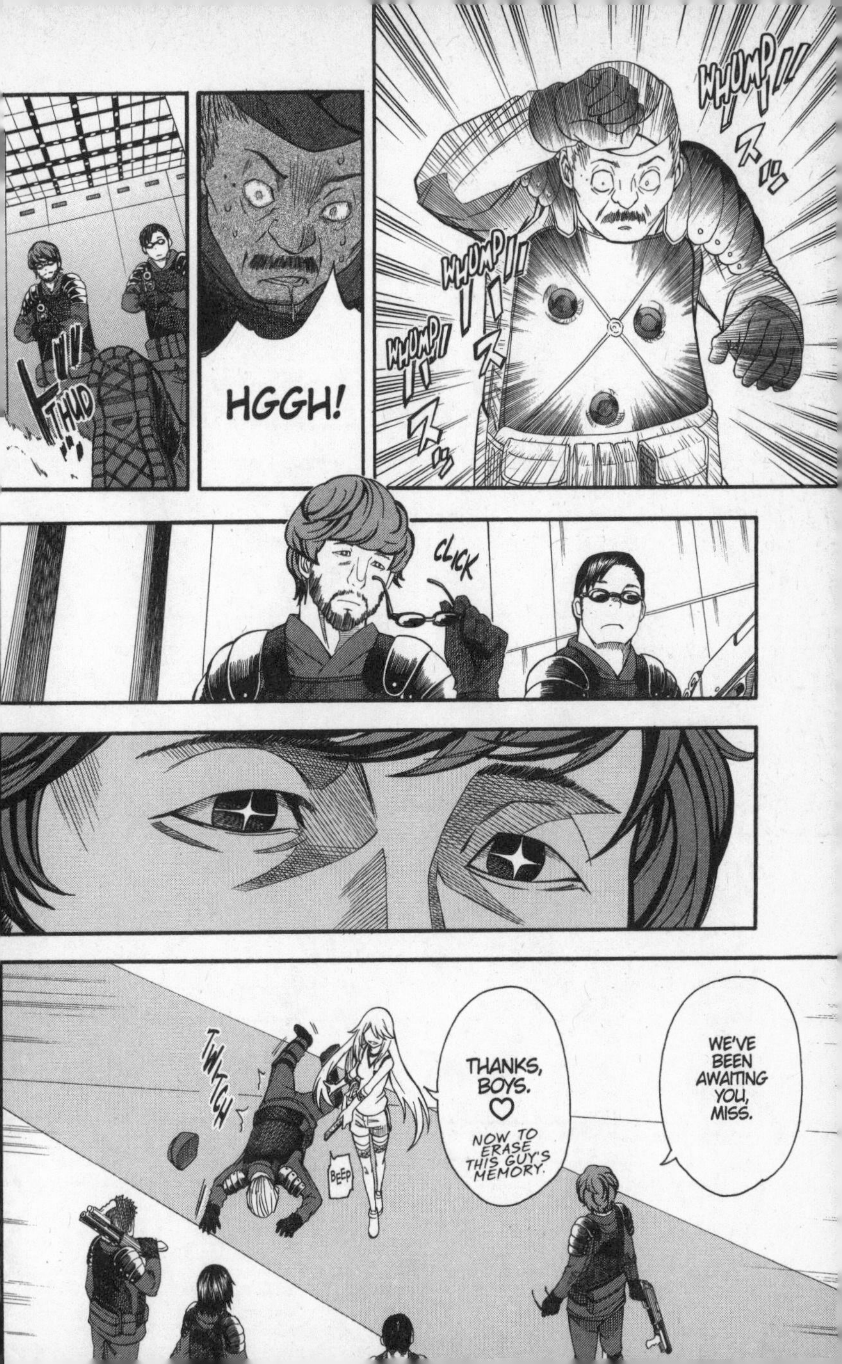
WHUMP!!
WHUMP!!
WHUMP!!
HGGH!
THUD
CLICK
WE'VE BEEN AWAITING YOU, MISS.
THANKS, BOYS. ♡
NOW TO ERASE THIS GUY'S MEMORY.
TWITCH
BEEP

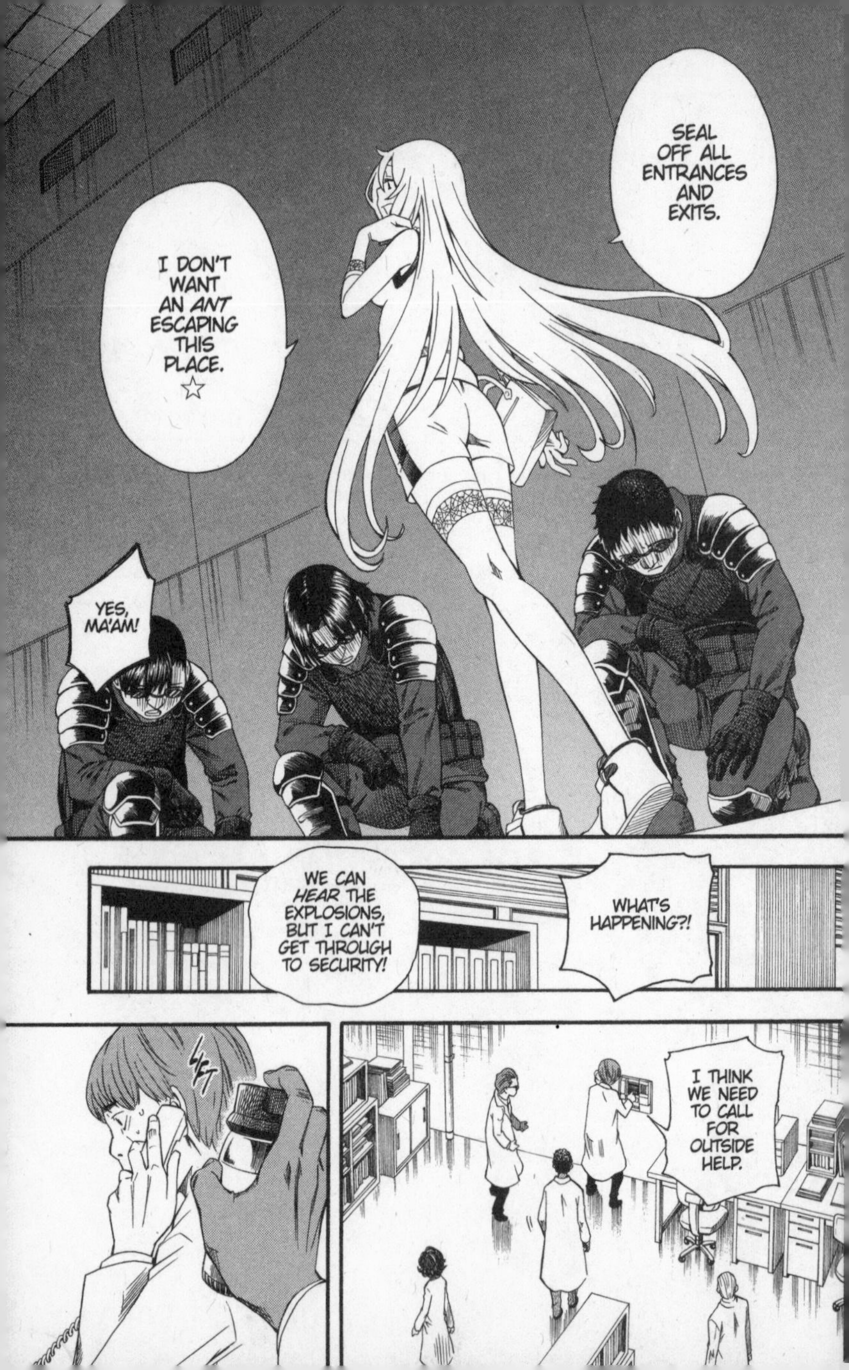
SEAL OFF ALL ENTRANCES AND EXITS.
I DON'T WANT AN *ANT* ESCAPING THIS PLACE. ☆
YES, MA'AM!
WHAT'S HAPPENING?!
WE CAN *HEAR* THE EXPLOSIONS, BUT I CAN'T GET THROUGH TO SECURITY!
I THINK WE NEED TO CALL FOR OUTSIDE HELP.

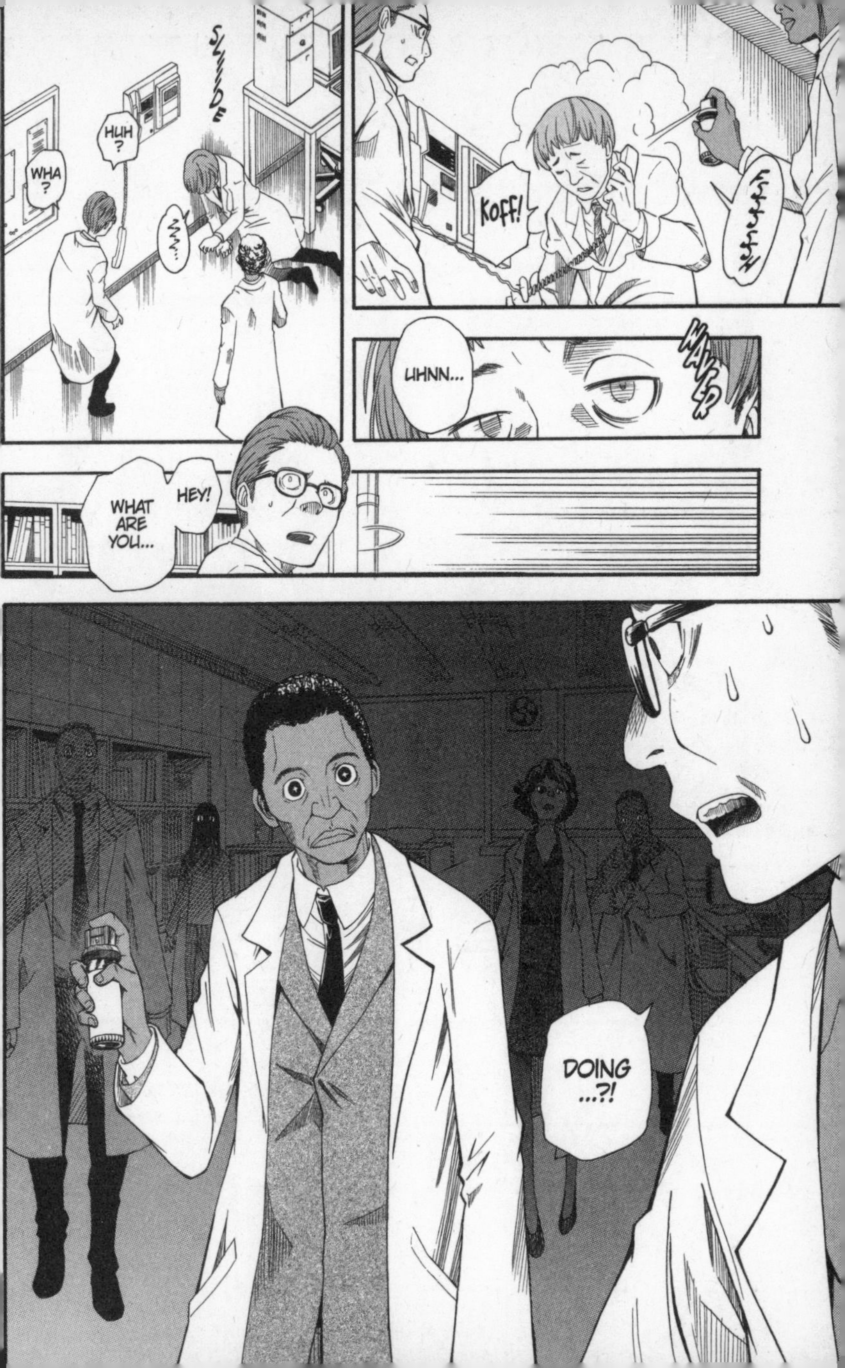
KOFF!
SLIIIDE
HUH?
WHA?
Zzz...
WAVER
UHNN...
HEY!
WHAT ARE YOU...
DOING ...?!

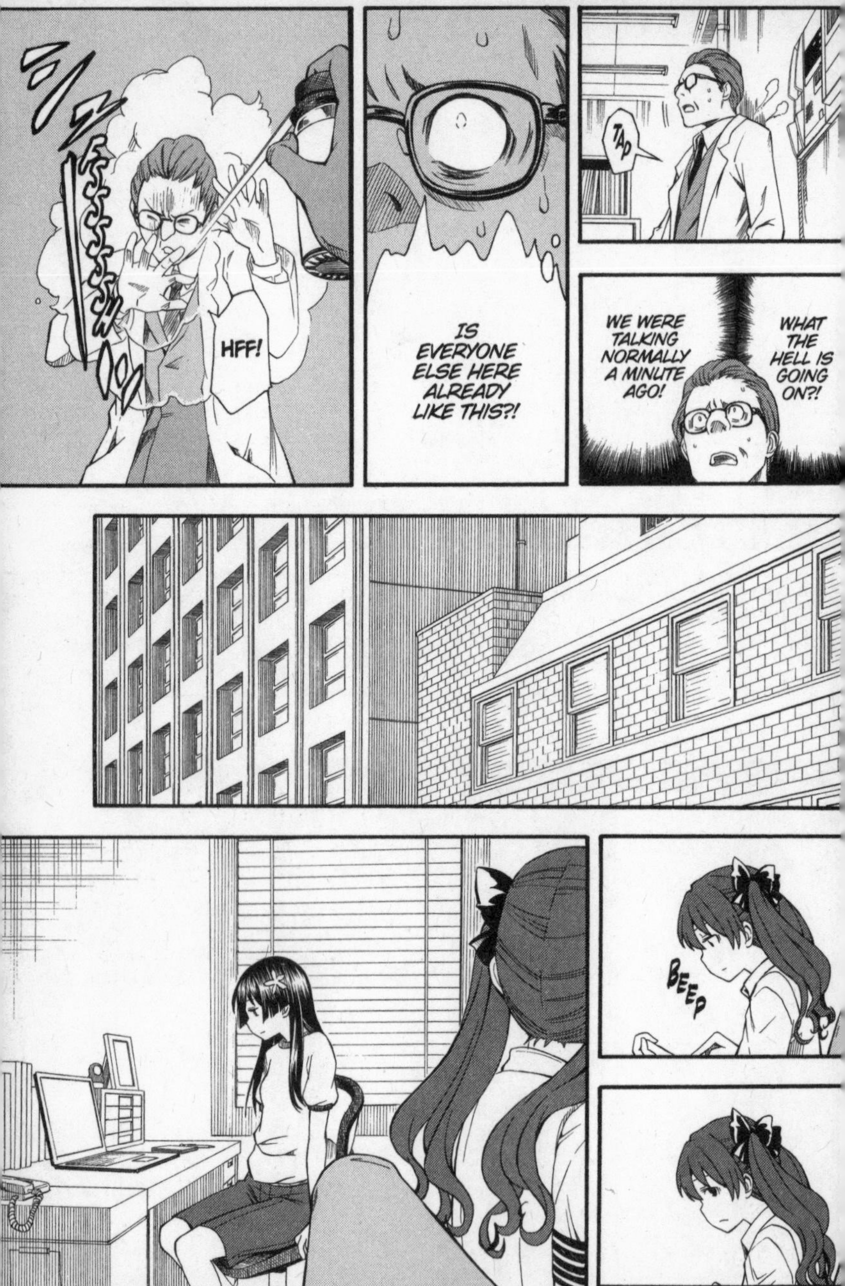
TAP
WHAT THE HELL IS GOING ON?!
WE WERE TALKING NORMALLY A MINUTE AGO!
IS EVERYONE ELSE HERE ALREADY LIKE THIS?!
HFF!
BEEP

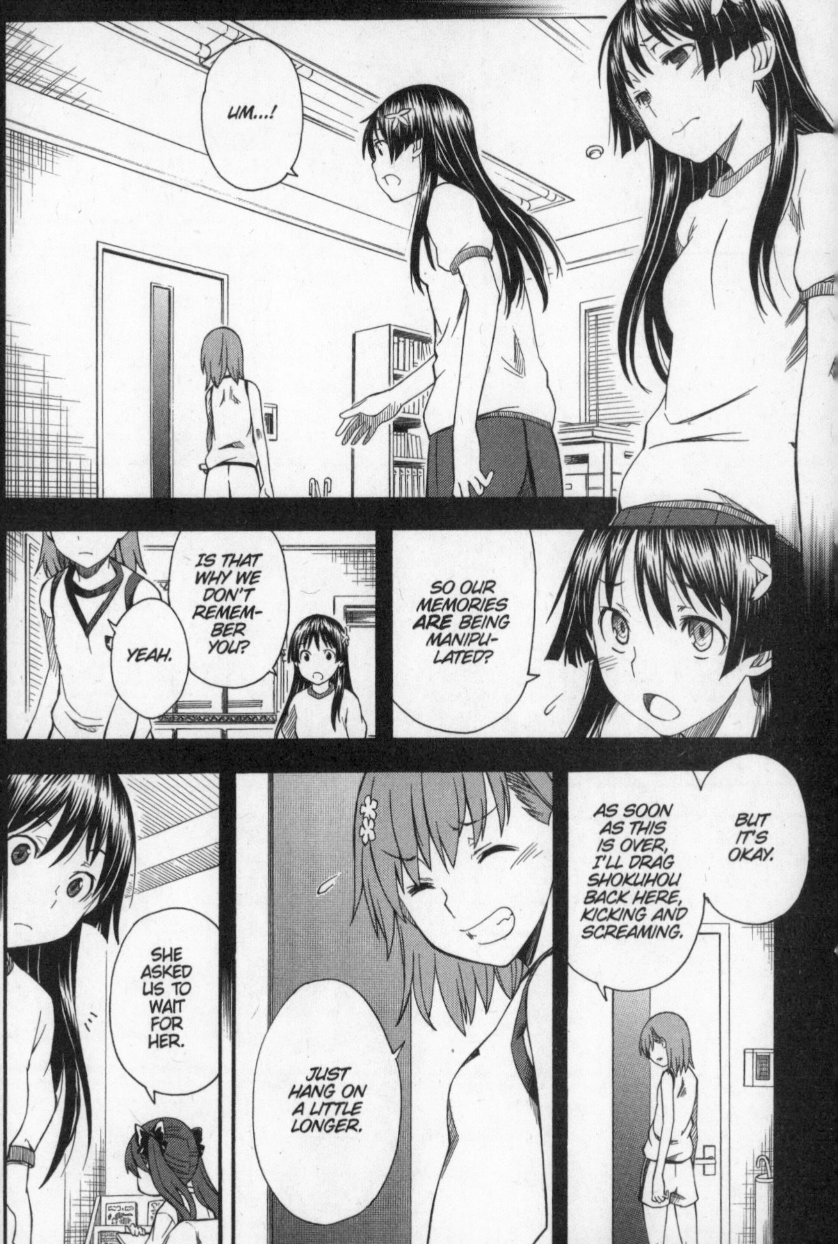
UM...!
SO OUR MEMORIES ARE BEING MANIPULATED?
IS THAT WHY WE DON'T REMEMBER YOU?
YEAH.
BUT IT'S OKAY.
AS SOON AS THIS IS OVER, I'LL DRAG SHOKUHOU BACK HERE, KICKING AND SCREAMING.
JUST HANG ON A LITTLE LONGER.
SHE ASKED US TO WAIT FOR HER.

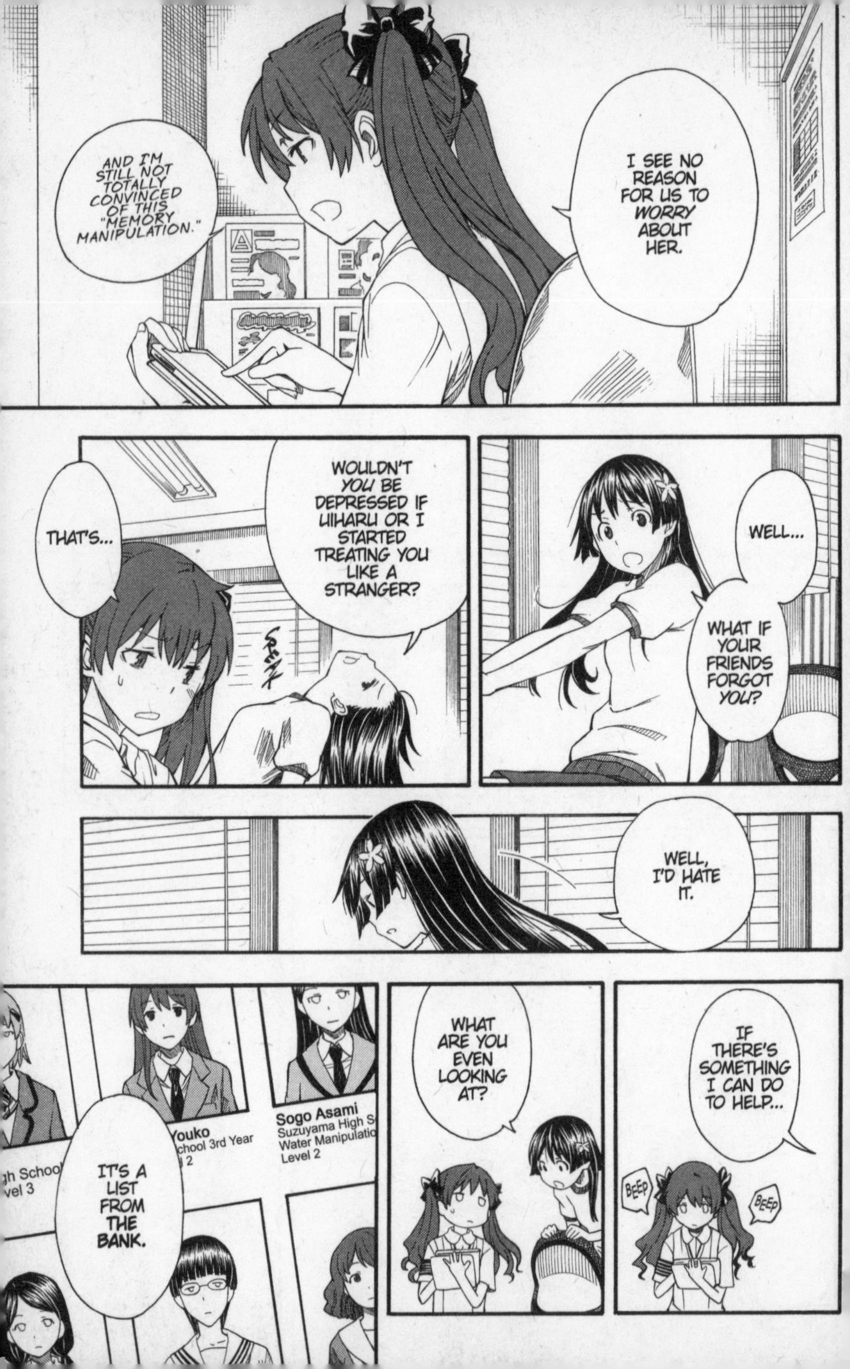
I SEE NO REASON FOR US TO *WORRY* ABOUT HER.
AND I'M STILL NOT TOTALLY CONVINCED OF THIS "MEMORY MANIPULATION."
WELL...
WHAT IF YOUR FRIENDS FORGOT *YOU?*
WOULDN'T *YOU* BE DEPRESSED IF UIHARU OR I STARTED TREATING YOU LIKE A STRANGER?
THAT'S...
WELL, I'D HATE IT.
IF THERE'S SOMETHING I CAN DO TO HELP...
BEEP
BEEP
WHAT ARE YOU EVEN LOOKING AT?
Sogo Asami
Suzuyama High S
Water Manipulatio
Level 2
Youko
chool 3rd Year
IT'S A LIST FROM THE BANK.

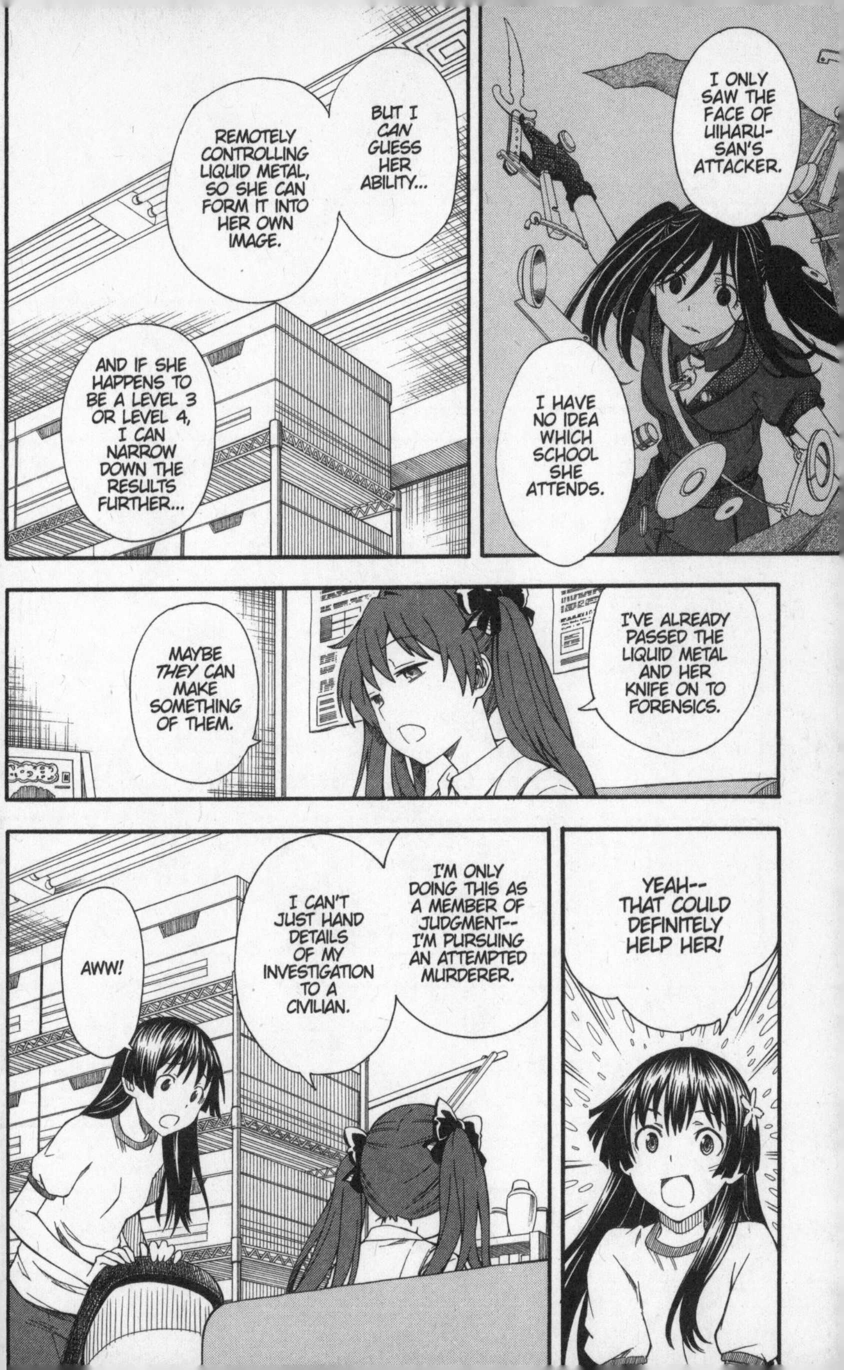
I ONLY SAW THE FACE OF UIHARU-SAN'S ATTACKER.
I HAVE NO IDEA WHICH SCHOOL SHE ATTENDS.
BUT I *CAN* GUESS HER ABILITY...
REMOTELY CONTROLLING LIQUID METAL, SO SHE CAN FORM IT INTO HER OWN IMAGE.
AND IF SHE HAPPENS TO BE A LEVEL 3 OR LEVEL 4, I CAN NARROW DOWN THE RESULTS FURTHER...
I'VE ALREADY PASSED THE LIQUID METAL AND HER KNIFE ON TO FORENSICS.
MAYBE *THEY* CAN MAKE SOMETHING OF THEM.
YEAH-- THAT COULD DEFINITELY HELP HER!
I'M ONLY DOING THIS AS A MEMBER OF JUDGMENT-- I'M PURSUING AN ATTEMPTED MURDERER.
I CAN'T JUST HAND DETAILS OF MY INVESTIGATION TO A CIVILIAN.
AWW!

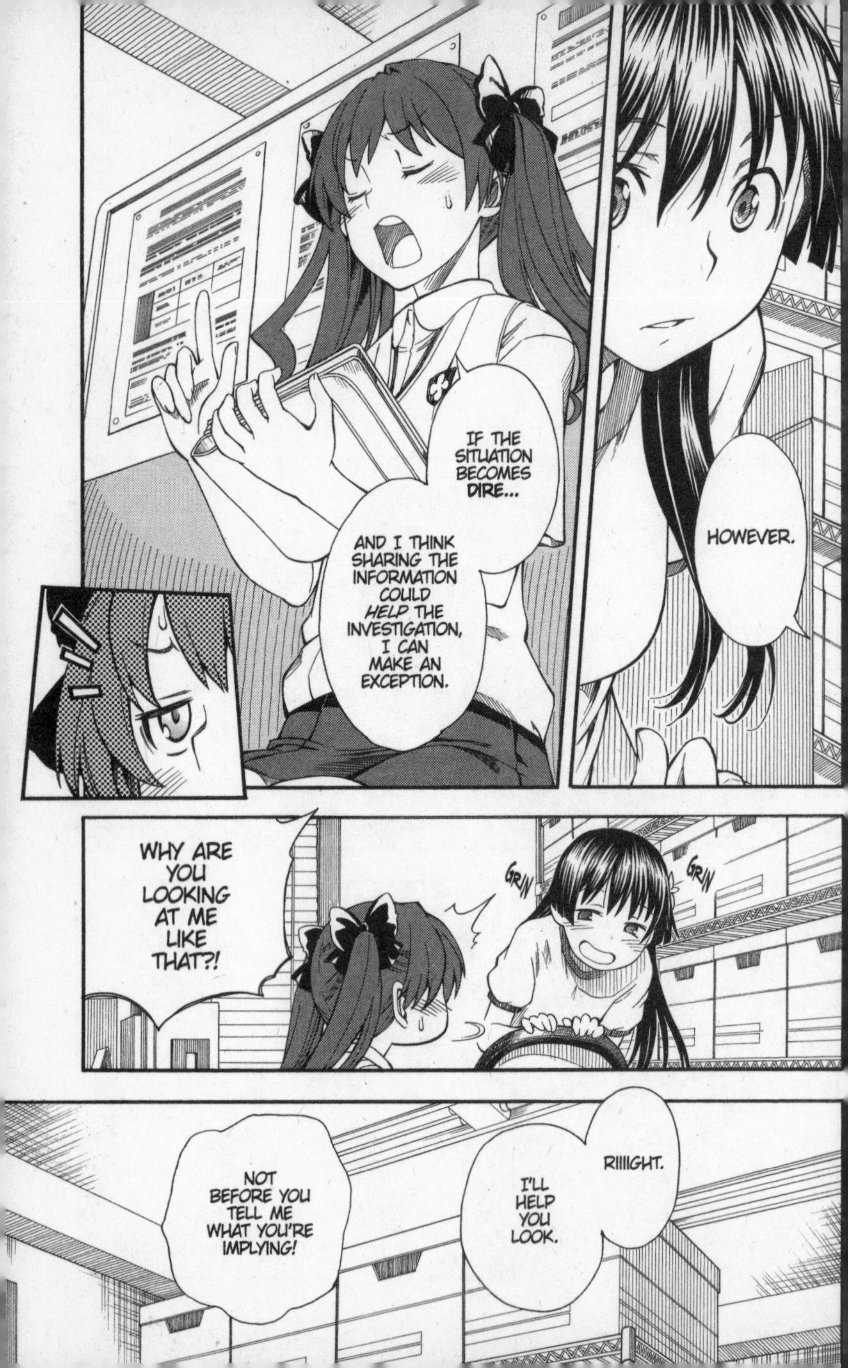
HOWEVER.
IF THE SITUATION BECOMES DIRE...
AND I THINK SHARING THE INFORMATION COULD HELP THE INVESTIGATION, I CAN MAKE AN EXCEPTION.
GRIN
GRIN
WHY ARE YOU LOOKING AT ME LIKE THAT?!
RIIIGHT.
I'LL HELP YOU LOOK.
NOT BEFORE YOU TELL ME WHAT YOU'RE IMPLYING!

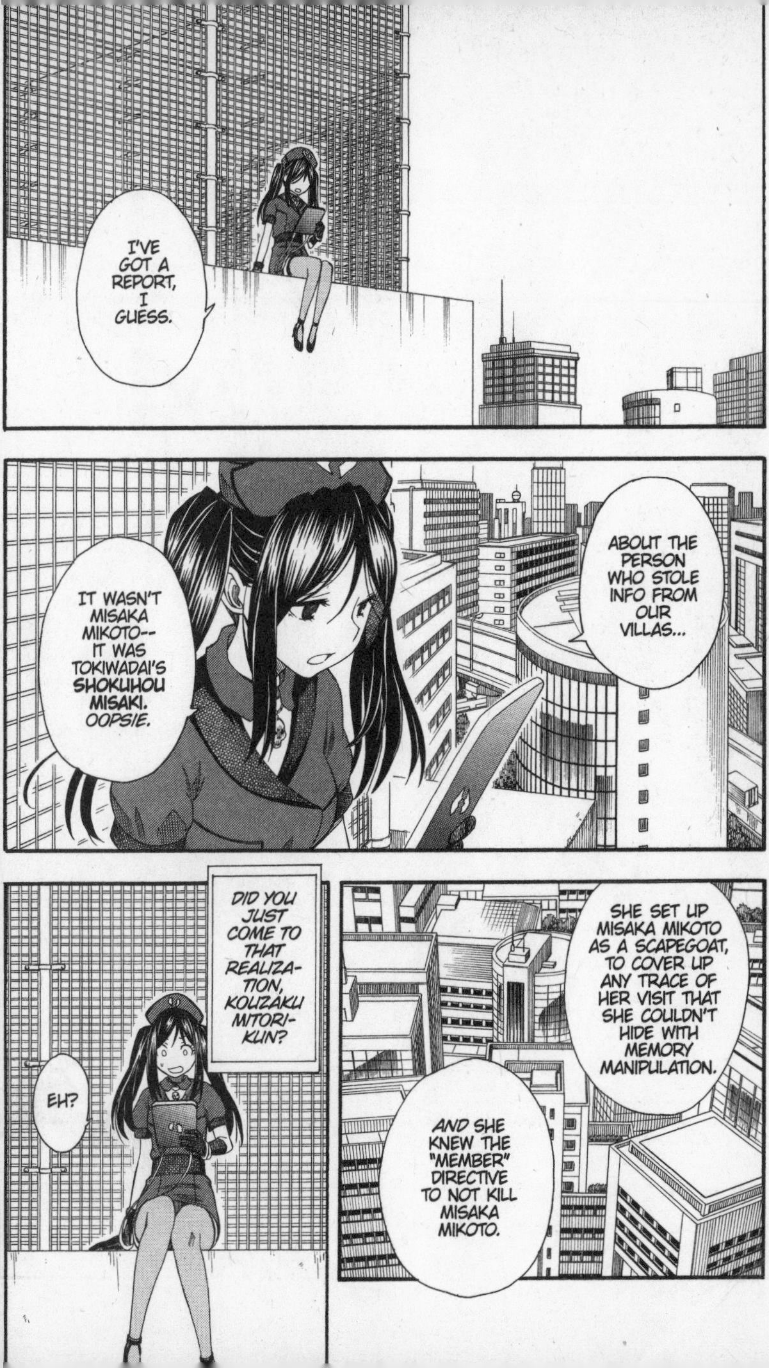
I'VE GOT A REPORT, I GUESS.
ABOUT THE PERSON WHO STOLE INFO FROM OUR VILLAS...
IT WASN'T MISAKA MIKOTO-- IT WAS TOKIWADAI'S SHOKUHOU MISAKI. OOPSIE.
SHE SET UP MISAKA MIKOTO AS A SCAPEGOAT, TO COVER UP ANY TRACE OF HER VISIT THAT SHE COULDN'T HIDE WITH MEMORY MANIPULATION.
AND SHE KNEW THE "MEMBER" DIRECTIVE TO NOT KILL MISAKA MIKOTO.
DID YOU JUST COME TO THAT REALIZA-TION, KOUZAKU MITORI-KUN?
EH?

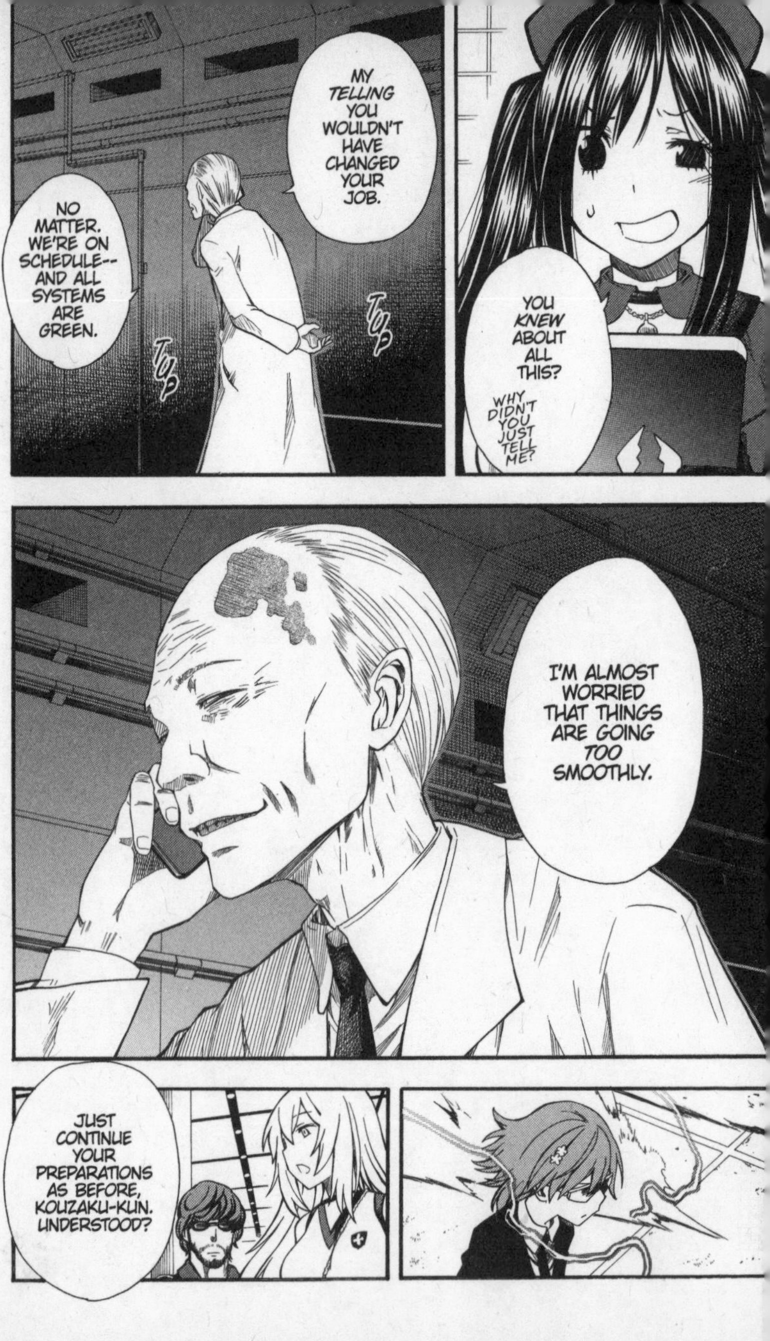
YOU KNEW ABOUT ALL THIS?
WHY DIDN'T YOU JUST TELL ME?
MY *TELLING* YOU WOULDN'T HAVE CHANGED YOUR JOB.
NO MATTER. WE'RE ON SCHEDULE-- AND ALL SYSTEMS ARE GREEN.
I'M ALMOST WORRIED THAT THINGS ARE GOING *TOO* SMOOTHLY.
JUST CONTINUE YOUR PREPARATIONS AS BEFORE, KOUZAKU-KUN. UNDERSTOOD?

A Certain SCIENTIFIC Railgun

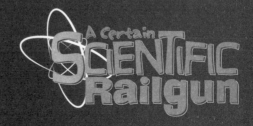

CHAPTER 57: SEARCH

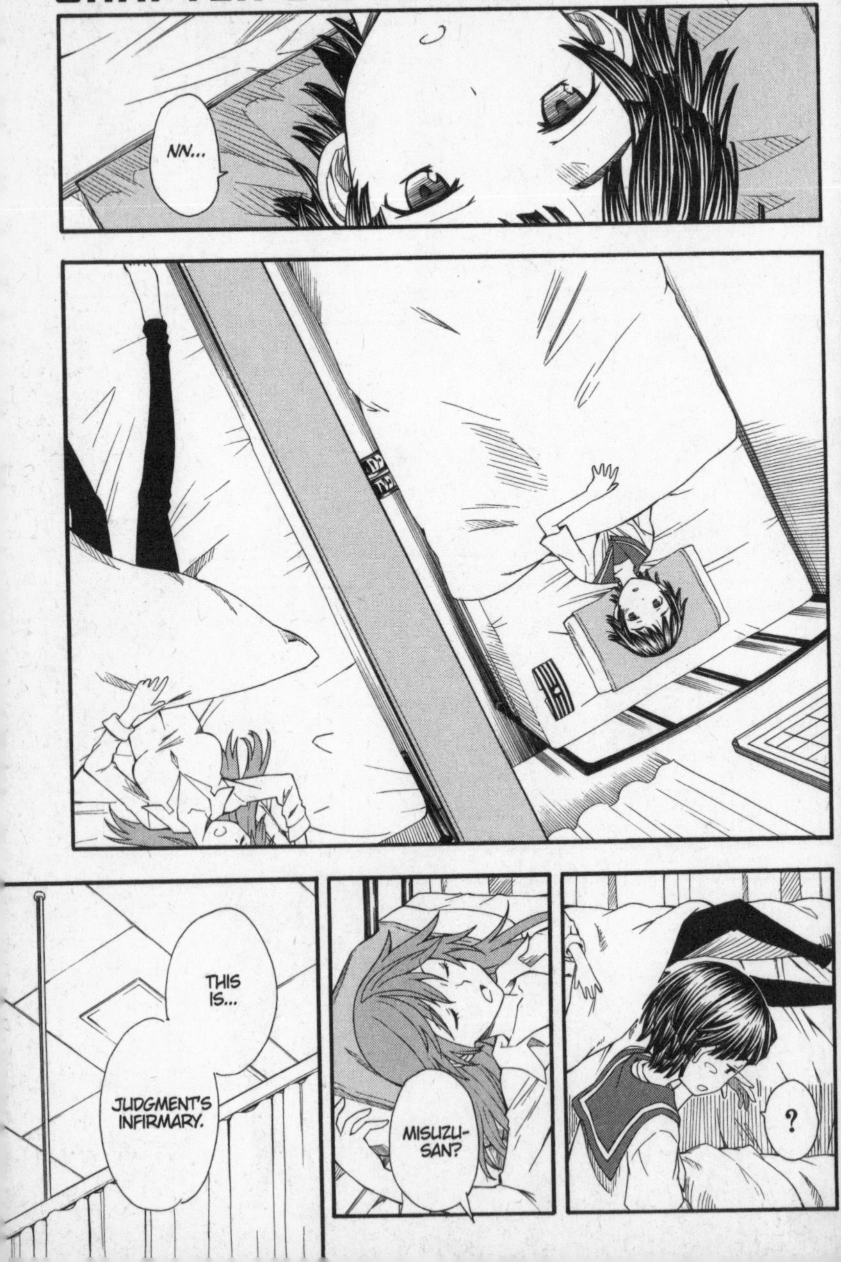
NN...
?
MISUZU-SAN?
THIS IS...
JUDGMENT'S INFIRMARY.

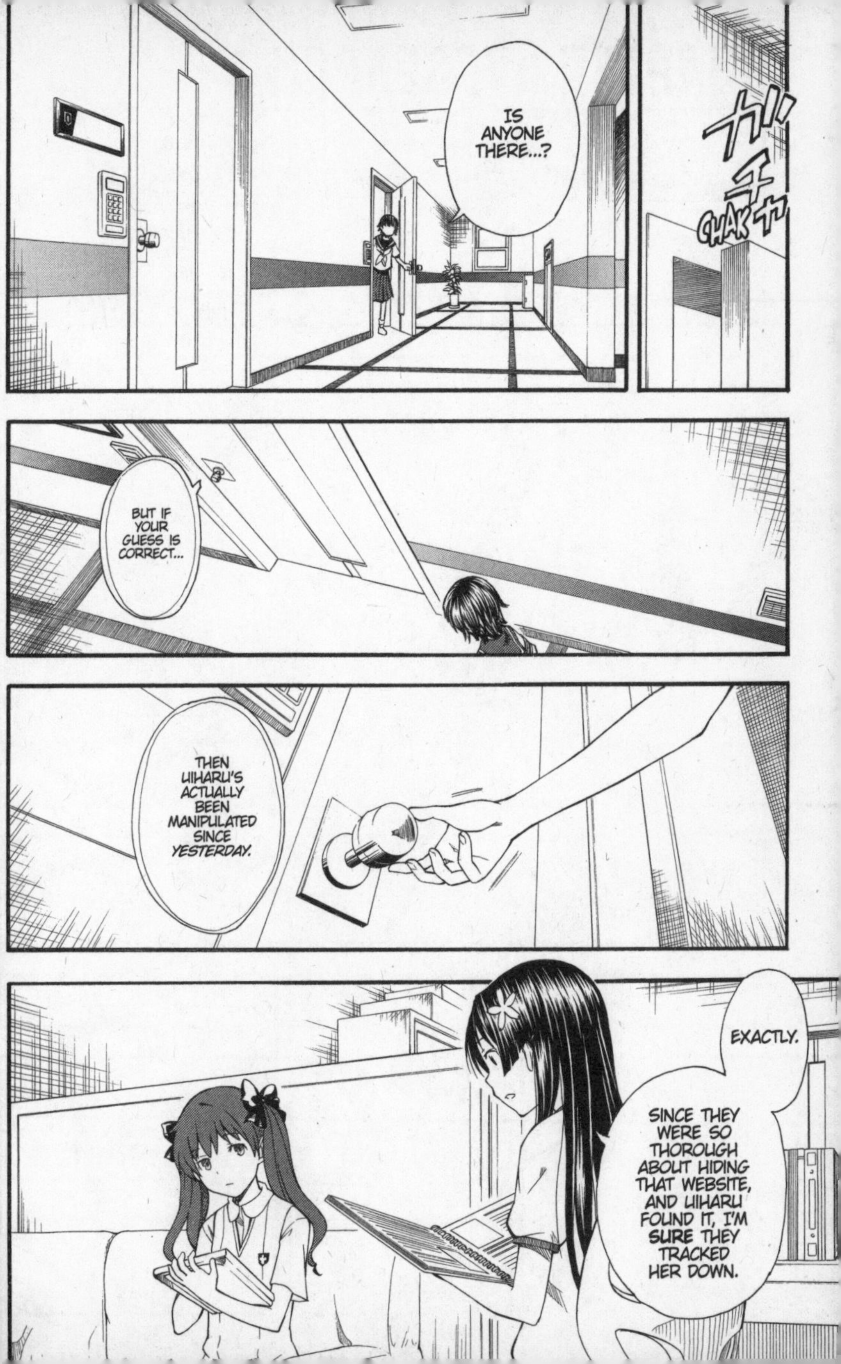
カチャ
CHAK
IS ANYONE THERE...?
BUT IF YOUR GUESS IS CORRECT...
THEN UIHARU'S ACTUALLY BEEN MANIPULATED SINCE *YESTERDAY.*
EXACTLY.
SINCE THEY WERE SO THOROUGH ABOUT HIDING THAT WEBSITE, AND UIHARU FOUND IT, I'M SURE THEY TRACKED HER DOWN.

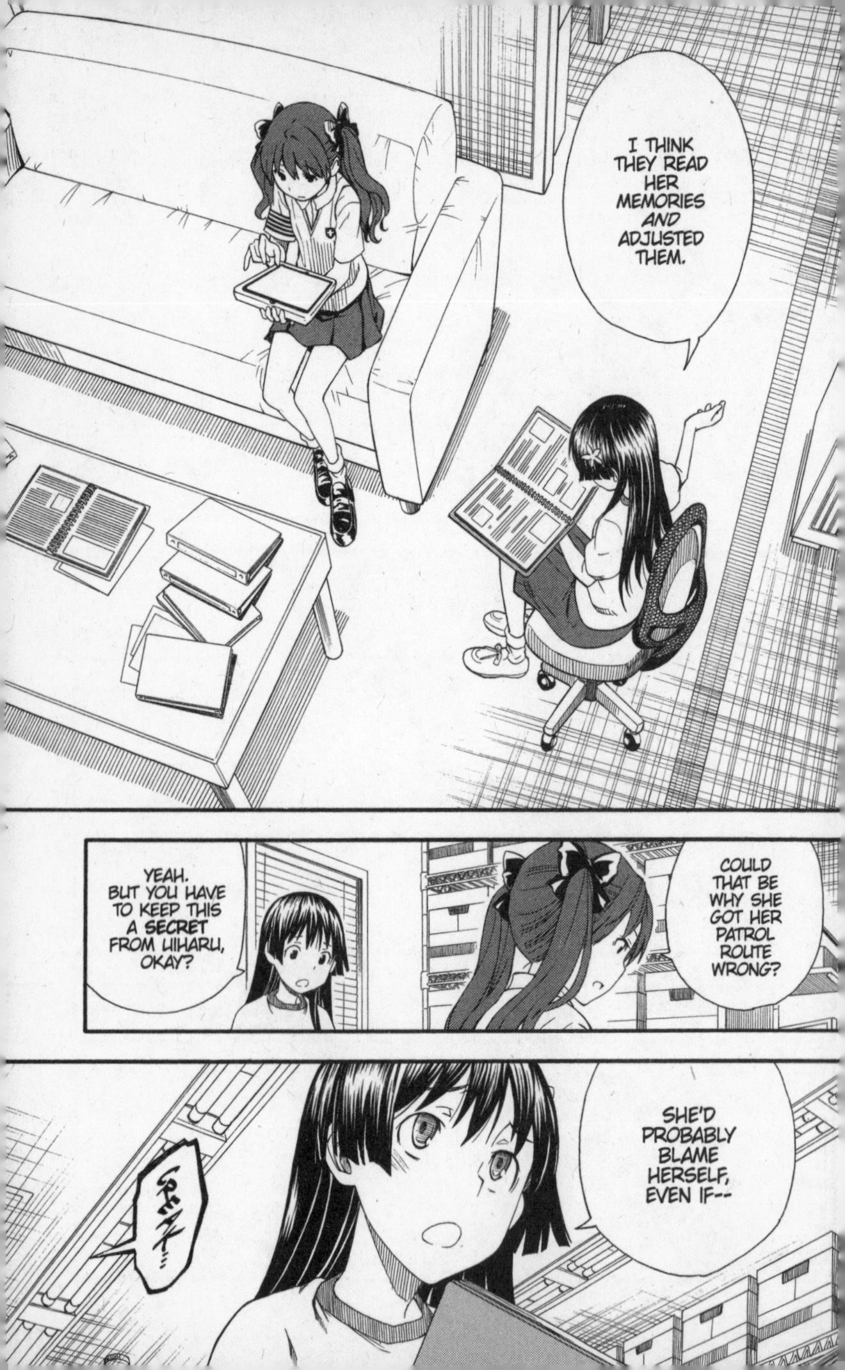
I THINK THEY READ HER MEMORIES AND ADJUSTED THEM.
COULD THAT BE WHY SHE GOT HER PATROL ROUTE WRONG?
YEAH. BUT YOU HAVE TO KEEP THIS A SECRET FROM UIHARU, OKAY?
SHE'D PROBABLY BLAME HERSELF, EVEN IF--
CREAK...

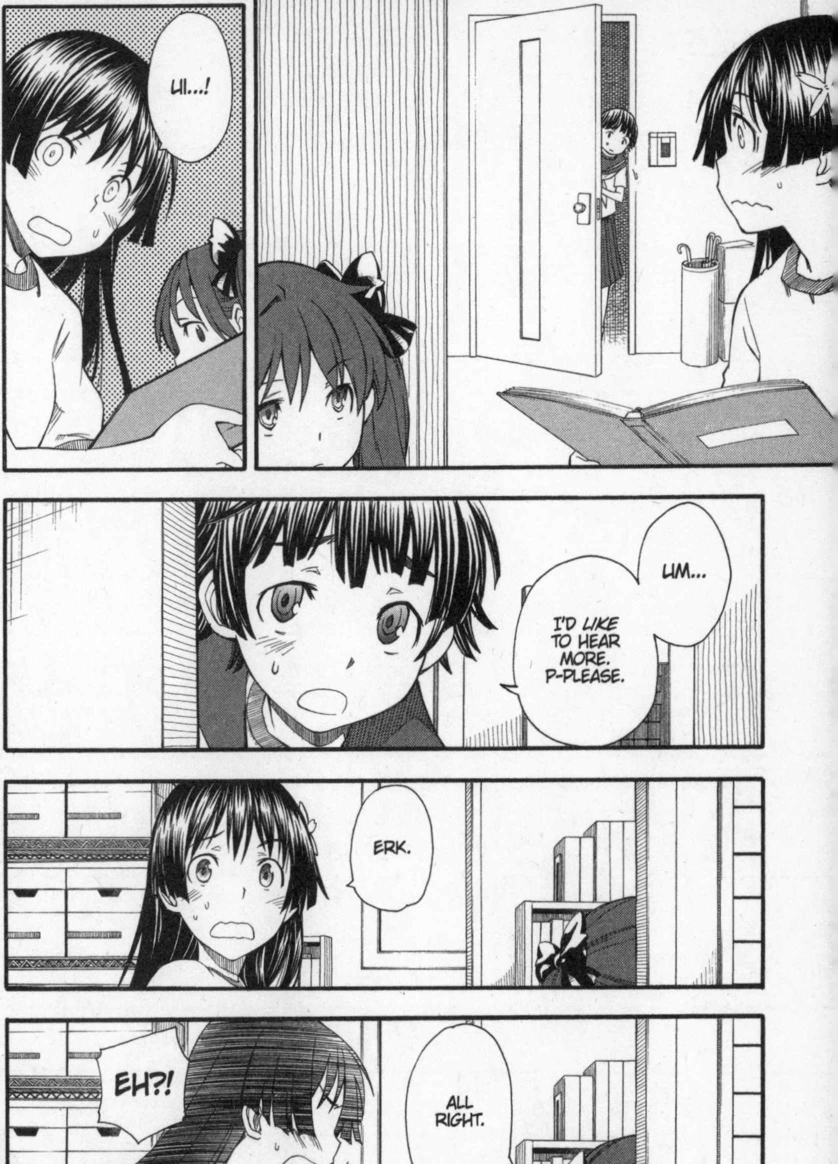
UI...!
UM...
I'D LIKE TO HEAR MORE. P-PLEASE.
ERK.
ALL RIGHT.
EH?!

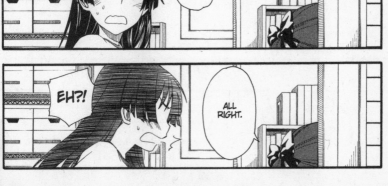

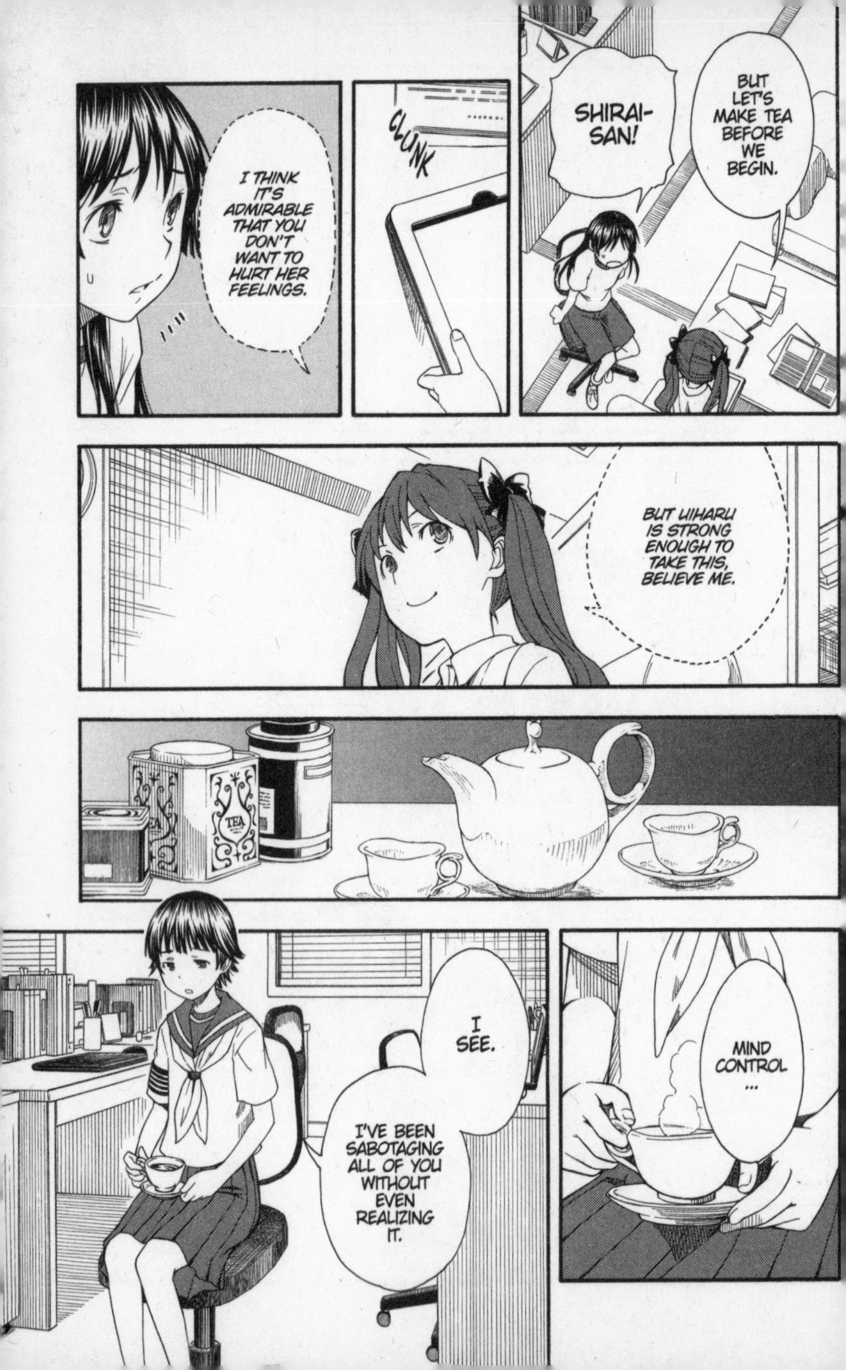
BUT LET'S MAKE TEA BEFORE WE BEGIN.
SHIRAI-SAN!
CLUNK
I THINK IT'S ADMIRABLE THAT YOU DON'T WANT TO HURT HER FEELINGS.
BUT UIHARU IS STRONG ENOUGH TO TAKE THIS, BELIEVE ME.
TEA
MIND CONTROL ...
I SEE.
I'VE BEEN SABOTAGING ALL OF YOU WITHOUT EVEN REALIZING IT.

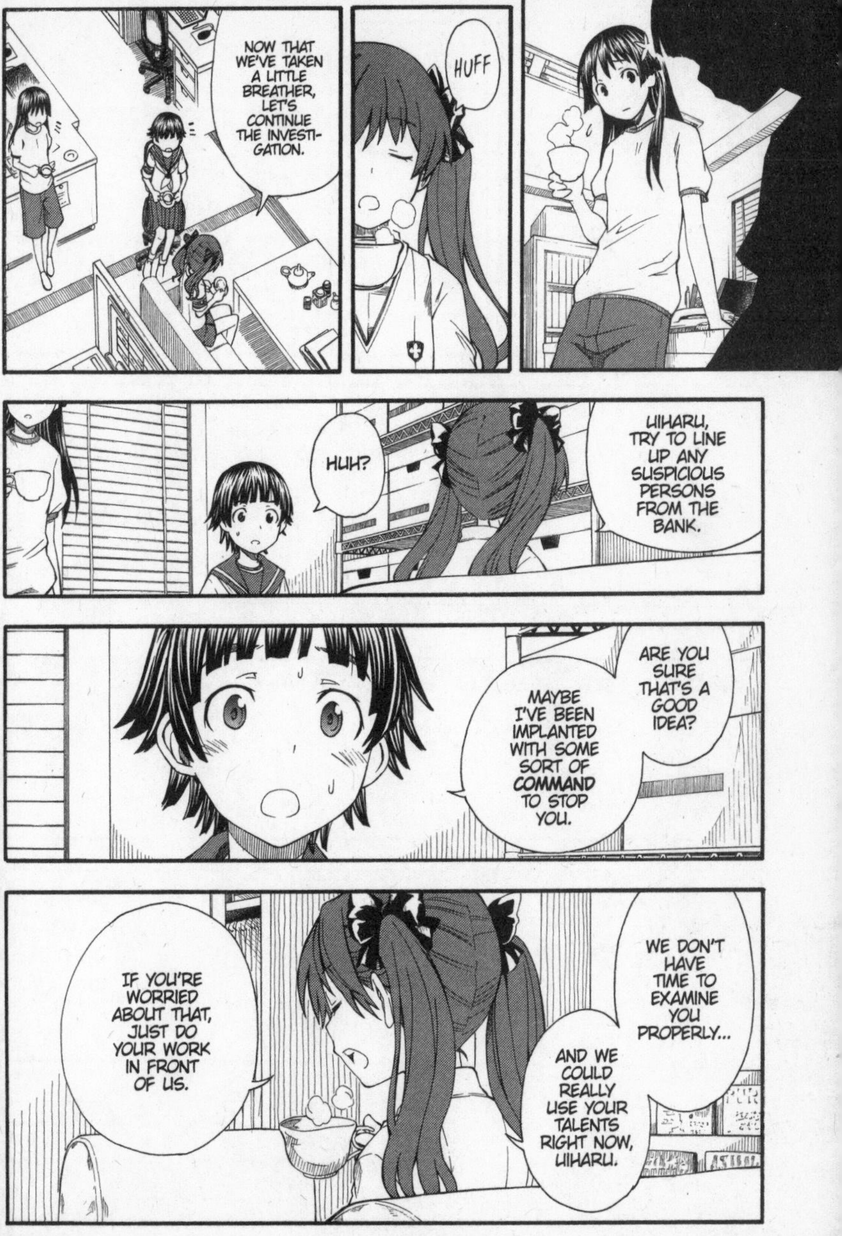
HUFF
NOW THAT WE'VE TAKEN A LITTLE BREATHER, LET'S CONTINUE THE INVESTIGATION.
UIHARU, TRY TO LINE UP ANY SUSPICIOUS PERSONS FROM THE BANK.
HUH?
ARE YOU SURE THAT'S A GOOD IDEA?
MAYBE I'VE BEEN IMPLANTED WITH SOME SORT OF COMMAND TO STOP YOU.
WE DON'T HAVE TIME TO EXAMINE YOU PROPERLY...
AND WE COULD REALLY USE YOUR TALENTS RIGHT NOW, UIHARU.
IF YOU'RE WORRIED ABOUT THAT, JUST DO YOUR WORK IN FRONT OF US.

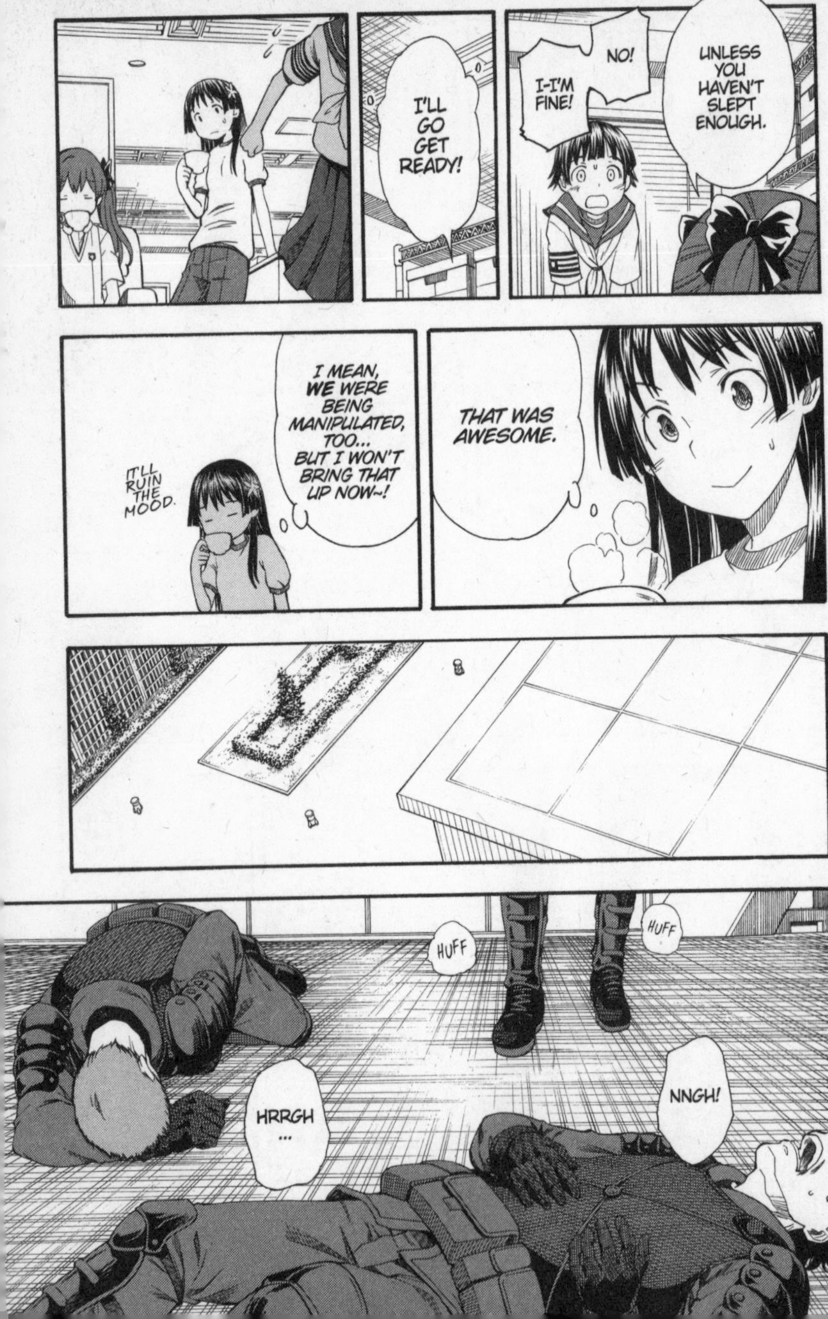
UNLESS YOU HAVEN'T SLEPT ENOUGH.
NO!
I-I'M FINE!
I'LL GO GET READY!
THAT WAS AWESOME.
I MEAN, WE WERE BEING MANIPULATED, TOO... BUT I WON'T BRING THAT UP NOW~!
IT'LL RUIN THE MOOD.
HUFF
HUFF
NNGH!
HRRGH ...

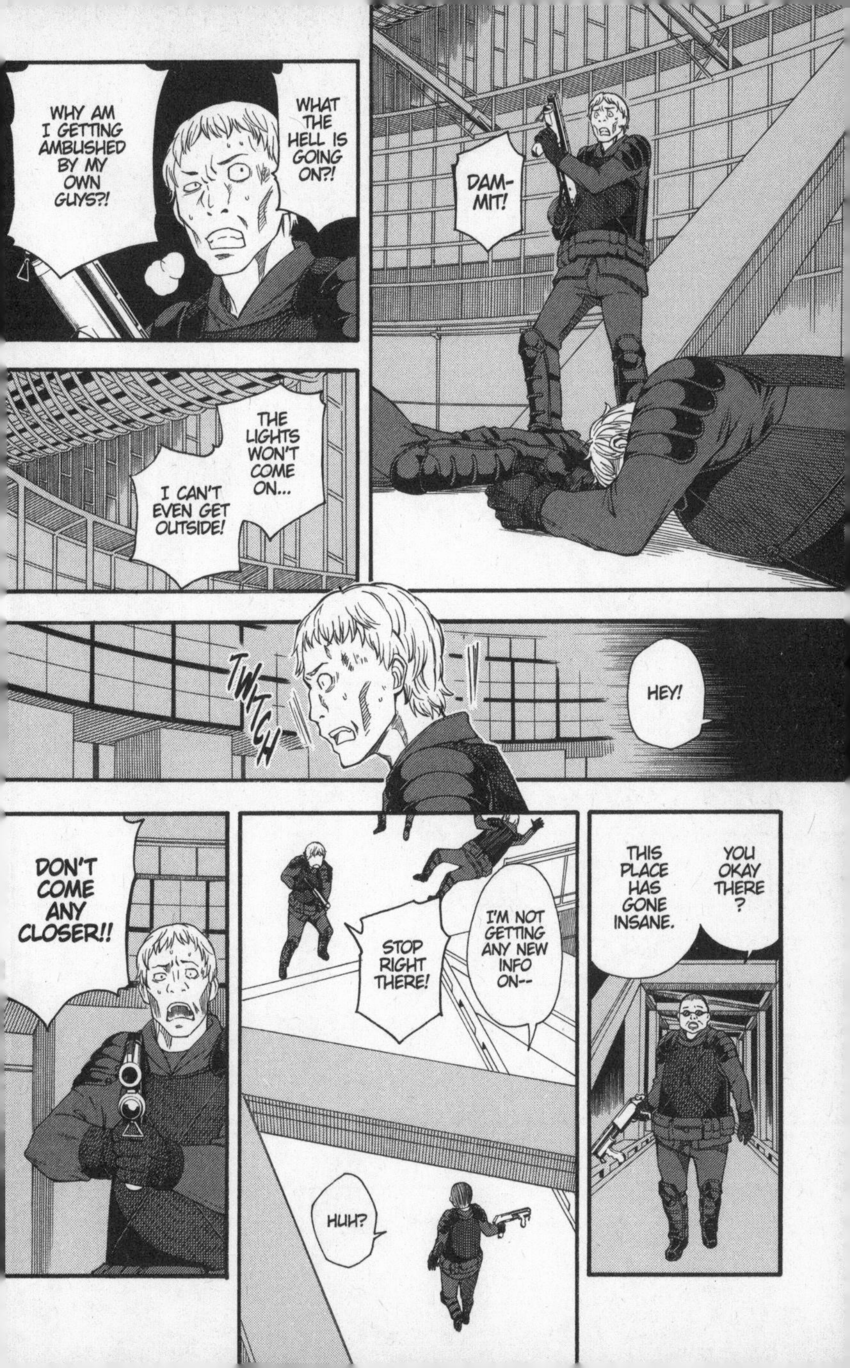
DAM-MIT!
WHAT THE HELL IS GOING ON?!
WHY AM I GETTING AMBUSHED BY MY OWN GUYS?!
THE LIGHTS WON'T COME ON...
I CAN'T EVEN GET OUTSIDE!
HEY!
TWITCH
YOU OKAY THERE?
THIS PLACE HAS GONE INSANE.
I'M NOT GETTING ANY NEW INFO ON--
STOP RIGHT THERE!
HUH?
DON'T COME ANY CLOSER!!

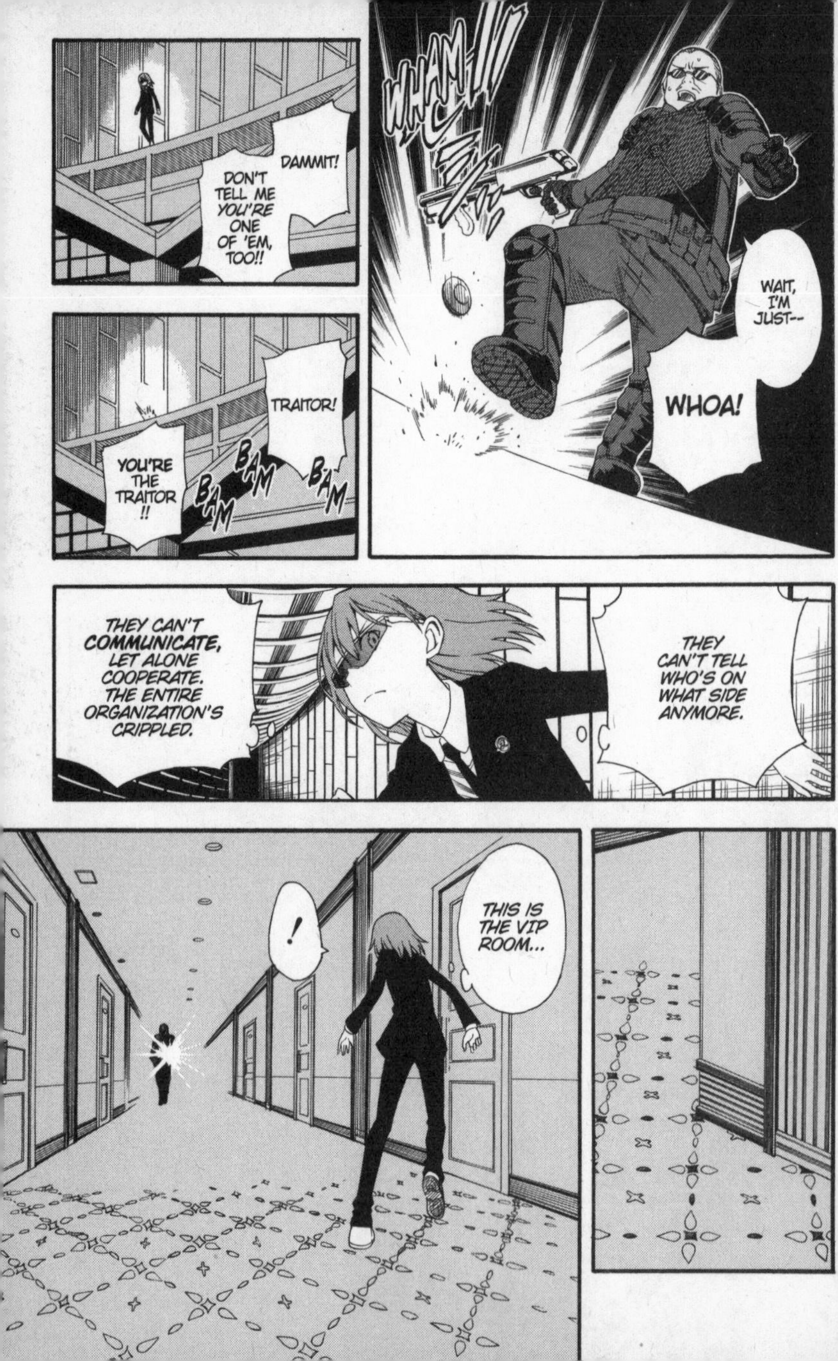
WHAM!!
WAIT, I'M JUST--
WHOA!
DAMMIT!
DON'T TELL ME YOU'RE ONE OF 'EM, TOO!!
TRAITOR!
BAM
BAM
BAM
YOU'RE THE TRAITOR!!
THEY CAN'T TELL WHO'S ON WHAT SIDE ANYMORE.
THEY CAN'T **COMMUNICATE**, LET ALONE COOPERATE. THE ENTIRE ORGANIZATION'S CRIPPLED.
THIS IS THE VIP ROOM...
!

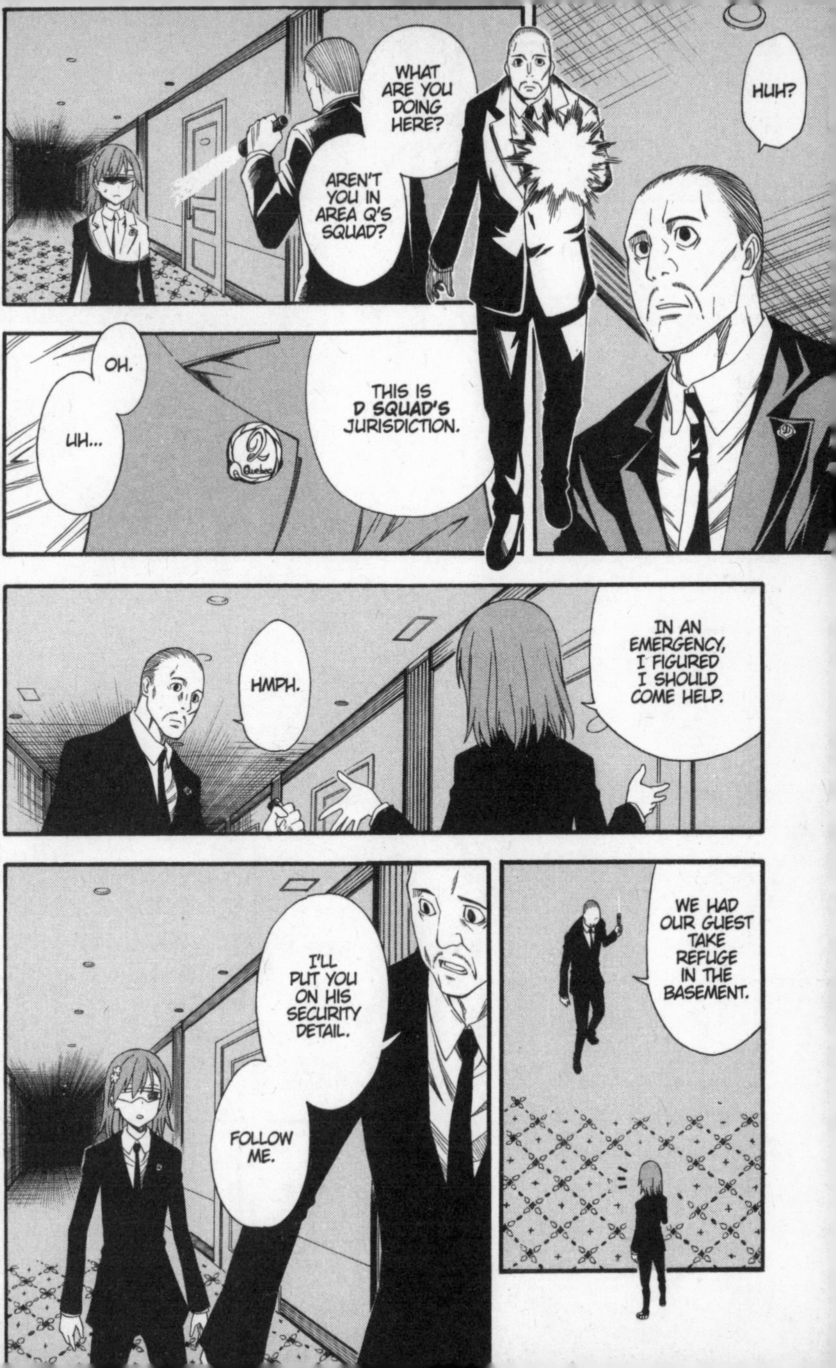
HUH?
WHAT ARE YOU DOING HERE?
AREN'T YOU IN AREA Q'S SQUAD?
THIS IS D SQUAD'S JURISDICTION.
OH.
UH...
Quebec
IN AN EMERGENCY, I FIGURED I SHOULD COME HELP.
HMPH.
WE HAD OUR GUEST TAKE REFUGE IN THE BASEMENT.
I'LL PUT YOU ON HIS SECURITY DETAIL.
FOLLOW ME.

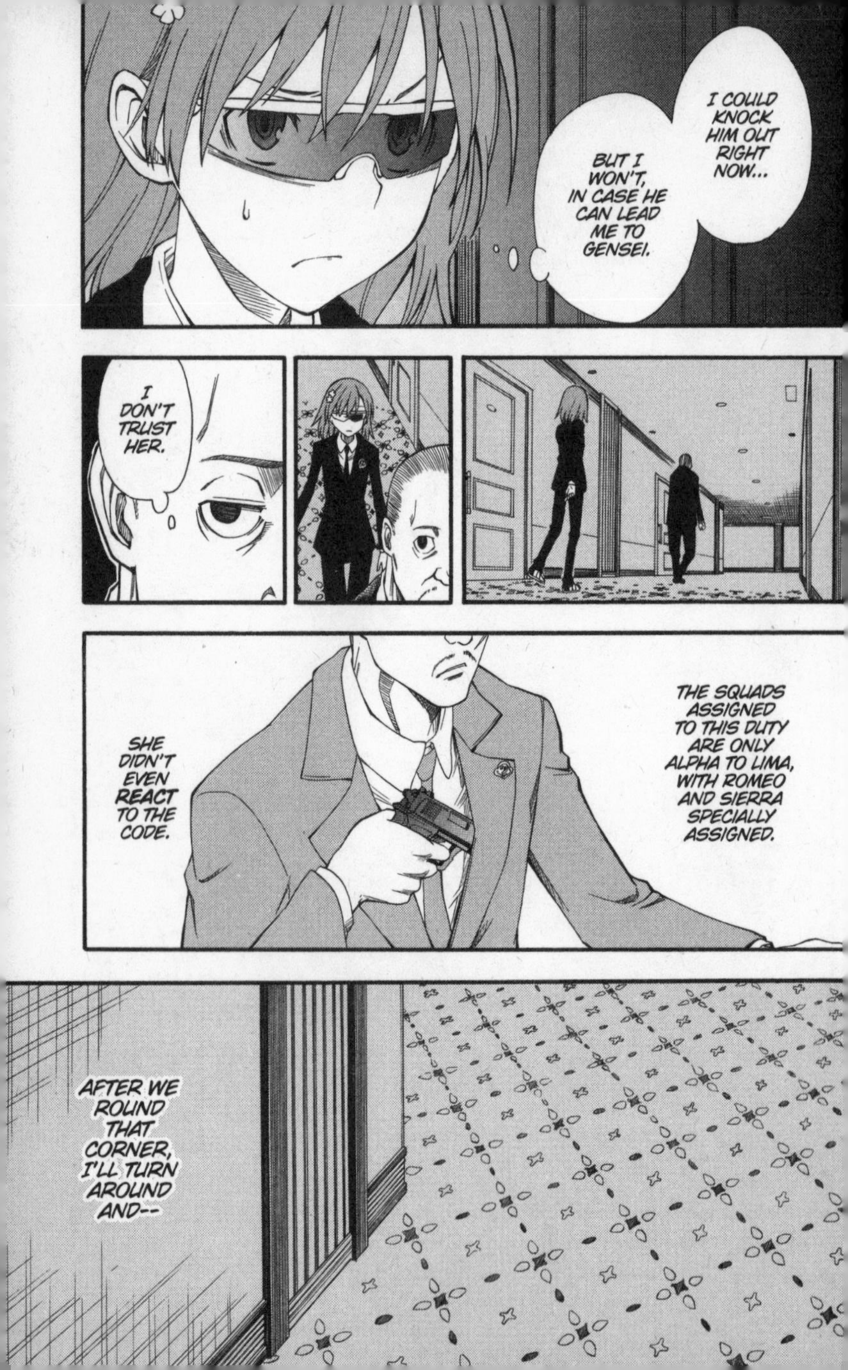
I COULD KNOCK HIM OUT RIGHT NOW...
BUT I WON'T, IN CASE HE CAN LEAD ME TO GENSEI.
I DON'T TRUST HER.
THE SQUADS ASSIGNED TO THIS DUTY ARE ONLY ALPHA TO LIMA, WITH ROMEO AND SIERRA SPECIALLY ASSIGNED.
SHE DIDN'T EVEN REACT TO THE CODE.
AFTER WE ROUND THAT CORNER, I'LL TURN AROUND AND--

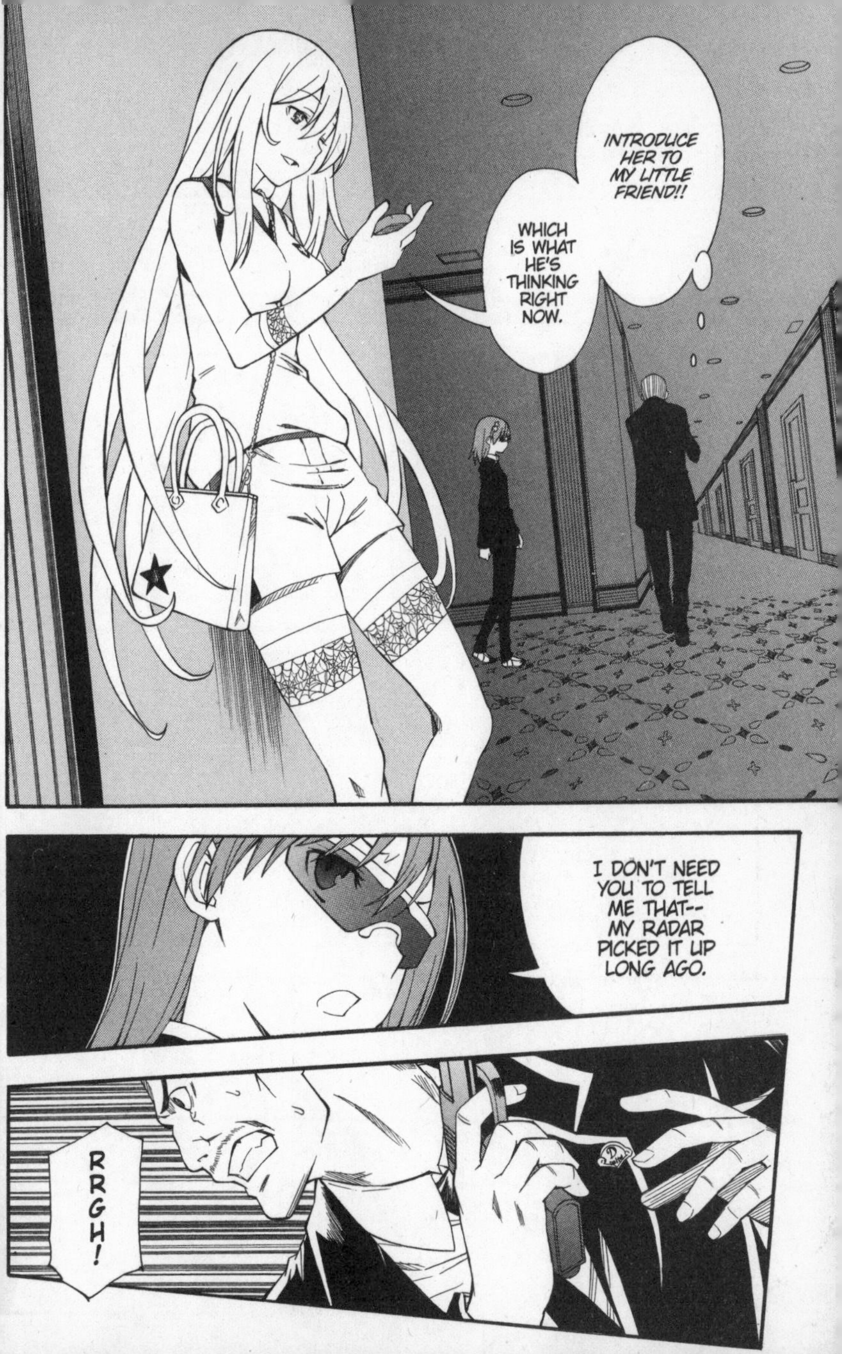
INTRODUCE HER TO MY LITTLE FRIEND!!
WHICH IS WHAT HE'S THINKING RIGHT NOW.
I DON'T NEED YOU TO TELL ME THAT-- MY RADAR PICKED IT UP LONG AGO.
RRGH!

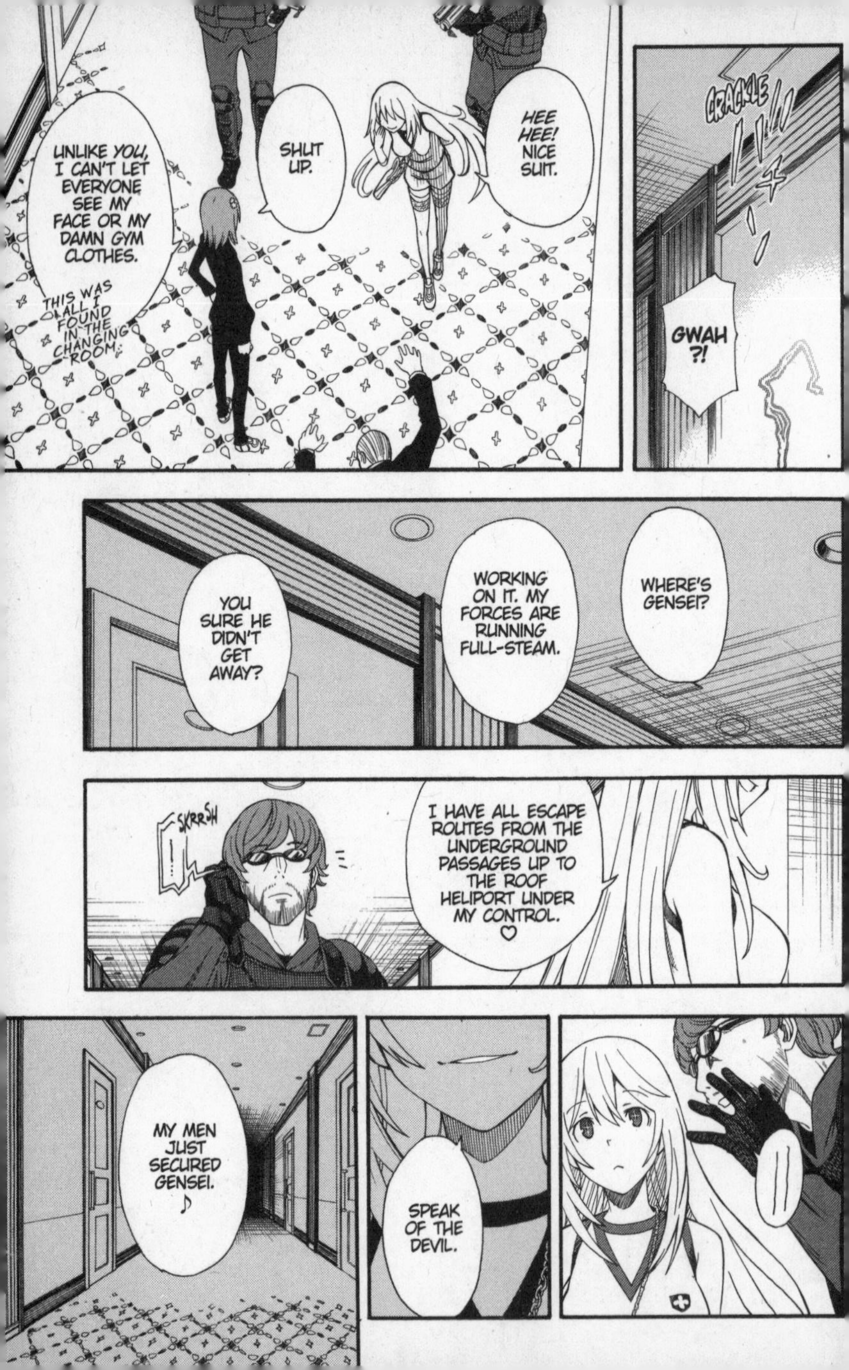
CRACKLE
GWAH?!
HEE HEE! NICE SUIT.
SHUT UP.
UNLIKE YOU, I CAN'T LET EVERYONE SEE MY FACE OR MY DAMN GYM CLOTHES.
THIS WAS ALL I FOUND IN THE CHANGING ROOM...
WHERE'S GENSEI?
WORKING ON IT. MY FORCES ARE RUNNING FULL-STEAM.
YOU SURE HE DIDN'T GET AWAY?
I HAVE ALL ESCAPE ROUTES FROM THE UNDERGROUND PASSAGES UP TO THE ROOF HELIPORT UNDER MY CONTROL. ♡
SKRRSH
SPEAK OF THE DEVIL.
MY MEN JUST SECURED GENSEI. ♪

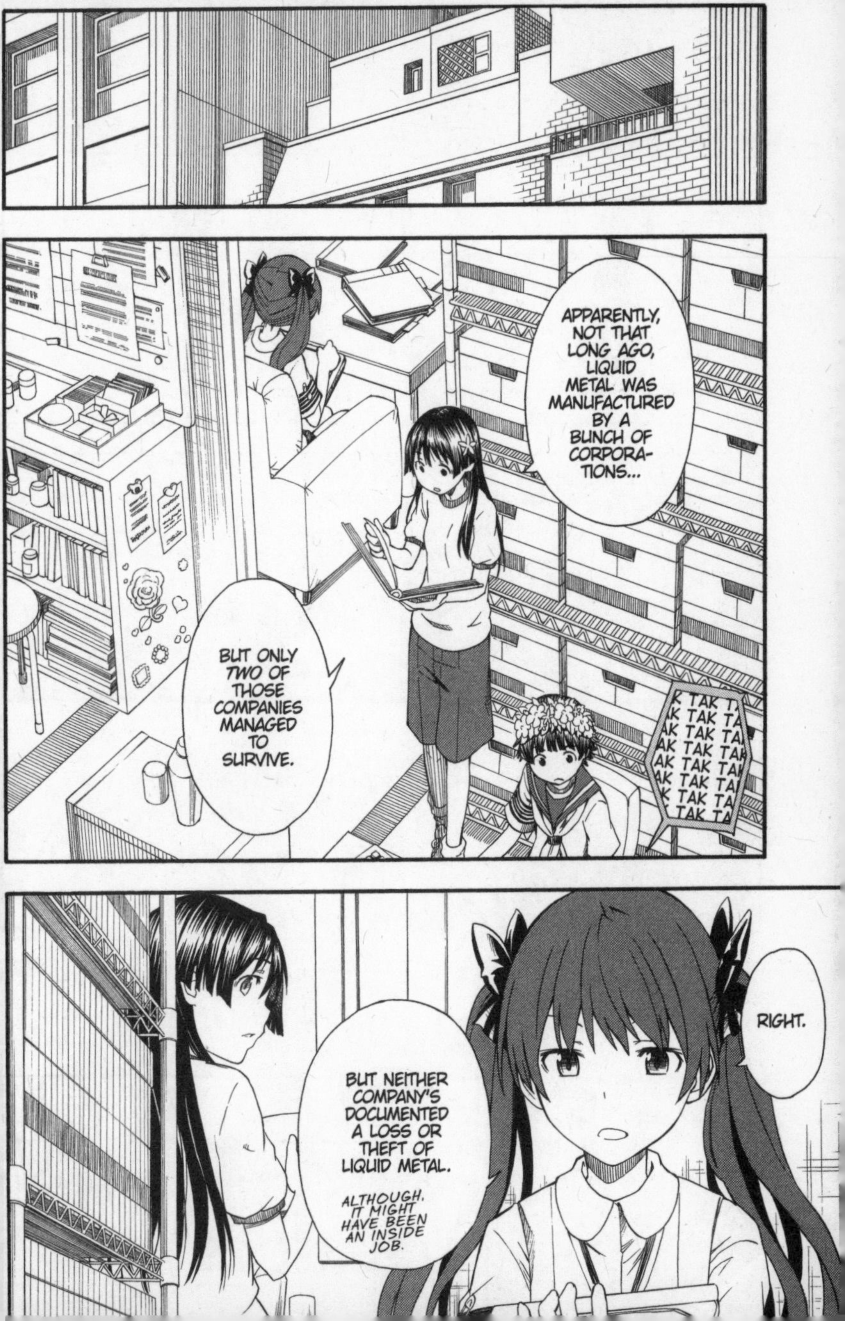
APPARENTLY, NOT THAT LONG AGO, LIQUID METAL WAS MANUFACTURED BY A BUNCH OF CORPORATIONS...
TAK TAK TAK TAK TAK TAK TAK TAK
BUT ONLY *TWO* OF THOSE COMPANIES MANAGED TO SURVIVE.
RIGHT.
BUT NEITHER COMPANY'S DOCUMENTED A LOSS OR THEFT OF LIQUID METAL.
ALTHOUGH, IT MIGHT HAVE BEEN AN INSIDE JOB.

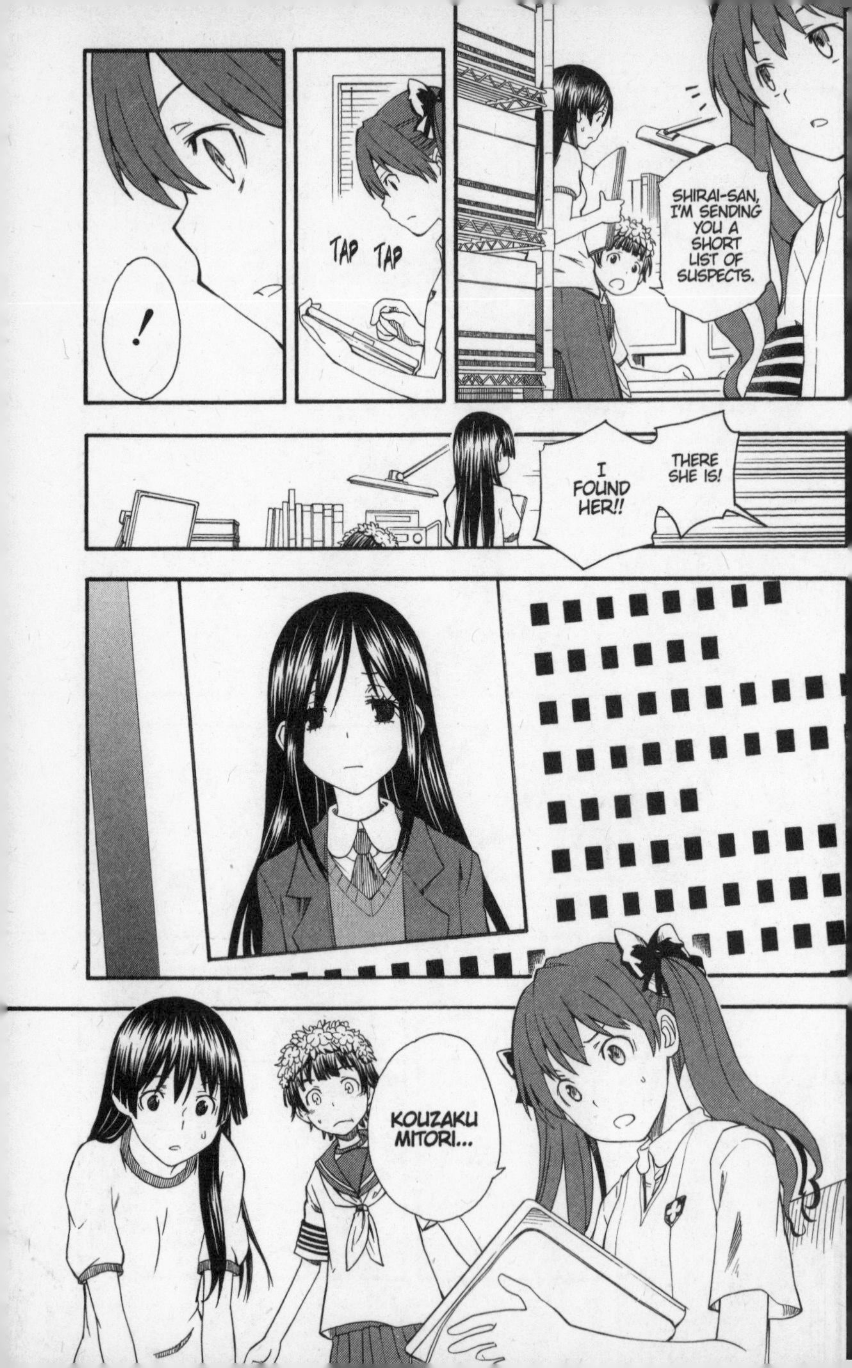
SHIRAI-SAN, I'M SENDING YOU A SHORT LIST OF SUSPECTS.
TAP TAP
!
THERE SHE IS!
I FOUND HER!!
KOUZAKU MITORI...

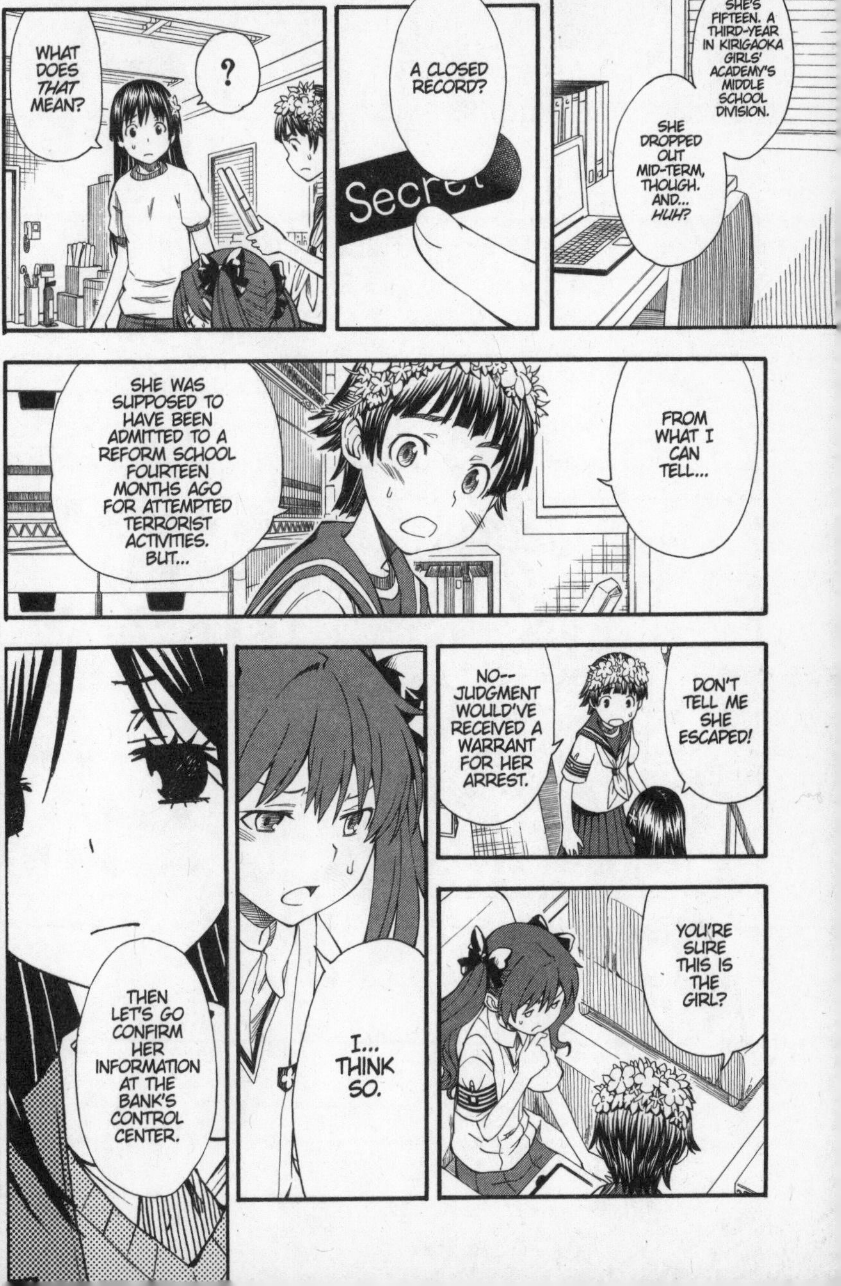
SHE'S FIFTEEN. A THIRD-YEAR IN KIRIGAOKA GIRLS' ACADEMY'S MIDDLE SCHOOL DIVISION.
SHE DROPPED OUT MID-TERM, THOUGH. AND... *HUH?*
A CLOSED RECORD?
Secret
?
WHAT DOES *THAT* MEAN?
FROM WHAT I CAN TELL...
SHE WAS SUPPOSED TO HAVE BEEN ADMITTED TO A REFORM SCHOOL FOURTEEN MONTHS AGO FOR ATTEMPTED TERRORIST ACTIVITIES. BUT...
DON'T TELL ME SHE ESCAPED!
NO-- JUDGMENT WOULD'VE RECEIVED A WARRANT FOR HER ARREST.
YOU'RE SURE THIS IS THE GIRL?
I... THINK SO.
THEN LET'S GO CONFIRM HER INFORMATION AT THE BANK'S CONTROL CENTER.

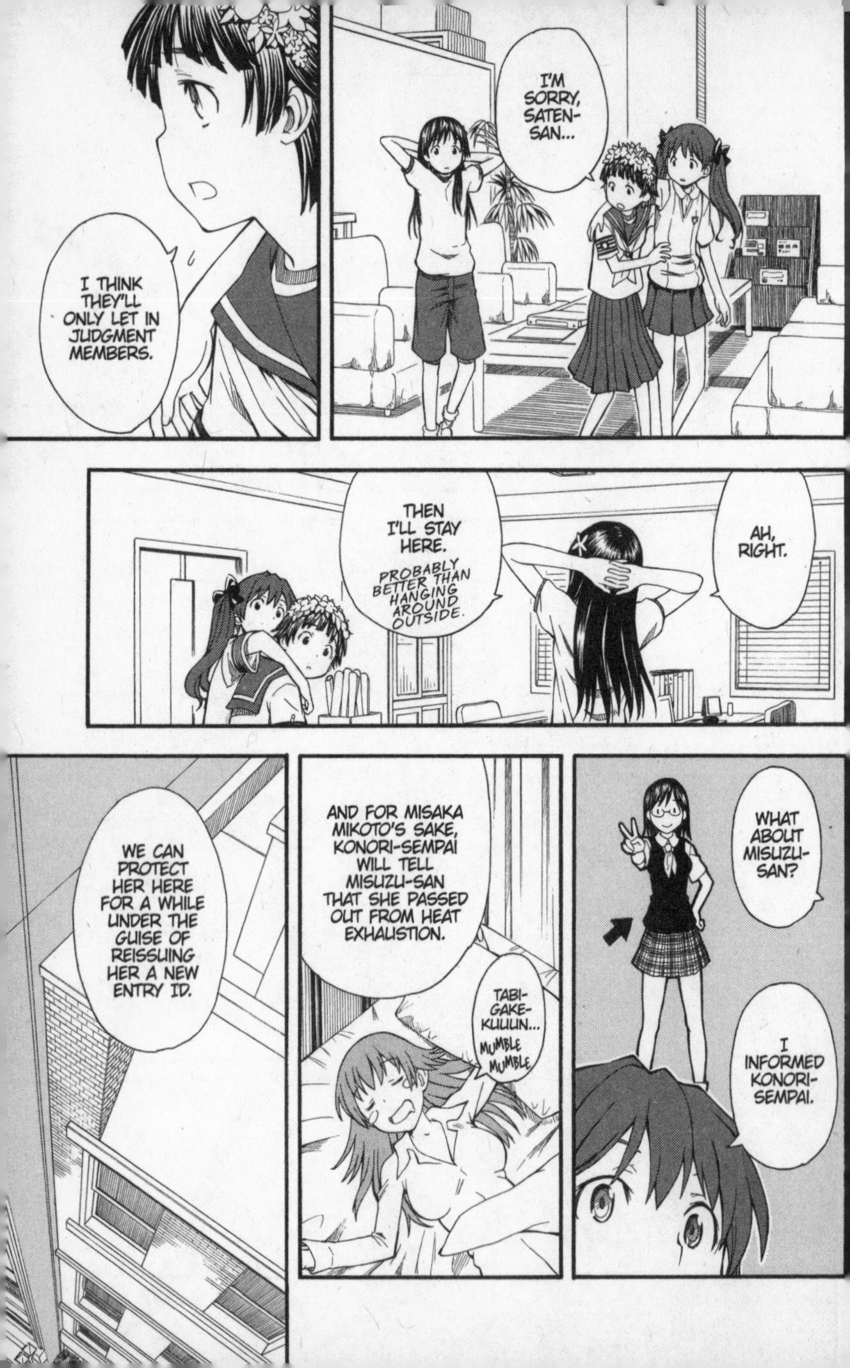
I'M SORRY, SATEN-SAN...
I THINK THEY'LL ONLY LET IN JUDGMENT MEMBERS.
AH, RIGHT.
THEN I'LL STAY HERE.
PROBABLY BETTER THAN HANGING AROUND OUTSIDE.
WHAT ABOUT MISUZU-SAN?
I INFORMED KONORI-SEMPAI.
AND FOR MISAKA MIKOTO'S SAKE, KONORI-SEMPAI WILL TELL MISUZU-SAN THAT SHE PASSED OUT FROM HEAT EXHAUSTION.
TABI-GAKE-KUUUN...
MUMBLE MUMBLE
WE CAN PROTECT HER HERE FOR A WHILE UNDER THE GUISE OF REISSUING HER A NEW ENTRY ID.

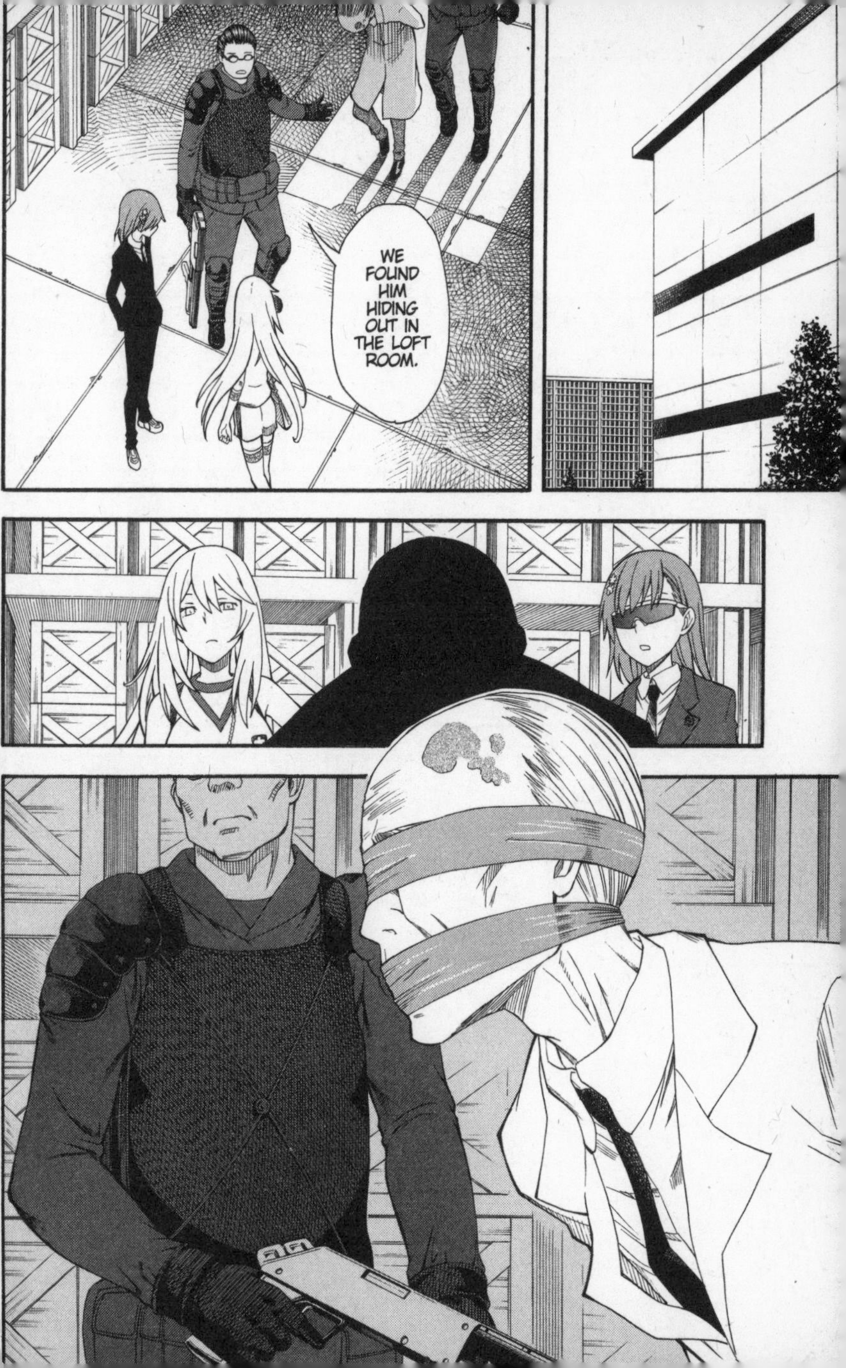
WE FOUND HIM HIDING OUT IN THE LOFT ROOM.

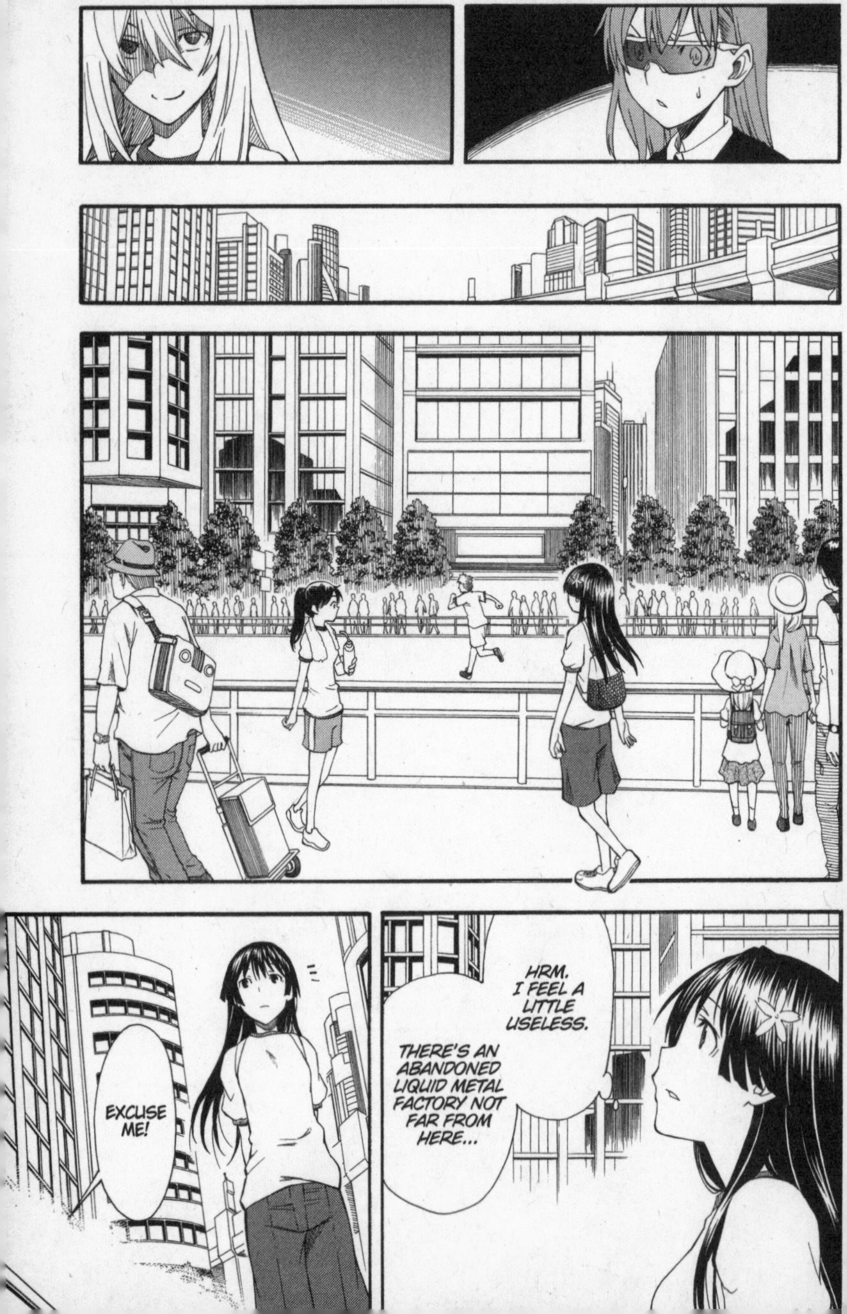
HRM. I FEEL A LITTLE USELESS.
THERE'S AN ABANDONED LIQUID METAL FACTORY NOT FAR FROM HERE...
EXCUSE ME!

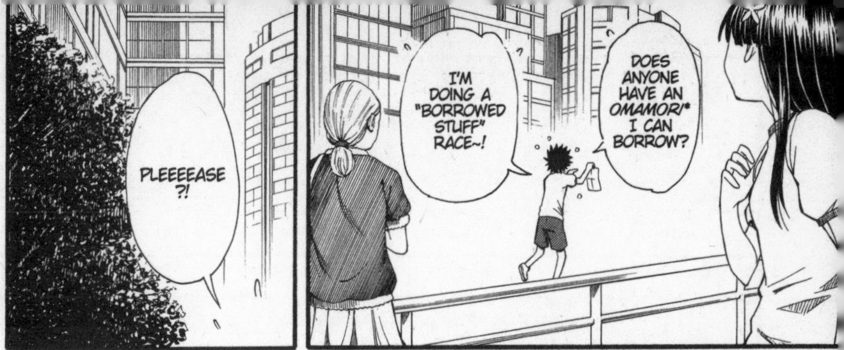
DOES ANYONE HAVE AN *OMAMORI** I CAN BORROW?
I'M DOING A "BORROWED STUFF" RACE~!
PLEEEEASE ?!

*An amulet or charm commonly sold at Shinto shrines and Buddhist temples.

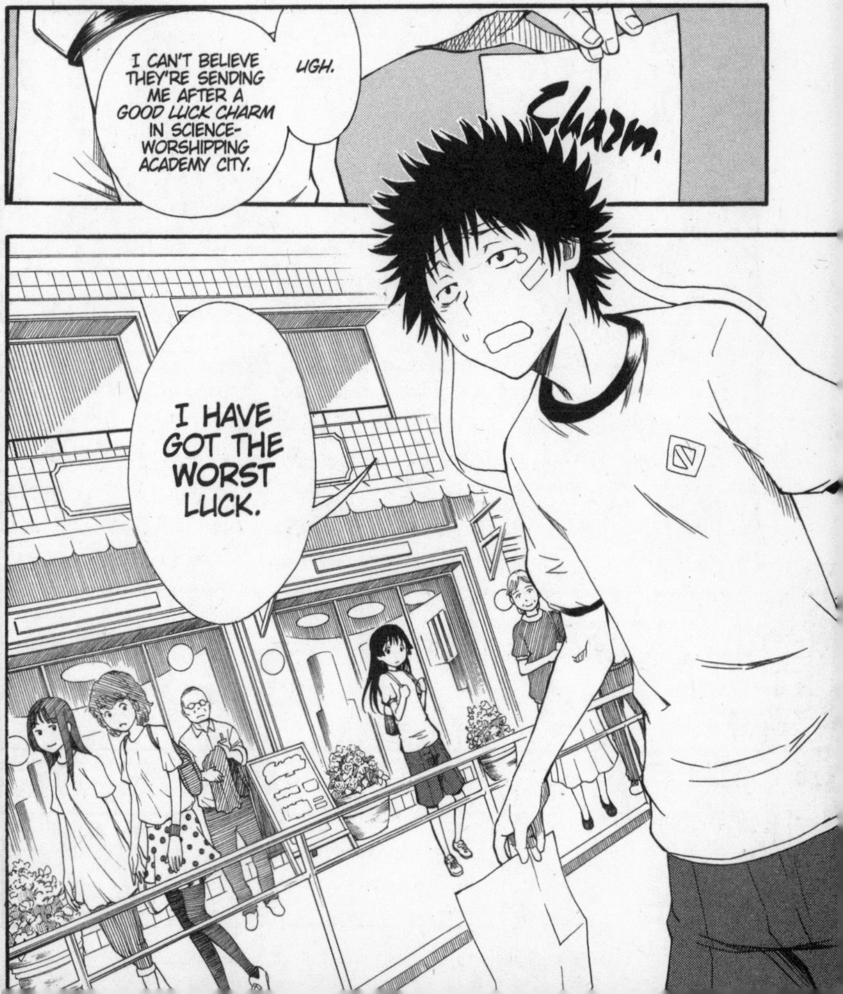
Charm.
UGH.
I CAN'T BELIEVE THEY'RE SENDING ME AFTER A *GOOD LUCK CHARM* IN SCIENCE-WORSHIPPING ACADEMY CITY.
I HAVE GOT THE WORST LUCK.

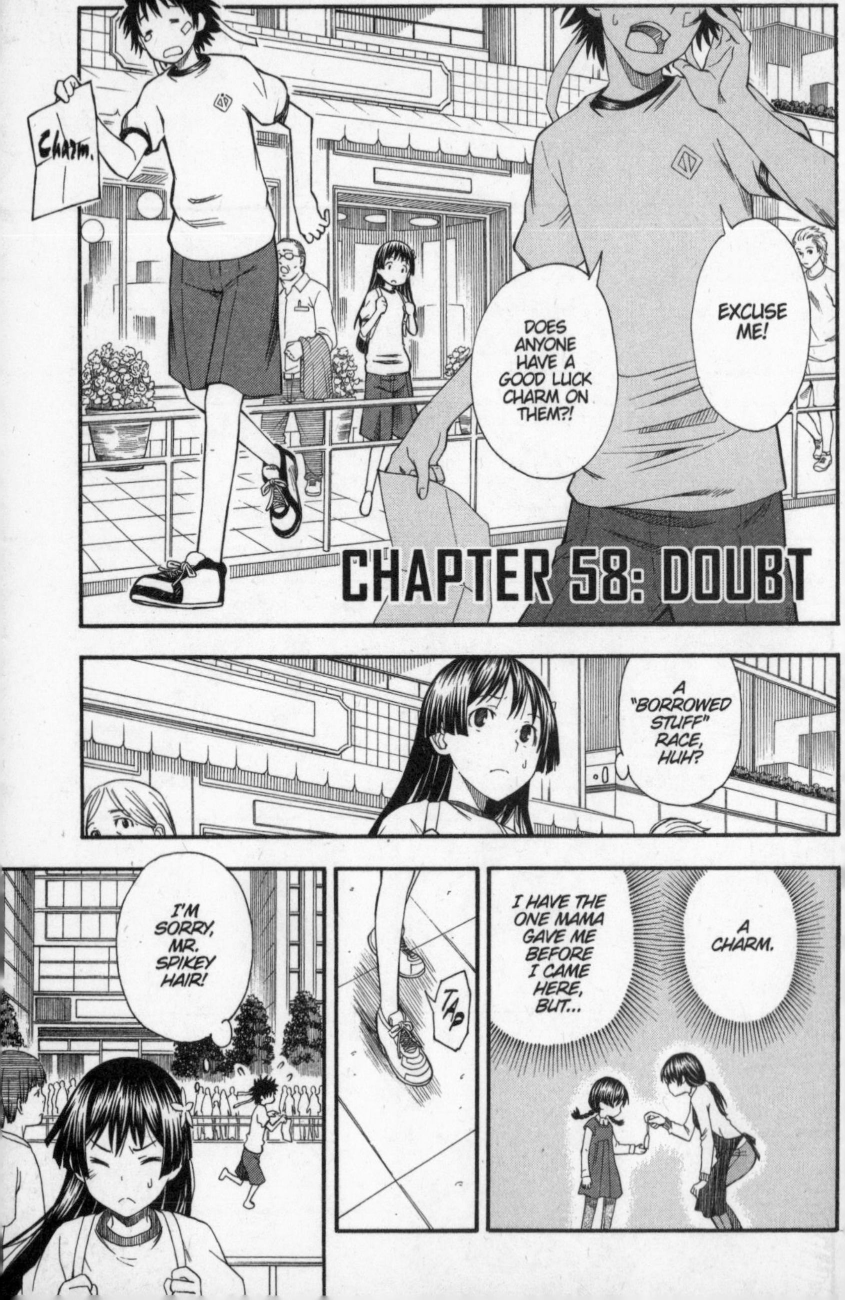
Charm.
EXCUSE ME!
DOES ANYONE HAVE A GOOD LUCK CHARM ON THEM?!
CHAPTER 58: DOUBT
A "BORROWED STUFF" RACE, HUH?
A CHARM.
I HAVE THE ONE MAMA GAVE ME BEFORE I CAME HERE, BUT...
TAP
I'M SORRY, MR. SPIKEY HAIR!

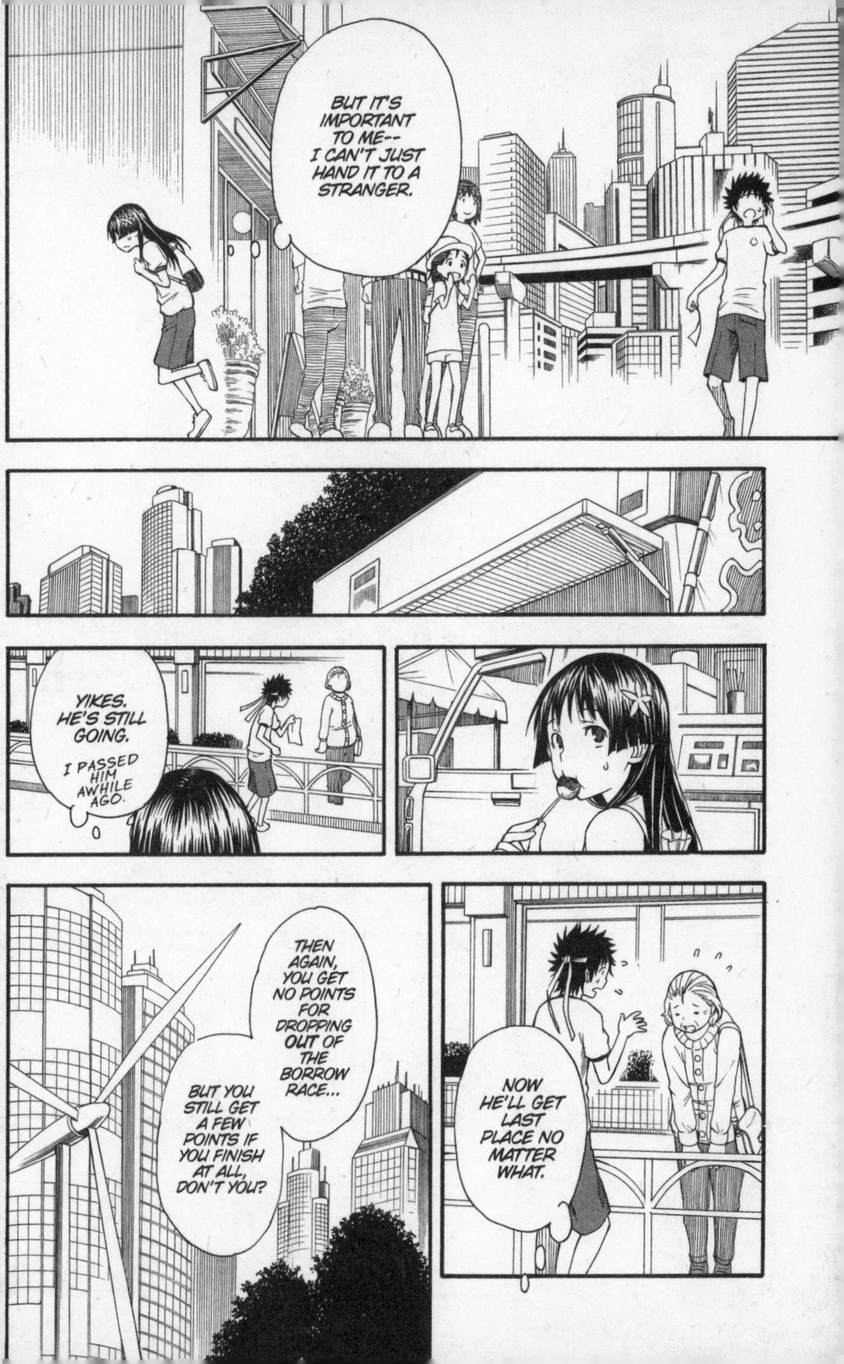
BUT IT'S IMPORTANT TO ME-- I CAN'T JUST HAND IT TO A STRANGER.
YIKES. HE'S STILL GOING.
I PASSED HIM AWHILE AGO.
NOW HE'LL GET LAST PLACE NO MATTER WHAT.
THEN AGAIN, YOU GET NO POINTS FOR DROPPING OUT OF THE BORROW RACE...
BUT YOU STILL GET A FEW POINTS IF YOU FINISH AT ALL, DON'T YOU?

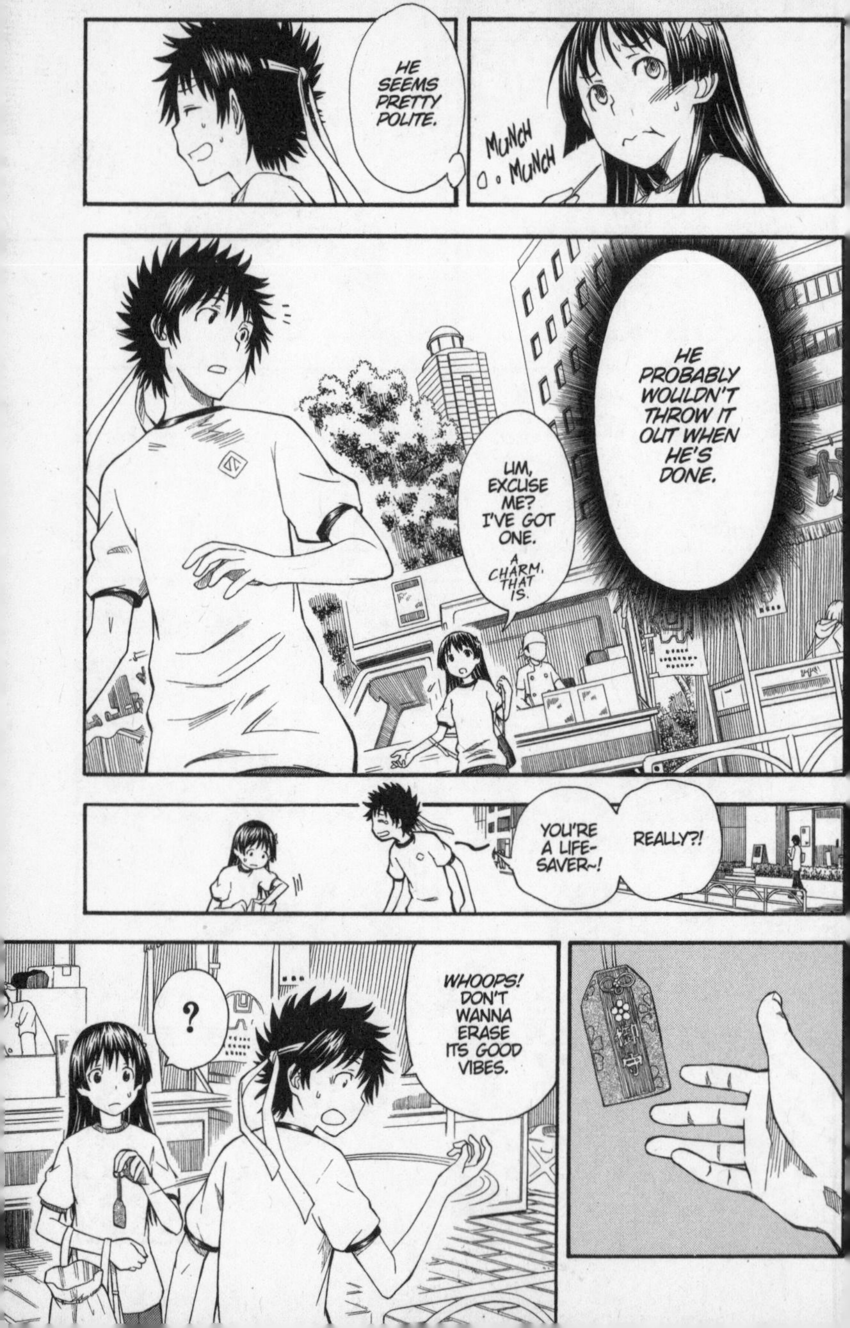
MUNCH MUNCH
HE SEEMS PRETTY POLITE.
HE PROBABLY WOULDN'T THROW IT OUT WHEN HE'S DONE.
UM, EXCUSE ME? I'VE GOT ONE. A CHARM, THAT IS.
REALLY?!
YOU'RE A LIFE-SAVER~!
WHOOPS! DON'T WANNA ERASE ITS GOOD VIBES.
?

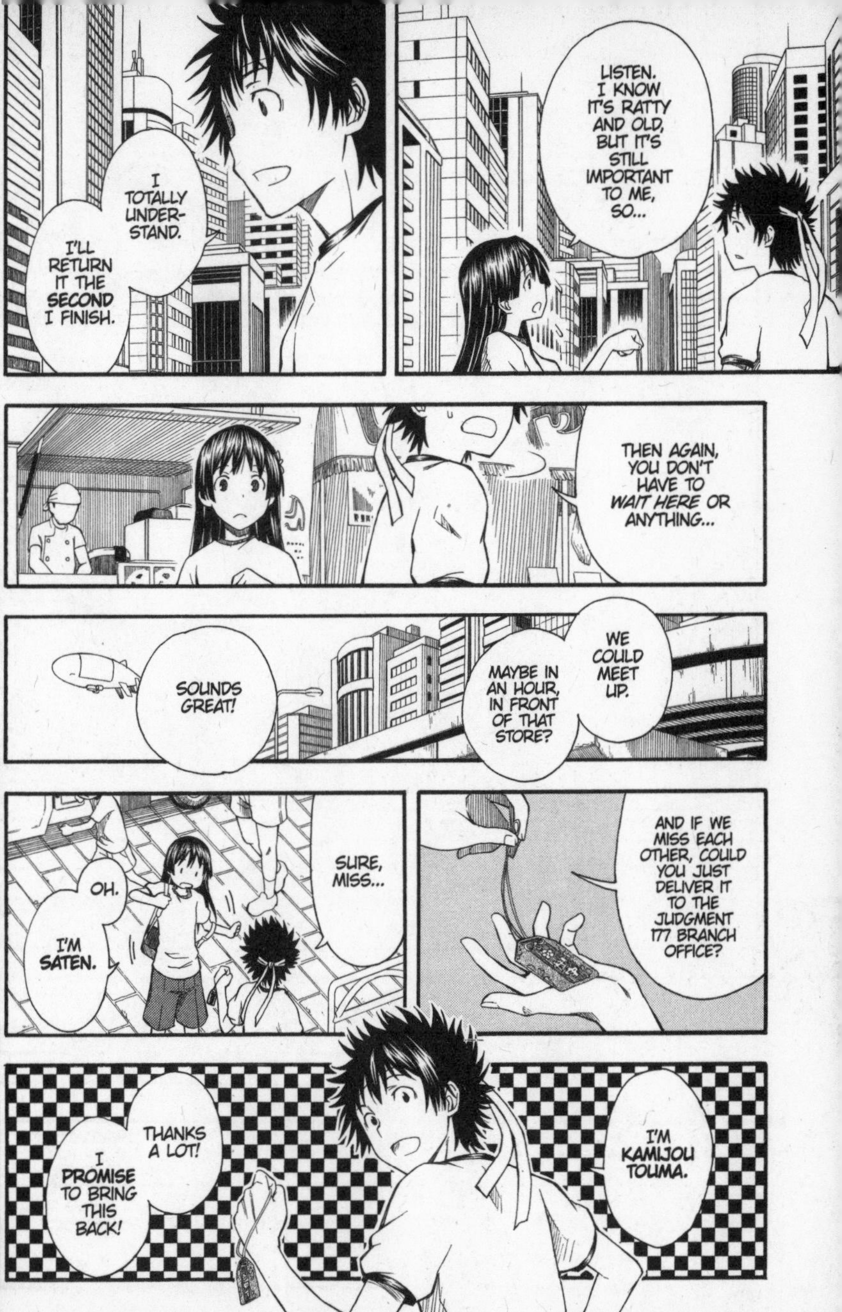
LISTEN. I KNOW IT'S RATTY AND OLD, BUT IT'S STILL IMPORTANT TO ME, SO...
I TOTALLY UNDER-STAND.
I'LL RETURN IT THE SECOND I FINISH.
THEN AGAIN, YOU DON'T HAVE TO *WAIT HERE* OR ANYTHING...
WE COULD MEET UP.
MAYBE IN AN HOUR, IN FRONT OF THAT STORE?
SOUNDS GREAT!
AND IF WE MISS EACH OTHER, COULD YOU JUST DELIVER IT TO THE JUDGMENT 177 BRANCH OFFICE?
SURE, MISS...
OH.
I'M SATEN.
I'M KAMIJOU TOUMA.
THANKS A LOT!
I PROMISE TO BRING THIS BACK!

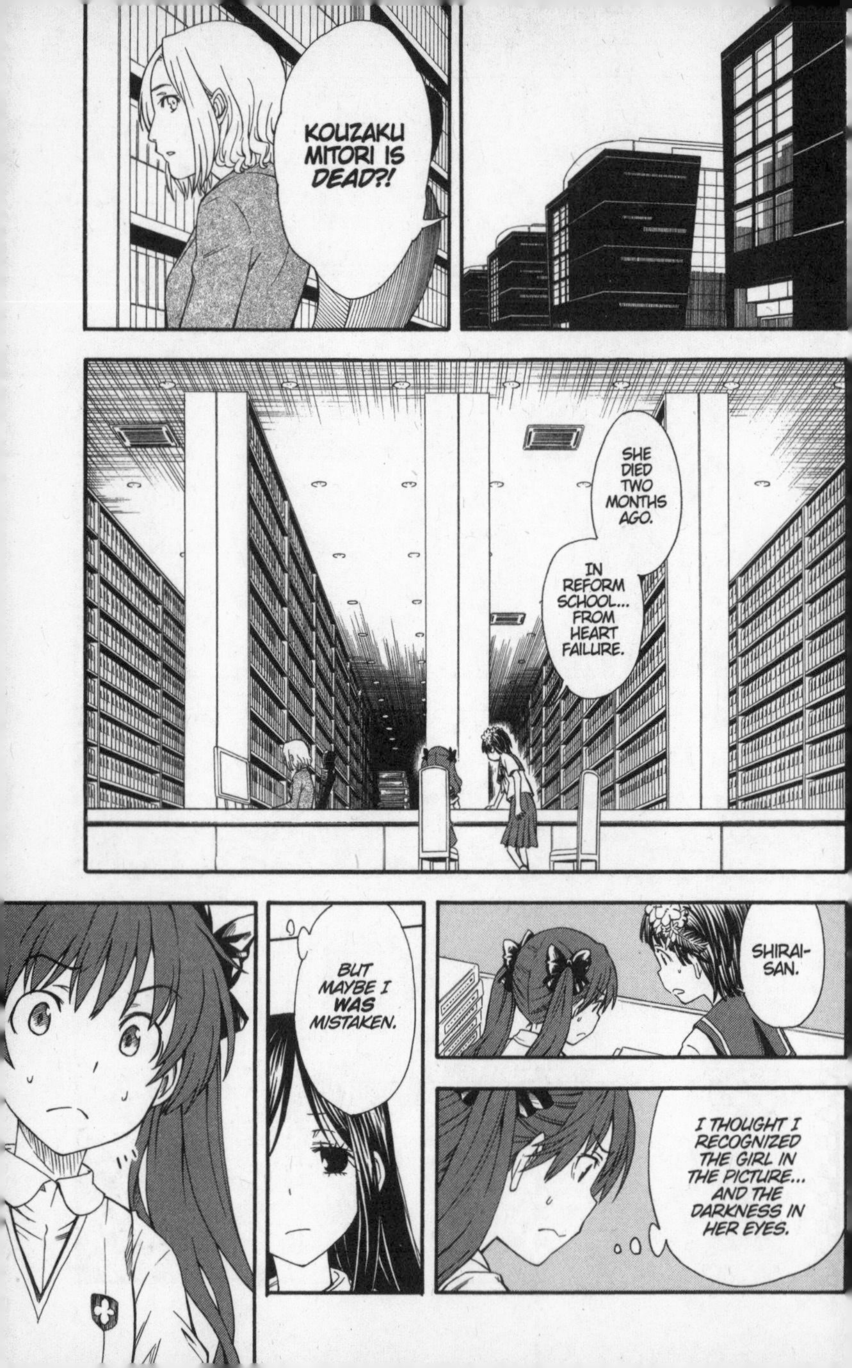
KOUZAKU MITORI IS DEAD?!
SHE DIED TWO MONTHS AGO.
IN REFORM SCHOOL... FROM HEART FAILURE.
BUT MAYBE I WAS MISTAKEN.
SHIRAI-SAN.
I THOUGHT I RECOGNIZED THE GIRL IN THE PICTURE... AND THE DARKNESS IN HER EYES.

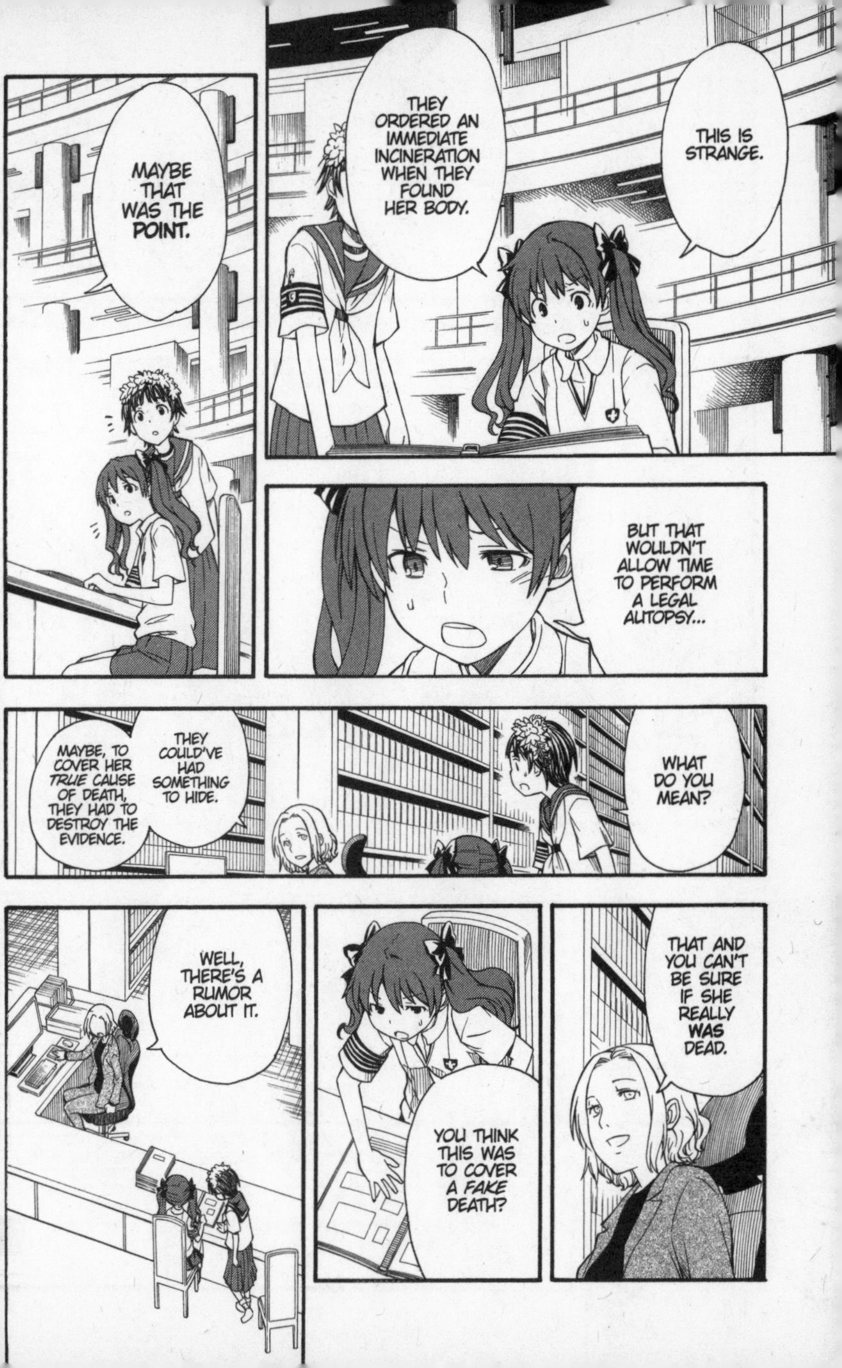
THIS IS STRANGE.
THEY ORDERED AN IMMEDIATE INCINERATION WHEN THEY FOUND HER BODY.
MAYBE THAT WAS THE POINT.
BUT THAT WOULDN'T ALLOW TIME TO PERFORM A LEGAL AUTOPSY...
WHAT DO YOU MEAN?
THEY COULD'VE HAD SOMETHING TO HIDE.
MAYBE, TO COVER HER *TRUE* CAUSE OF DEATH, THEY HAD TO DESTROY THE EVIDENCE.
THAT AND YOU CAN'T BE SURE IF SHE REALLY WAS DEAD.
YOU THINK THIS WAS TO COVER A *FAKE* DEATH?
WELL, THERE'S A RUMOR ABOUT IT.

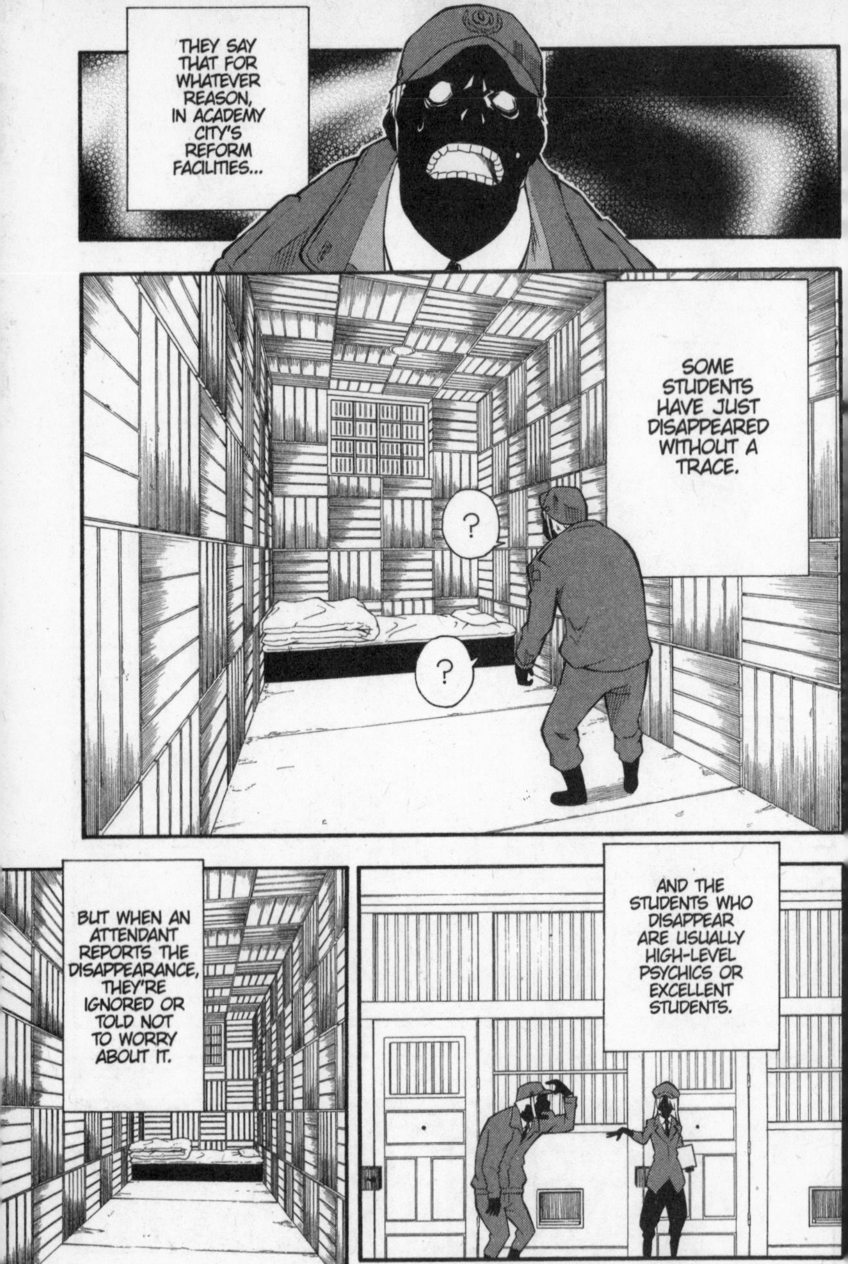
THEY SAY THAT FOR WHATEVER REASON, IN ACADEMY CITY'S REFORM FACILITIES...
SOME STUDENTS HAVE JUST DISAPPEARED WITHOUT A TRACE.
?
?
AND THE STUDENTS WHO DISAPPEAR ARE USUALLY HIGH-LEVEL PSYCHICS OR EXCELLENT STUDENTS.
BUT WHEN AN ATTENDANT REPORTS THE DISAPPEARANCE, THEY'RE IGNORED OR TOLD NOT TO WORRY ABOUT IT.

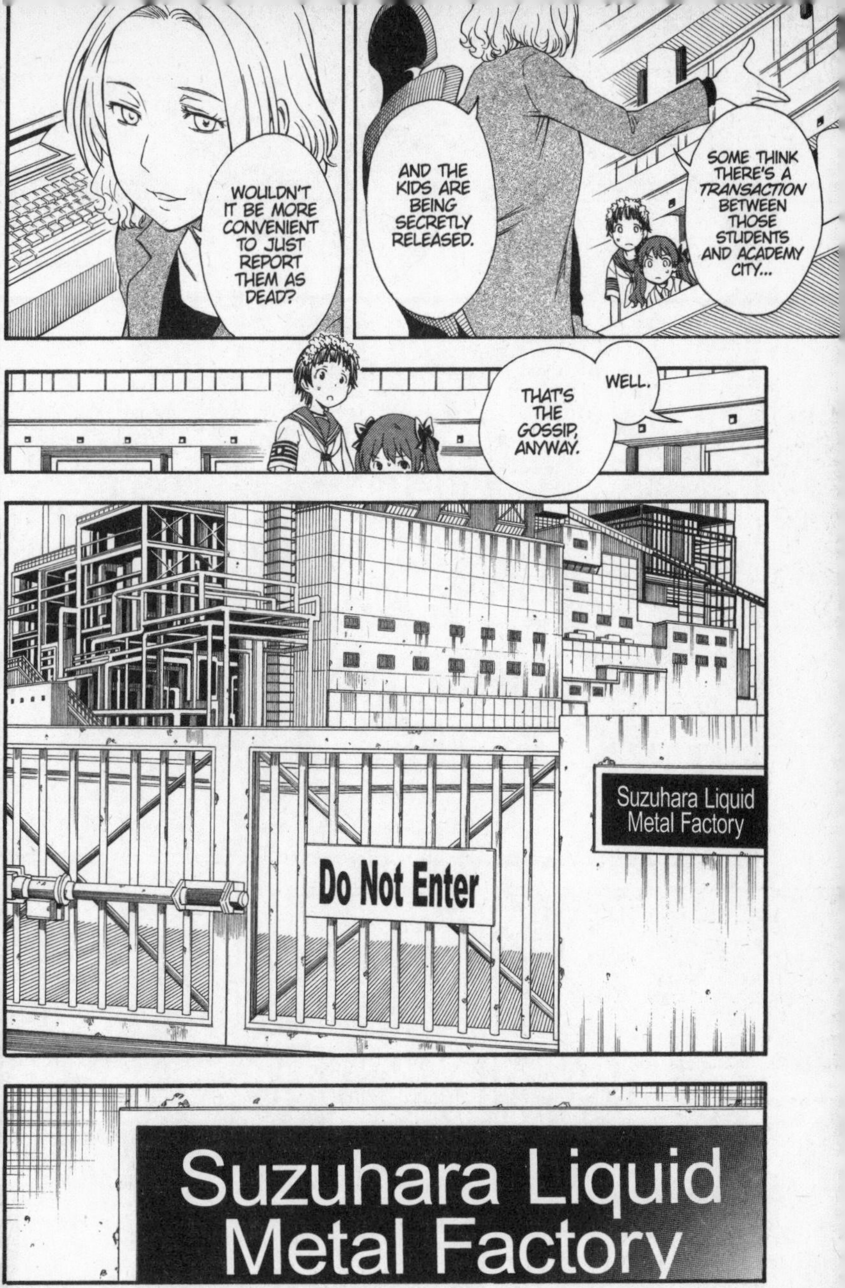
SOME THINK THERE'S A TRANSACTION BETWEEN THOSE STUDENTS AND ACADEMY CITY...
AND THE KIDS ARE BEING SECRETLY RELEASED.
WOULDN'T IT BE MORE CONVENIENT TO JUST REPORT THEM AS DEAD?
WELL.
THAT'S THE GOSSIP, ANYWAY.
Suzuhara Liquid Metal Factory
Do Not Enter
Suzuhara Liquid Metal Factory

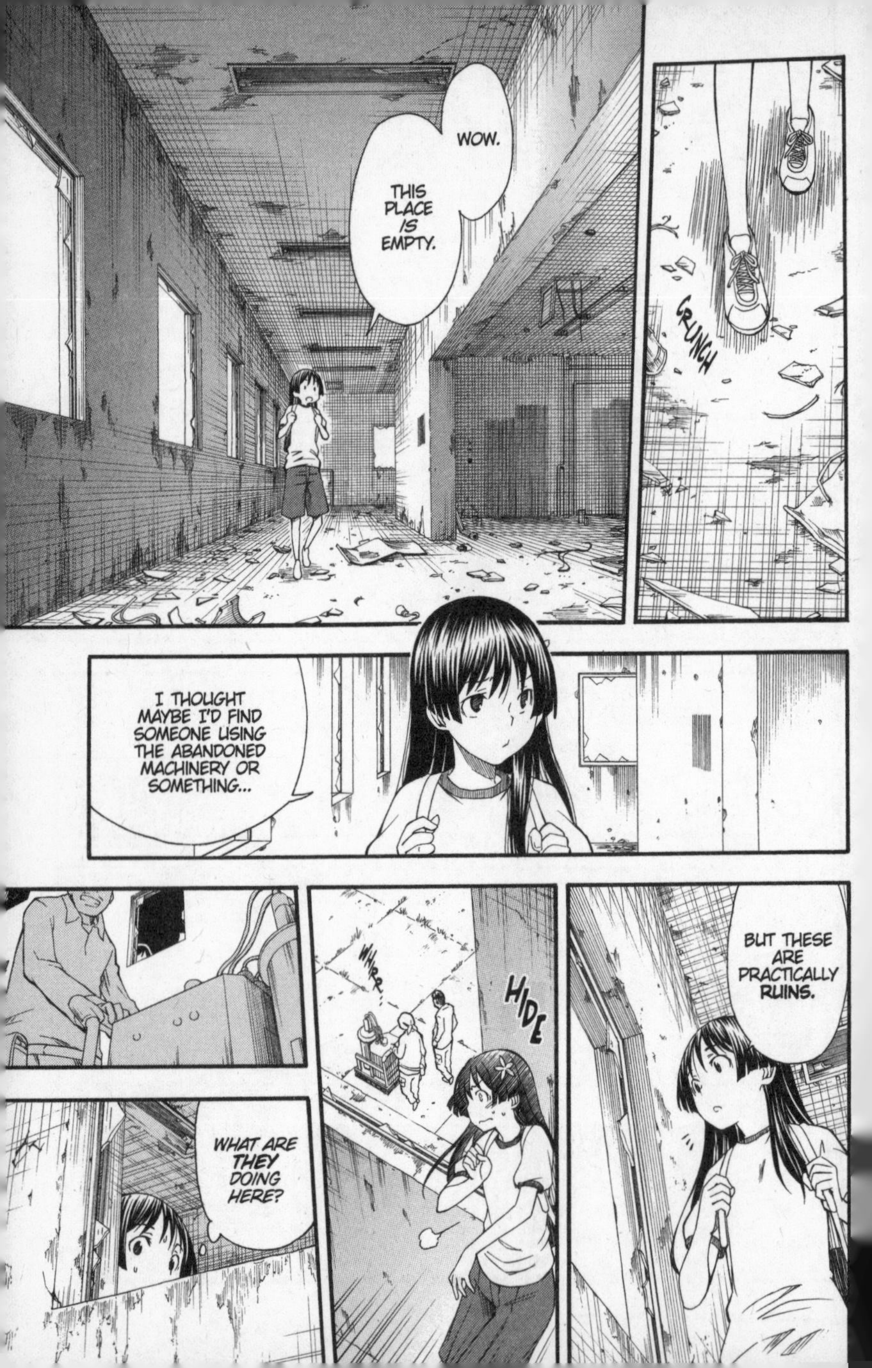
CRUNCH
WOW.
THIS PLACE IS EMPTY.
I THOUGHT MAYBE I'D FIND SOMEONE USING THE ABANDONED MACHINERY OR SOMETHING...
BUT THESE ARE PRACTICALLY RUINS.
HIDE
WHRR
WHAT ARE THEY DOING HERE?

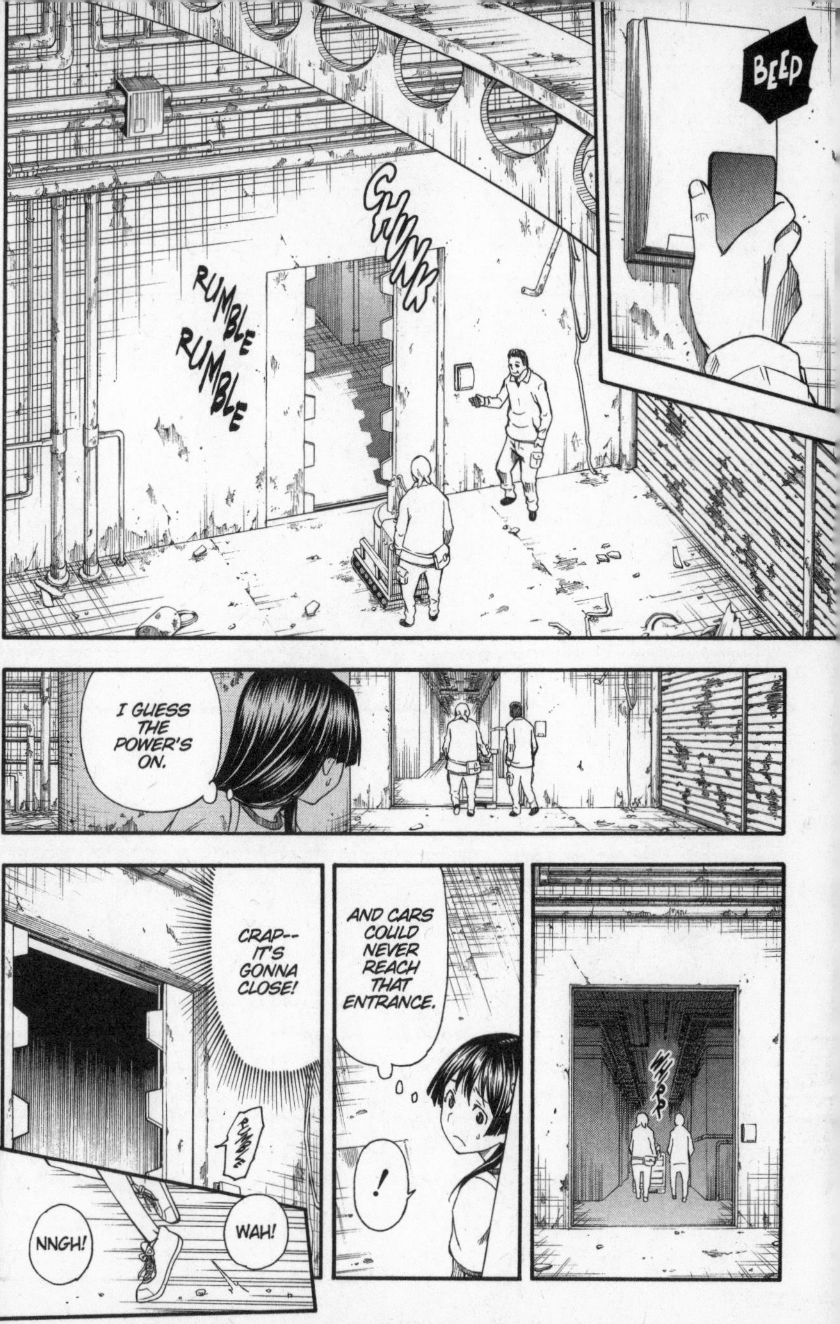

BEEP
CHUNK
RUMBLE RUMBLE
I GUESS THE POWER'S ON.
WHIRR
AND CARS COULD NEVER REACH THAT ENTRANCE.
!
CRAP-- IT'S GONNA CLOSE!
RUMBLE
WAH!
NNGH!

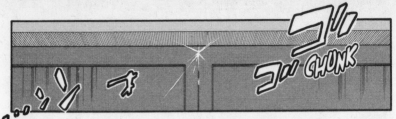
CHUNK

PHEW!

JUST BAAARELY.

WAIT, WHY DID I JUST DO THAT?!

I-IT WON'T OPEN --!

NO, YOU NEED A *SPECIAL CARD* TO OPEN IT?!

!!!

THIS WAS SO STUPID!

I HAVE TO AT LEAST CONTACT UIHARU--

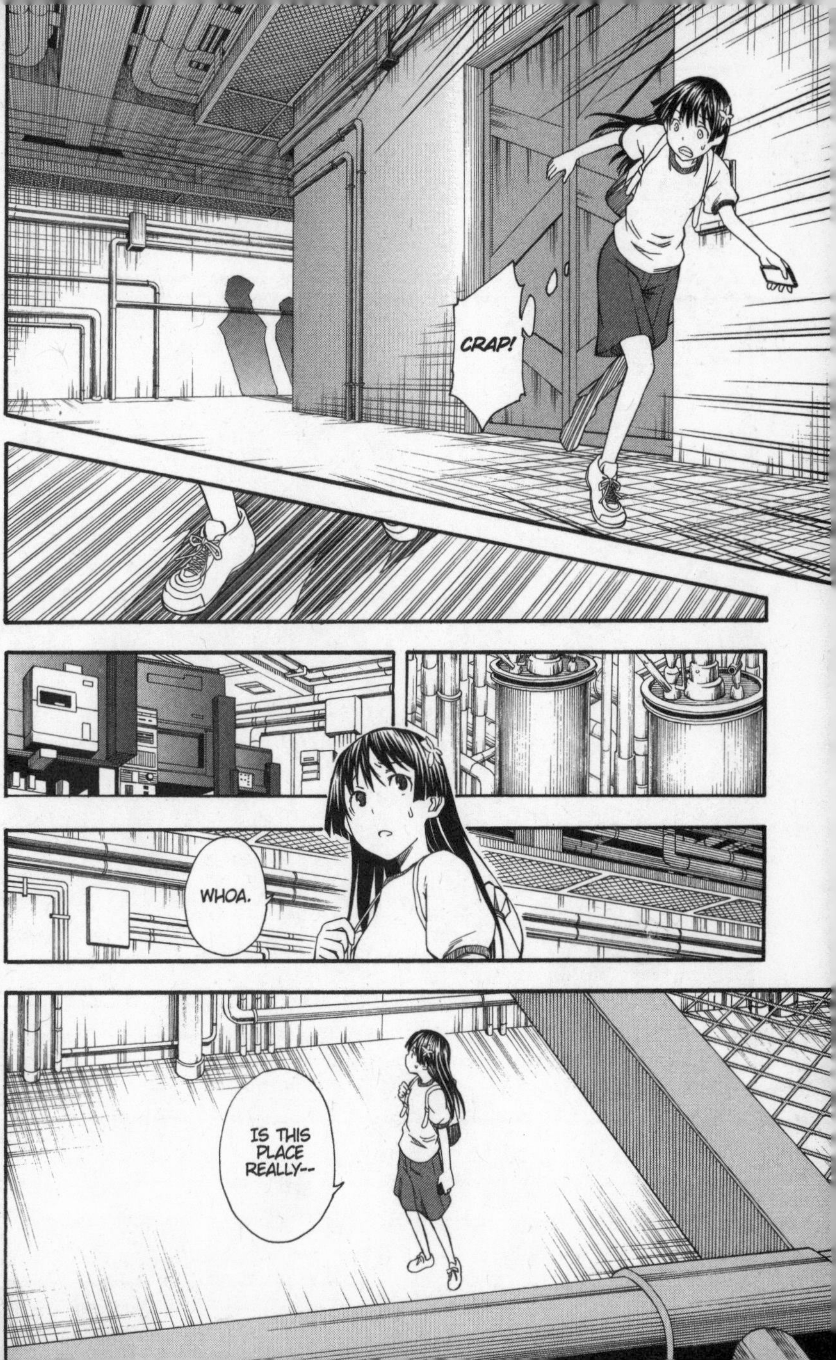
CRAP!
WHOA.
IS THIS PLACE REALLY--

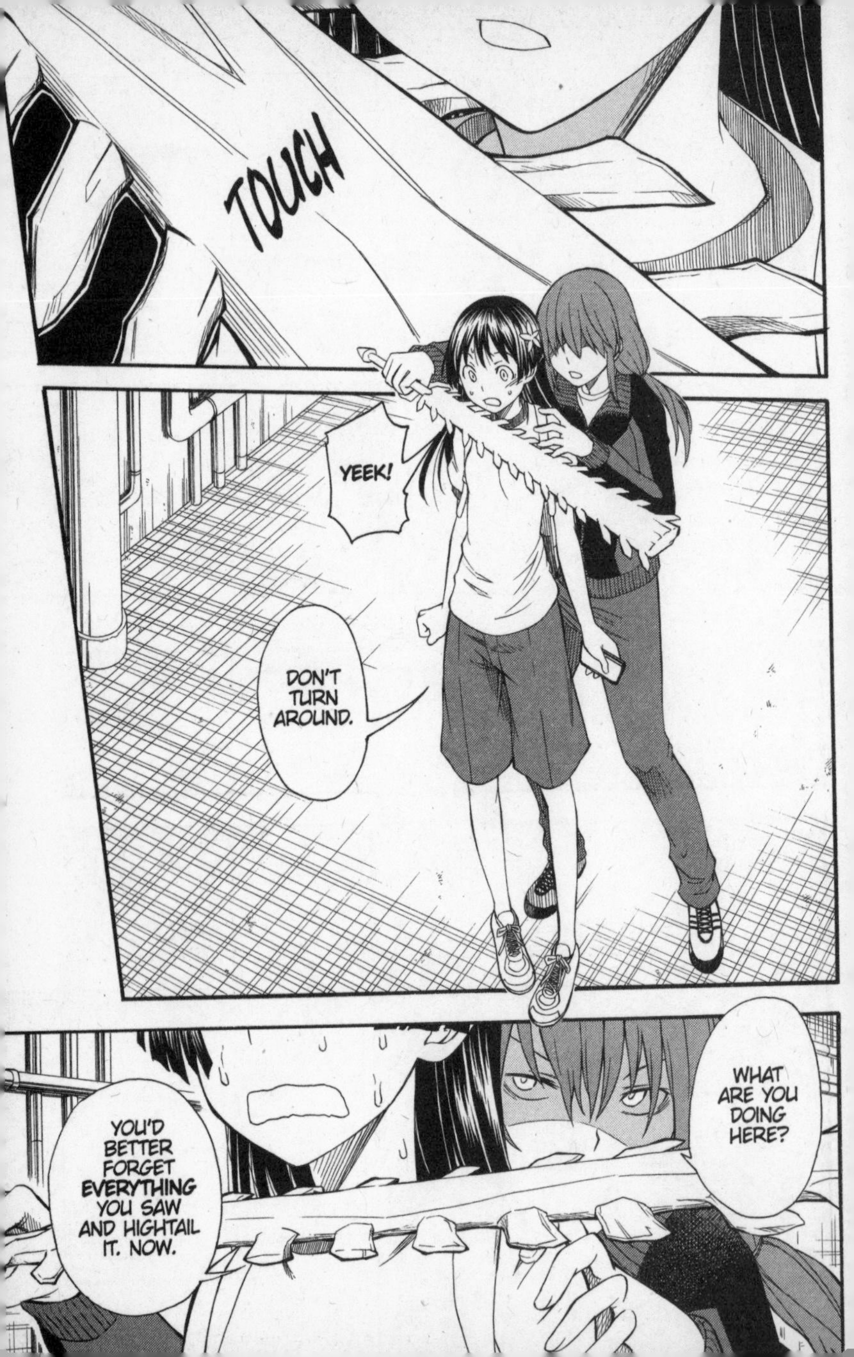
TOUCH
YEEK!
DON'T TURN AROUND.
WHAT ARE YOU DOING HERE?
YOU'D BETTER FORGET EVERYTHING YOU SAW AND HIGHTAIL IT. NOW.

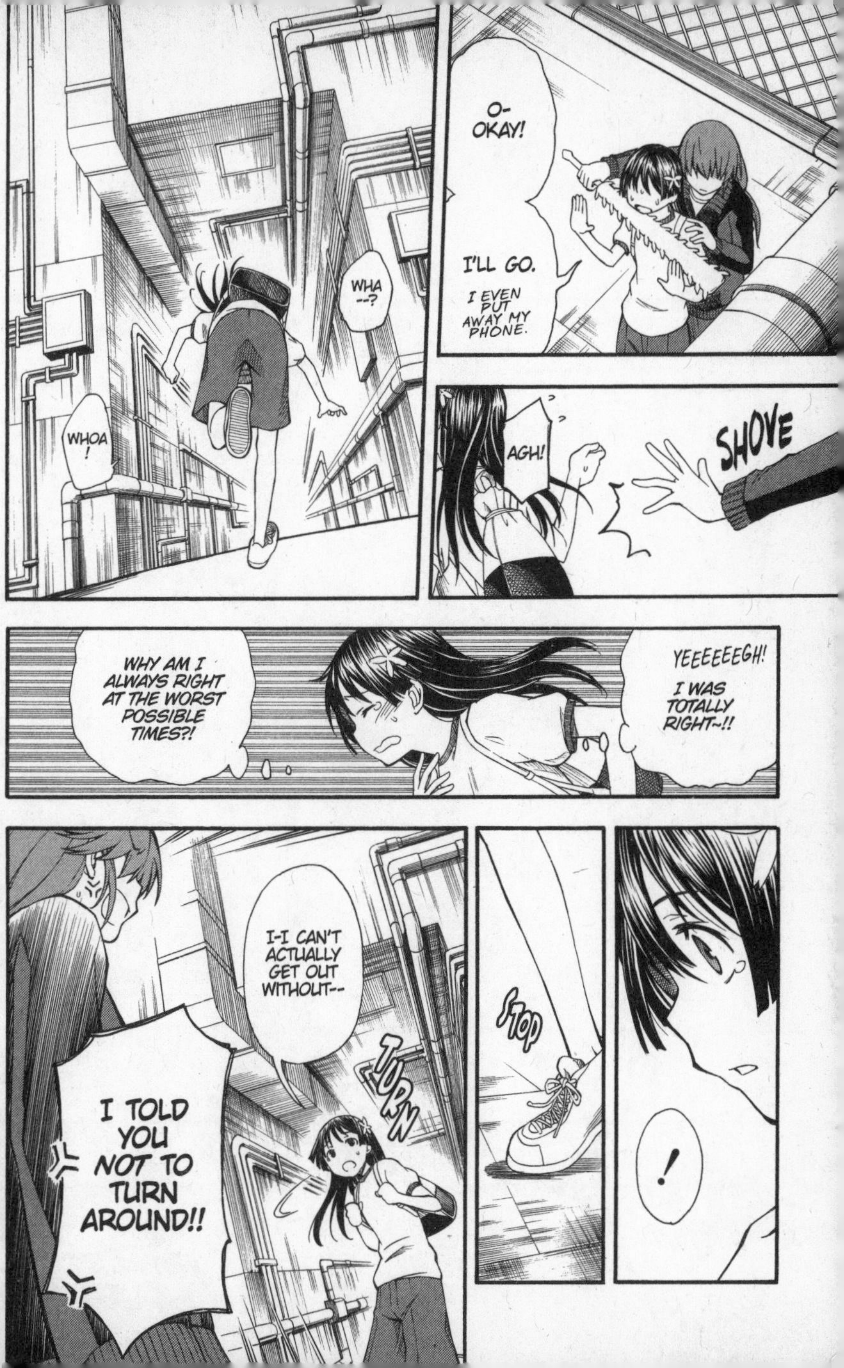
O- OKAY!
I'LL GO.
I EVEN PUT AWAY MY PHONE.
SHOVE
AGH!
WHA --?
WHOA !
YEEEEEEGH!
I WAS TOTALLY RIGHT~!!
WHY AM I ALWAYS RIGHT AT THE WORST POSSIBLE TIMES?!
!
STOP
I-I CAN'T ACTUALLY GET OUT WITHOUT--
TURN
I TOLD YOU NOT TO TURN AROUND!!

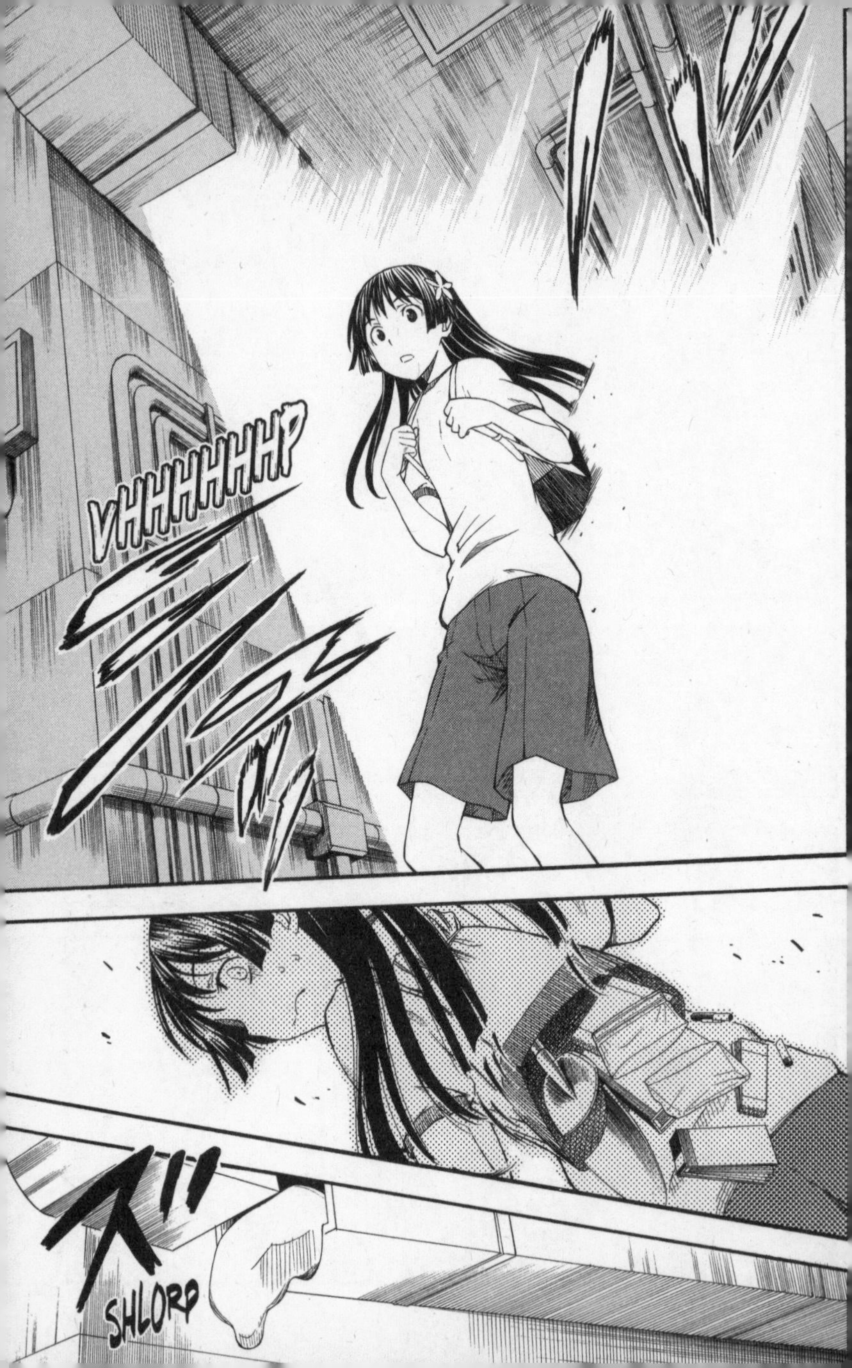
VHHHHHHP
SHLORP

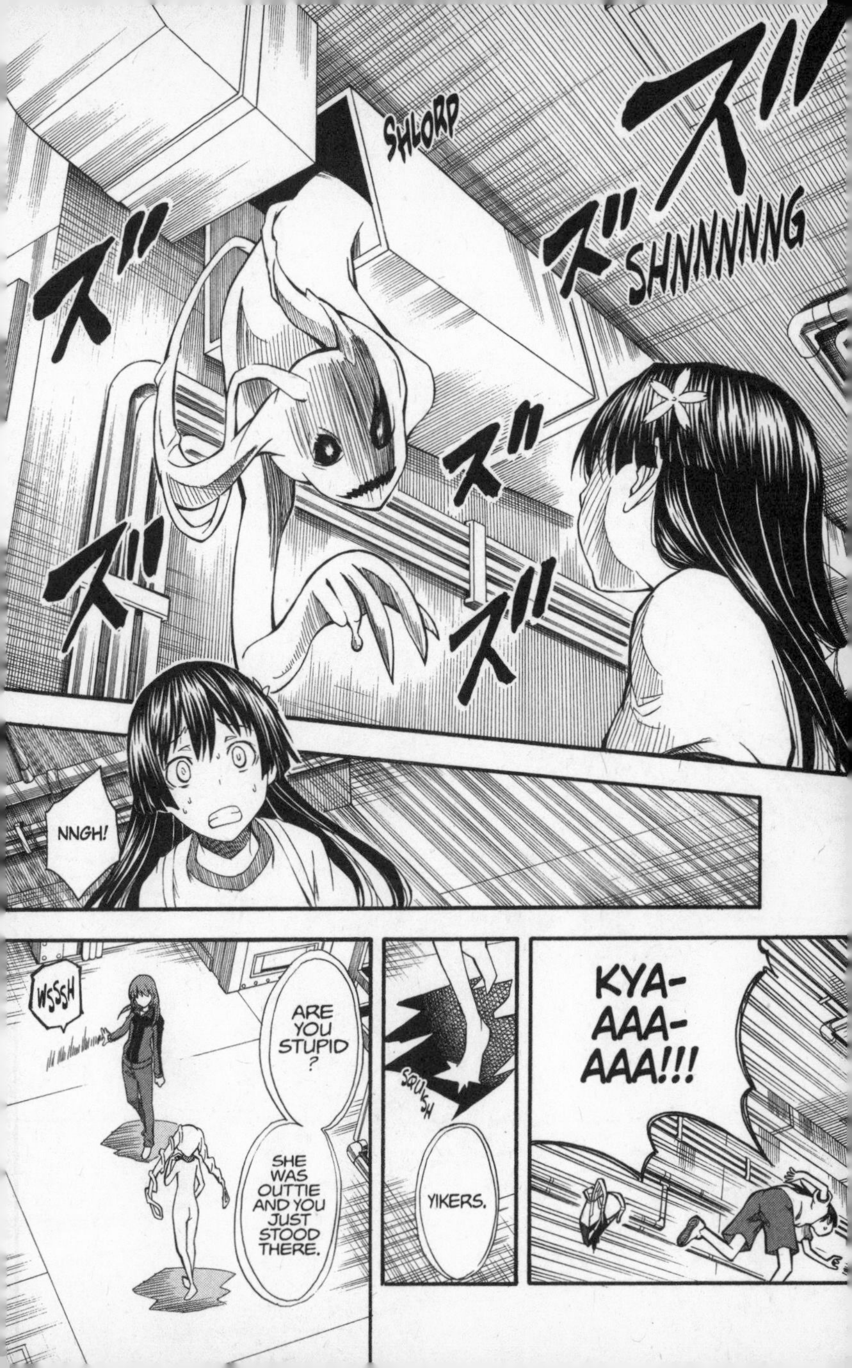
ズ
SHNNNNG
SHLORP
ズ
ズ
ズ
ズ
ズ
NNGH!
KYA-AAA-AAA!!!
SQUISH
YIKERS.
ARE YOU STUPID?
SHE WAS OUTTIE AND YOU JUST STOOD THERE.
WSSSH

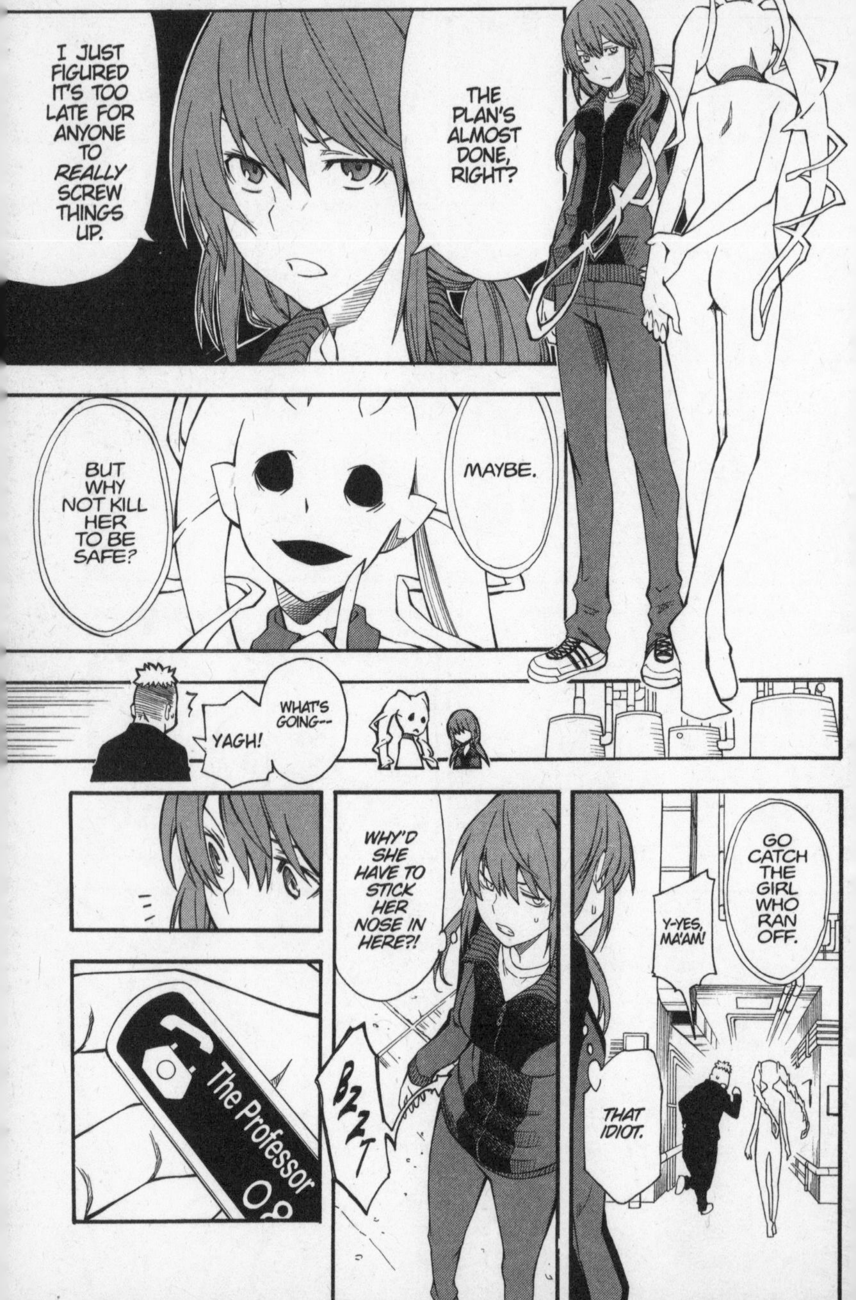
I JUST FIGURED IT'S TOO LATE FOR ANYONE TO *REALLY* SCREW THINGS UP.
THE PLAN'S ALMOST DONE, RIGHT?
MAYBE.
BUT WHY NOT KILL HER TO BE SAFE?
WHAT'S GOING--
YAGH!
GO CATCH THE GIRL WHO RAN OFF.
Y-YES, MA'AM!
THAT IDIOT.
WHY'D SHE HAVE TO STICK HER NOSE IN HERE?!
BZZT
The Professor
08

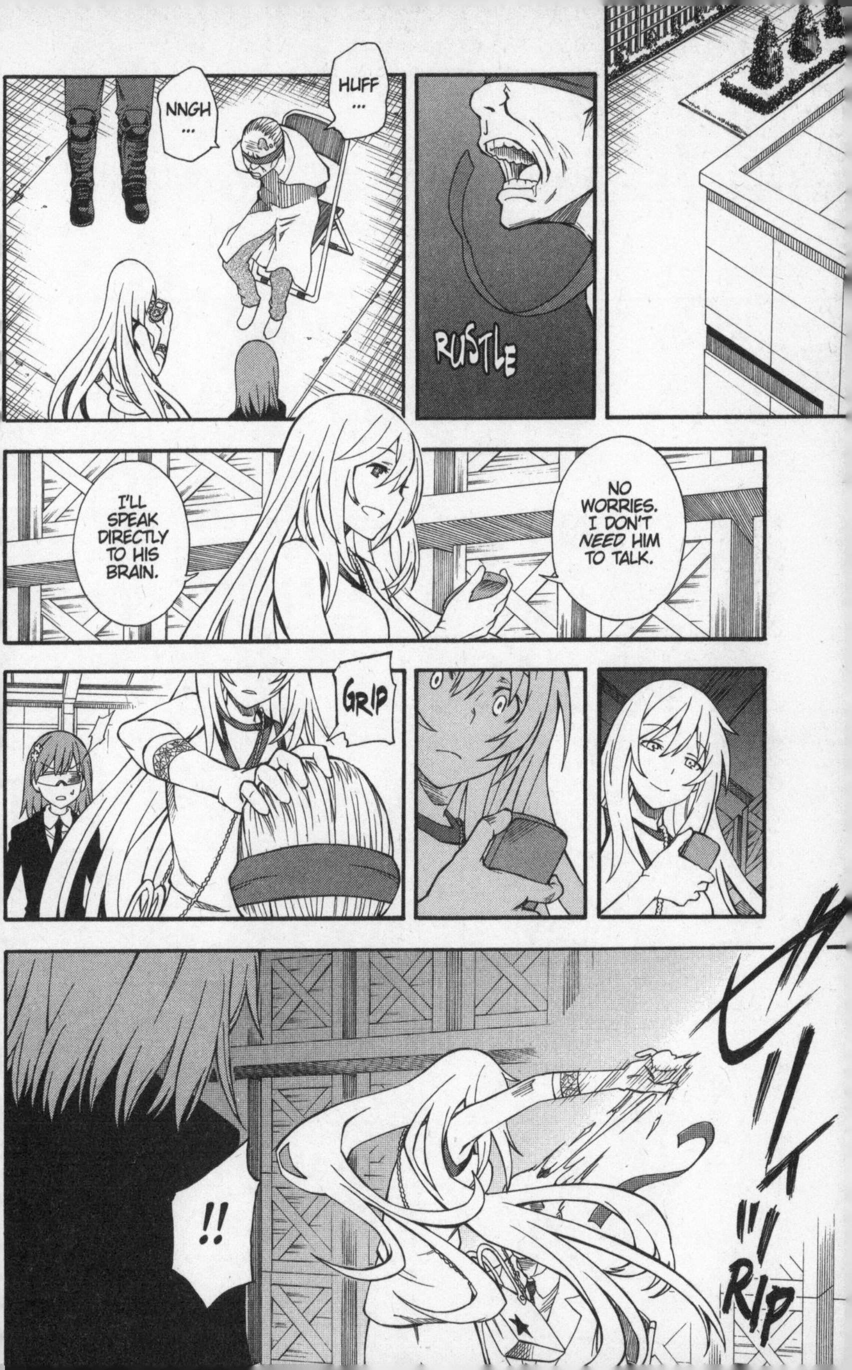
RUSTLE
HUFF ...
NNGH ...
NO WORRIES. I DON'T *NEED* HIM TO TALK.
I'LL SPEAK DIRECTLY TO HIS BRAIN.
GRIP
RIP
!!

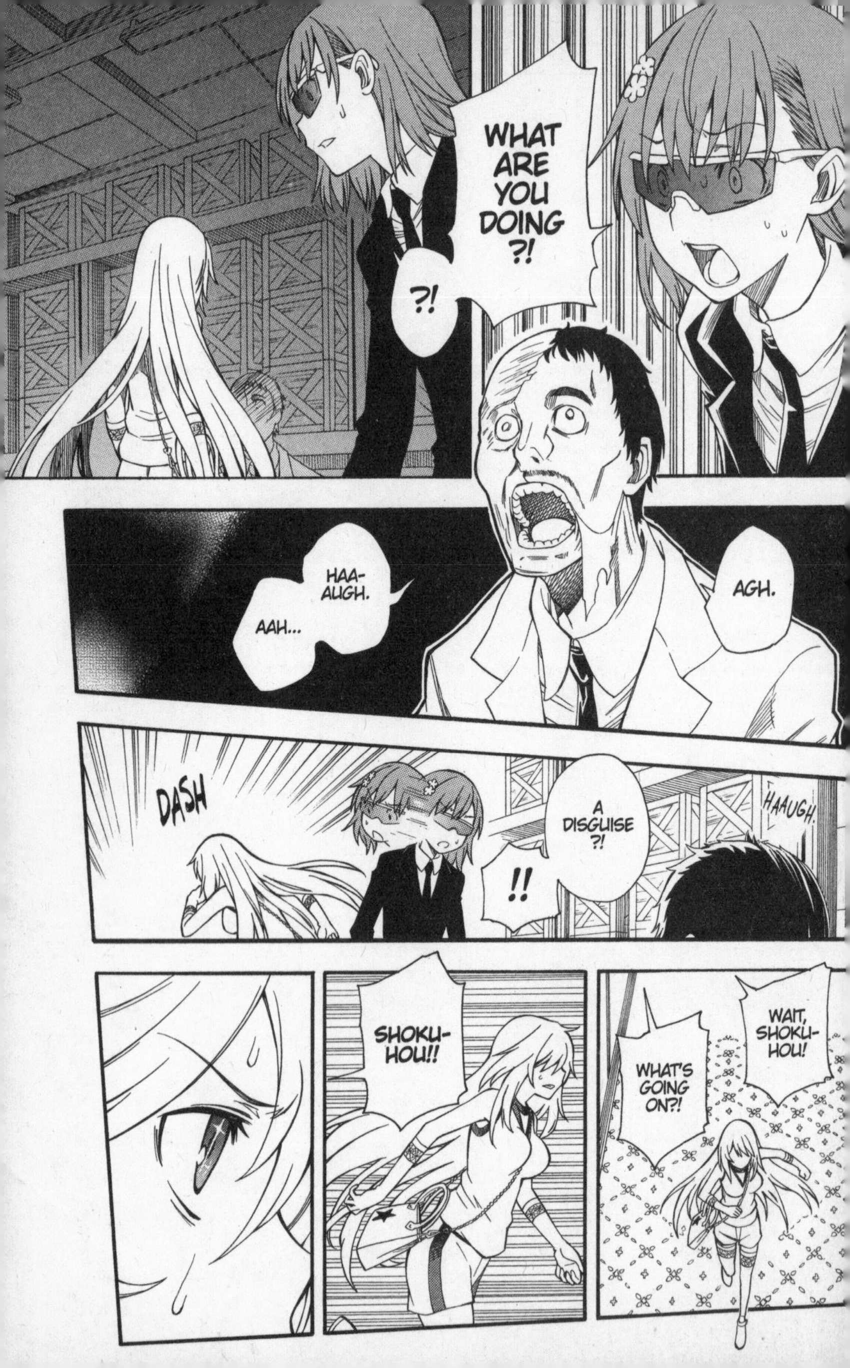

WHAT ARE YOU DOING ?!
?!
AGH.
HAA-AUGH.
AAH...
HAAAUGH.
A DISGUISE ?!
!!
DASH
WAIT, SHOKU-HOU!
WHAT'S GOING ON?!
SHOKU-HOU!!

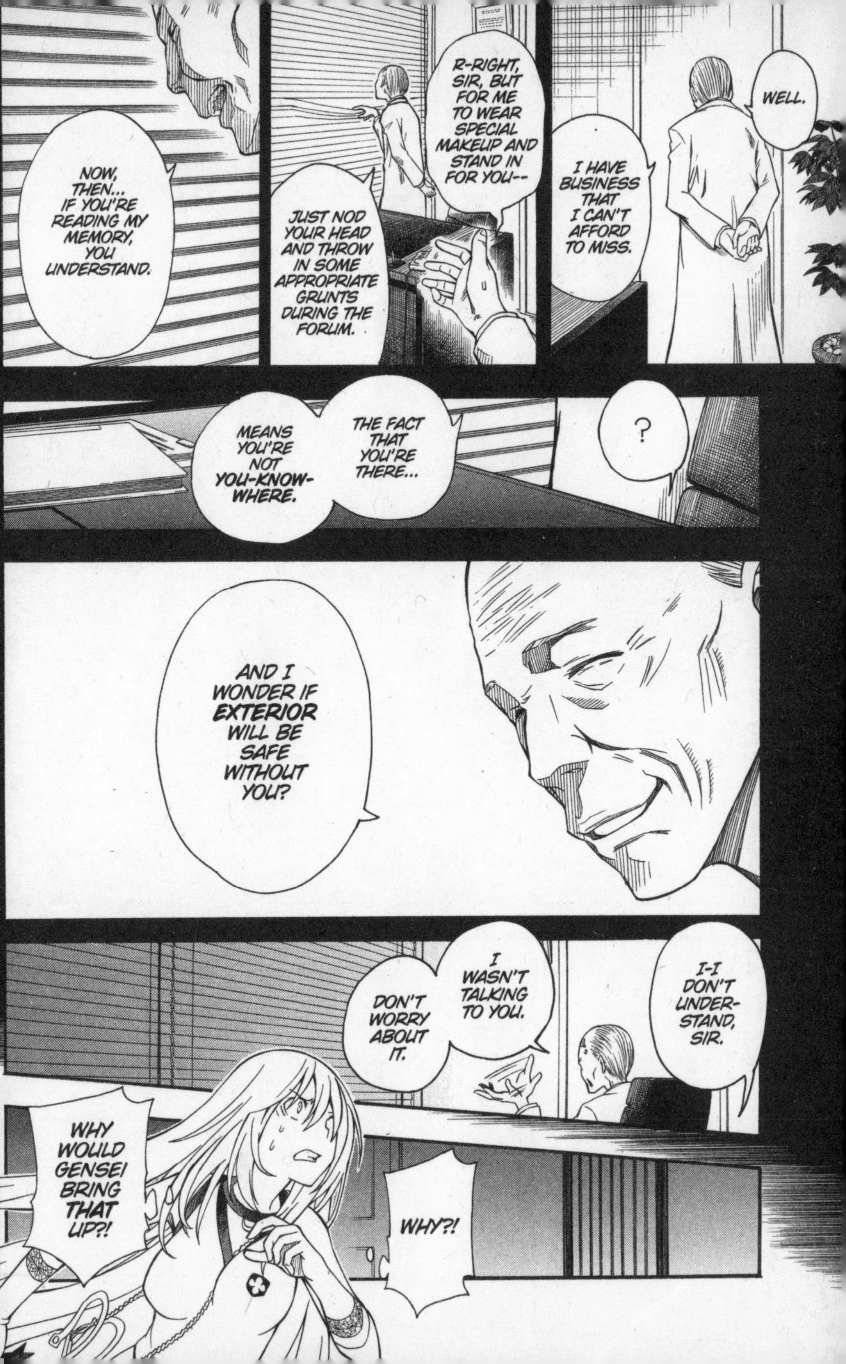
WELL.
I HAVE BUSINESS THAT I CAN'T AFFORD TO MISS.
R-RIGHT, SIR, BUT FOR ME TO WEAR SPECIAL MAKEUP AND STAND IN FOR YOU--
JUST NOD YOUR HEAD AND THROW IN SOME APPROPRIATE GRUNTS DURING THE FORUM.
NOW, THEN... IF YOU'RE READING MY MEMORY, YOU UNDERSTAND.
?
THE FACT THAT YOU'RE THERE...
MEANS YOU'RE NOT YOU-KNOW-WHERE.
AND I WONDER IF **EXTERIOR** WILL BE SAFE WITHOUT YOU?
I-I DON'T UNDER-STAND, SIR.
I WASN'T TALKING TO YOU.
DON'T WORRY ABOUT IT.
WHY?!
WHY WOULD GENSEI BRING **THAT** UP?!

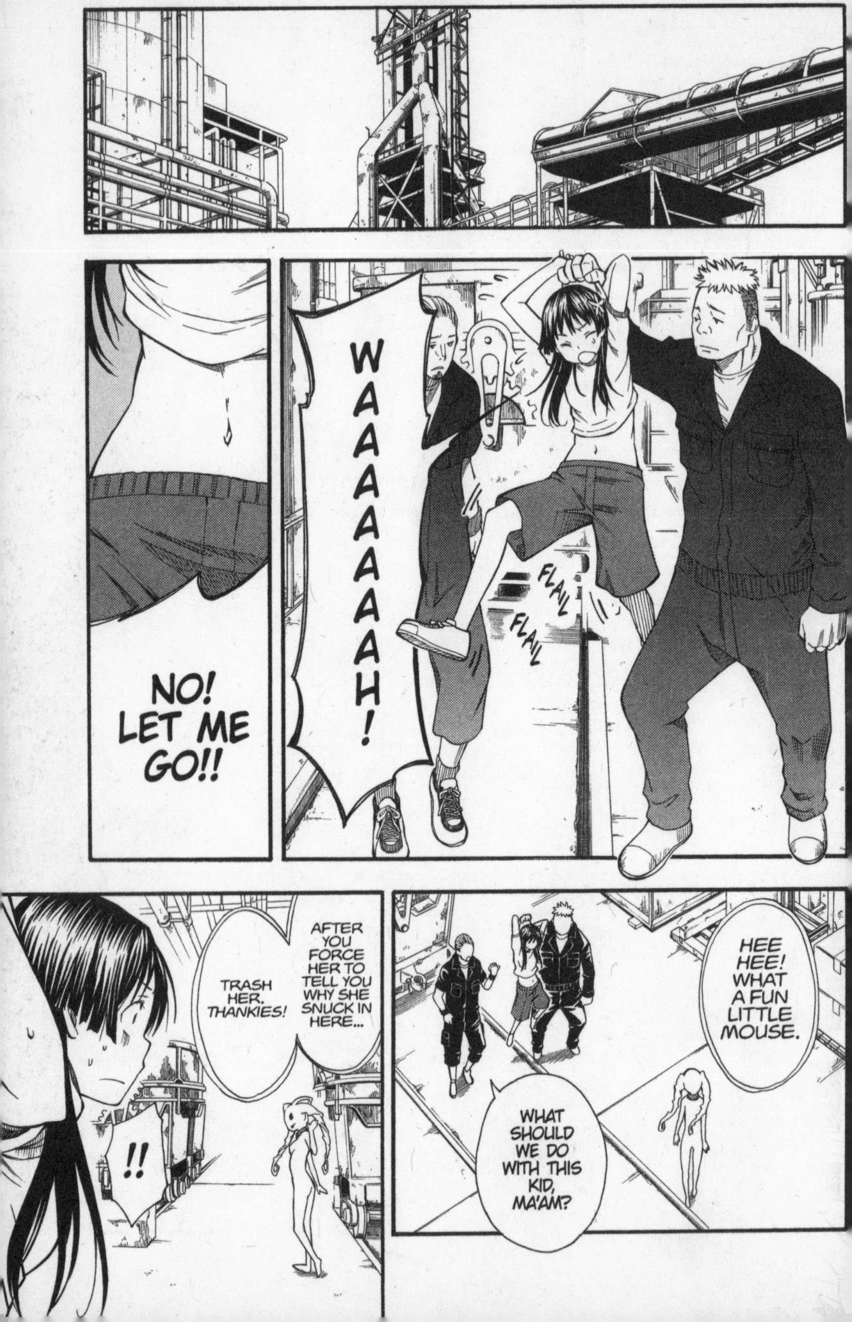
WAAAAAAAAAH!
FLAIL
FLAIL
NO! LET ME GO!!
HEE HEE! WHAT A FUN LITTLE MOUSE.
WHAT SHOULD WE DO WITH THIS KID, MA'AM?
AFTER YOU FORCE HER TO TELL YOU WHY SHE SNUCK IN HERE...
TRASH HER. THANKIES!
!!

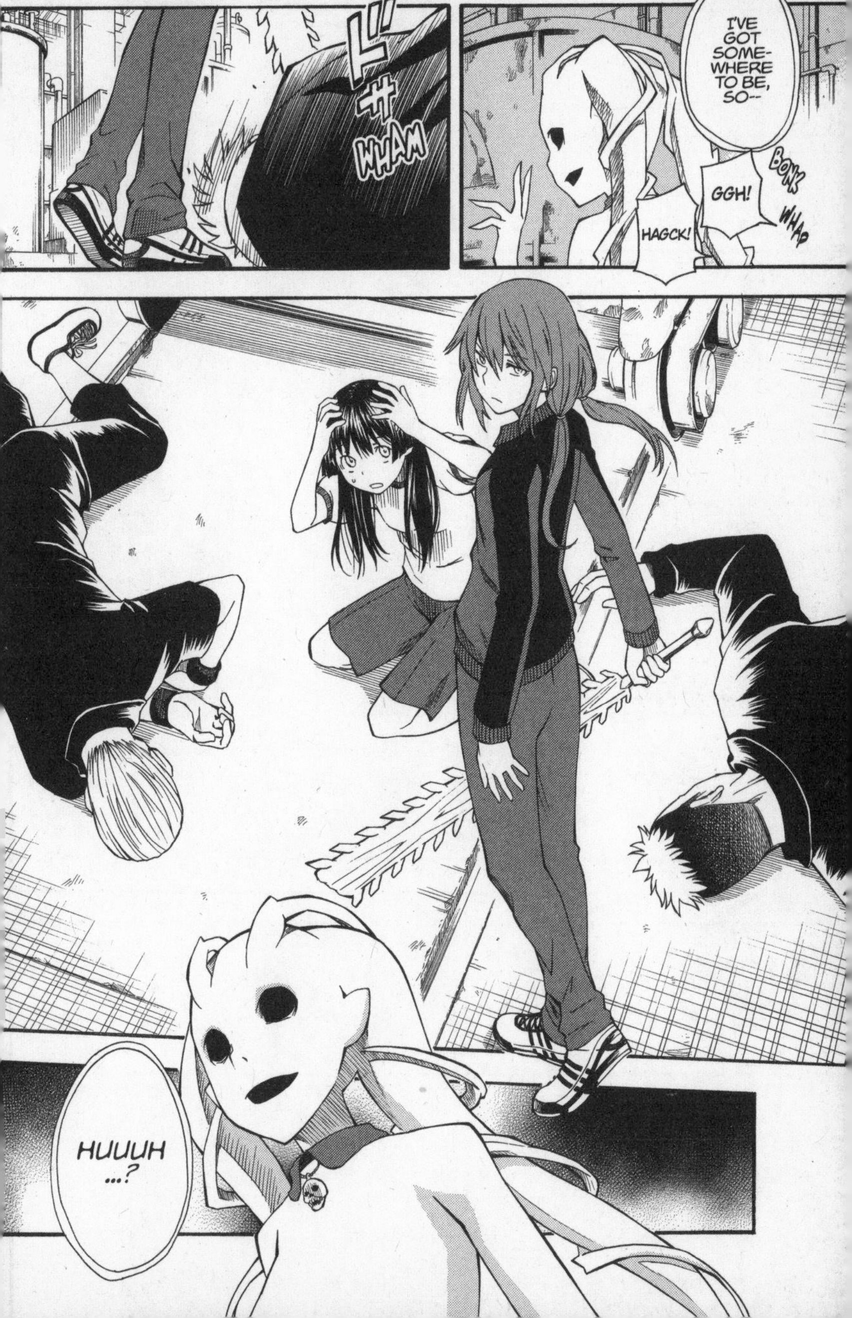

I'VE GOT SOMEWHERE TO BE, SO--
BONK
WHAP
GGH!
HAGCK!
ドザ
WHAM
HUUUH ...?

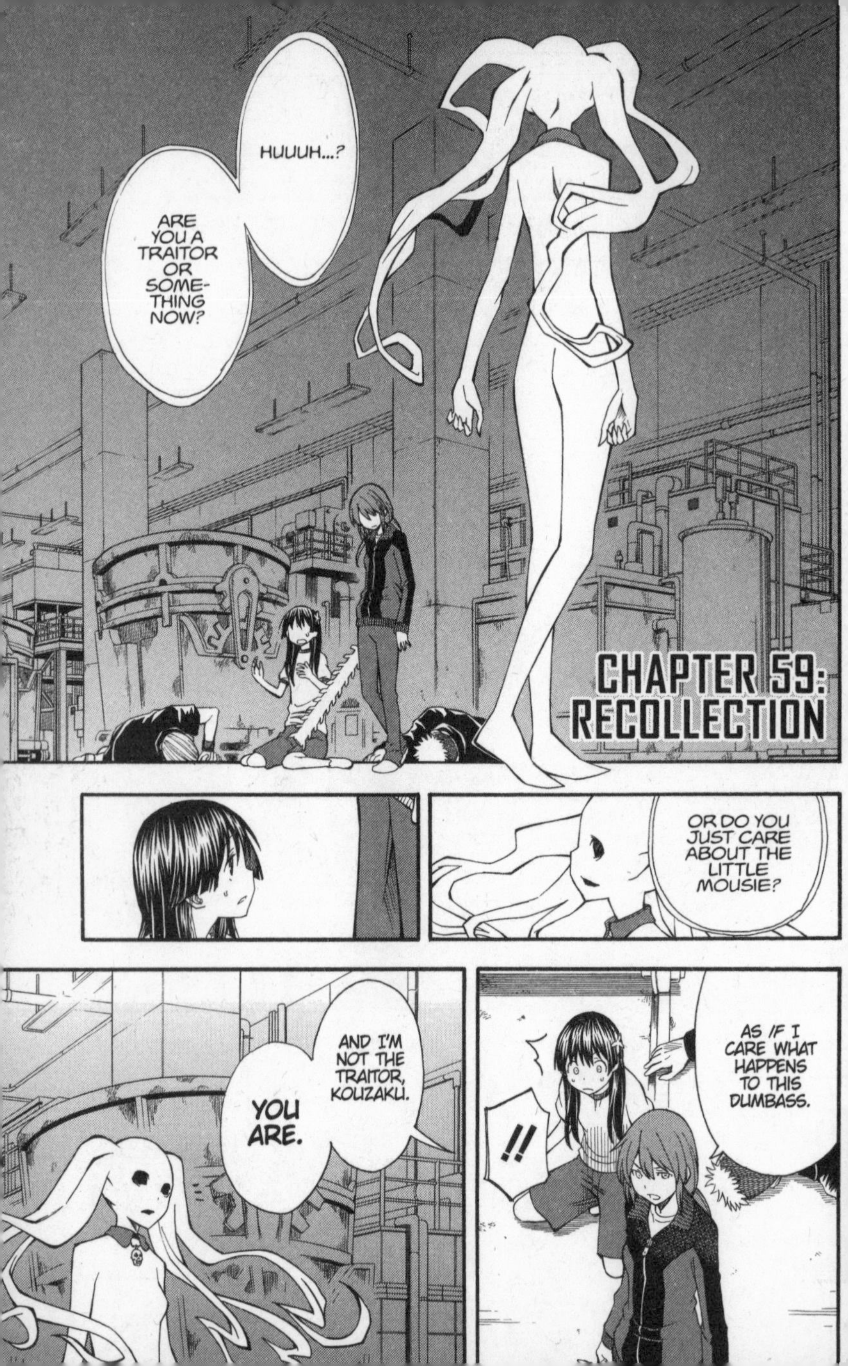
HUUUH...?
ARE YOU A TRAITOR OR SOME-THING NOW?
CHAPTER 59: RECOLLECTION
OR DO YOU JUST CARE ABOUT THE LITTLE MOUSIE?
AS IF I CARE WHAT HAPPENS TO THIS DUMBASS.
!!
AND I'M NOT THE TRAITOR, KOUZAKU.
YOU ARE.

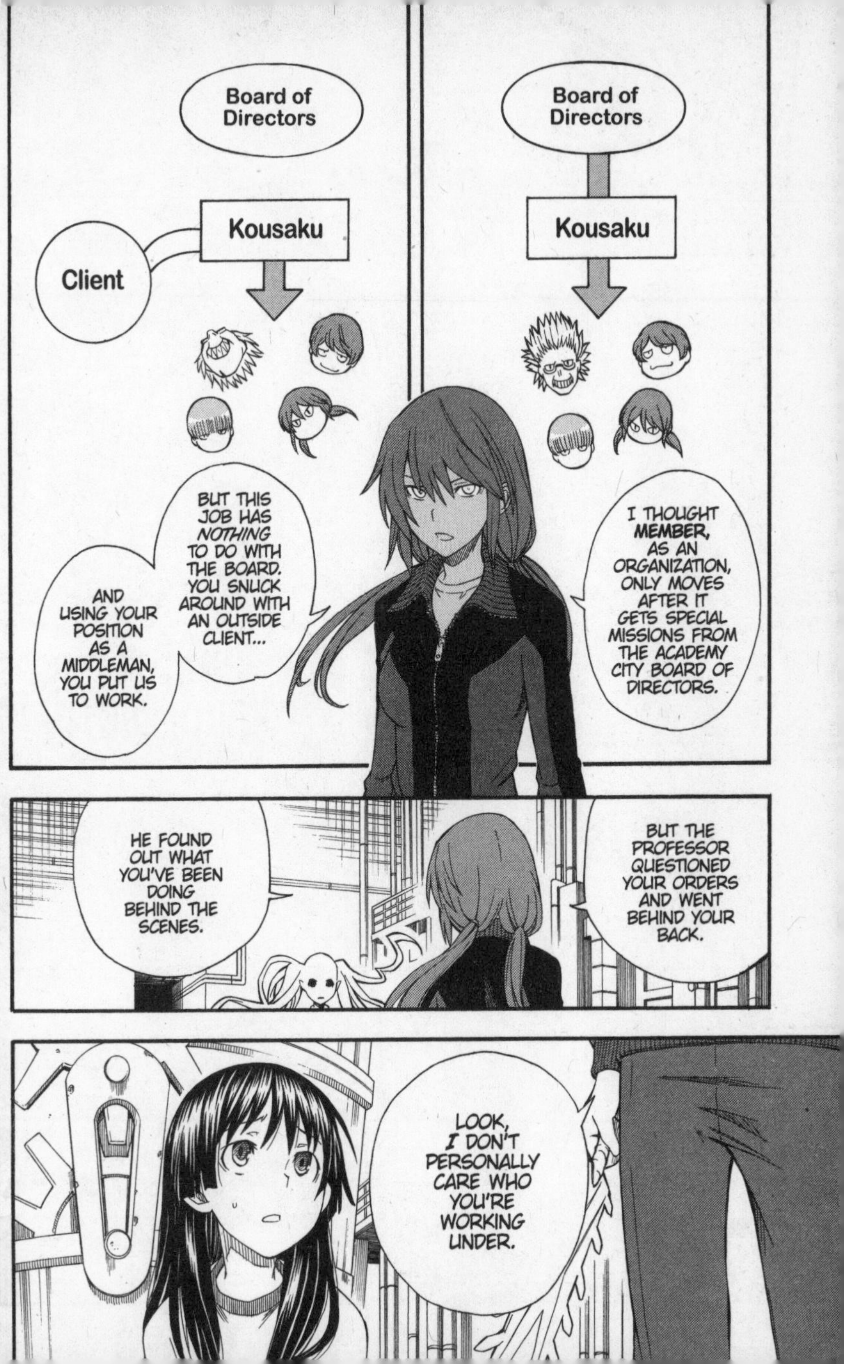
Board of Directors
Kousaku
I THOUGHT MEMBER, AS AN ORGANIZATION, ONLY MOVES AFTER IT GETS SPECIAL MISSIONS FROM THE ACADEMY CITY BOARD OF DIRECTORS.
Board of Directors
Kousaku
Client
BUT THIS JOB HAS NOTHING TO DO WITH THE BOARD. YOU SNUCK AROUND WITH AN OUTSIDE CLIENT...
AND USING YOUR POSITION AS A MIDDLEMAN, YOU PUT US TO WORK.
BUT THE PROFESSOR QUESTIONED YOUR ORDERS AND WENT BEHIND YOUR BACK.
HE FOUND OUT WHAT YOU'VE BEEN DOING BEHIND THE SCENES.
LOOK, I DON'T PERSONALLY CARE WHO YOU'RE WORKING UNDER.

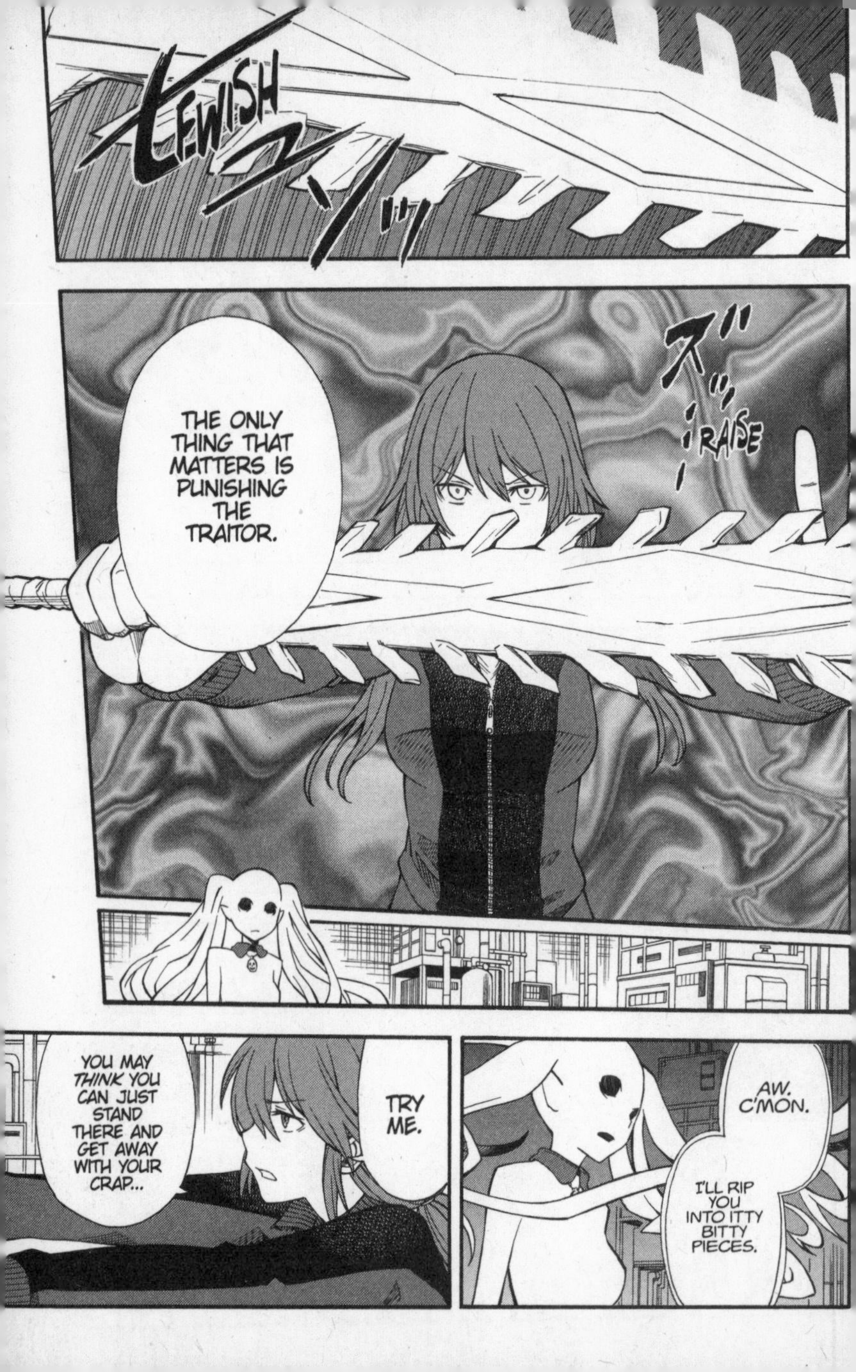
SWISH
RAISE
THE ONLY THING THAT MATTERS IS PUNISHING THE TRAITOR.
AW. C'MON.
I'LL RIP YOU INTO ITTY BITTY PIECES.
TRY ME.
YOU MAY *THINK* YOU CAN JUST STAND THERE AND GET AWAY WITH YOUR CRAP...

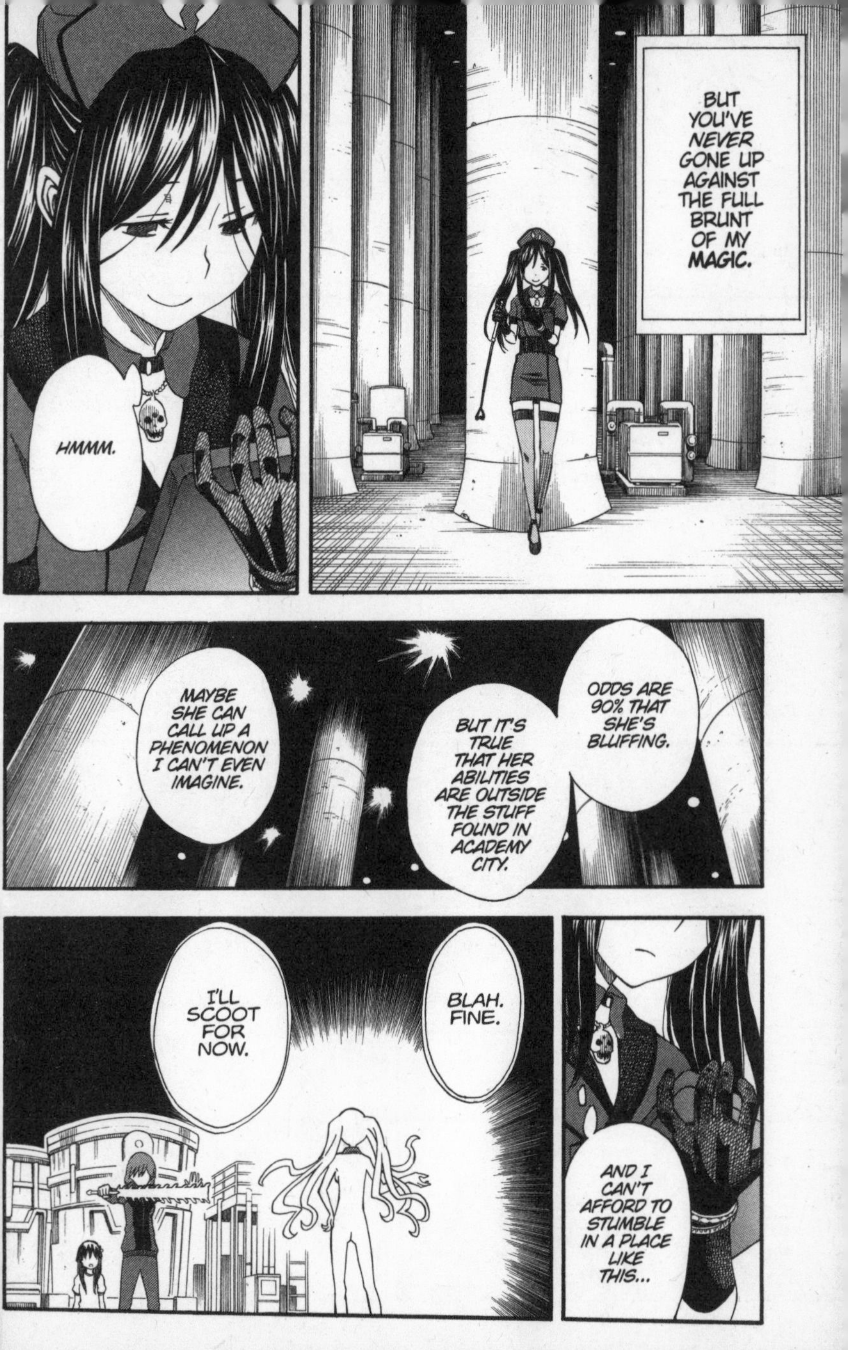
BUT YOU'VE NEVER GONE UP AGAINST THE FULL BRUNT OF MY MAGIC.
HMMM.
ODDS ARE 90% THAT SHE'S BLUFFING.
BUT IT'S TRUE THAT HER ABILITIES ARE OUTSIDE THE STUFF FOUND IN ACADEMY CITY.
MAYBE SHE CAN CALL UP A PHENOMENON I CAN'T EVEN IMAGINE.
AND I CAN'T AFFORD TO STUMBLE IN A PLACE LIKE THIS...
BLAH. FINE.
I'LL SCOOT FOR NOW.

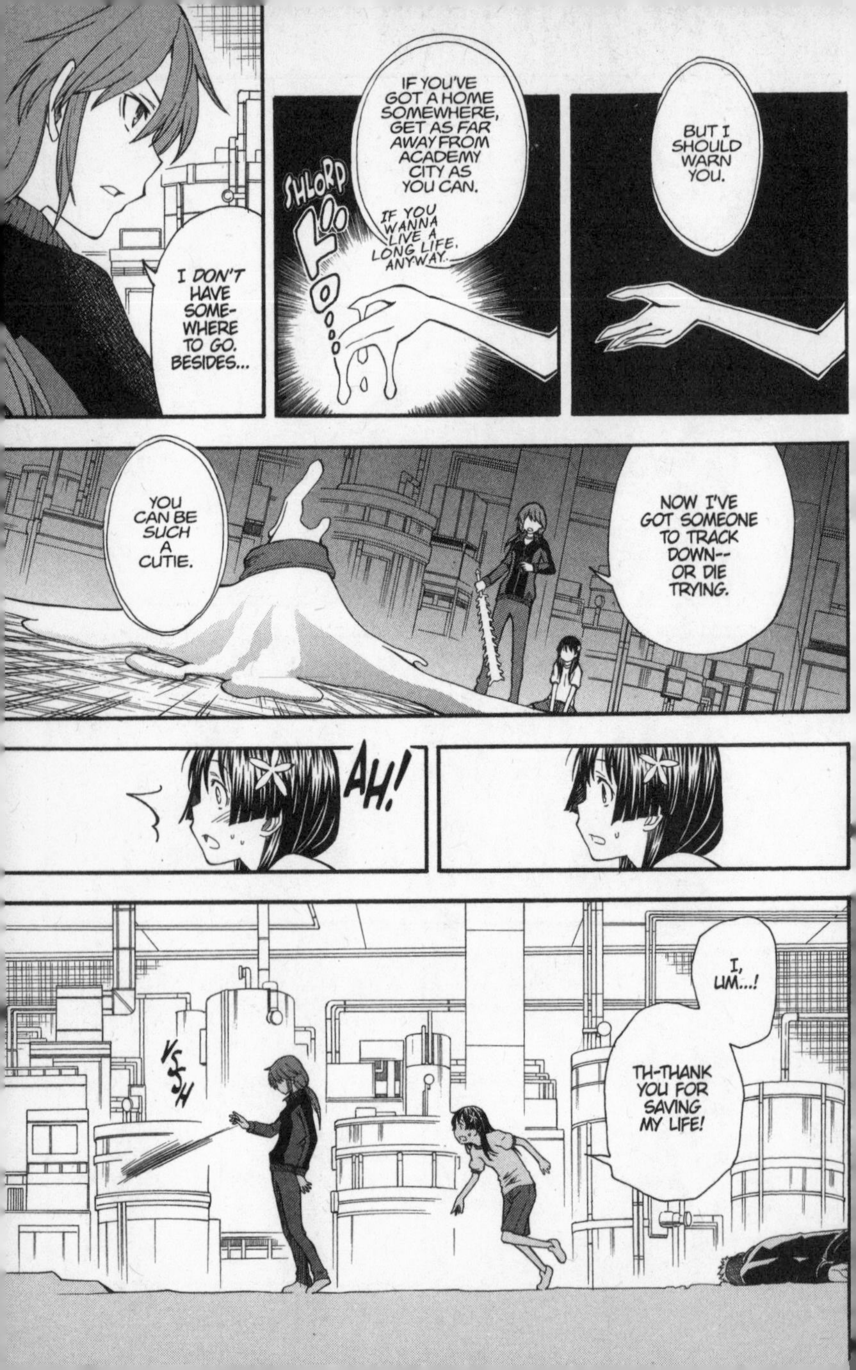
BUT I SHOULD WARN YOU.
IF YOU'VE GOT A HOME SOMEWHERE, GET AS FAR AWAY FROM ACADEMY CITY AS YOU CAN.
IF YOU WANNA LIVE A LONG LIFE, ANYWAY.
SHLORP
I DON'T HAVE SOMEWHERE TO GO. BESIDES...
NOW I'VE GOT SOMEONE TO TRACK DOWN-- OR DIE TRYING.
YOU CAN BE SUCH A CUTIE.
AH!
I, UM...!
TH-THANK YOU FOR SAVING MY LIFE!
VSSH

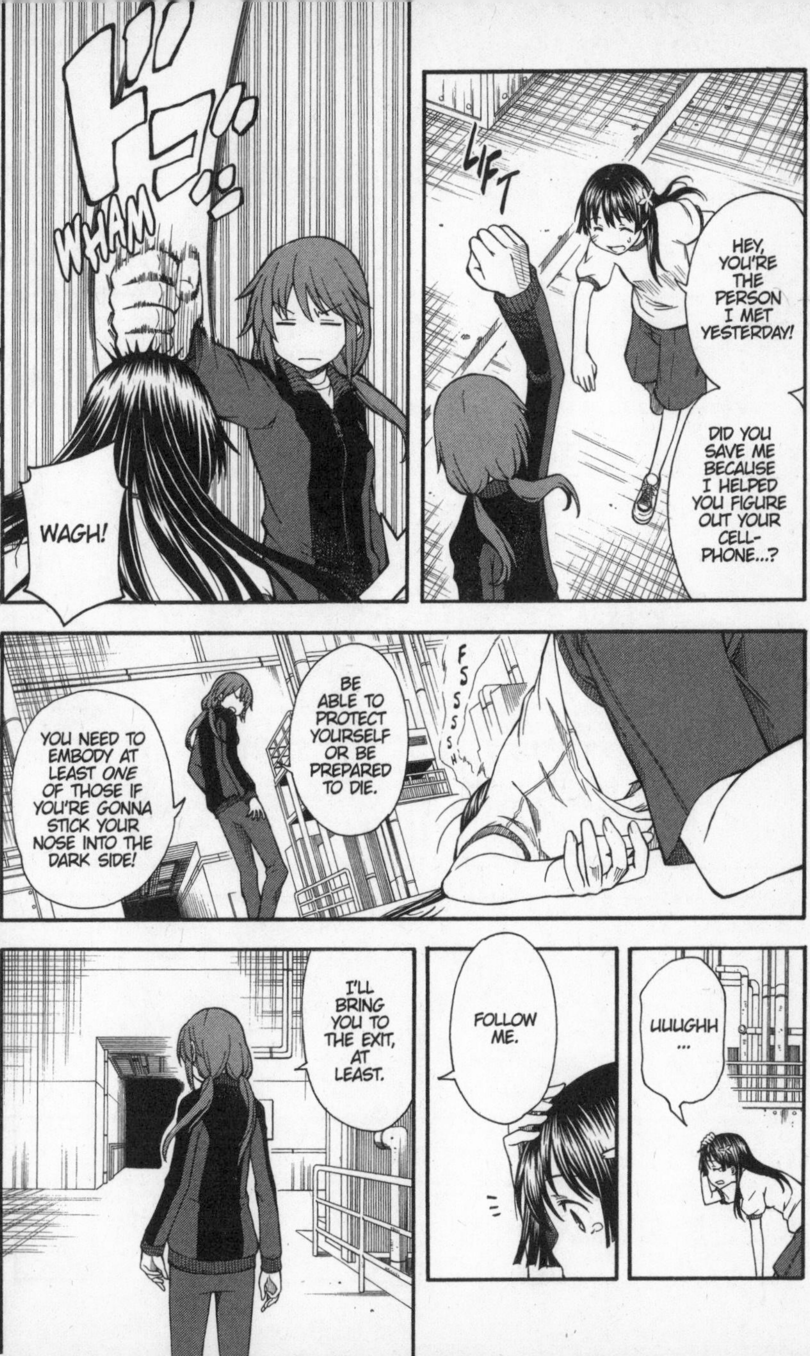
LIFT
HEY, YOU'RE THE PERSON I MET YESTERDAY!
DID YOU SAVE ME BECAUSE I HELPED YOU FIGURE OUT YOUR CELL-PHONE...?
WHAM
WAGH!
FSSSSH
BE ABLE TO PROTECT YOURSELF OR BE PREPARED TO DIE.
YOU NEED TO EMBODY AT LEAST ONE OF THOSE IF YOU'RE GONNA STICK YOUR NOSE INTO THE DARK SIDE!
UUUGHH...
FOLLOW ME.
I'LL BRING YOU TO THE EXIT, AT LEAST.

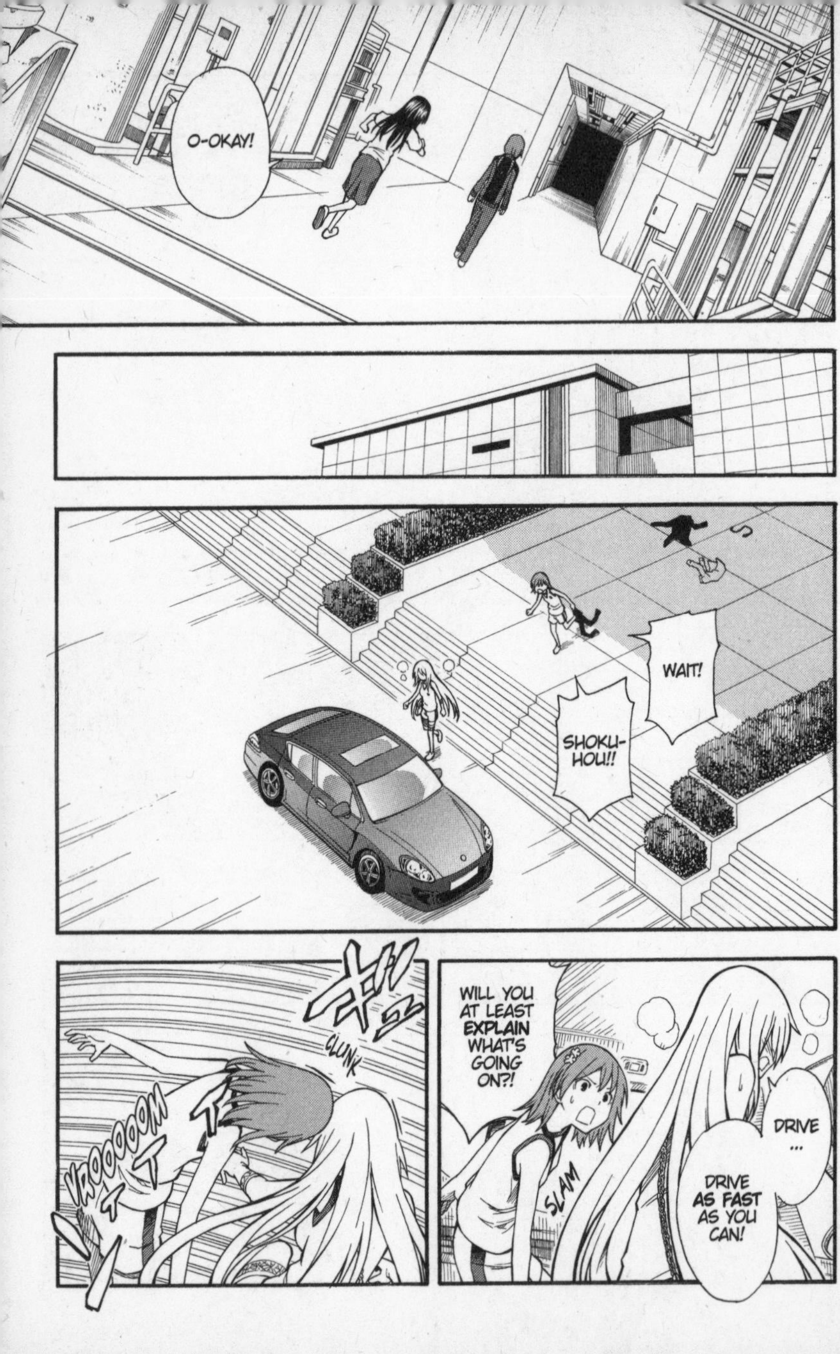
O-OKAY!
WAIT!
SHOKU-HOU!!
DRIVE ...
DRIVE AS FAST AS YOU CAN!
WILL YOU AT LEAST EXPLAIN WHAT'S GOING ON?!
SLAM
CLUNK
VROOOOOM

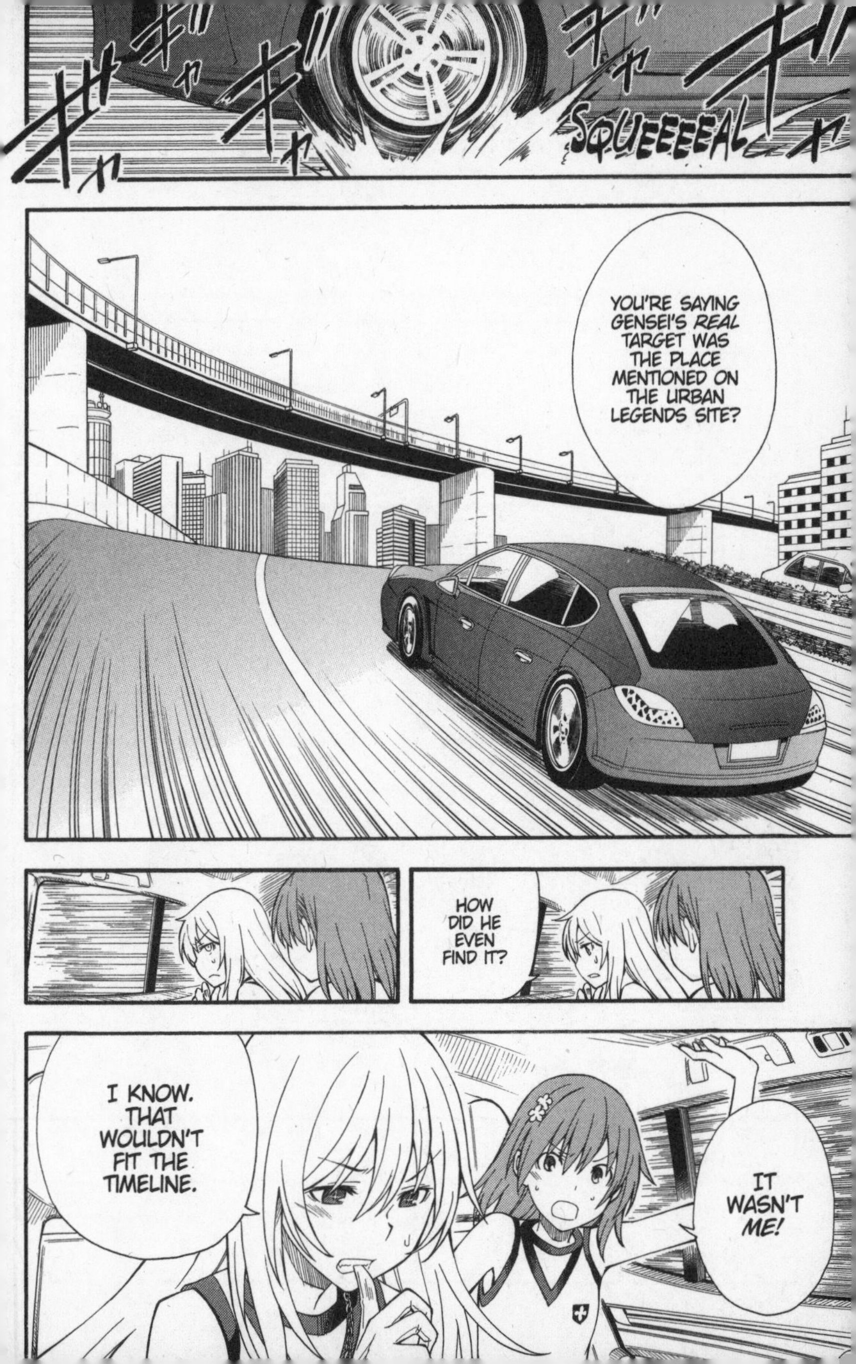
SQUEEEEEAL
YOU'RE SAYING GENSEI'S *REAL* TARGET WAS THE PLACE MENTIONED ON THE URBAN LEGENDS SITE?
HOW DID HE EVEN FIND IT?
IT WASN'T *ME!*
I KNOW. THAT WOULDN'T FIT THE TIMELINE.

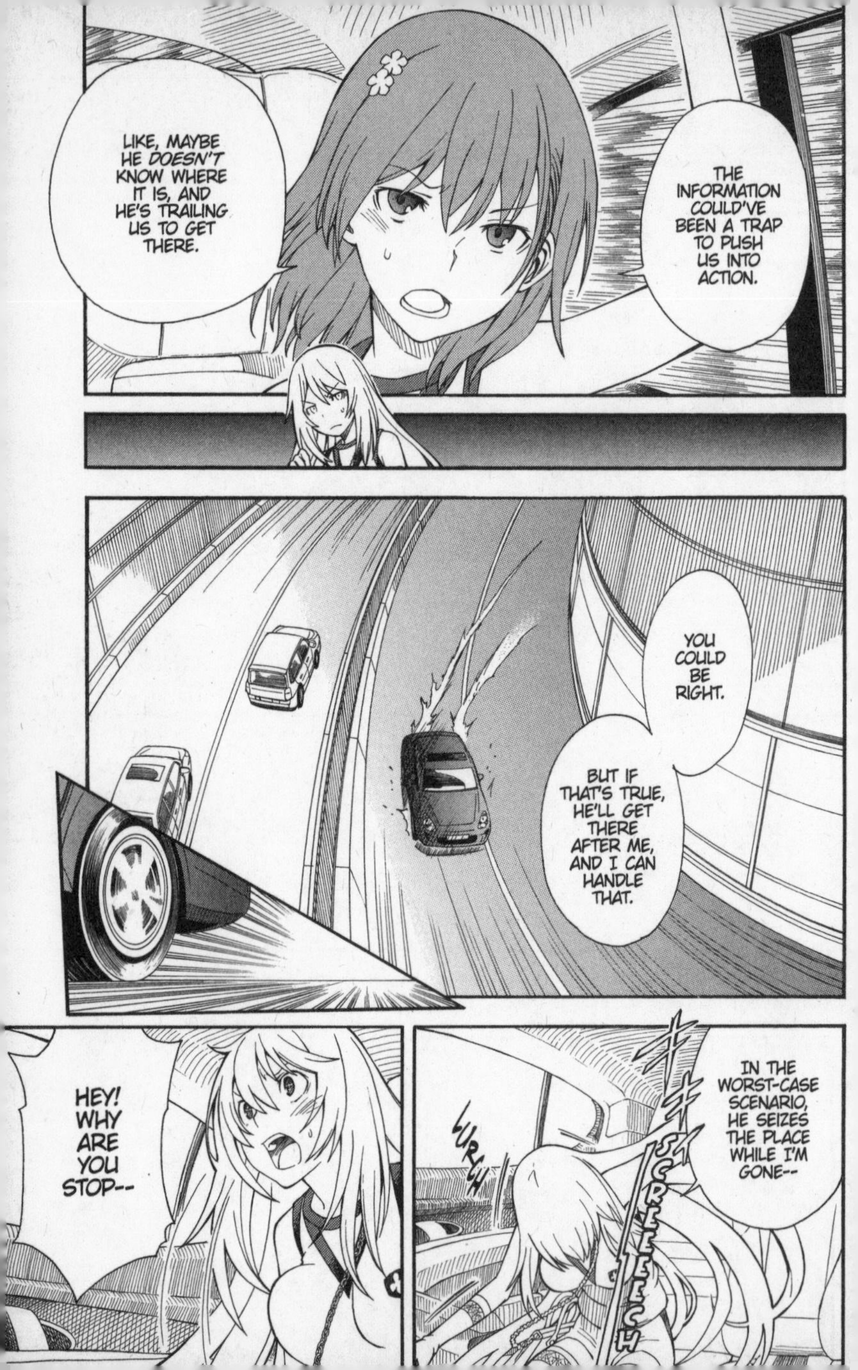
THE INFORMATION COULD'VE BEEN A TRAP TO PUSH US INTO ACTION.
LIKE, MAYBE HE DOESN'T KNOW WHERE IT IS, AND HE'S TRAILING US TO GET THERE.
YOU COULD BE RIGHT.
BUT IF THAT'S TRUE, HE'LL GET THERE AFTER ME, AND I CAN HANDLE THAT.
IN THE WORST-CASE SCENARIO, HE SEIZES THE PLACE WHILE I'M GONE--
SCREEEECH
LURCH
HEY! WHY ARE YOU STOP--

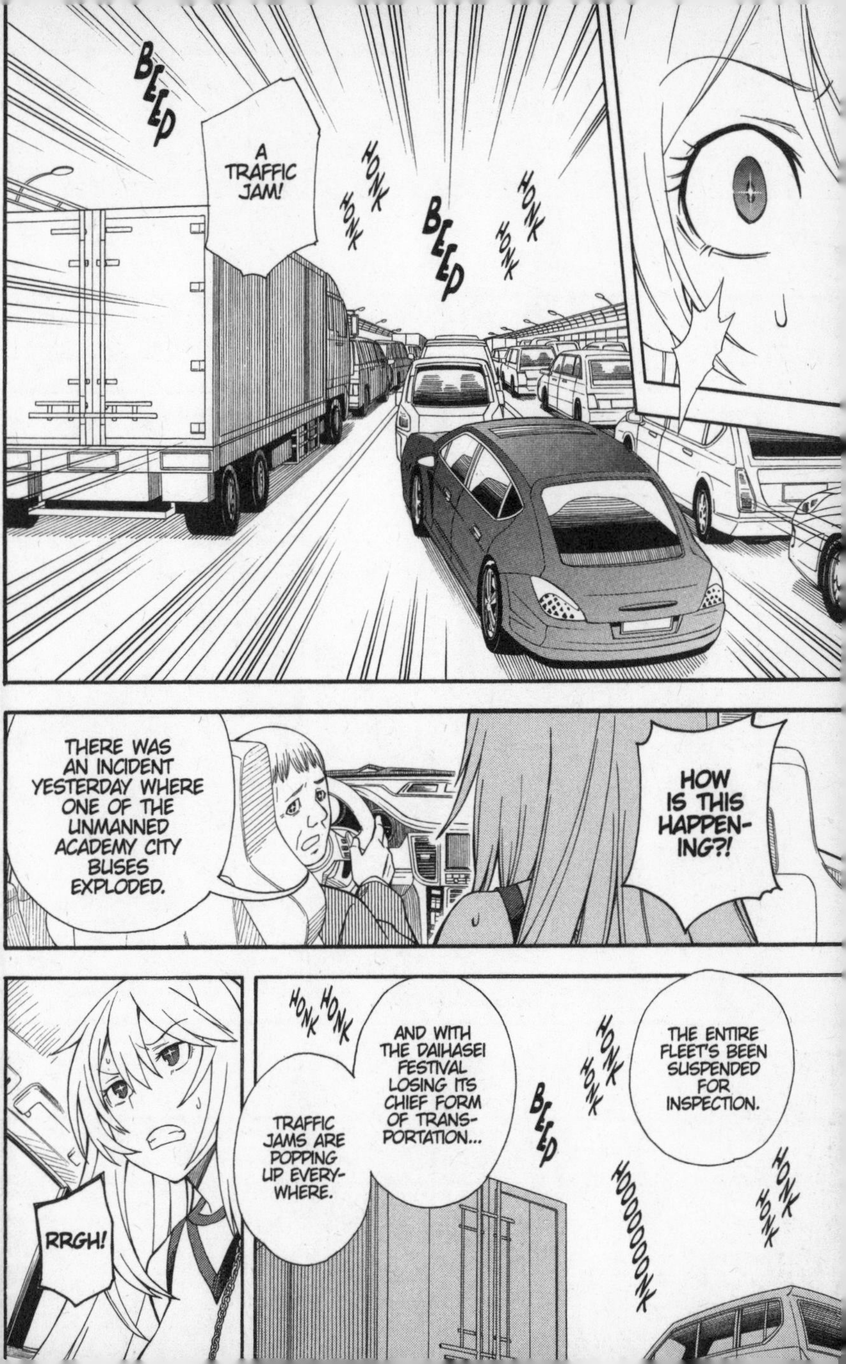

HONK HONK
BEEP
HONK HONK
A TRAFFIC JAM!
BEEP
HOW IS THIS HAPPENING?!
THERE WAS AN INCIDENT YESTERDAY WHERE ONE OF THE UNMANNED ACADEMY CITY BUSES EXPLODED.
HONK HONK
THE ENTIRE FLEET'S BEEN SUSPENDED FOR INSPECTION.
HOOOOOONK
BEEP
HONK HONK
AND WITH THE DAIHASEI FESTIVAL LOSING ITS CHIEF FORM OF TRANSPORTATION...
TRAFFIC JAMS ARE POPPING UP EVERYWHERE.
HONK HONK
RRGH!

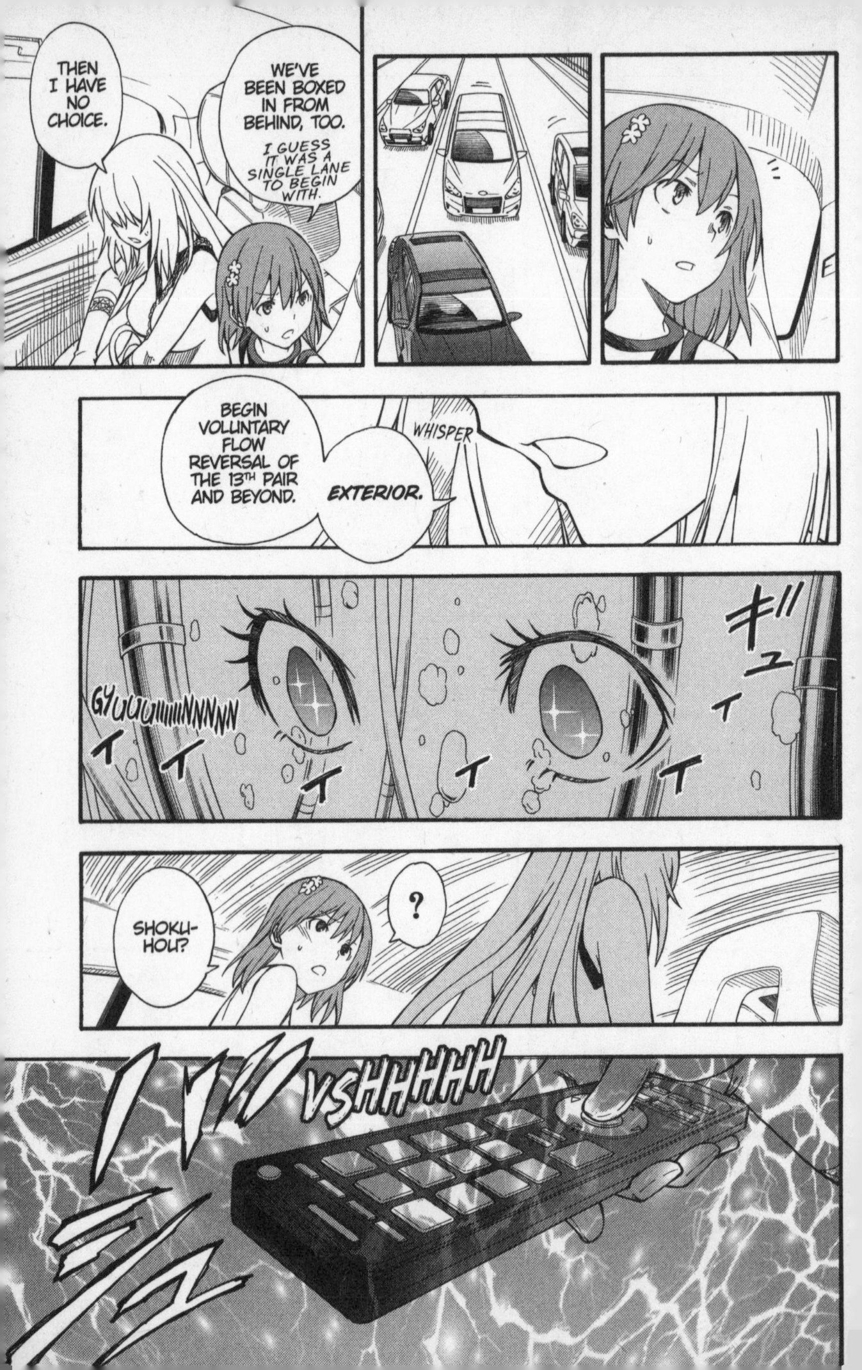

WE'VE BEEN BOXED IN FROM BEHIND, TOO.
I GUESS IT WAS A SINGLE LANE TO BEGIN WITH.
THEN I HAVE NO CHOICE.
WHISPER
EXTERIOR.
BEGIN VOLUNTARY FLOW REVERSAL OF THE 13TH PAIR AND BEYOND.
ギュイイイイイ
GYUUUIIIIIINNNNN
?
SHOKU-HOU?
VSHHHHHH

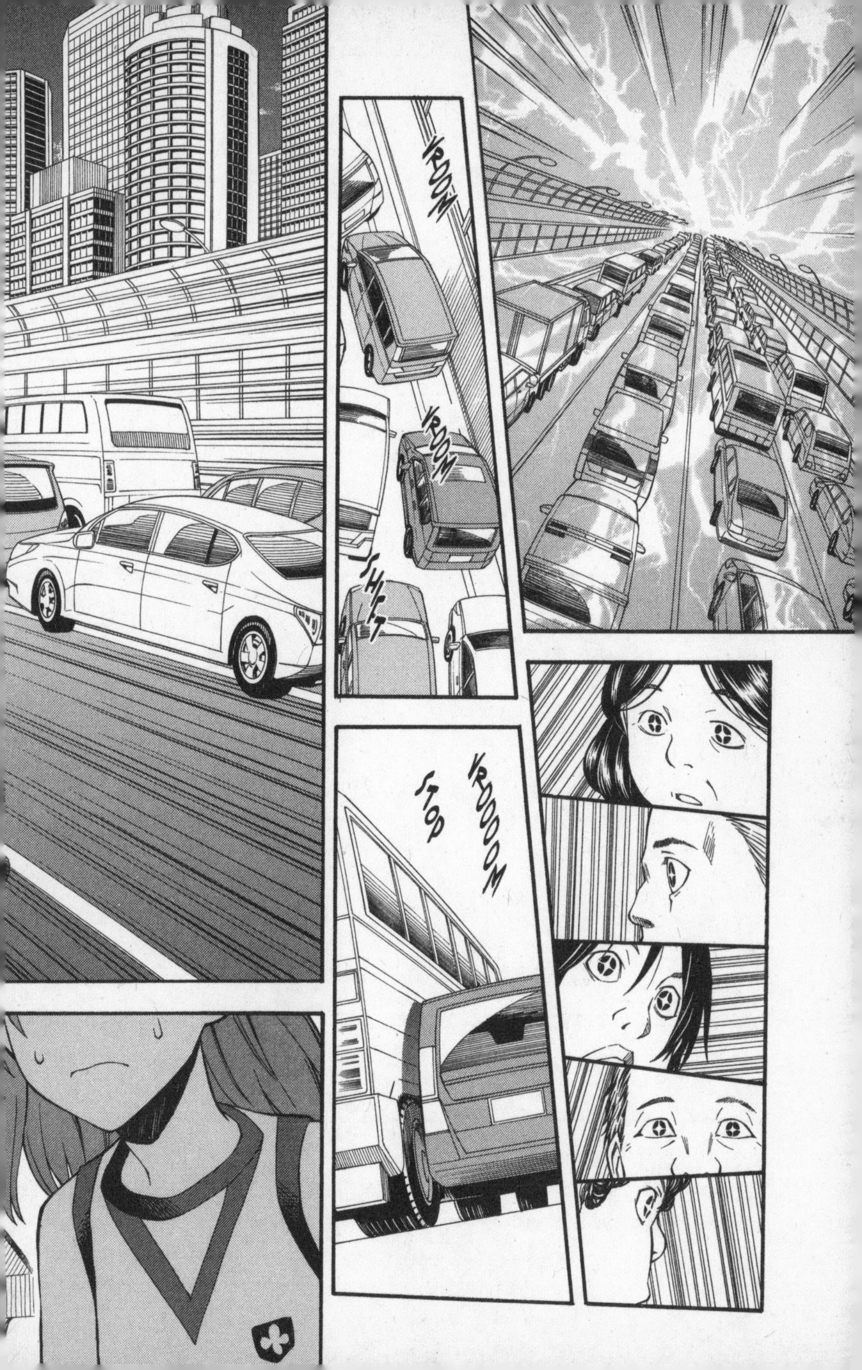
VROOM
VROOM
SHIFT
VROOOOOM
STOP

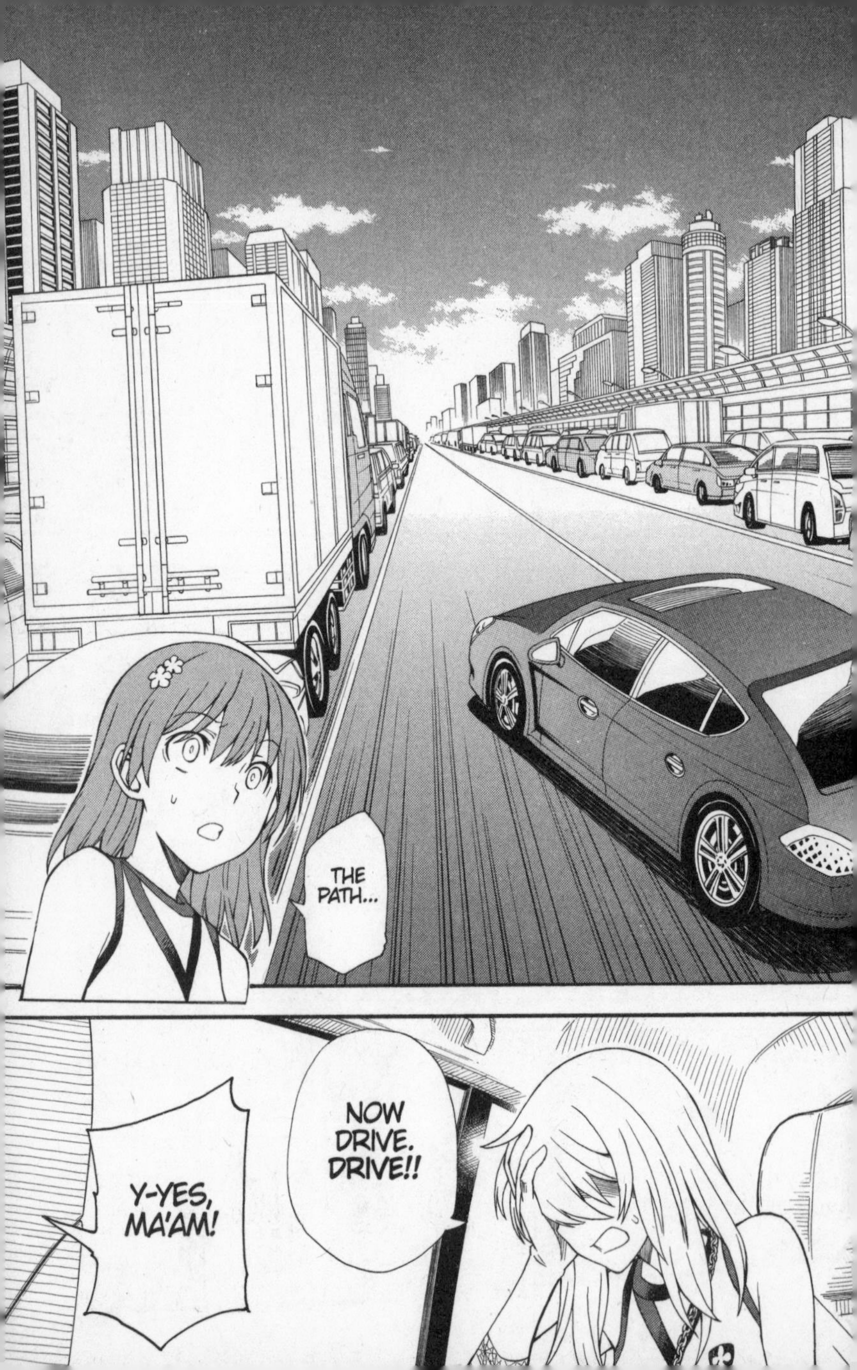
THE PATH...
NOW DRIVE. DRIVE!!
Y-YES, MA'AM!

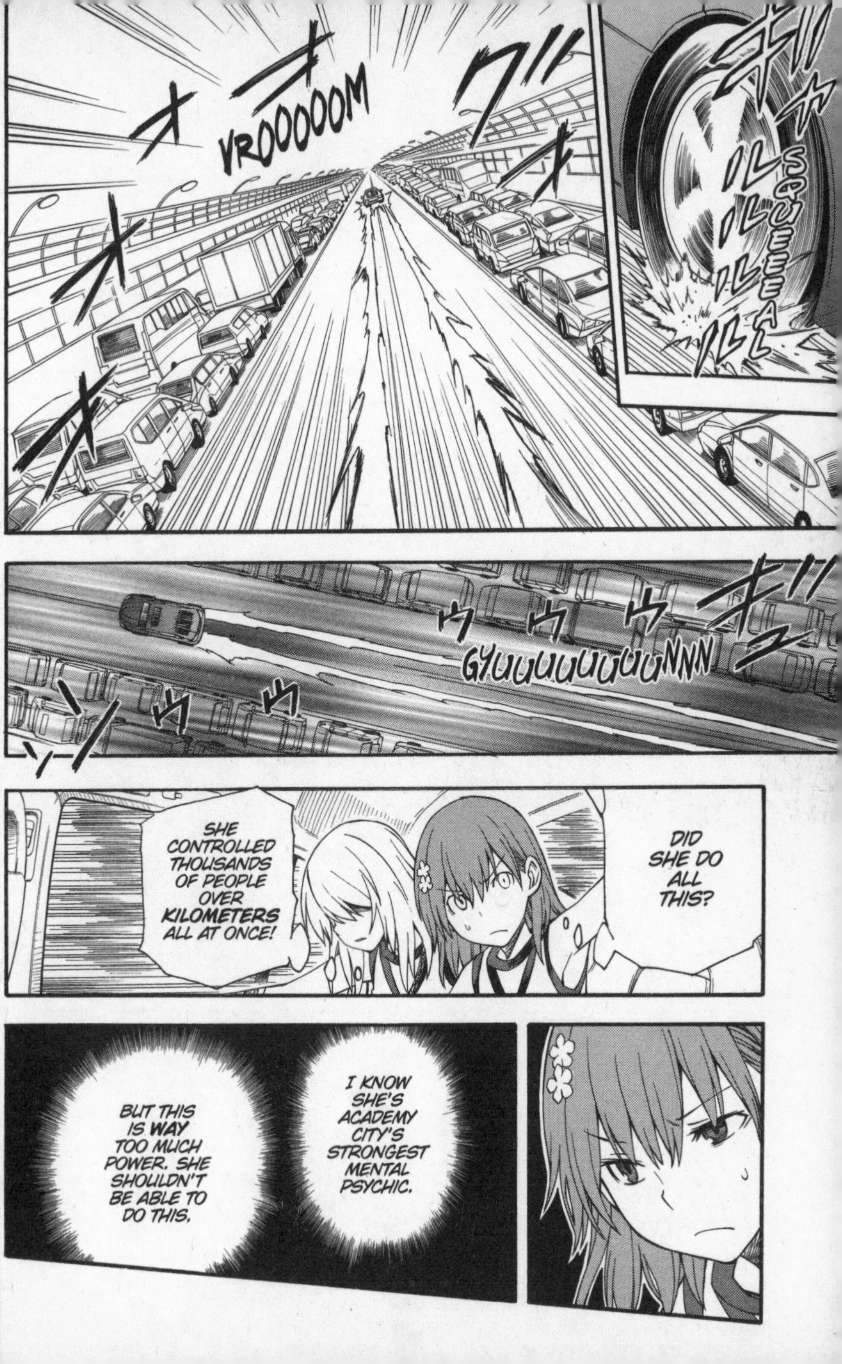
SQUEEEAL
VROOOOOM
GYUUUUUUUUNNN
DID SHE DO ALL THIS?
SHE CONTROLLED THOUSANDS OF PEOPLE OVER KILOMETERS ALL AT ONCE!
I KNOW SHE'S ACADEMY CITY'S STRONGEST MENTAL PSYCHIC.
BUT THIS IS WAY TOO MUCH POWER. SHE SHOULDN'T BE ABLE TO DO THIS.

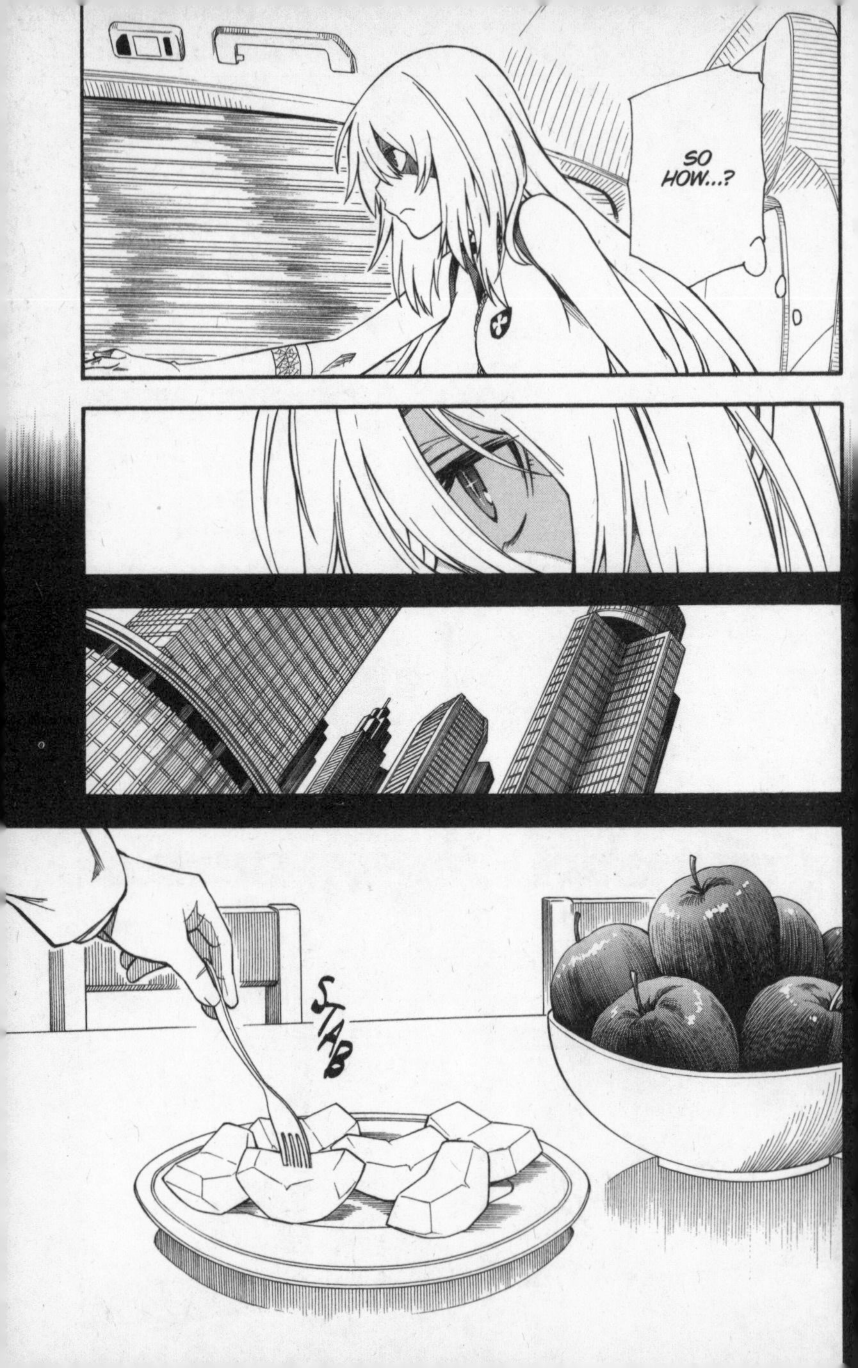
SO HOW...?
STAB

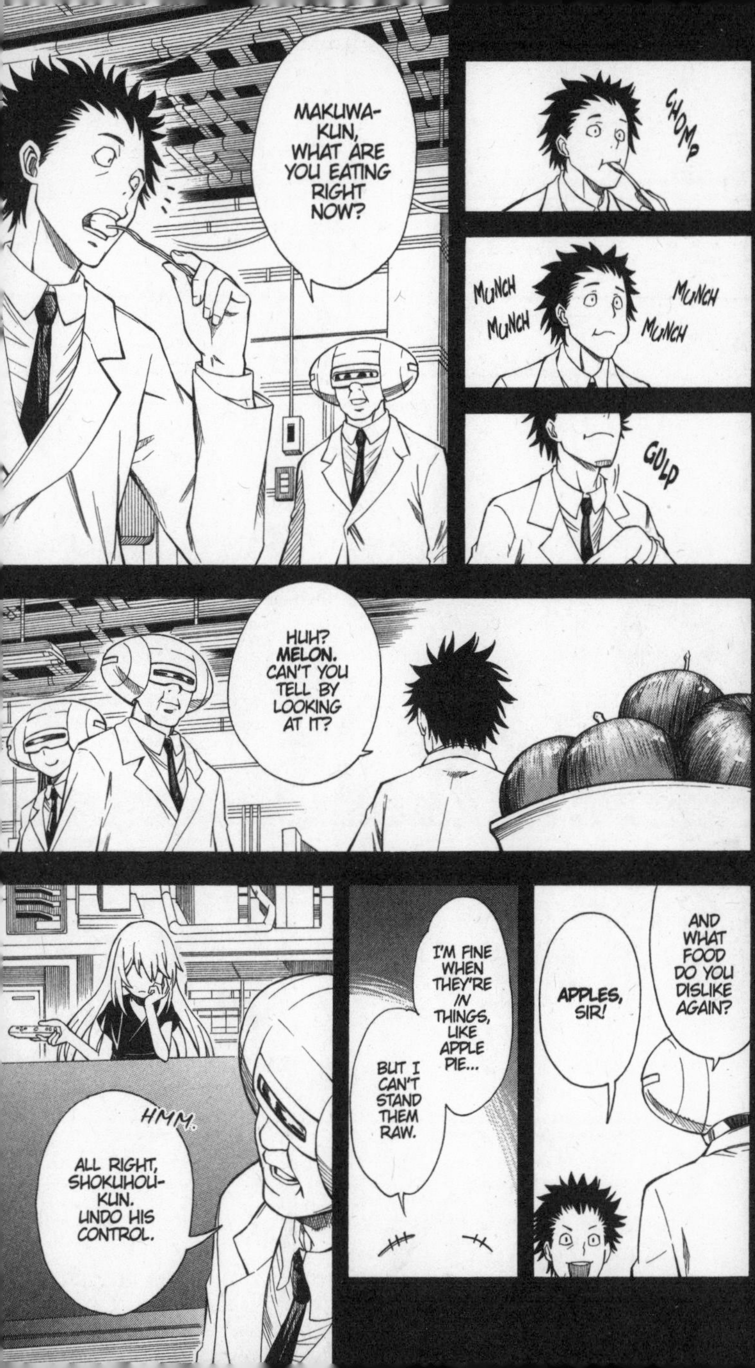

CHOMP
MUNCH MUNCH
MUNCH MUNCH
GULP
MAKUWA-KUN, WHAT ARE YOU EATING RIGHT NOW?
HUH? MELON. CAN'T YOU TELL BY LOOKING AT IT?
AND WHAT FOOD DO YOU DISLIKE AGAIN?
APPLES, SIR!
I'M FINE WHEN THEY'RE *IN* THINGS, LIKE APPLE PIE...
BUT I CAN'T STAND THEM RAW.
HMM.
ALL RIGHT, SHOKUHOU-KUN. UNDO HIS CONTROL.

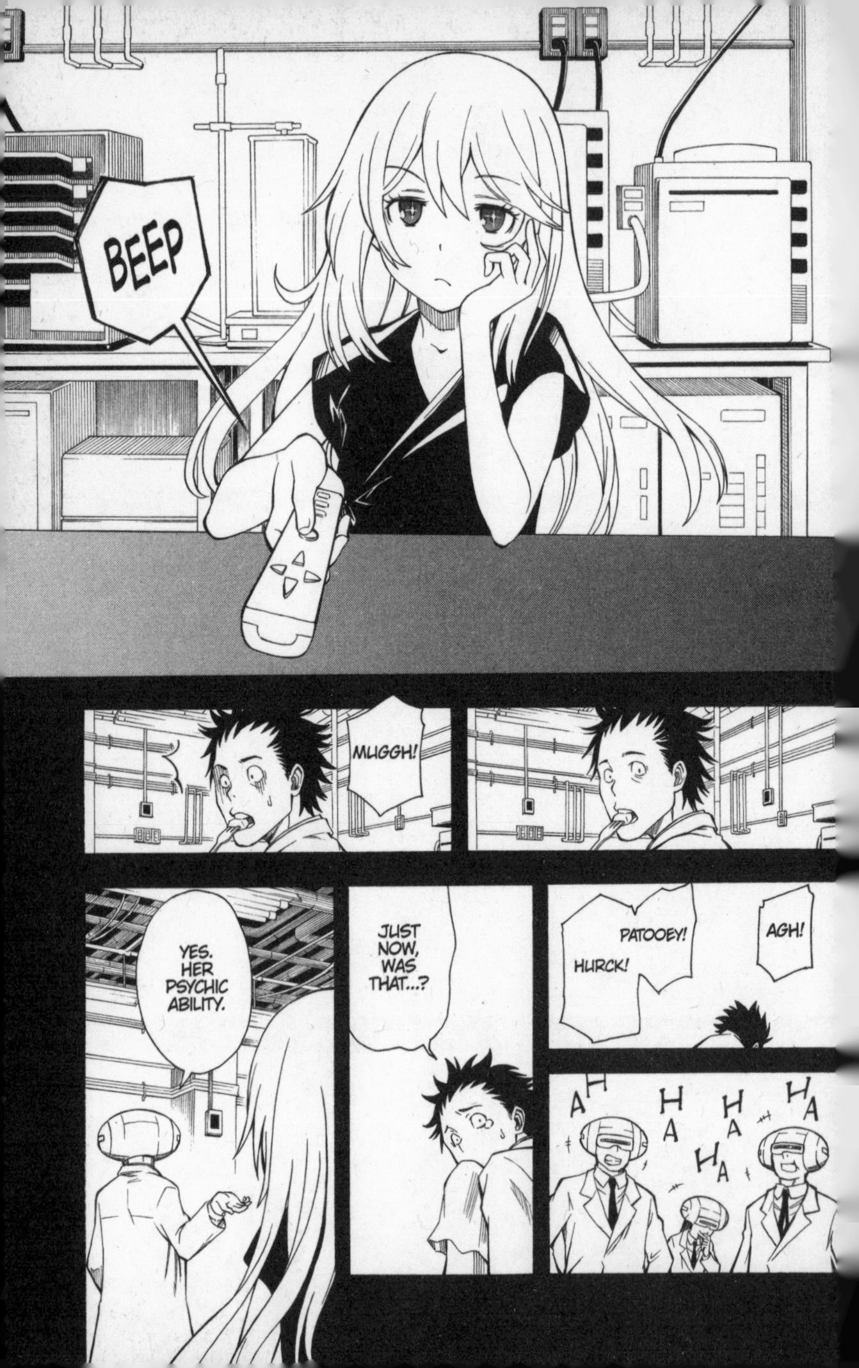
BEEP
MUGGH!
AGH!
PATOOEY!
HURCK!
AH HA HA HA HA HA
JUST NOW, WAS THAT...?
YES. HER PSYCHIC ABILITY.

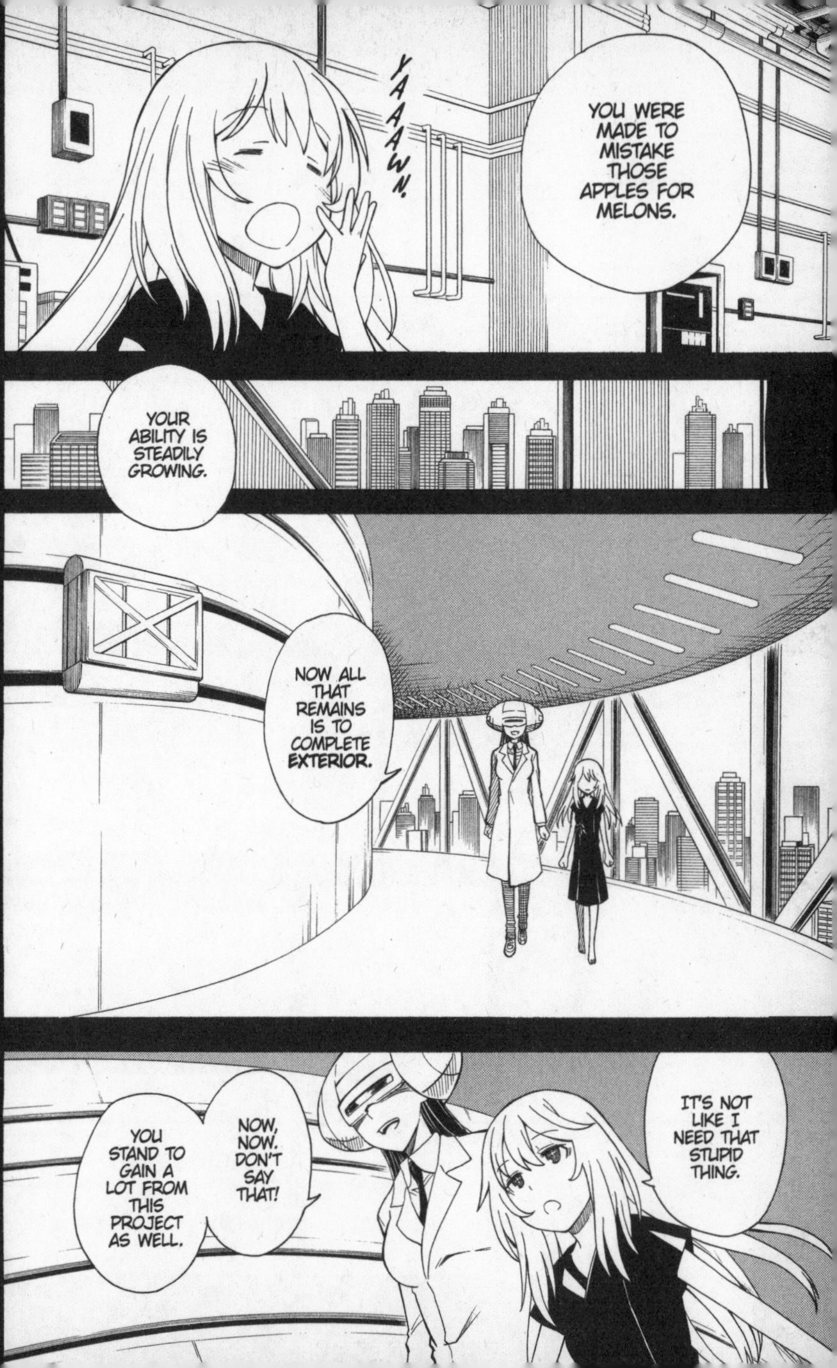
YOU WERE MADE TO MISTAKE THOSE APPLES FOR MELONS.
YAAAAWN.
YOUR ABILITY IS STEADILY GROWING.
NOW ALL THAT REMAINS IS TO COMPLETE EXTERIOR.
IT'S NOT LIKE I NEED THAT STUPID THING.
NOW, NOW. DON'T SAY THAT!
YOU STAND TO GAIN A LOT FROM THIS PROJECT AS WELL.

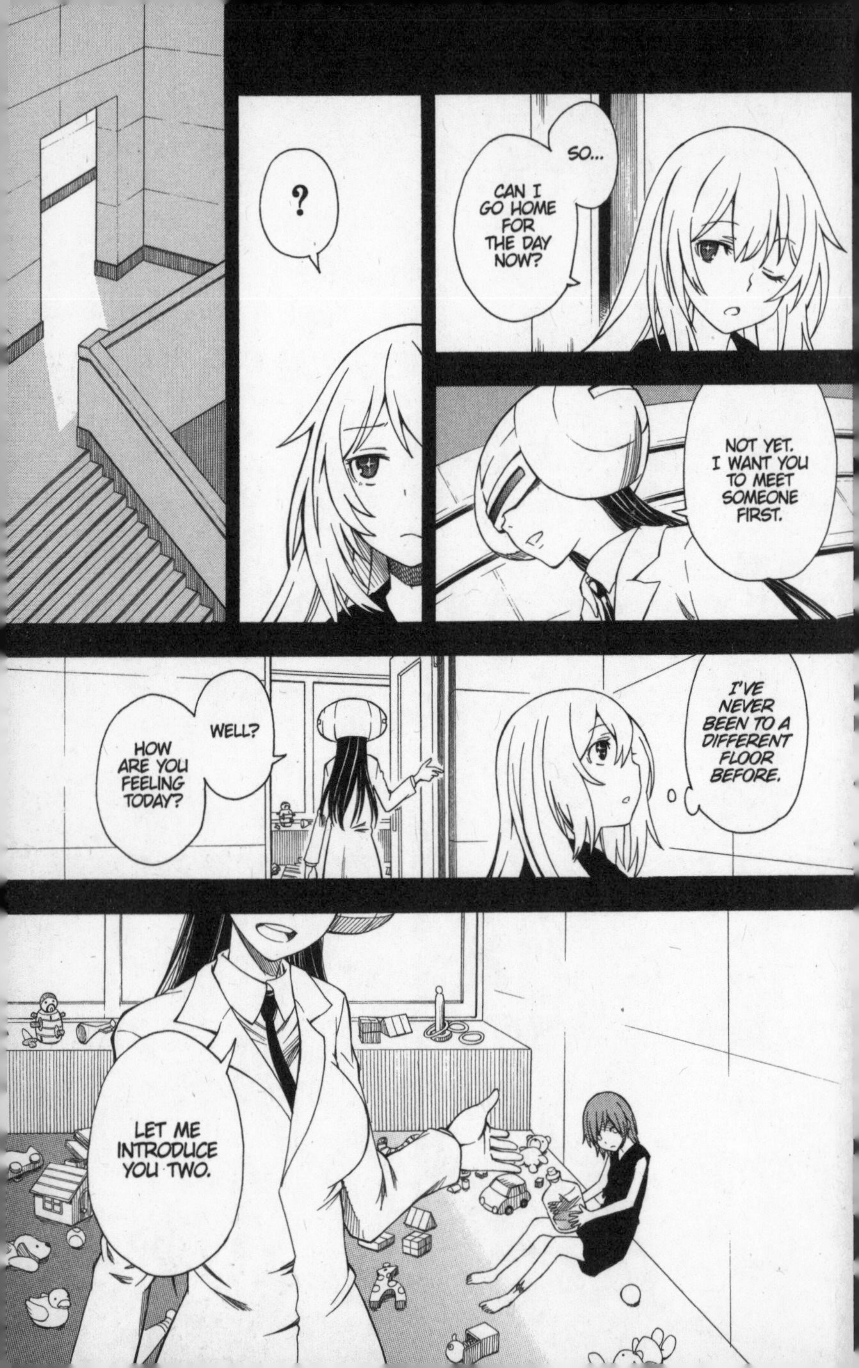
SO...
CAN I GO HOME FOR THE DAY NOW?
?
NOT YET. I WANT YOU TO MEET SOMEONE FIRST.
I'VE NEVER BEEN TO A DIFFERENT FLOOR BEFORE.
WELL? HOW ARE YOU FEELING TODAY?
LET ME INTRODUCE YOU TWO.

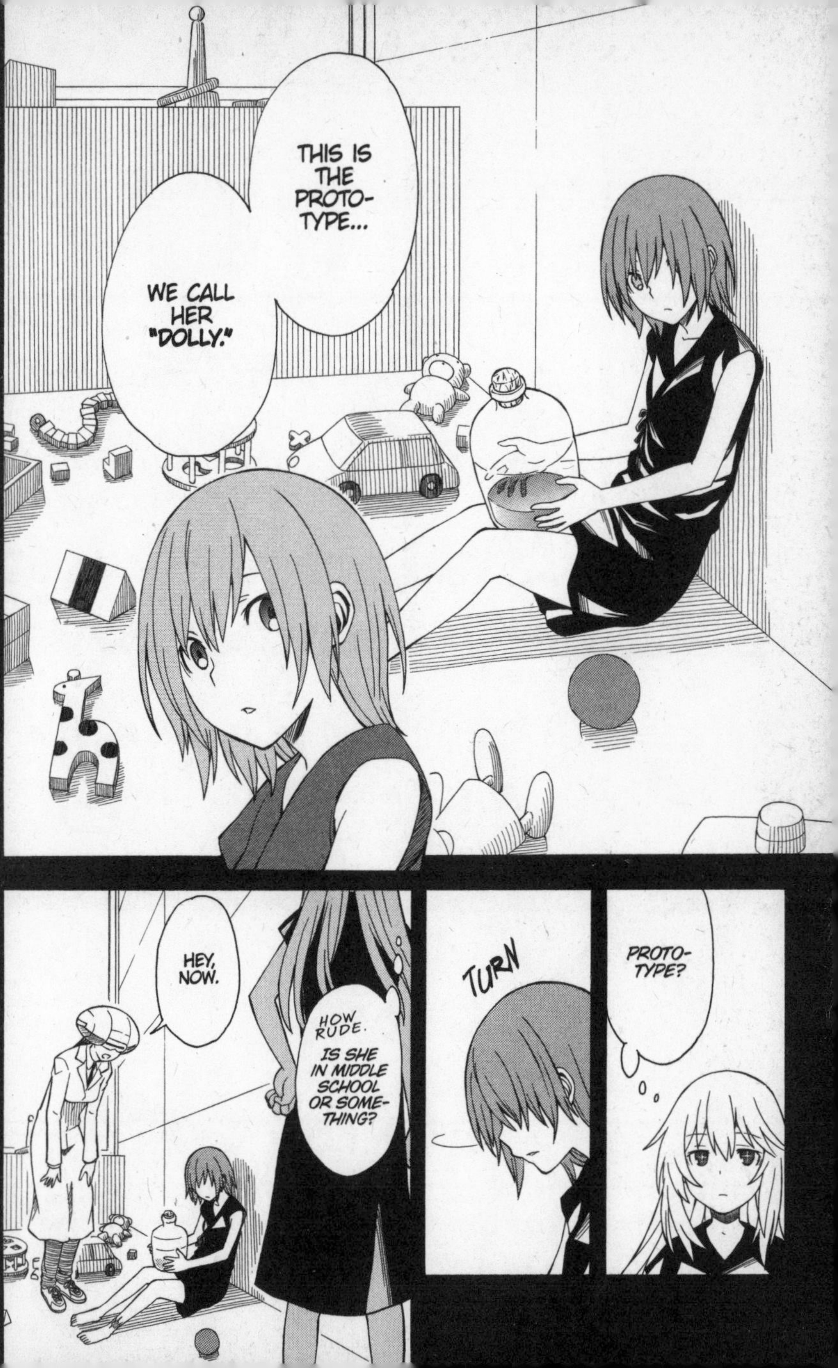
THIS IS THE PROTO-TYPE...
WE CALL HER "DOLLY."
PROTO-TYPE?
TURN
HEY, NOW.
HOW RUDE. IS SHE IN MIDDLE SCHOOL OR SOME-THING?

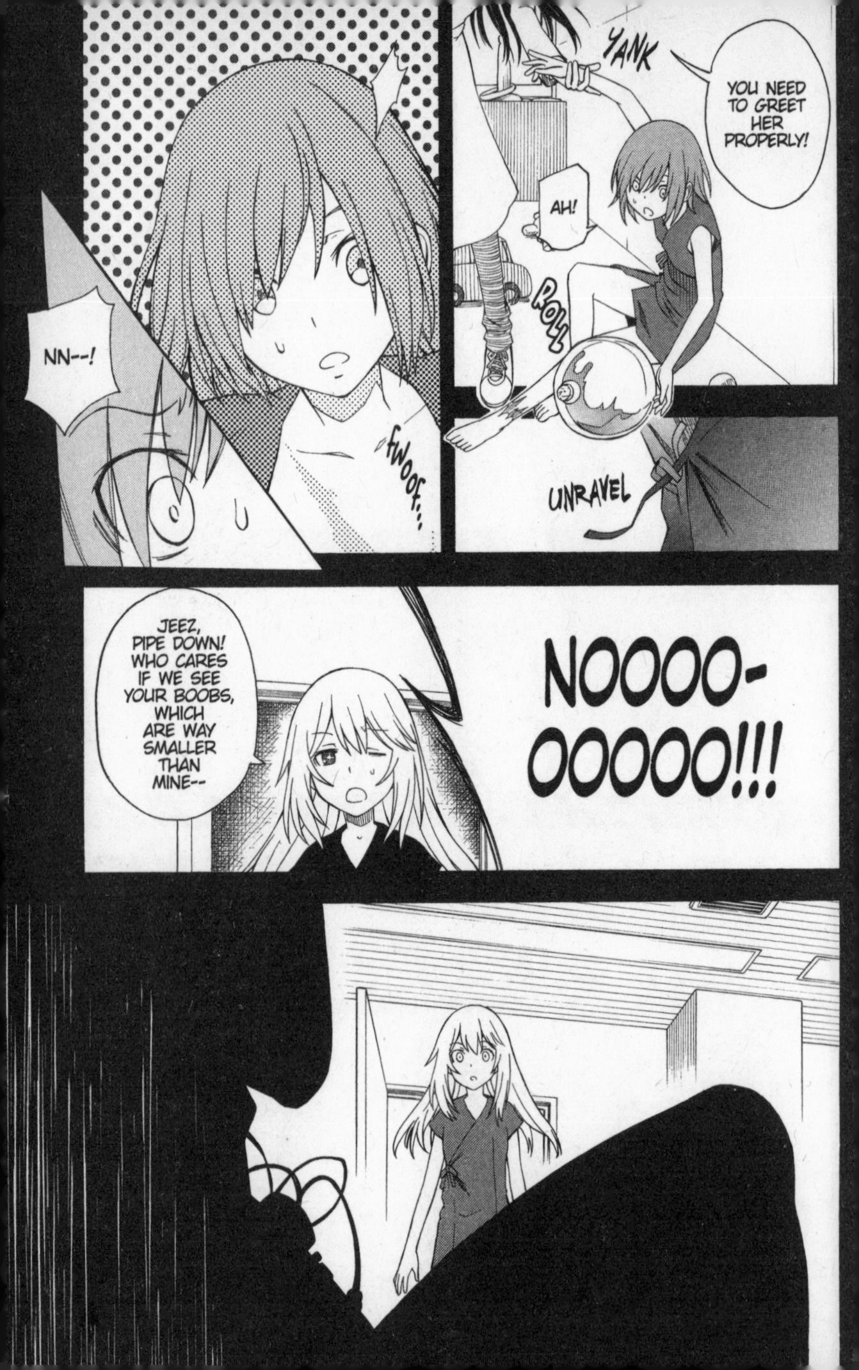
YANK
YOU NEED TO GREET HER PROPERLY!
AH!
ROLL
UNRAVEL
NN--!
FWOOF...
NOOOO-OOOOO!!!
JEEZ, PIPE DOWN! WHO CARES IF WE SEE YOUR BOOBS, WHICH ARE WAY SMALLER THAN MINE--

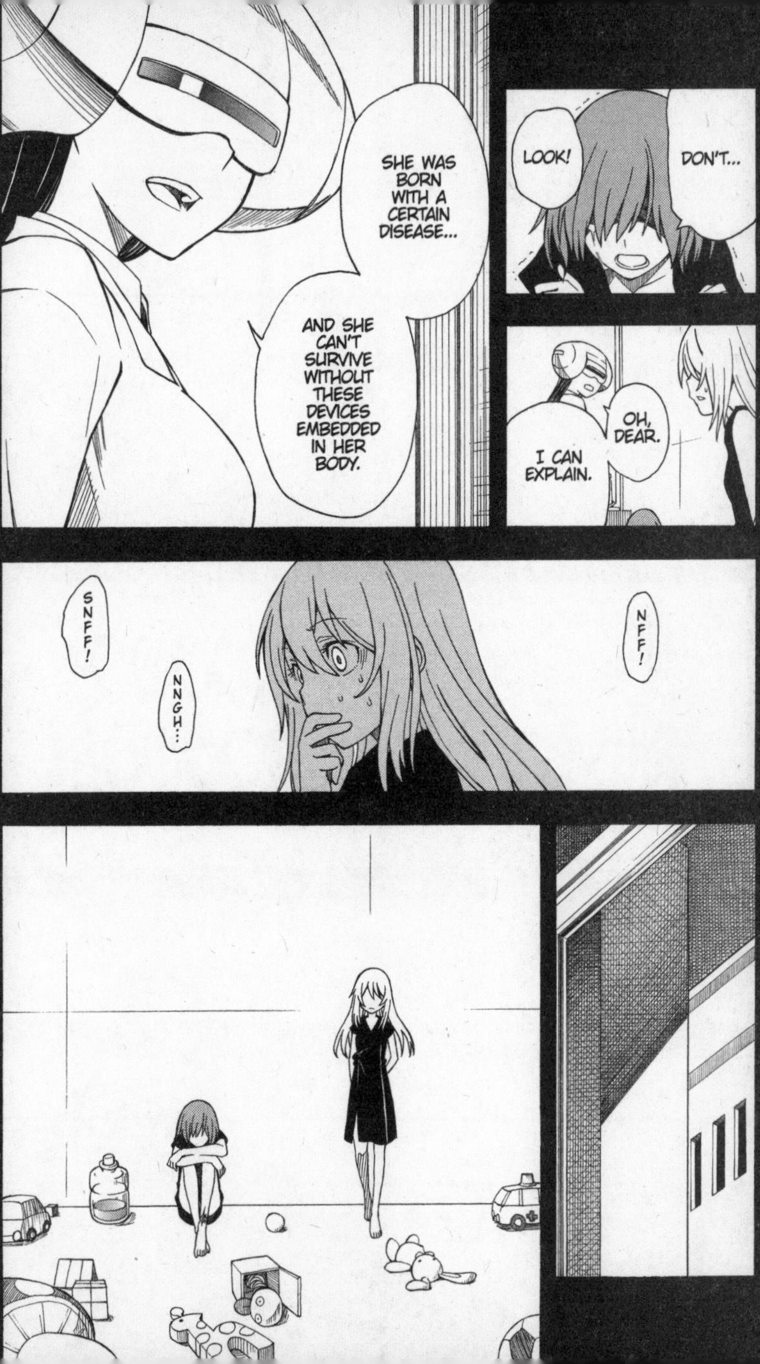
DON'T...
LOOK!
SHE WAS BORN WITH A CERTAIN DISEASE...
AND SHE CAN'T SURVIVE WITHOUT THESE DEVICES EMBEDDED IN HER BODY.
OH, DEAR.
I CAN EXPLAIN.
NFF!
SNFF!
NNGH...

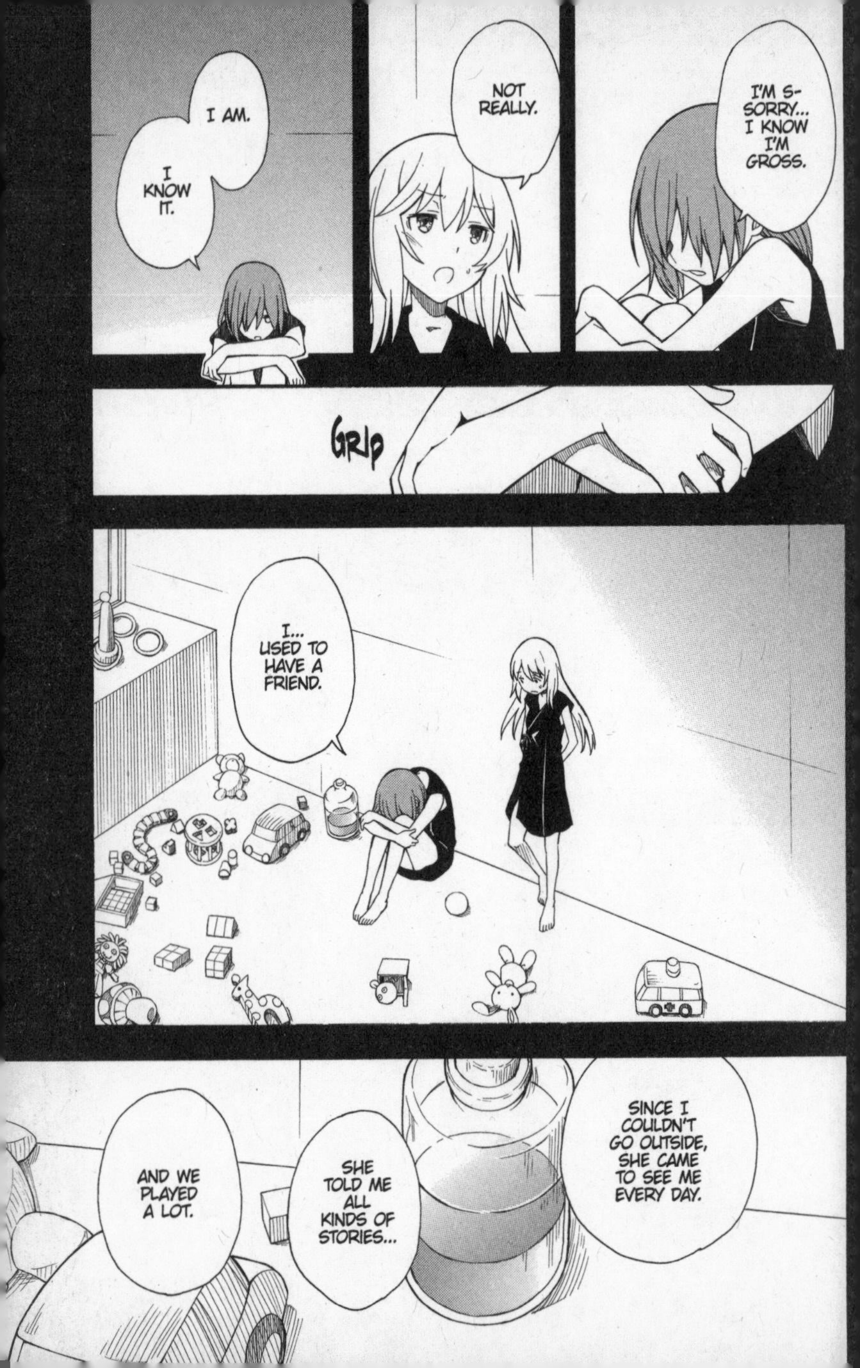
I'M S-SORRY... I KNOW I'M GROSS.
NOT REALLY.
I AM.
I KNOW IT.
GRIP
I... USED TO HAVE A FRIEND.
SINCE I COULDN'T GO OUTSIDE, SHE CAME TO SEE ME EVERY DAY.
SHE TOLD ME ALL KINDS OF STORIES...
AND WE PLAYED A LOT.

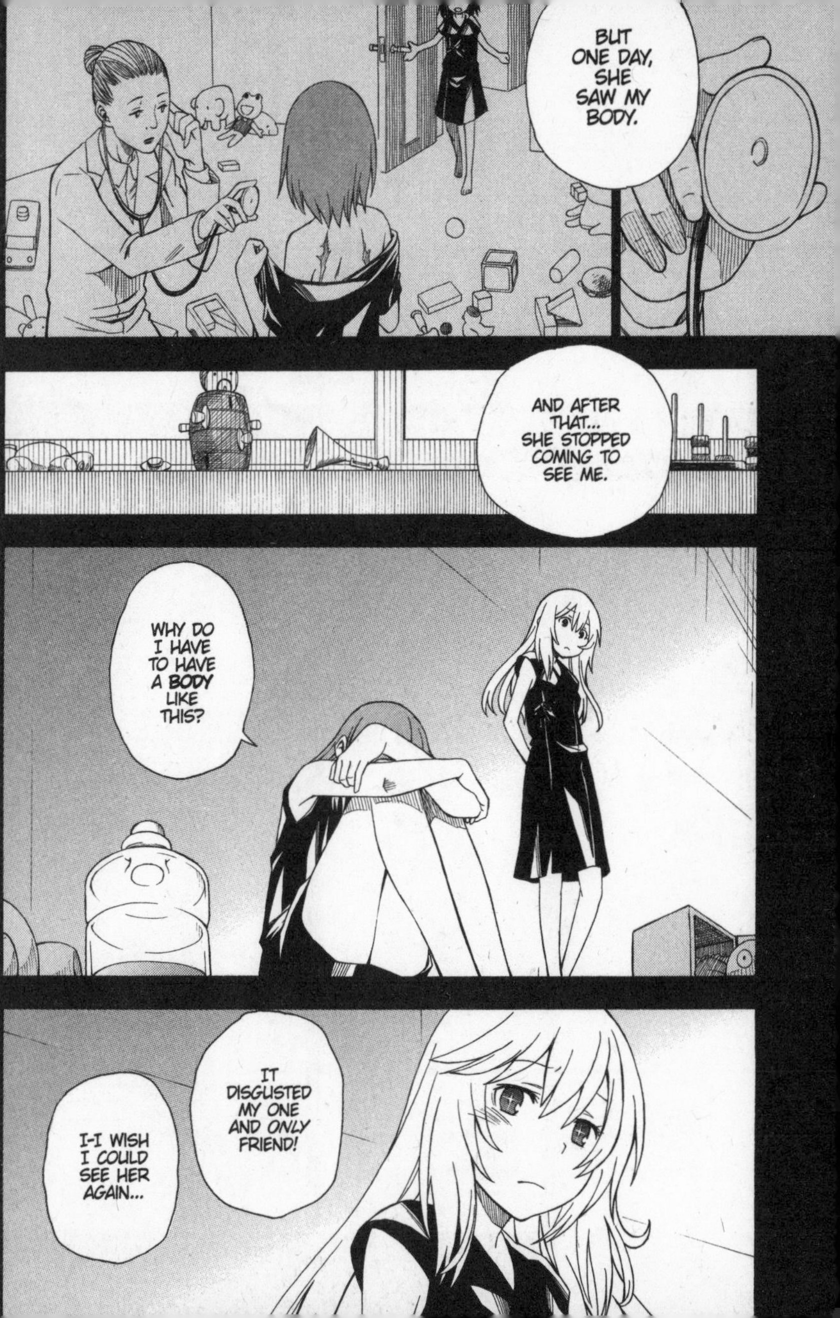
BUT ONE DAY, SHE SAW MY BODY.
AND AFTER THAT... SHE STOPPED COMING TO SEE ME.
WHY DO I HAVE TO HAVE A BODY LIKE THIS?
IT DISGUSTED MY ONE AND ONLY FRIEND!
I-I WISH I COULD SEE HER AGAIN...

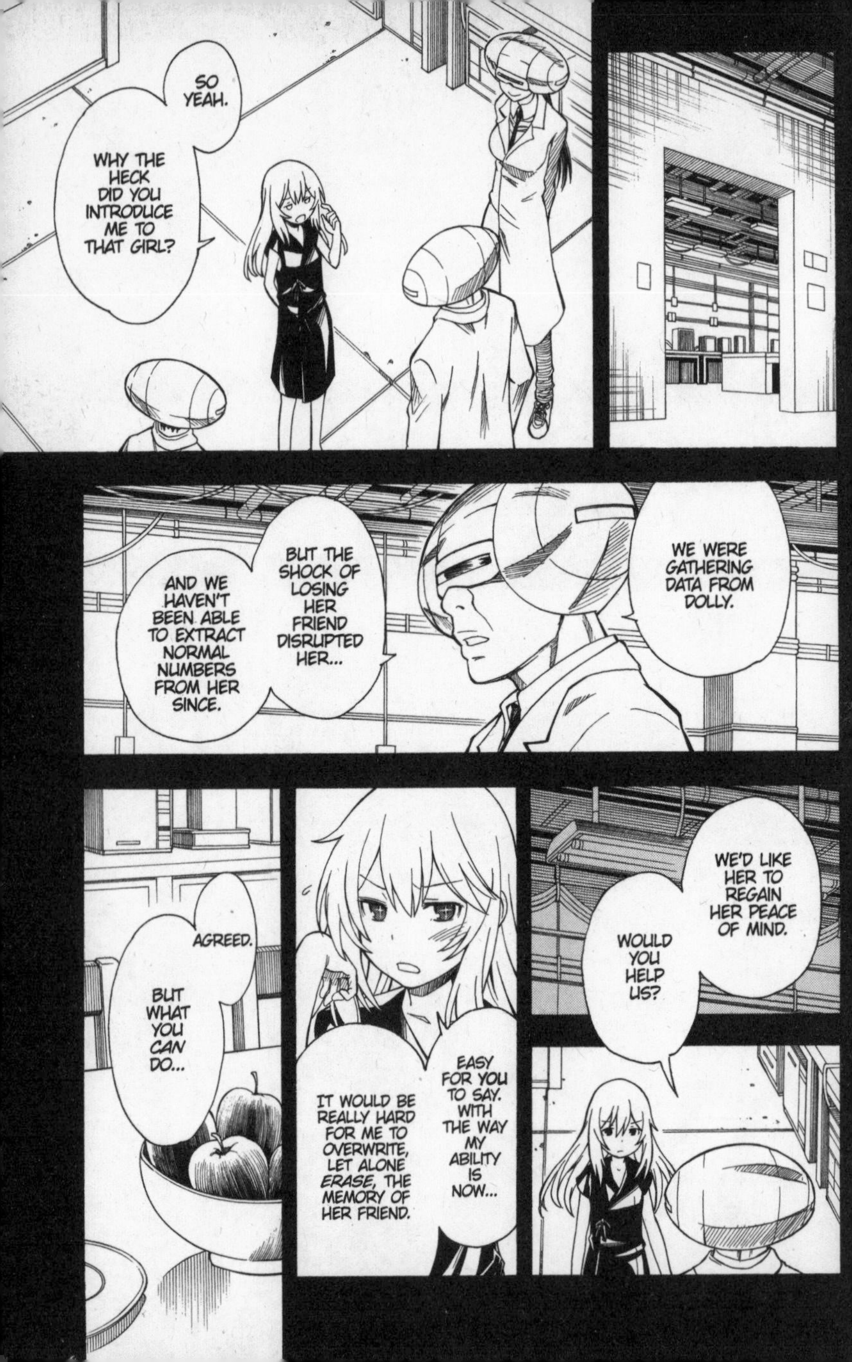
SO YEAH.
WHY THE HECK DID YOU INTRODUCE ME TO THAT GIRL?
WE WERE GATHERING DATA FROM DOLLY.
BUT THE SHOCK OF LOSING HER FRIEND DISRUPTED HER...
AND WE HAVEN'T BEEN ABLE TO EXTRACT NORMAL NUMBERS FROM HER SINCE.
WE'D LIKE HER TO REGAIN HER PEACE OF MIND.
WOULD YOU HELP US?
AGREED.
BUT WHAT YOU CAN DO...
EASY FOR YOU TO SAY. WITH THE WAY MY ABILITY IS NOW...
IT WOULD BE REALLY HARD FOR ME TO OVERWRITE, LET ALONE ERASE, THE MEMORY OF HER FRIEND.

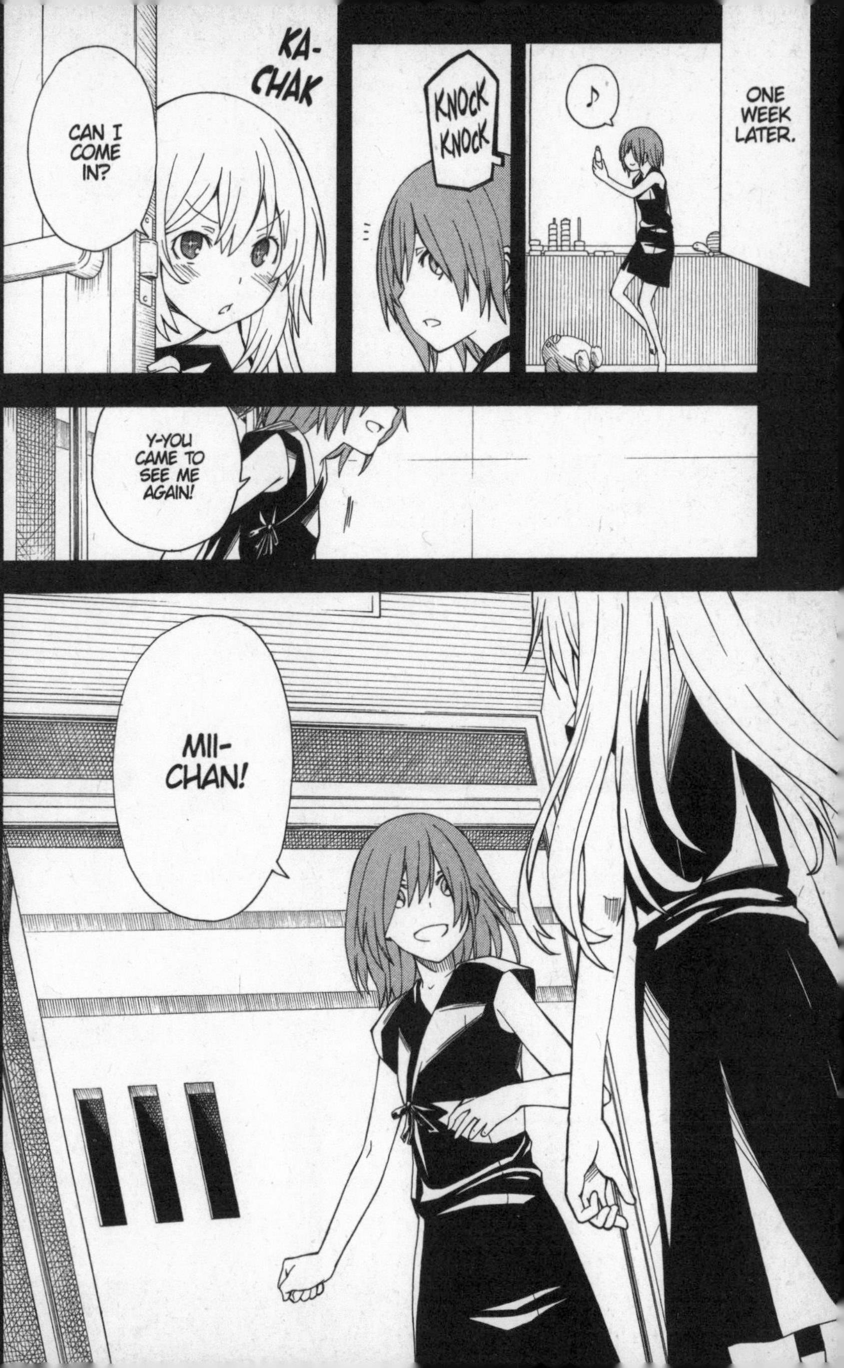
ONE WEEK LATER.
♪
KNOCK KNOCK
KA-CHAK
CAN I COME IN?
Y-YOU CAME TO SEE ME AGAIN!
MII-CHAN!

A Certain SCIENTIFIC Railgun

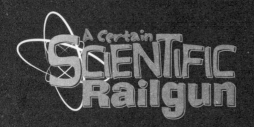

とある魔術の禁書目録外伝

とある科学の超電磁砲

レールガン

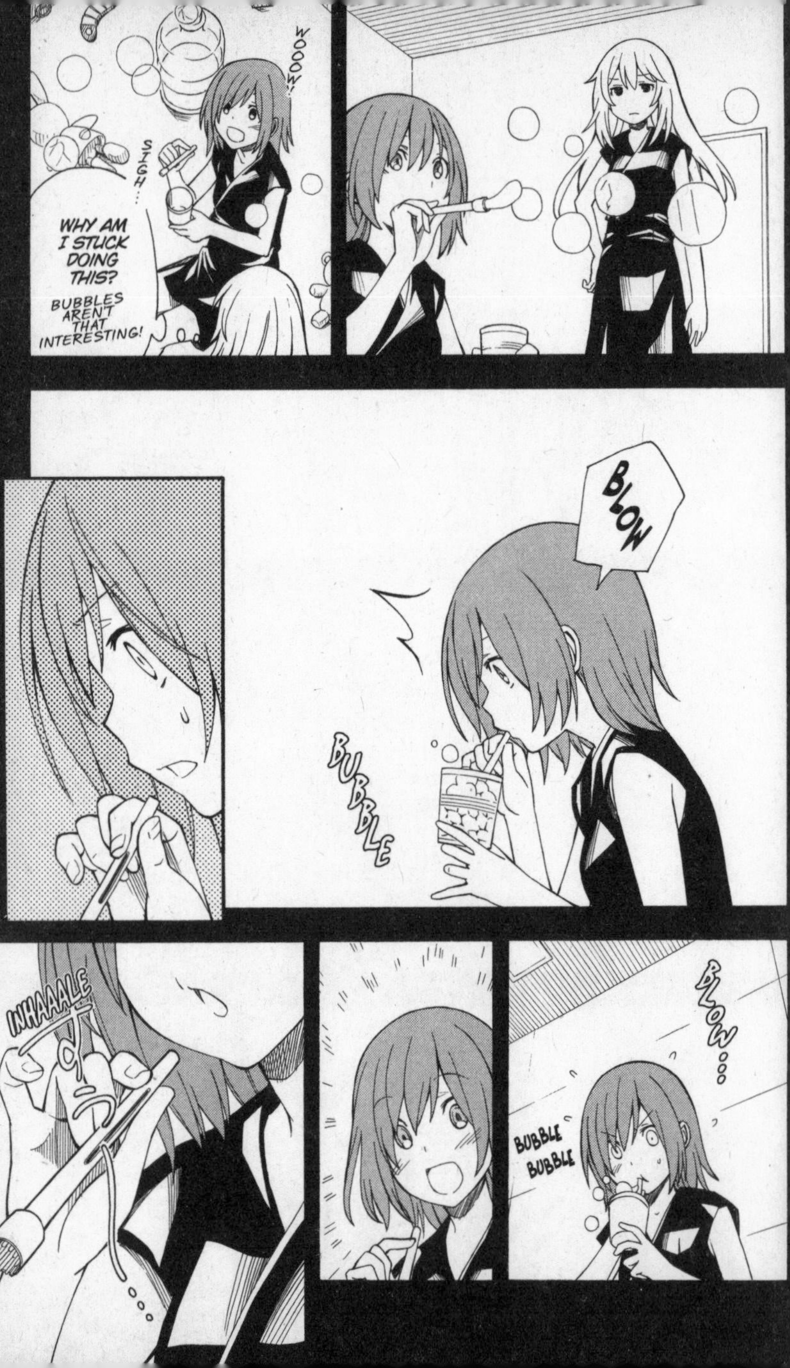
WOOOOW!
SIGH...
WHY AM I STUCK DOING THIS?
BUBBLES AREN'T THAT INTERESTING!
BLOW
BUBBLE
INHAAALE
BLOW...
BUBBLE BUBBLE

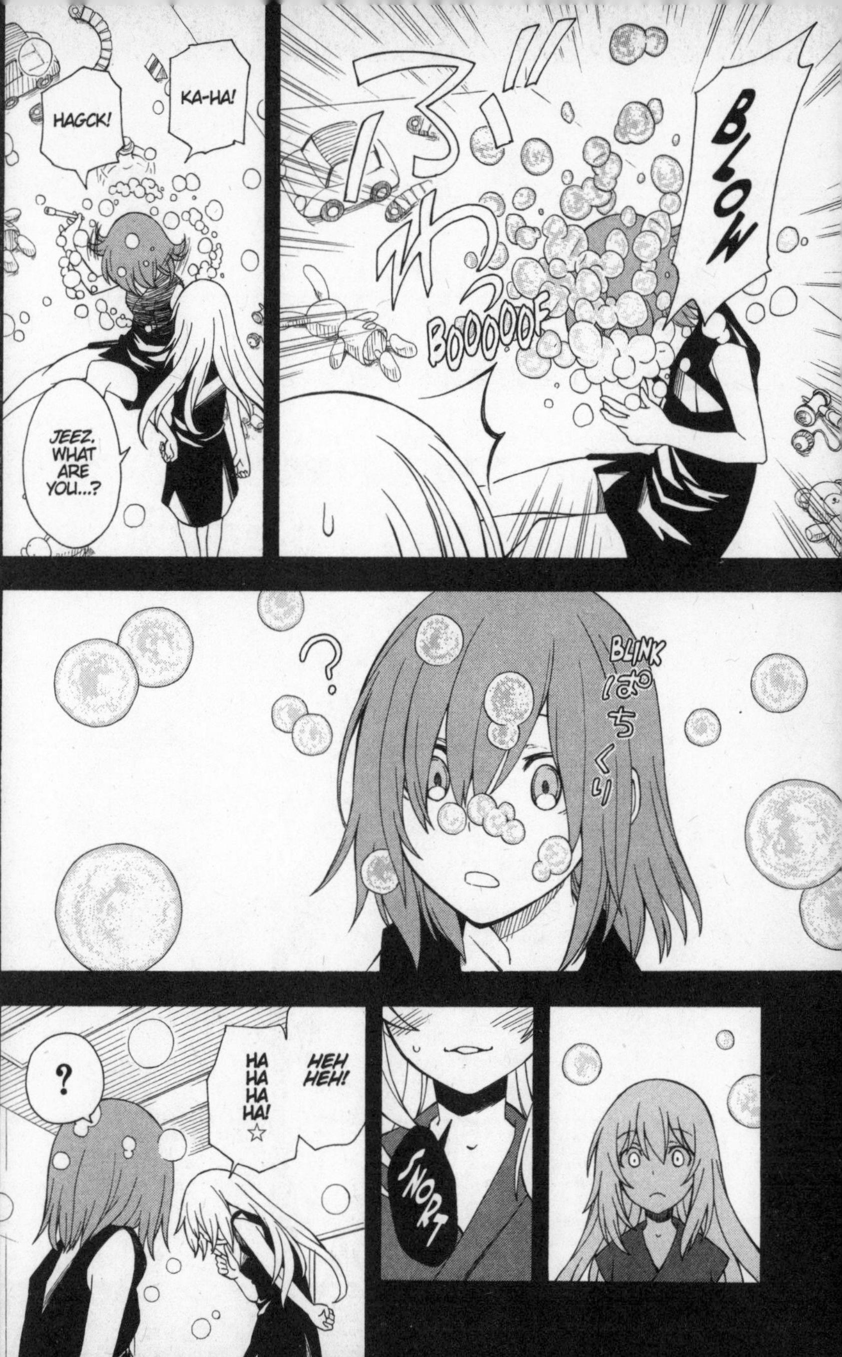

BLOW
ふぅ~
わっ
BOOOOOF
KA-HA!
HAGCK!
JEEZ. WHAT ARE YOU...?
?
BLINK
ぱちくり
SNORT
HEH HEH!
HA HA HA HA! ☆
?

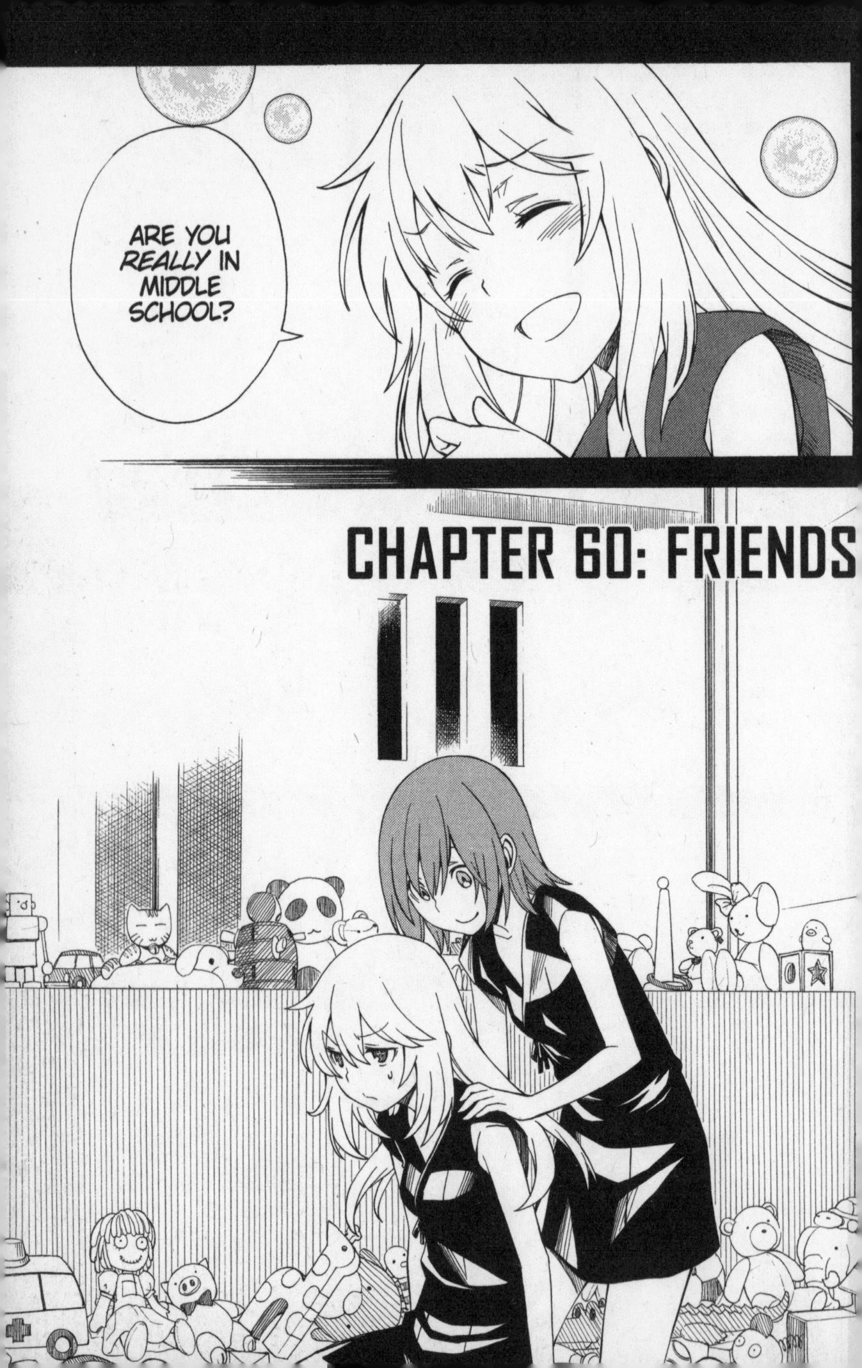
ARE YOU REALLY IN MIDDLE SCHOOL?
CHAPTER 60: FRIENDS

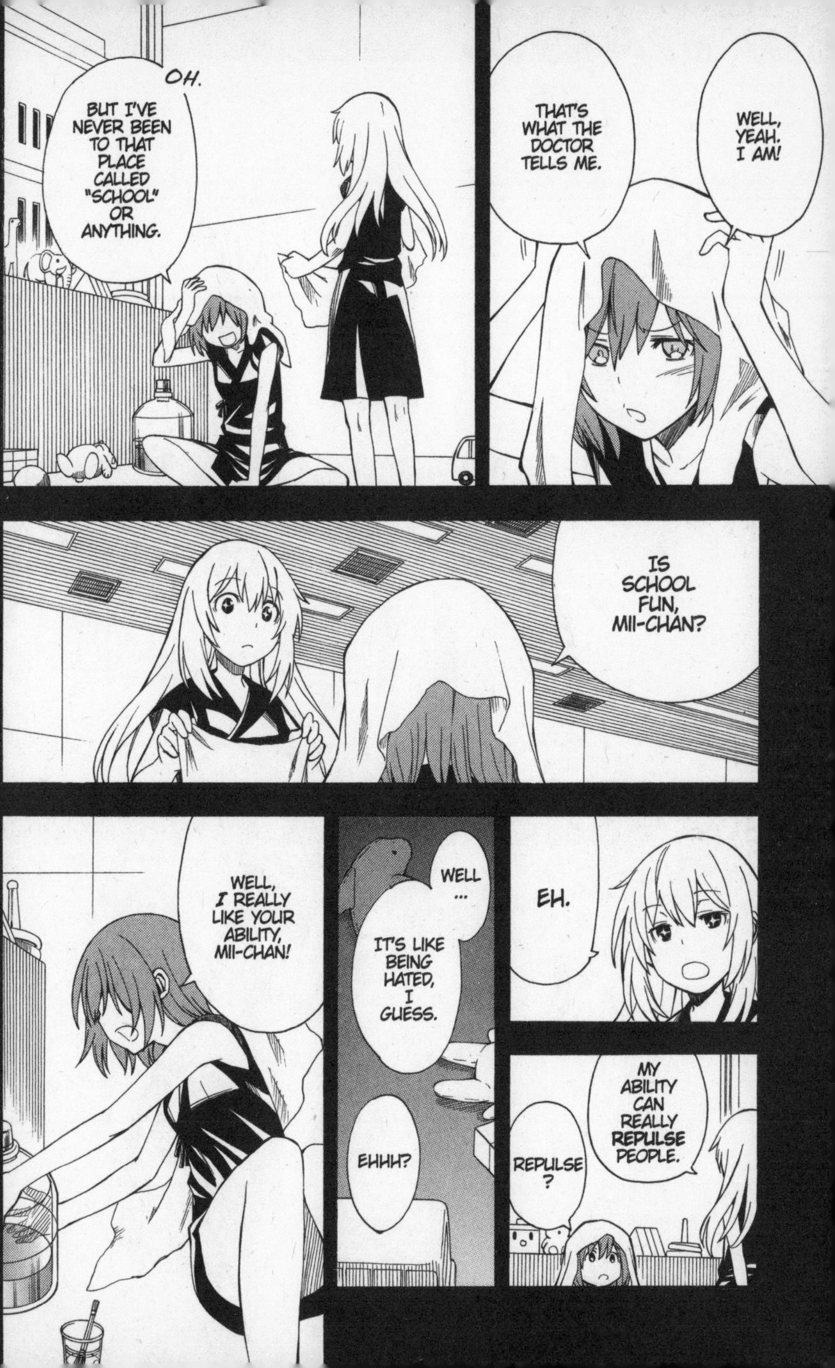
WELL, YEAH. I AM!
THAT'S WHAT THE DOCTOR TELLS ME.
OH.
BUT I'VE NEVER BEEN TO THAT PLACE CALLED "SCHOOL" OR ANYTHING.
IS SCHOOL FUN, MII-CHAN?
EH.
MY ABILITY CAN REALLY REPULSE PEOPLE.
REPULSE?
WELL...
IT'S LIKE BEING HATED, I GUESS.
EHHH?
WELL, *I* REALLY LIKE YOUR ABILITY, MII-CHAN!

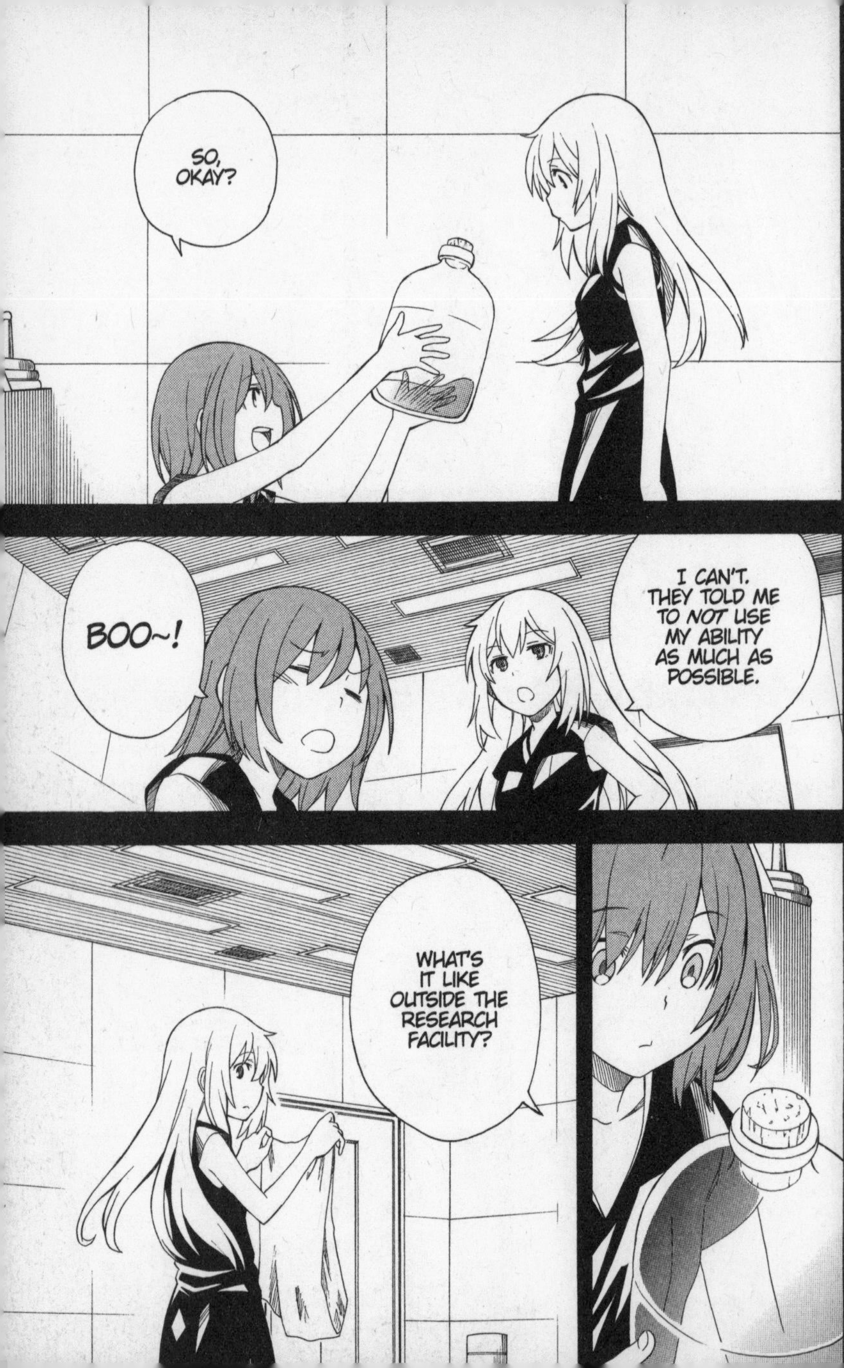
SO, OKAY?
I CAN'T. THEY TOLD ME TO *NOT* USE MY ABILITY AS MUCH AS POSSIBLE.
BOO~!
WHAT'S IT LIKE OUTSIDE THE RESEARCH FACILITY?

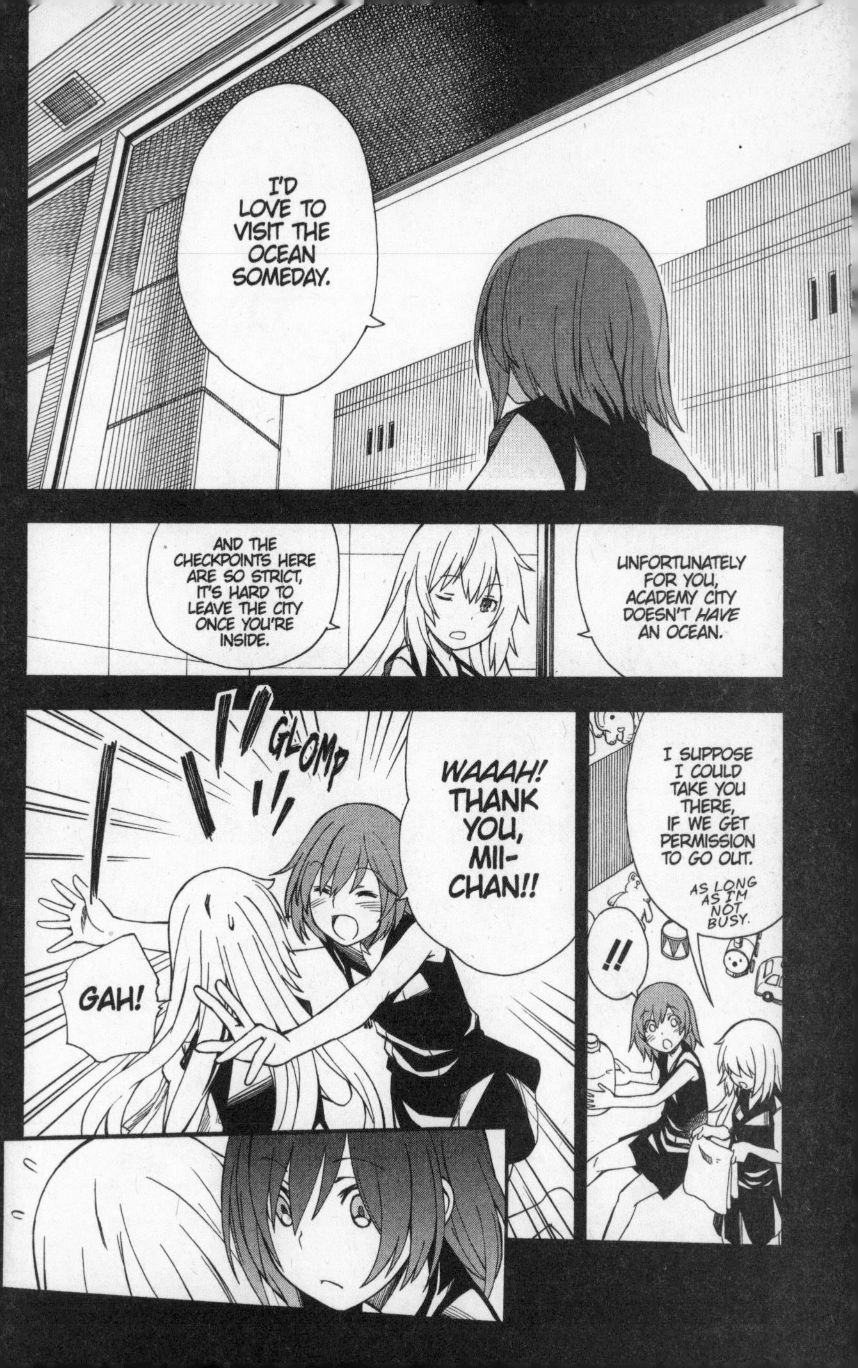
I'D LOVE TO VISIT THE OCEAN SOMEDAY.
UNFORTUNATELY FOR YOU, ACADEMY CITY DOESN'T *HAVE* AN OCEAN.
AND THE CHECKPOINTS HERE ARE SO STRICT, IT'S HARD TO LEAVE THE CITY ONCE YOU'RE INSIDE.
I SUPPOSE I COULD TAKE YOU THERE, IF WE GET PERMISSION TO GO OUT.
AS LONG AS I'M NOT BUSY.
!!
WAAAH! THANK YOU, MII-CHAN!!
GLOMP
GAH!

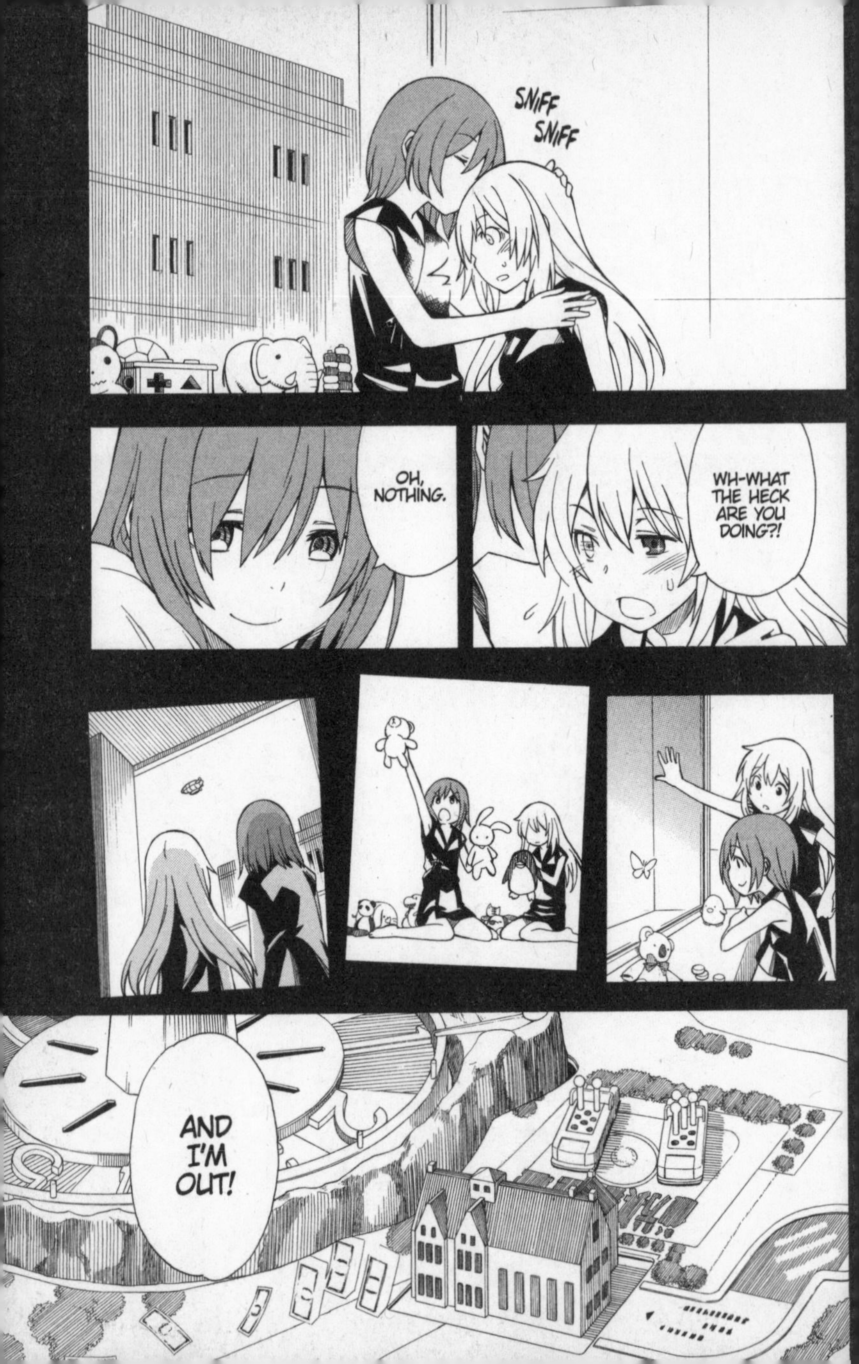
SNIFF
SNIFF
WH-WHAT THE HECK ARE YOU DOING?!
OH, NOTHING.
AND I'M OUT!

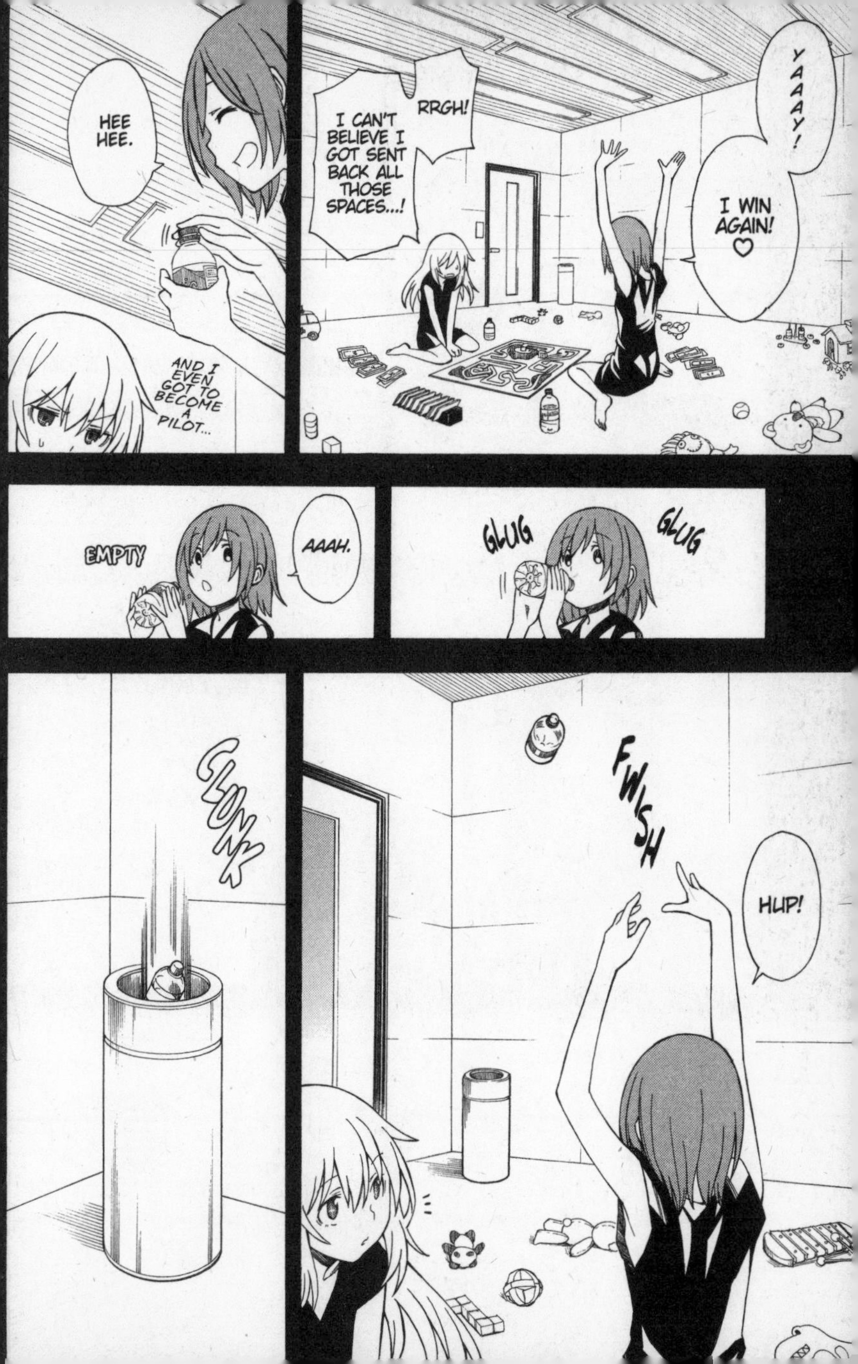
YAAAAY!
I WIN AGAIN! ♡
RRGH!
I CAN'T BELIEVE I GOT SENT BACK ALL THOSE SPACES...!
HEE HEE.
AND I EVEN GOT TO BECOME A PILOT...
GLUG
GLUG
AAAH.
EMPTY
HUP!
FWISH
CLONK

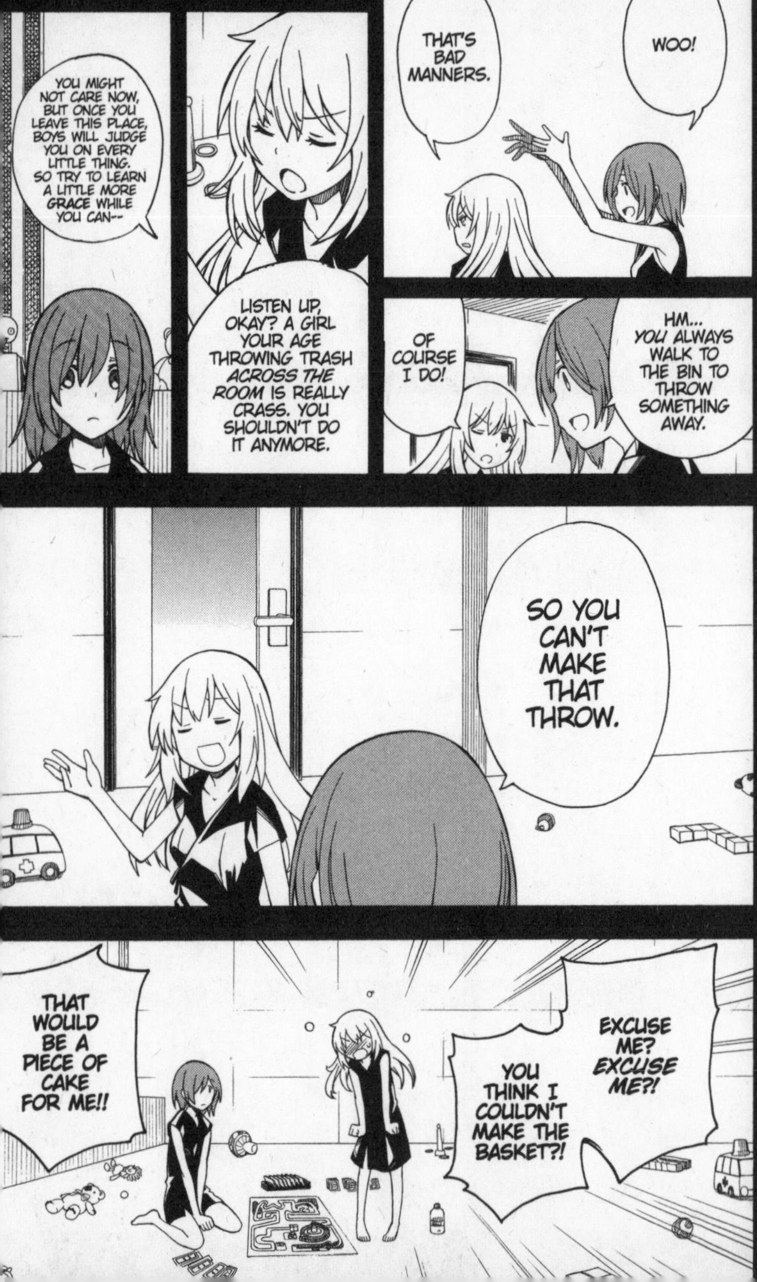
WOO!
THAT'S BAD MANNERS.
HM... YOU ALWAYS WALK TO THE BIN TO THROW SOMETHING AWAY.
OF COURSE I DO!
LISTEN UP, OKAY? A GIRL YOUR AGE THROWING TRASH ACROSS THE ROOM IS REALLY CRASS. YOU SHOULDN'T DO IT ANYMORE.
YOU MIGHT NOT CARE NOW, BUT ONCE YOU LEAVE THIS PLACE, BOYS WILL JUDGE YOU ON EVERY LITTLE THING. SO TRY TO LEARN A LITTLE MORE GRACE WHILE YOU CAN--
SO YOU CAN'T MAKE THAT THROW.
EXCUSE ME? EXCUSE ME?!
YOU THINK I COULDN'T MAKE THE BASKET?!
THAT WOULD BE A PIECE OF CAKE FOR ME!!

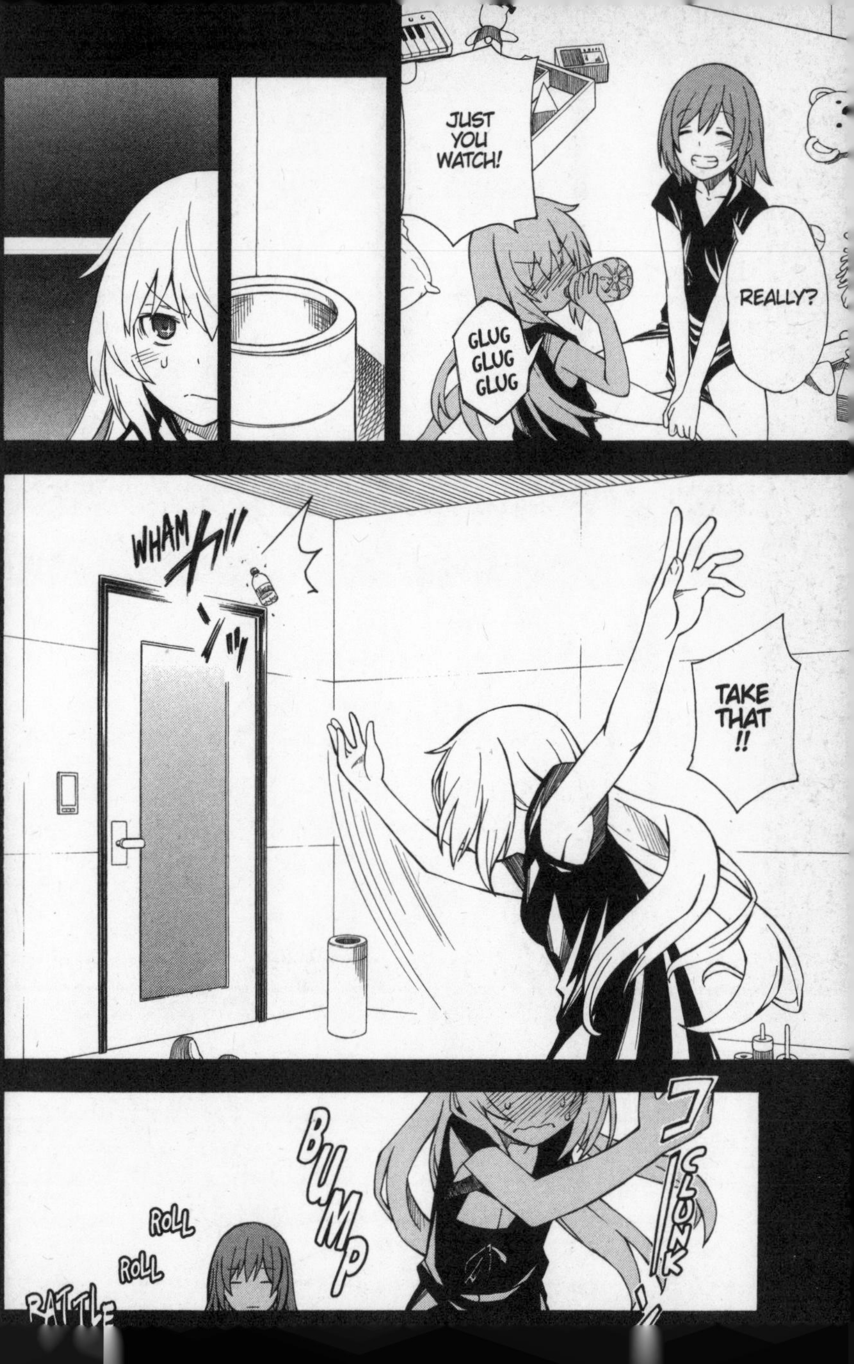
REALLY?
JUST YOU WATCH!
GLUG GLUG GLUG
TAKE THAT!!
WHAM
CLONK
BUMP
ROLL
ROLL
RATTLE

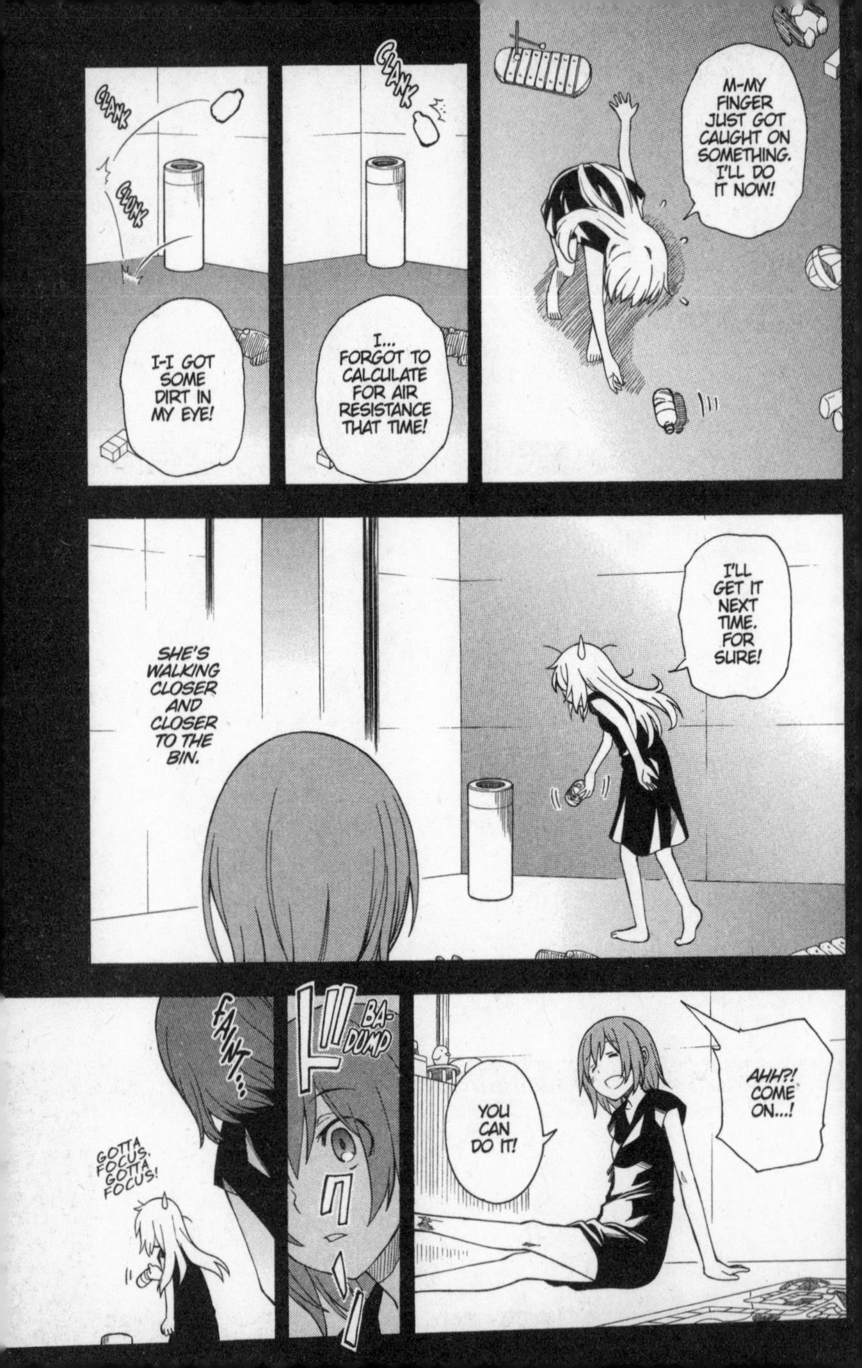
M-MY FINGER JUST GOT CAUGHT ON SOMETHING. I'LL DO IT NOW!
CLANK
I... FORGOT TO CALCULATE FOR AIR RESISTANCE THAT TIME!
CLANK
CLUNK
I-I GOT SOME DIRT IN MY EYE!
I'LL GET IT NEXT TIME. FOR SURE!
SHE'S WALKING CLOSER AND CLOSER TO THE BIN.
AHH?! COME ON...!
YOU CAN DO IT!
BA-DUMP
FAINT...
GOTTA FOCUS. GOTTA FOCUS!

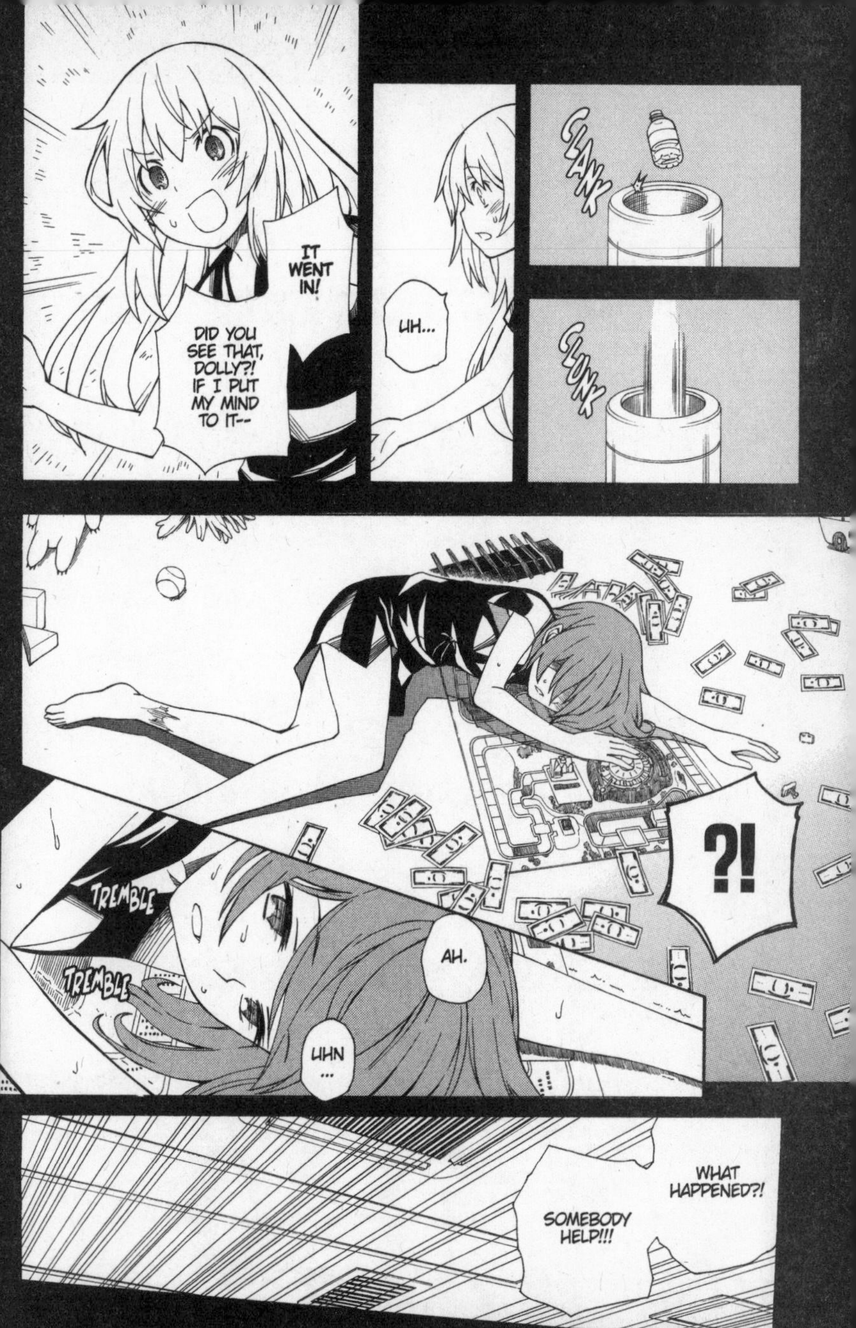
IT WENT IN!
DID YOU SEE THAT, DOLLY?! IF I PUT MY MIND TO IT--
UH...
CLANK
CLUNK
?!
TREMBLE
TREMBLE
AH.
UHN ...
WHAT HAPPENED?!
SOMEBODY HELP!!!

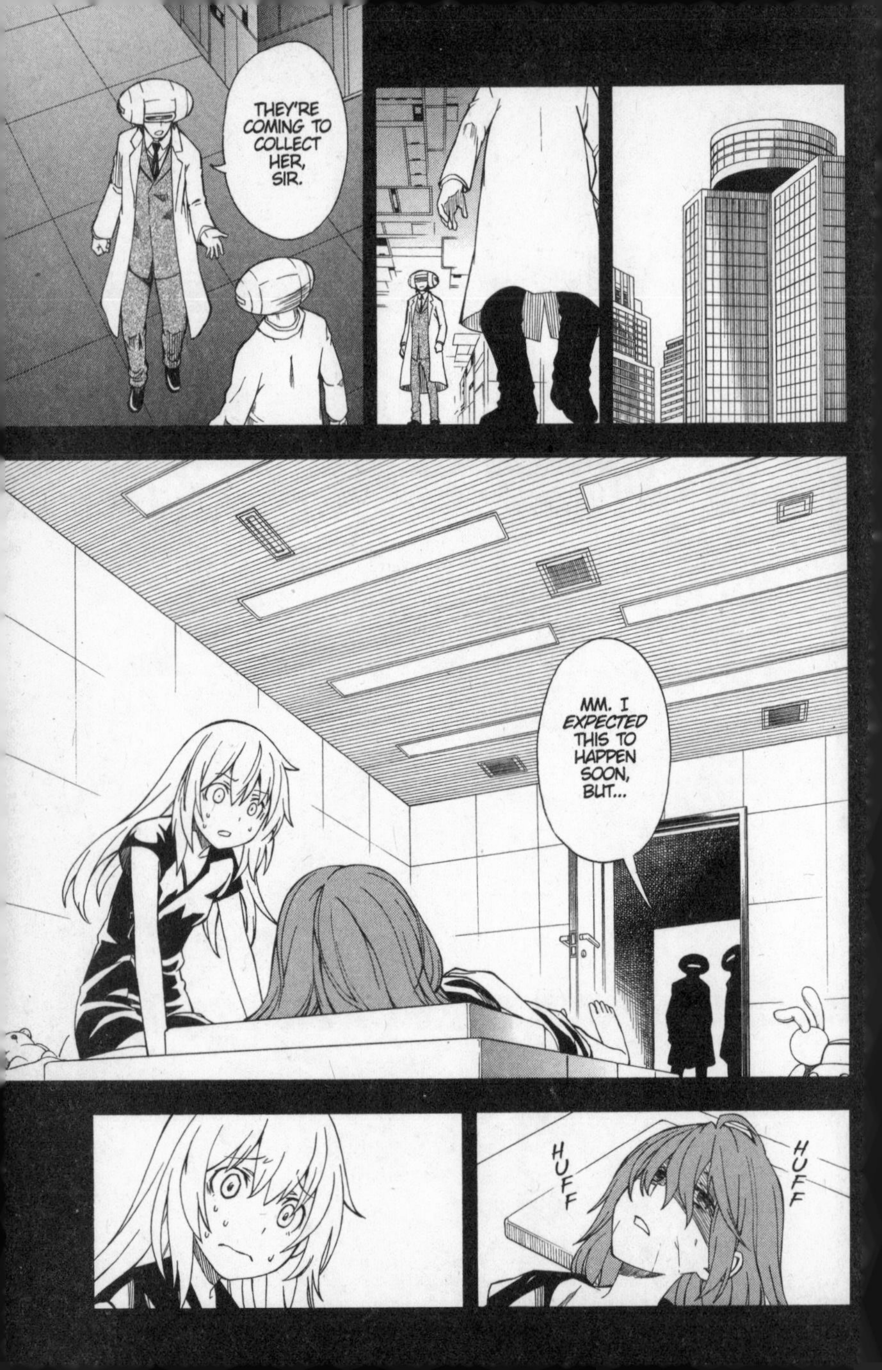
THEY'RE COMING TO COLLECT HER, SIR.
MM. I EXPECTED THIS TO HAPPEN SOON, BUT...
HUFF
HUFF

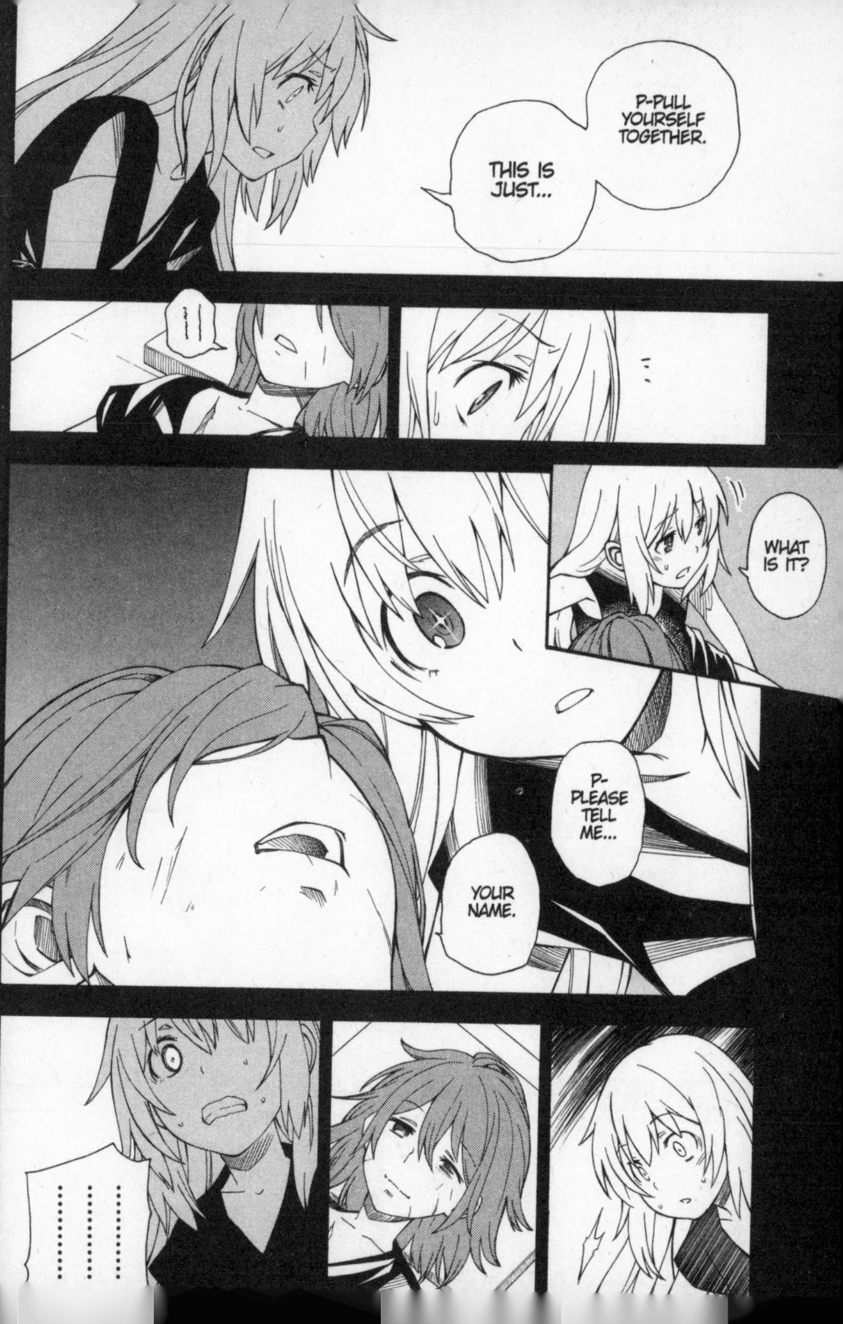
P-PULL YOURSELF TOGETHER.
THIS IS JUST...
WHAT IS IT?
P-PLEASE TELL ME...
YOUR NAME.

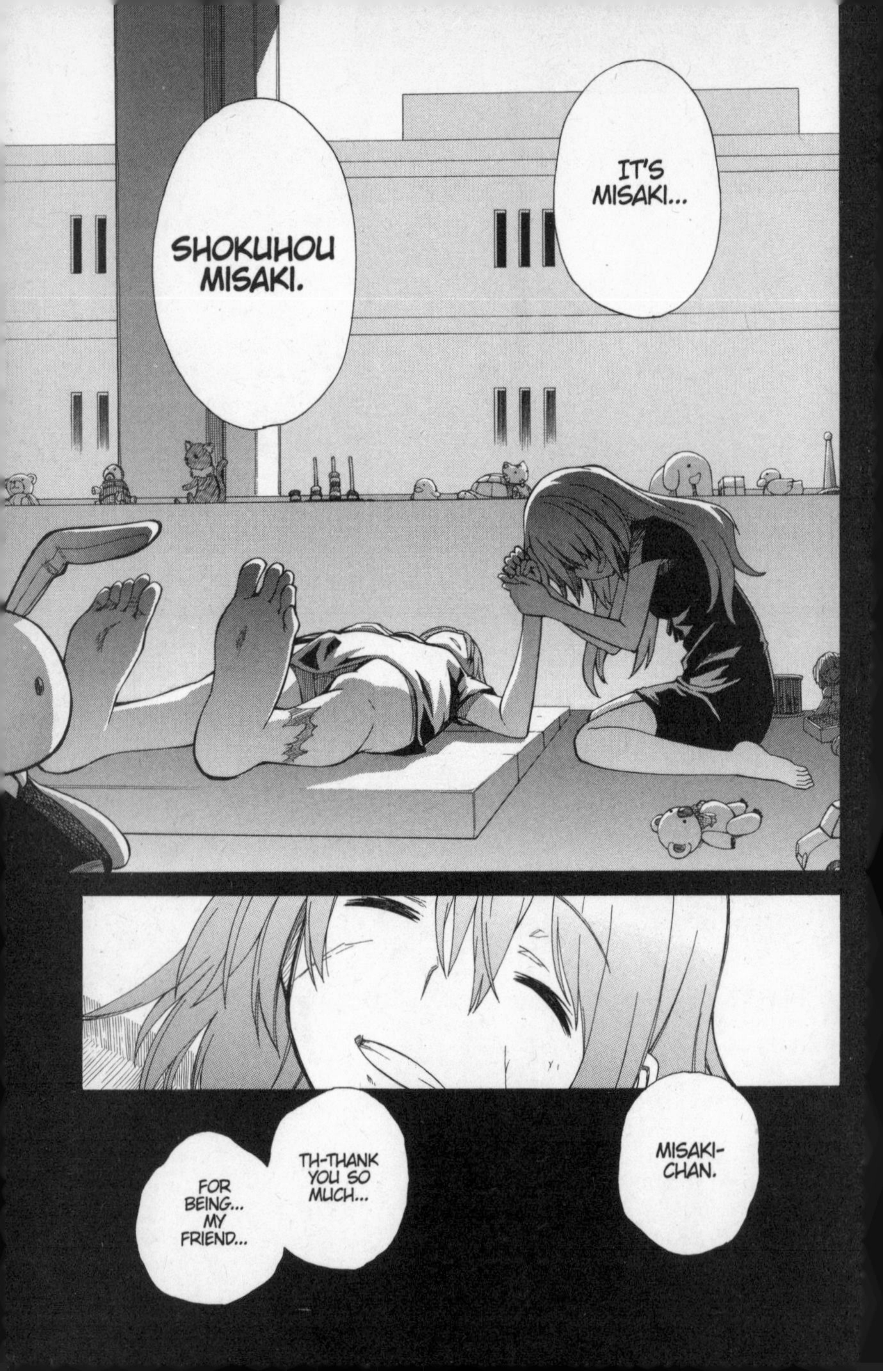
IT'S MISAKI...
SHOKUHOU MISAKI.
MISAKI-CHAN.
TH-THANK YOU SO MUCH...
FOR BEING... MY FRIEND...

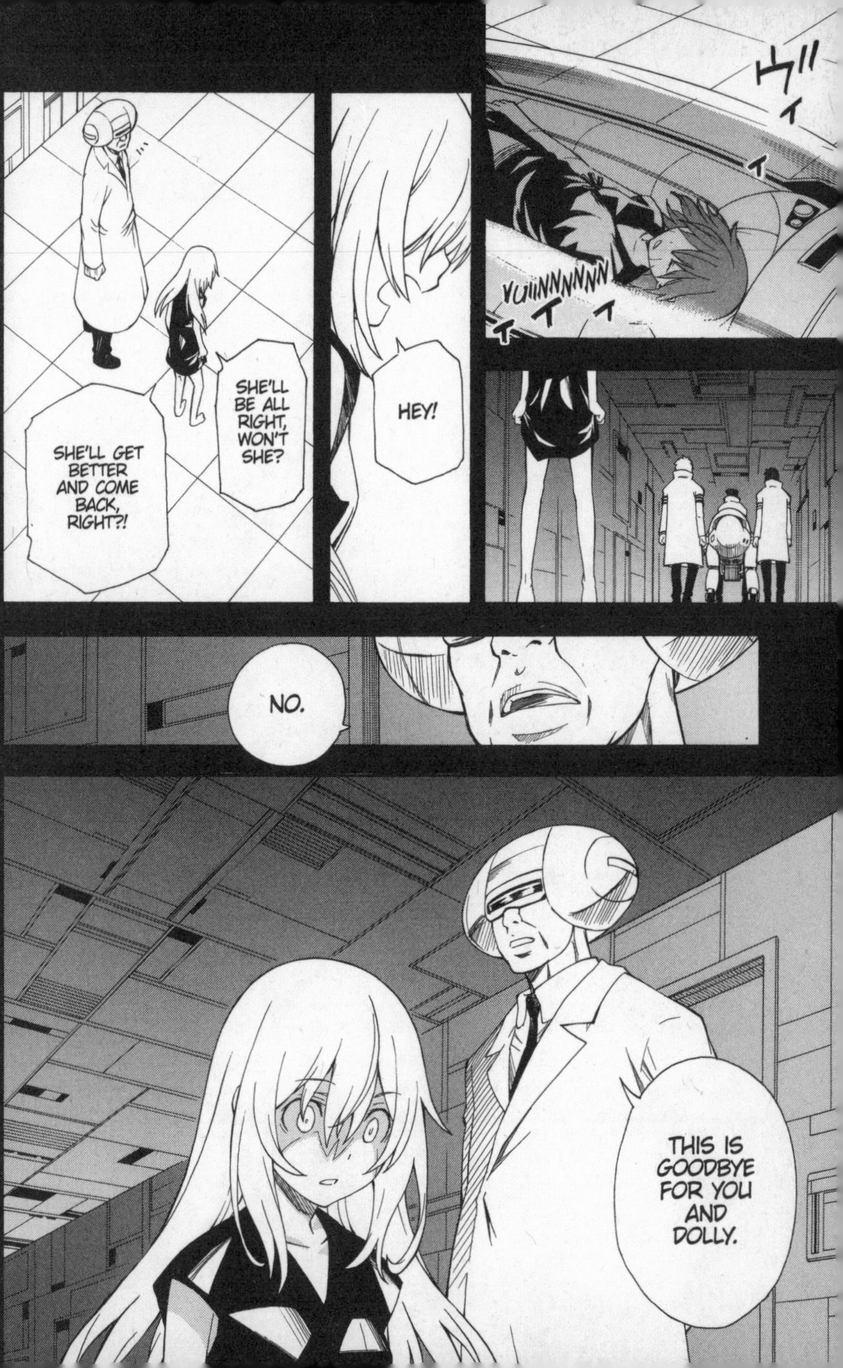
VUIINNNNNN
HEY!
SHE'LL BE ALL RIGHT, WON'T SHE?
SHE'LL GET BETTER AND COME BACK, RIGHT?!
NO.
THIS IS GOODBYE FOR YOU AND DOLLY.

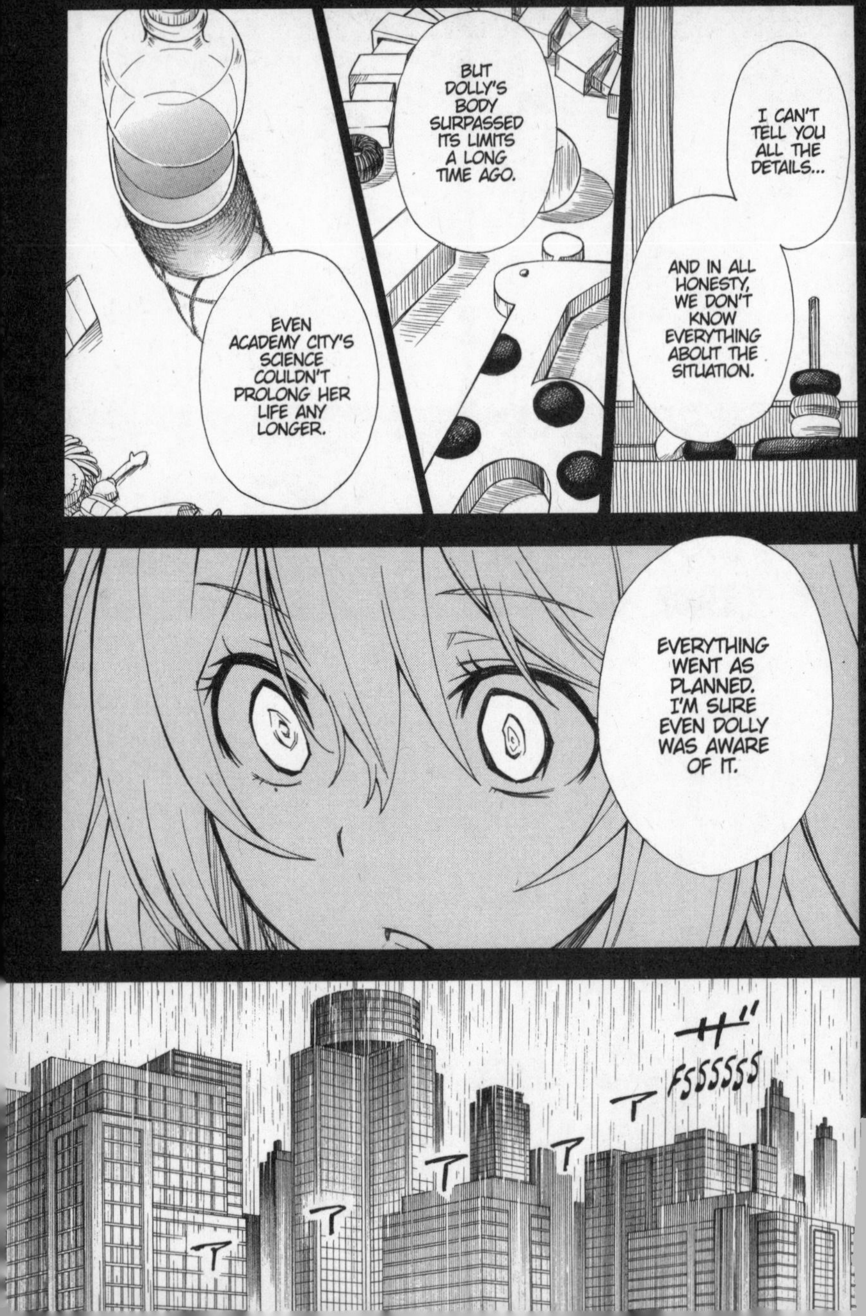
I CAN'T TELL YOU ALL THE DETAILS...
AND IN ALL HONESTY, WE DON'T KNOW EVERYTHING ABOUT THE SITUATION.
BUT DOLLY'S BODY SURPASSED ITS LIMITS A LONG TIME AGO.
EVEN ACADEMY CITY'S SCIENCE COULDN'T PROLONG HER LIFE ANY LONGER.
EVERYTHING WENT AS PLANNED. I'M SURE EVEN DOLLY WAS AWARE OF IT.
FSSSSSS

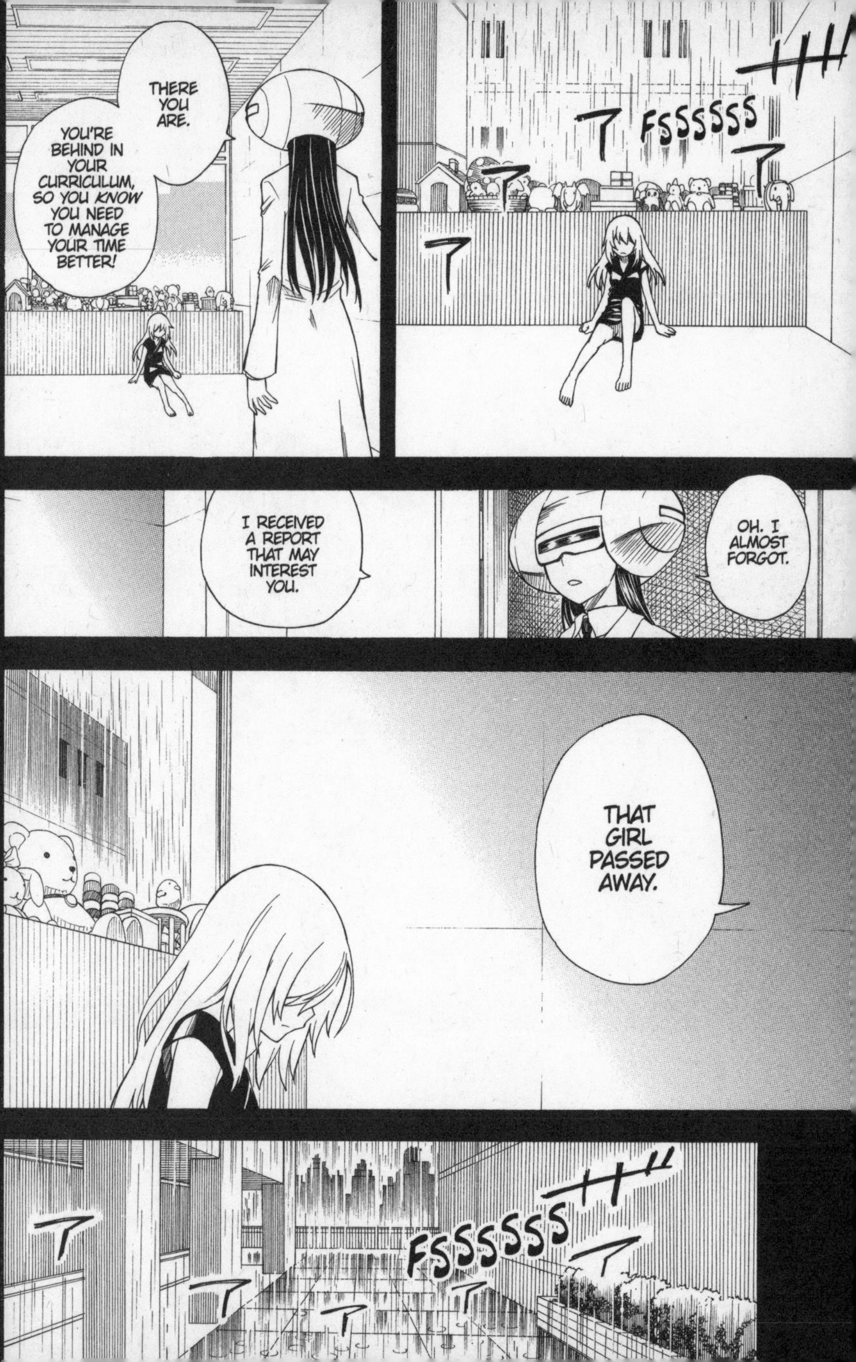

THERE YOU ARE.
YOU'RE BEHIND IN YOUR CURRICULUM, SO YOU *KNOW* YOU NEED TO MANAGE YOUR TIME BETTER!
FSSSSSS
I RECEIVED A REPORT THAT MAY INTEREST YOU.
OH. I ALMOST FORGOT.
THAT GIRL PASSED AWAY.
FSSSSSS

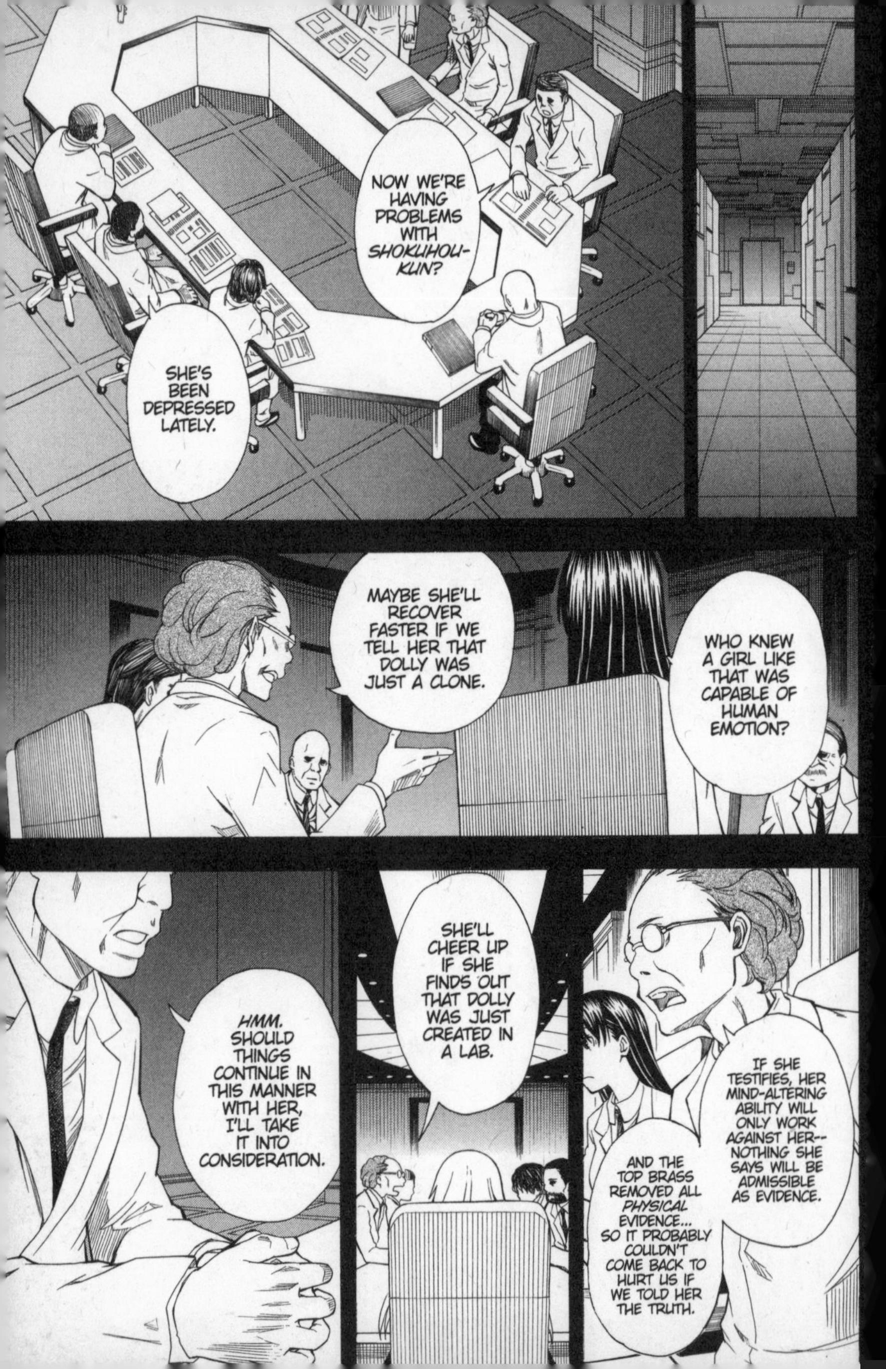
NOW WE'RE HAVING PROBLEMS WITH *SHOKUHOU-KUN*?
SHE'S BEEN DEPRESSED LATELY.
WHO KNEW A GIRL LIKE THAT WAS CAPABLE OF HUMAN EMOTION?
MAYBE SHE'LL RECOVER FASTER IF WE TELL HER THAT DOLLY WAS JUST A CLONE.
IF SHE TESTIFIES, HER MIND-ALTERING ABILITY WILL ONLY WORK AGAINST HER-- NOTHING SHE SAYS WILL BE ADMISSIBLE AS EVIDENCE.
AND THE TOP BRASS REMOVED ALL *PHYSICAL* EVIDENCE... SO IT PROBABLY COULDN'T COME BACK TO HURT US IF WE TOLD HER THE TRUTH.
SHE'LL CHEER UP IF SHE FINDS OUT THAT DOLLY WAS JUST CREATED IN A LAB.
HMM. SHOULD THINGS CONTINUE IN THIS MANNER WITH HER, I'LL TAKE IT INTO CONSIDERATION.

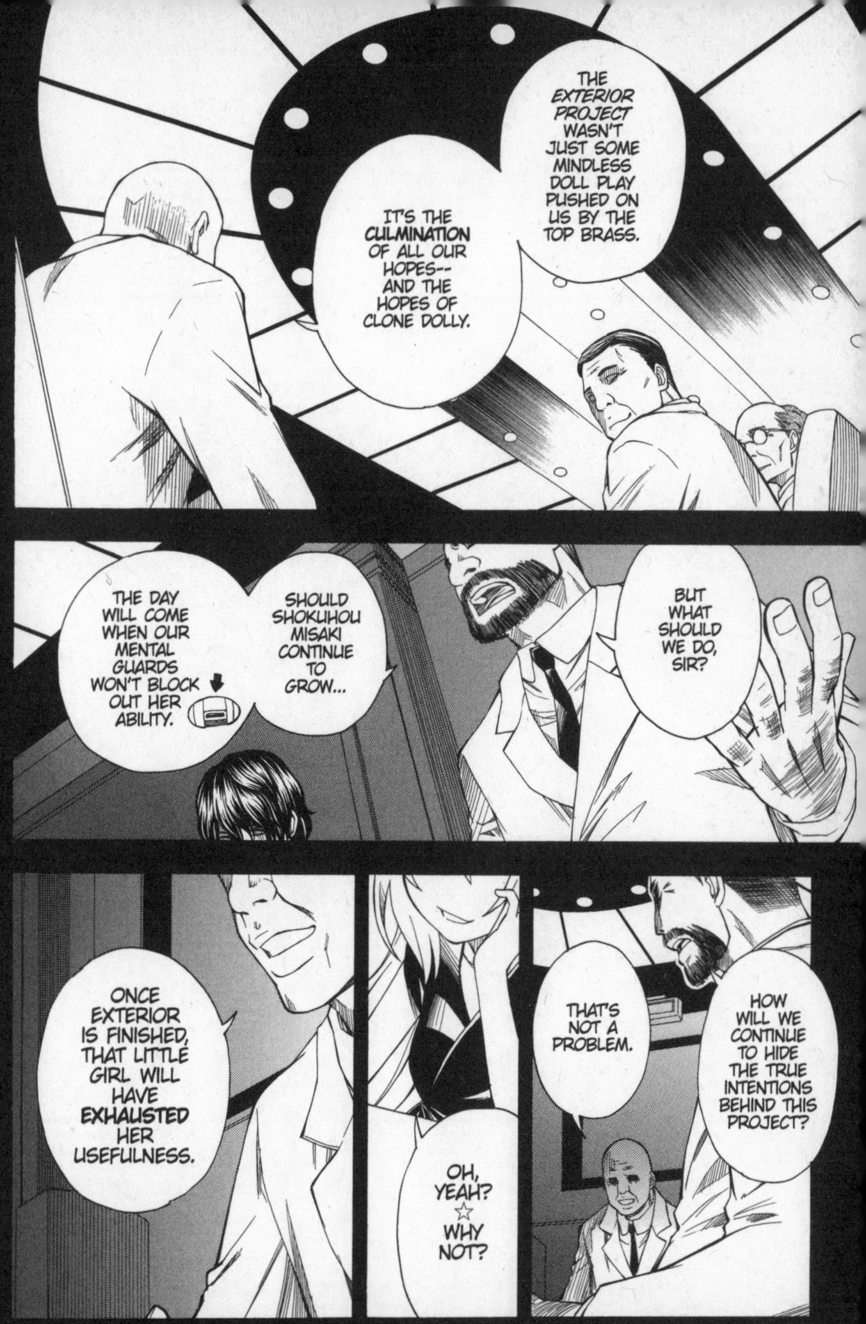
THE EXTERIOR PROJECT WASN'T JUST SOME MINDLESS DOLL PLAY PUSHED ON US BY THE TOP BRASS.
IT'S THE CULMINATION OF ALL OUR HOPES-- AND THE HOPES OF CLONE DOLLY.
BUT WHAT SHOULD WE DO, SIR?
SHOULD SHOKUHOU MISAKI CONTINUE TO GROW...
THE DAY WILL COME WHEN OUR MENTAL GUARDS WON'T BLOCK OUT HER ABILITY.
HOW WILL WE CONTINUE TO HIDE THE TRUE INTENTIONS BEHIND THIS PROJECT?
THAT'S NOT A PROBLEM.
OH, YEAH? ☆ WHY NOT?
ONCE EXTERIOR IS FINISHED, THAT LITTLE GIRL WILL HAVE EXHAUSTED HER USEFULNESS.

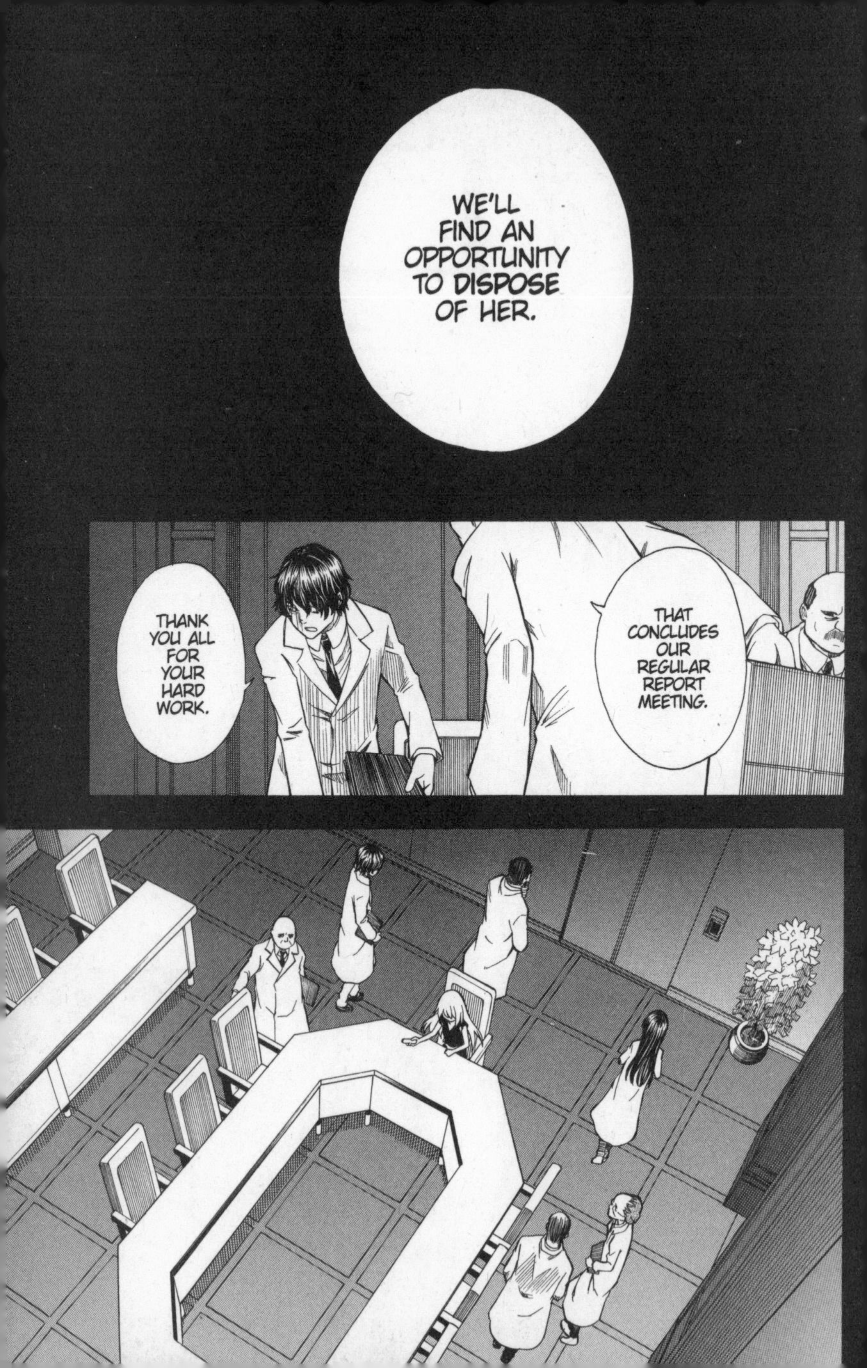
WE'LL FIND AN OPPORTUNITY TO DISPOSE OF HER.
THAT CONCLUDES OUR REGULAR REPORT MEETING.
THANK YOU ALL FOR YOUR HARD WORK.

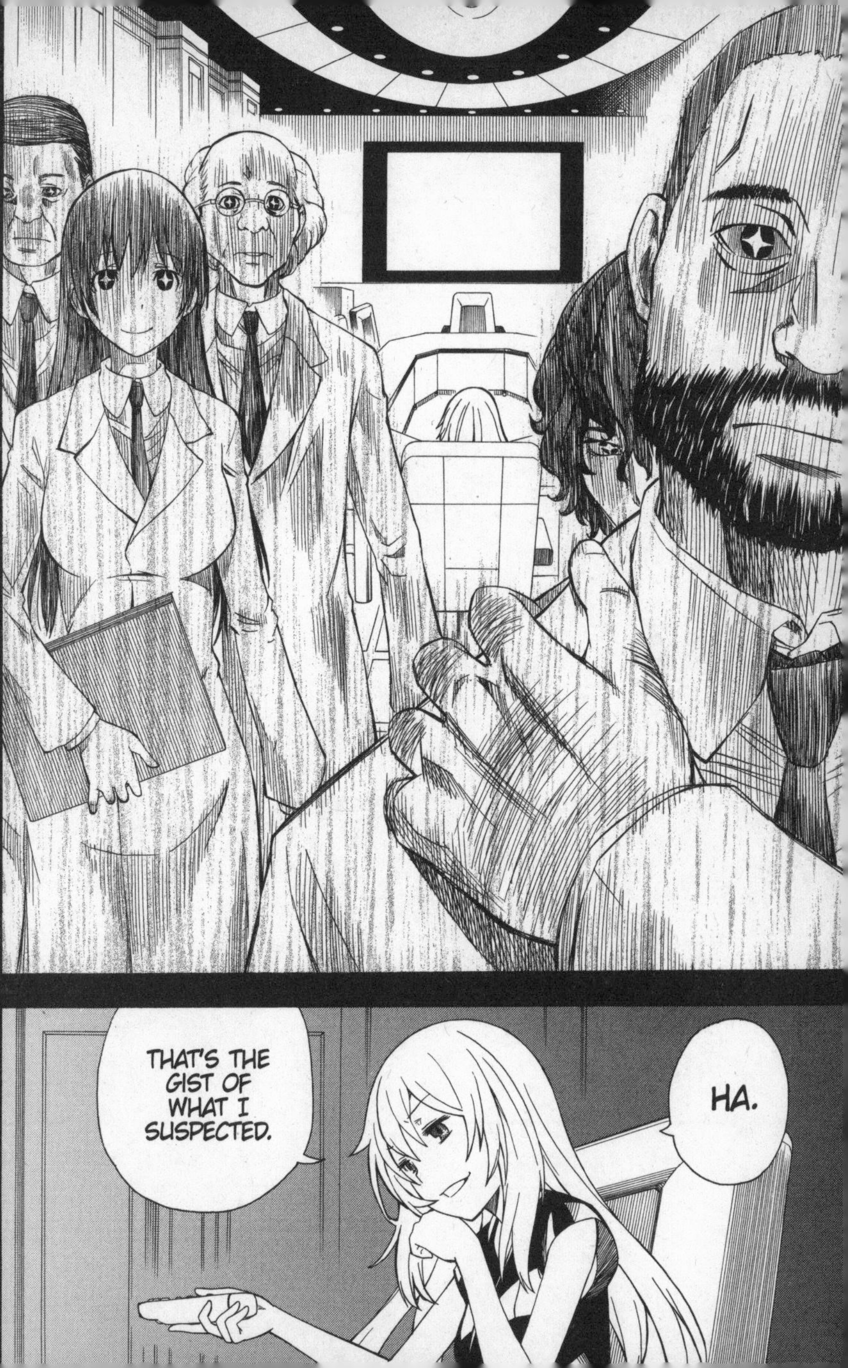
HA.
THAT'S THE GIST OF WHAT I SUSPECTED.

IN THE CONFUSION OF THE EXPERIMENTS, I HAD A LOWER-LEVEL RESEARCHER UNDER MY CONTROL SABOTAGE THE MENTAL GUARD...

LETTING ME EXTEND MY RULE WITHOUT THEM KNOWING.

BEFORE I ENTERED TOKIWADAI, I MADE SURE TO BRAINWASH ANYONE THAT HAD ANYTHING TO DO WITH THE EXTERIOR PROJECT.

SO NO MATTER WHAT WAS DONE TO THEM, THEY'D NEVER TALK.

HOW DID GENSEI...?

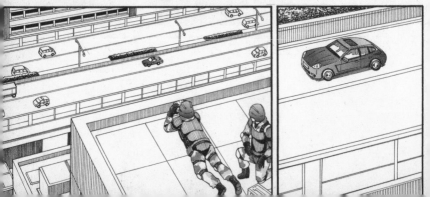

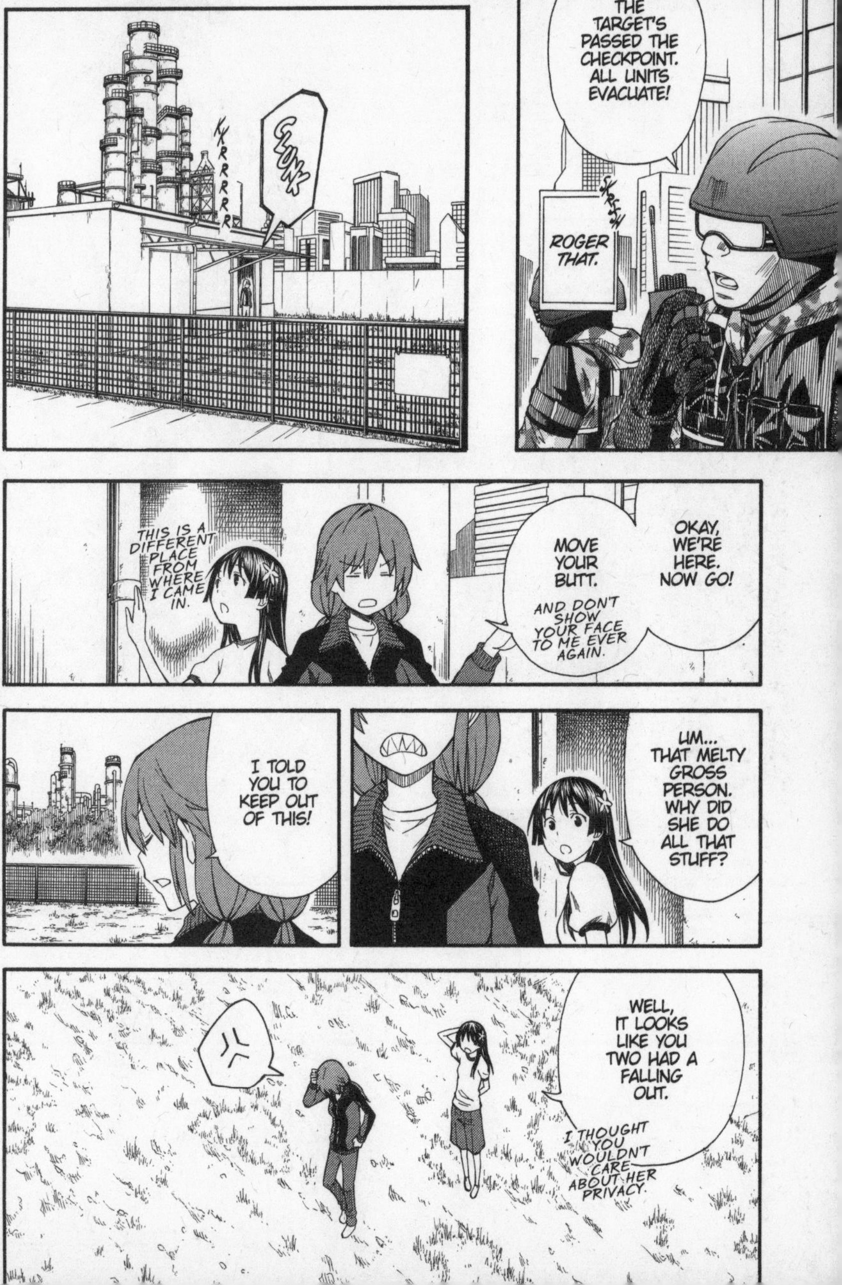
THE TARGET'S PASSED THE CHECKPOINT. ALL UNITS EVACUATE!
ROGER THAT.
CLUNK
OKAY, WE'RE HERE. NOW GO!
MOVE YOUR BUTT.
AND DON'T SHOW YOUR FACE TO ME EVER AGAIN.
THIS IS A DIFFERENT PLACE FROM WHERE I CAME IN.
UM... THAT MELTY GROSS PERSON. WHY DID SHE DO ALL THAT STUFF?
I TOLD YOU TO KEEP OUT OF THIS!
WELL, IT LOOKS LIKE YOU TWO HAD A FALLING OUT.
I THOUGHT YOU WOULDN'T CARE ABOUT HER PRIVACY.

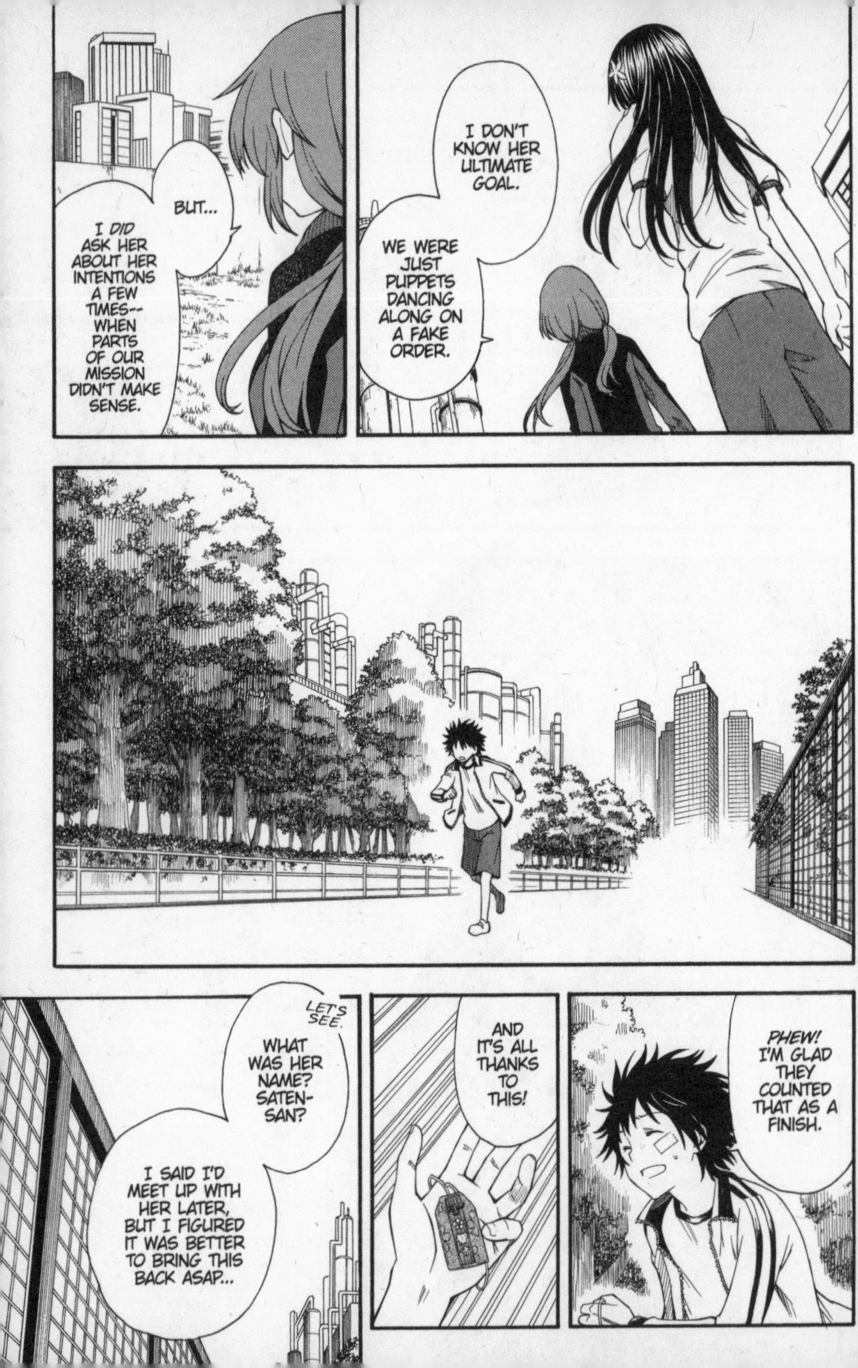
I DON'T KNOW HER ULTIMATE GOAL.
WE WERE JUST PUPPETS DANCING ALONG ON A FAKE ORDER.
BUT...
I *DID* ASK HER ABOUT HER INTENTIONS A FEW TIMES-- WHEN PARTS OF OUR MISSION DIDN'T MAKE SENSE.
PHEW! I'M GLAD THEY COUNTED THAT AS A FINISH.
AND IT'S ALL THANKS TO THIS!
LET'S SEE.
WHAT WAS HER NAME? SATEN-SAN?
I SAID I'D MEET UP WITH HER LATER, BUT I FIGURED IT WAS BETTER TO BRING THIS BACK ASAP...

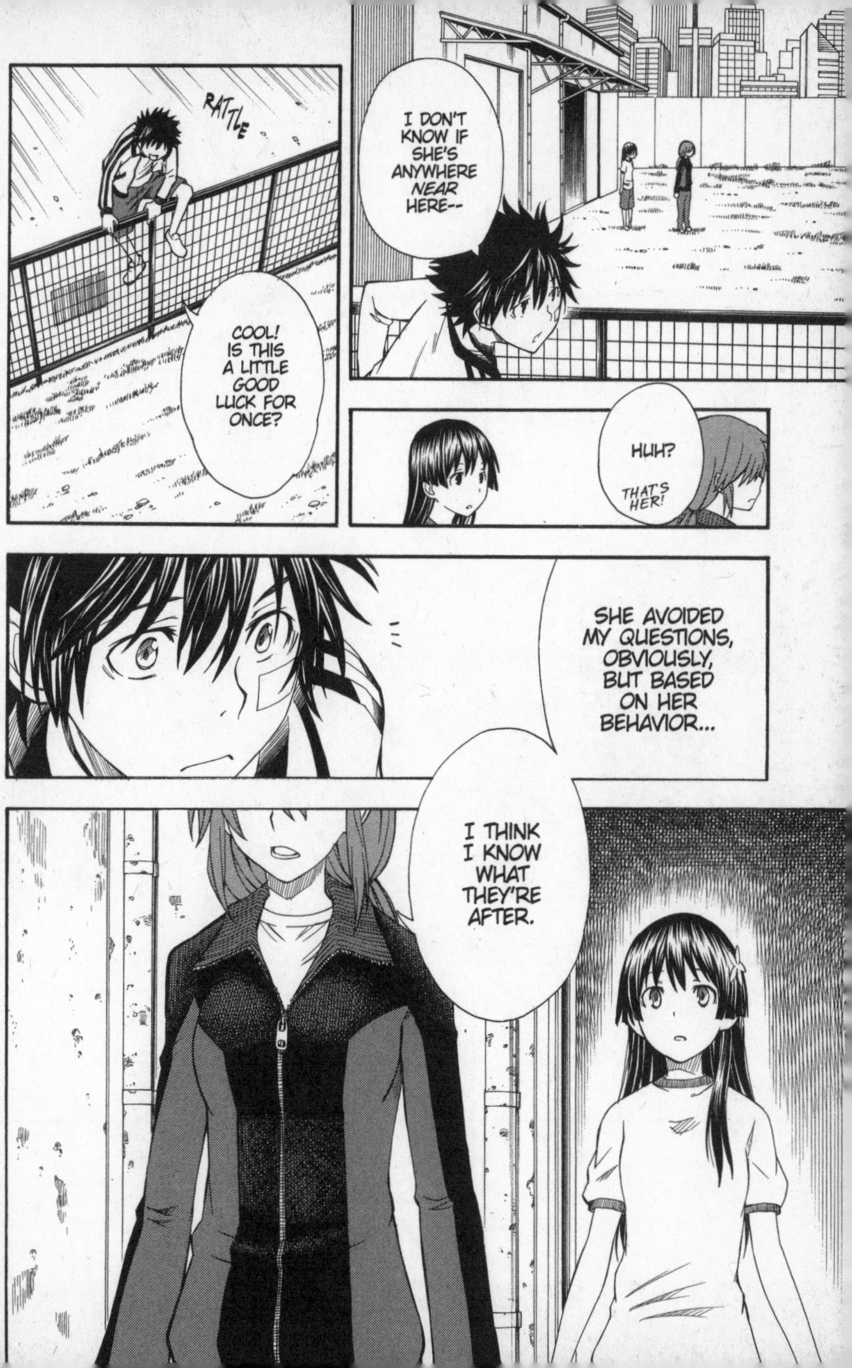
I DON'T KNOW IF SHE'S ANYWHERE NEAR HERE--
RATTLE
COOL! IS THIS A LITTLE GOOD LUCK FOR ONCE?
HUH?
THAT'S HER!
SHE AVOIDED MY QUESTIONS, OBVIOUSLY, BUT BASED ON HER BEHAVIOR...
I THINK I KNOW WHAT THEY'RE AFTER.

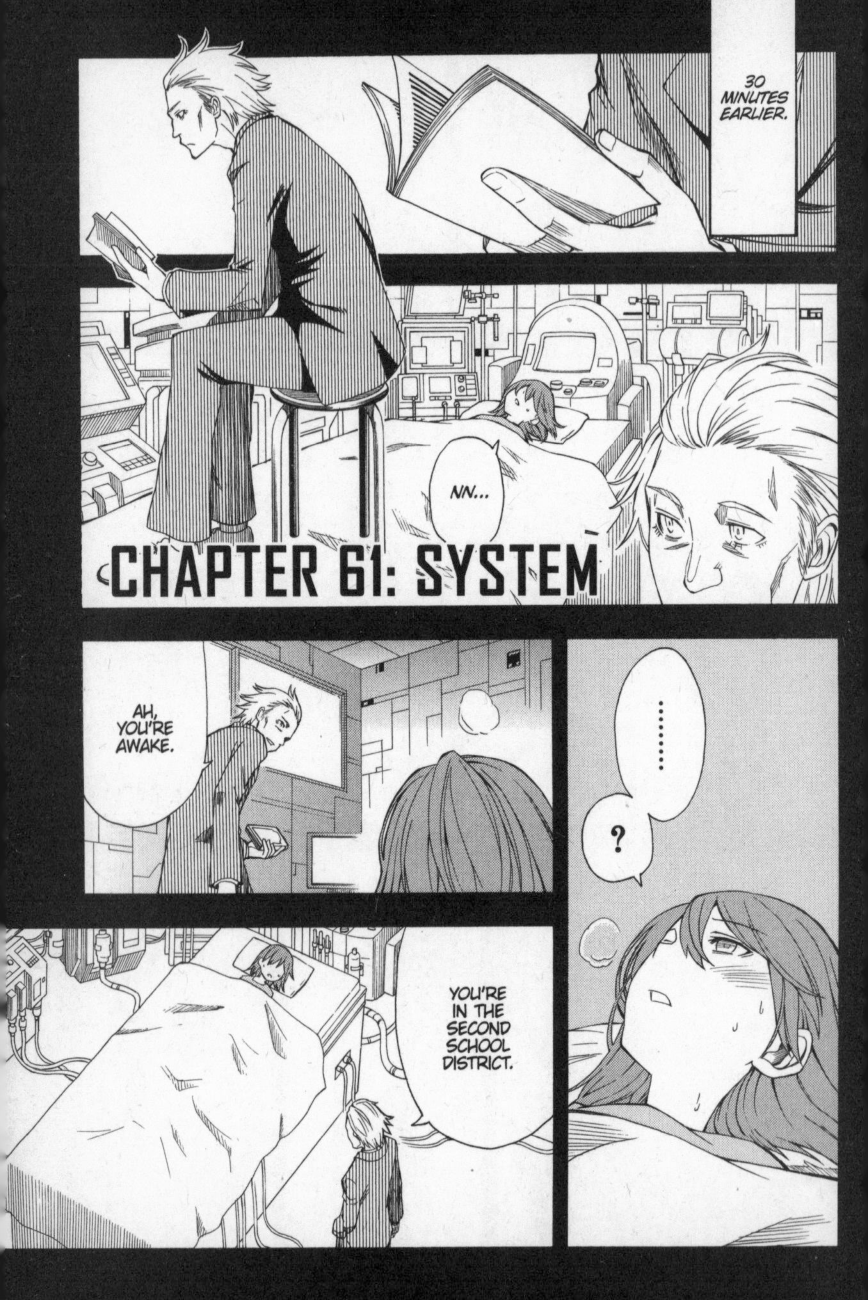
30 MINUTES EARLIER.
NN...
CHAPTER 61: SYSTEM
......
?
AH, YOU'RE AWAKE.
YOU'RE IN THE SECOND SCHOOL DISTRICT.

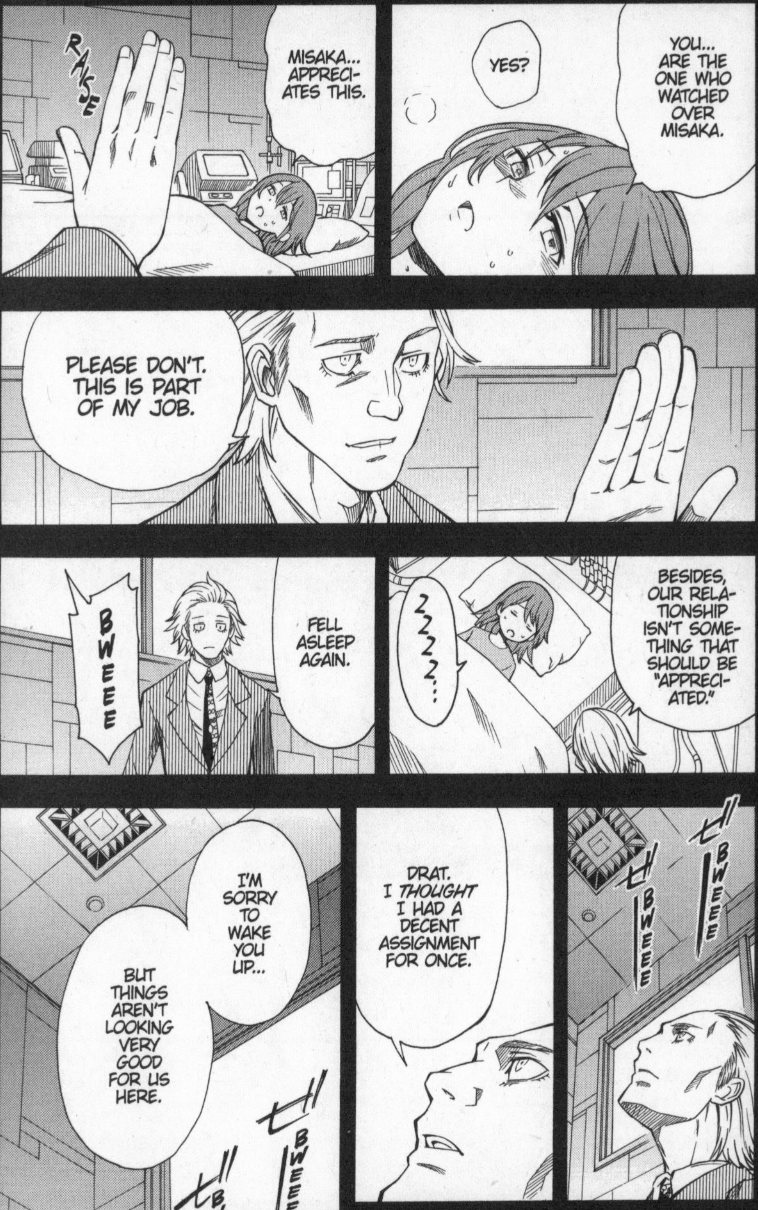
YOU... ARE THE ONE WHO WATCHED OVER MISAKA.
YES?
MISAKA... APPRECIATES THIS.
RAISE
PLEASE DON'T. THIS IS PART OF MY JOB.
BESIDES, OUR RELATIONSHIP ISN'T SOMETHING THAT SHOULD BE "APPRECIATED."
ZZZZ...
FELL ASLEEP AGAIN.
BWEEE
BWEEE
BWEEE
DRAT. I THOUGHT I HAD A DECENT ASSIGNMENT FOR ONCE.
I'M SORRY TO WAKE YOU UP...
BUT THINGS AREN'T LOOKING VERY GOOD FOR US HERE.
BWEEE
BWEEE

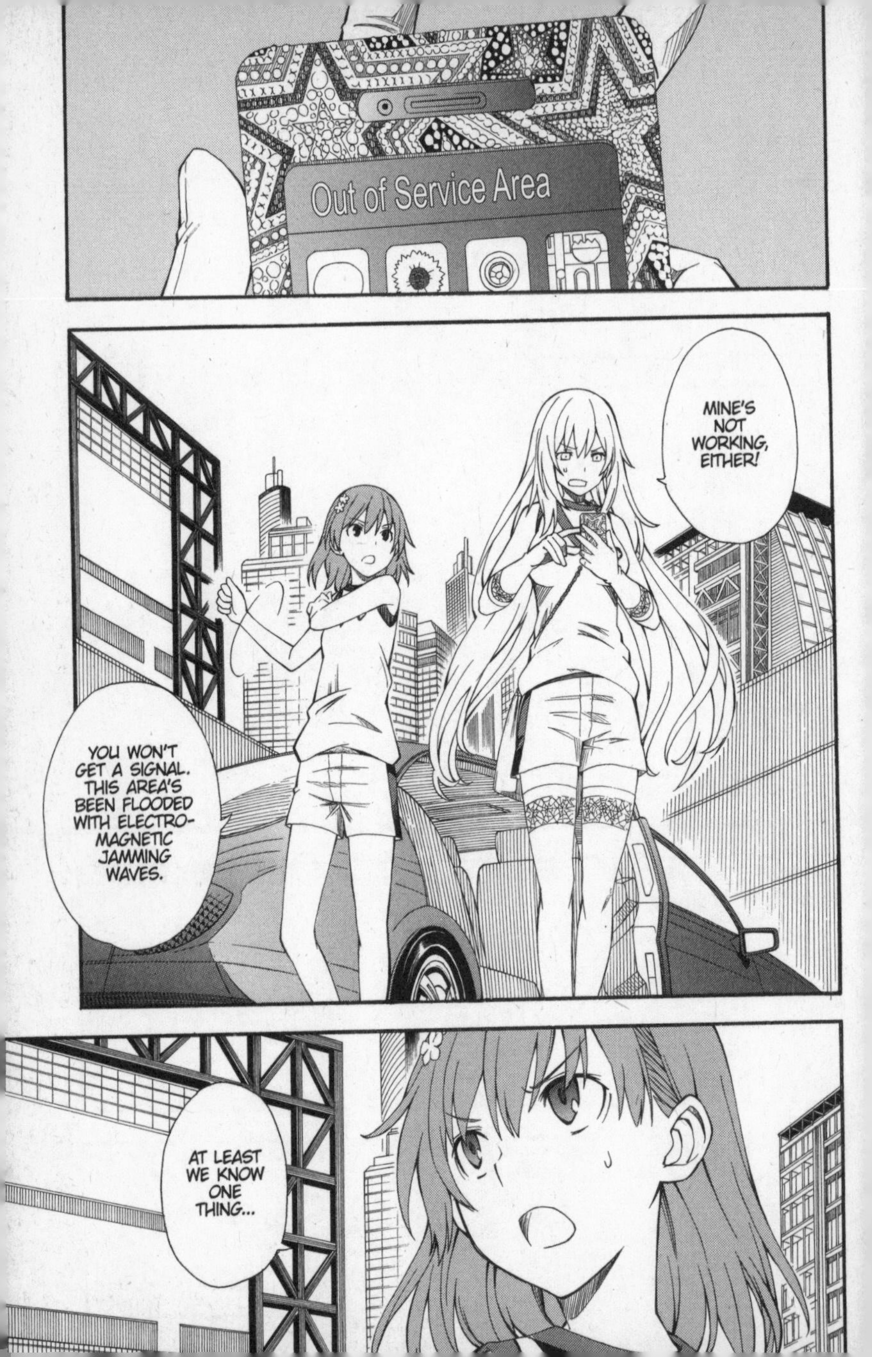
Out of Service Area
MINE'S NOT WORKING, EITHER!
YOU WON'T GET A SIGNAL. THIS AREA'S BEEN FLOODED WITH ELECTRO-MAGNETIC JAMMING WAVES.
AT LEAST WE KNOW ONE THING...

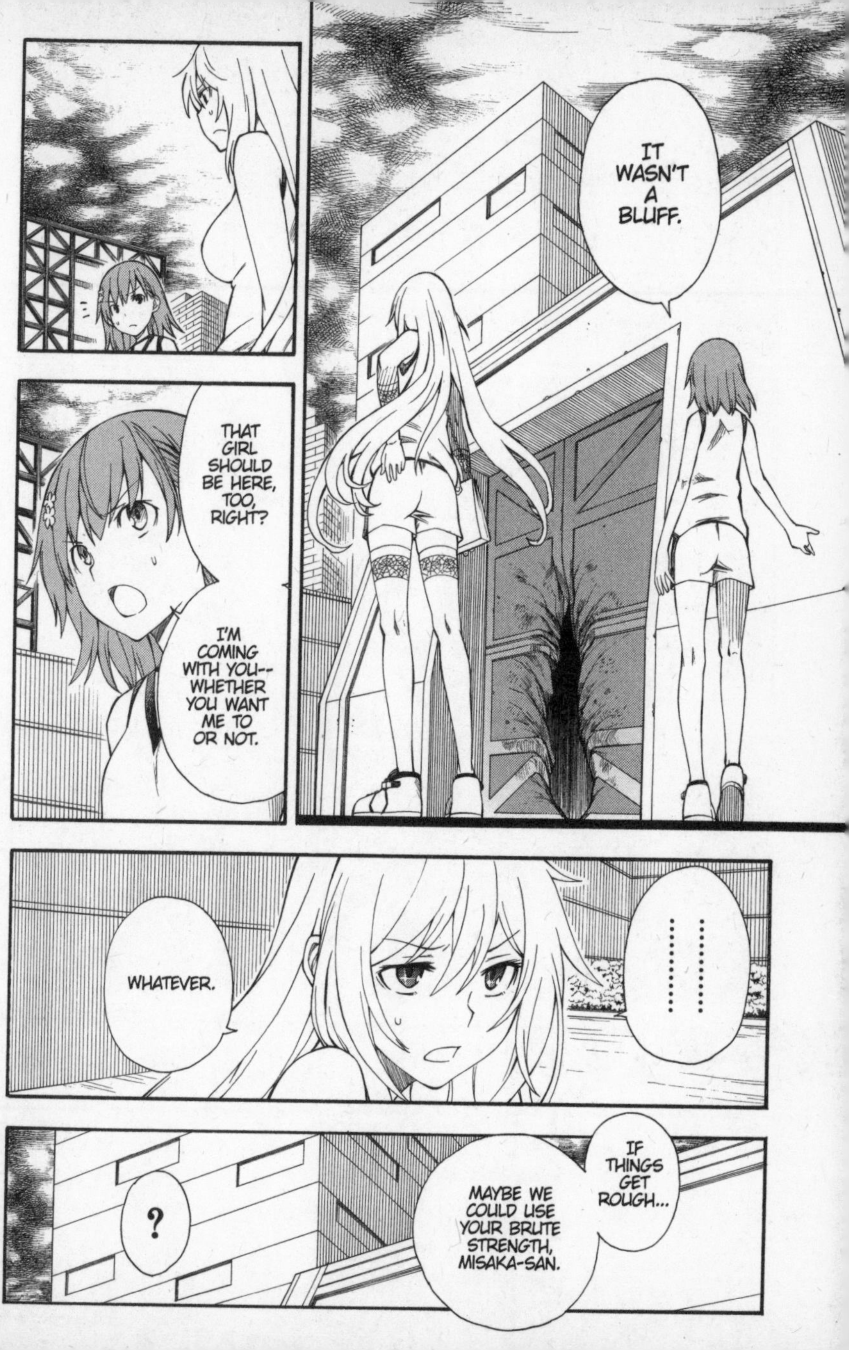
IT WASN'T A BLUFF.
THAT GIRL SHOULD BE HERE, TOO, RIGHT?
I'M COMING WITH YOU--WHETHER YOU WANT ME TO OR NOT.
......
WHATEVER.
IF THINGS GET ROUGH...
MAYBE WE COULD USE YOUR BRUTE STRENGTH, MISAKA-SAN.
?

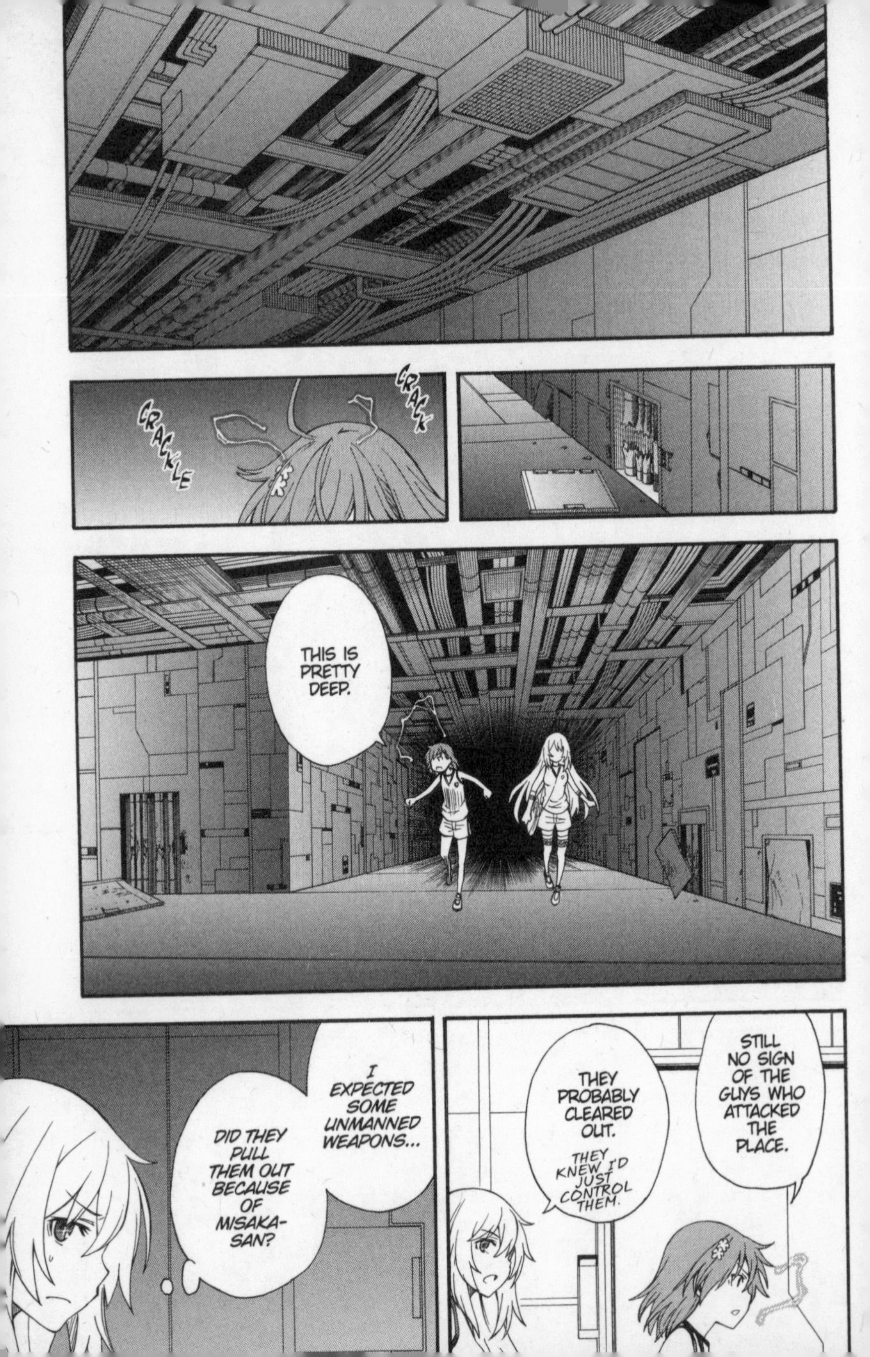
CRACK
CRACKLE
THIS IS PRETTY DEEP.
STILL NO SIGN OF THE GUYS WHO ATTACKED THE PLACE.
THEY PROBABLY CLEARED OUT.
THEY KNEW I'D JUST CONTROL THEM.
I EXPECTED SOME UNMANNED WEAPONS...
DID THEY PULL THEM OUT BECAUSE OF MISAKA-SAN?

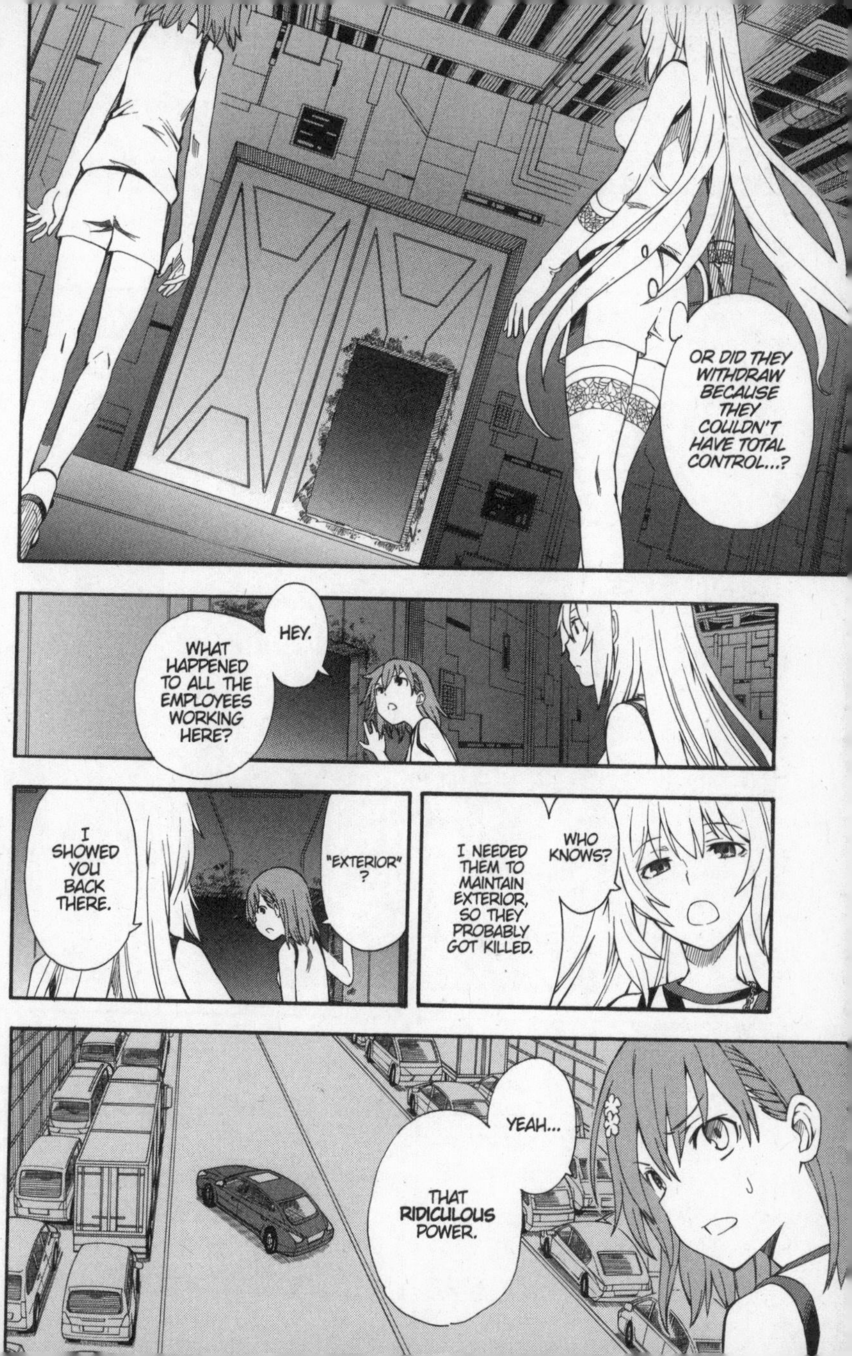
OR DID THEY WITHDRAW BECAUSE THEY COULDN'T HAVE TOTAL CONTROL...?
HEY.
WHAT HAPPENED TO ALL THE EMPLOYEES WORKING HERE?
WHO KNOWS?
I NEEDED THEM TO MAINTAIN EXTERIOR, SO THEY PROBABLY GOT KILLED.
"EXTERIOR"?
I SHOWED YOU BACK THERE.
YEAH...
THAT RIDICULOUS POWER.

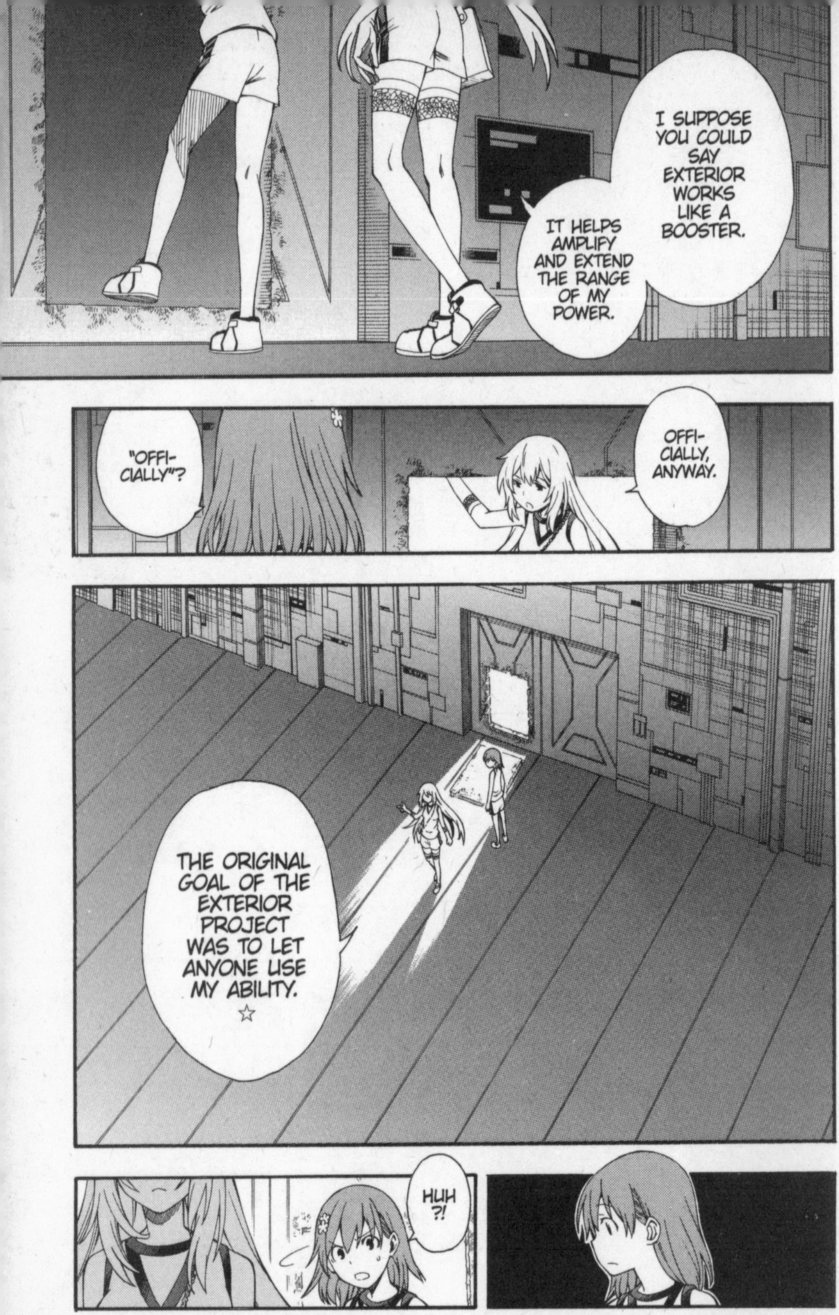
I SUPPOSE YOU COULD SAY EXTERIOR WORKS LIKE A BOOSTER.
IT HELPS AMPLIFY AND EXTEND THE RANGE OF MY POWER.
OFFI-CIALLY, ANYWAY.
"OFFI-CIALLY"?
THE ORIGINAL GOAL OF THE EXTERIOR PROJECT WAS TO LET ANYONE USE MY ABILITY. ☆
HUH ?!

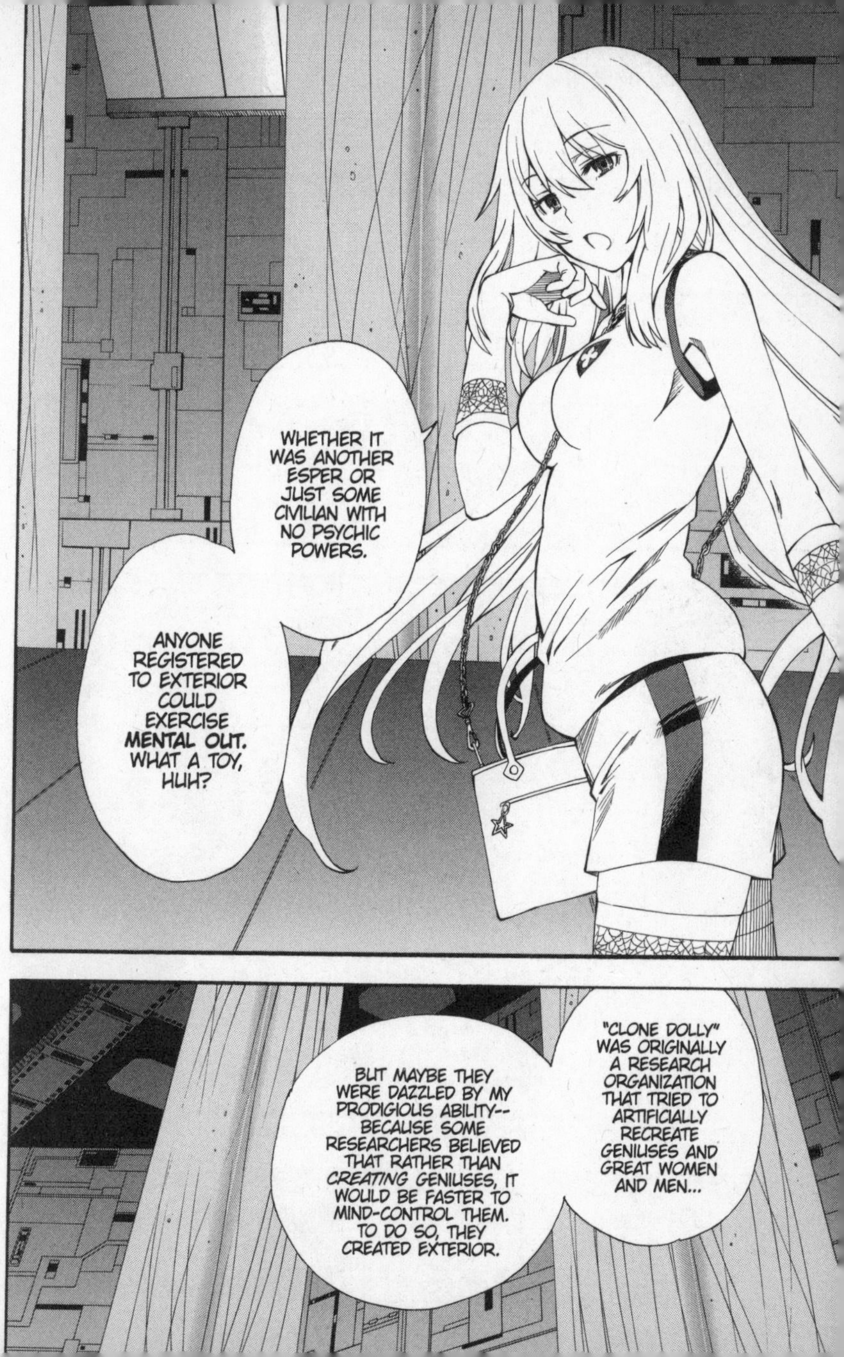
WHETHER IT WAS ANOTHER ESPER OR JUST SOME CIVILIAN WITH NO PSYCHIC POWERS.
ANYONE REGISTERED TO EXTERIOR COULD EXERCISE MENTAL OUT. WHAT A TOY, HUH?
"CLONE DOLLY" WAS ORIGINALLY A RESEARCH ORGANIZATION THAT TRIED TO ARTIFICIALLY RECREATE GENIUSES AND GREAT WOMEN AND MEN...
BUT MAYBE THEY WERE DAZZLED BY MY PRODIGIOUS ABILITY-- BECAUSE SOME RESEARCHERS BELIEVED THAT RATHER THAN *CREATING* GENIUSES, IT WOULD BE FASTER TO MIND-CONTROL THEM. TO DO SO, THEY CREATED EXTERIOR.

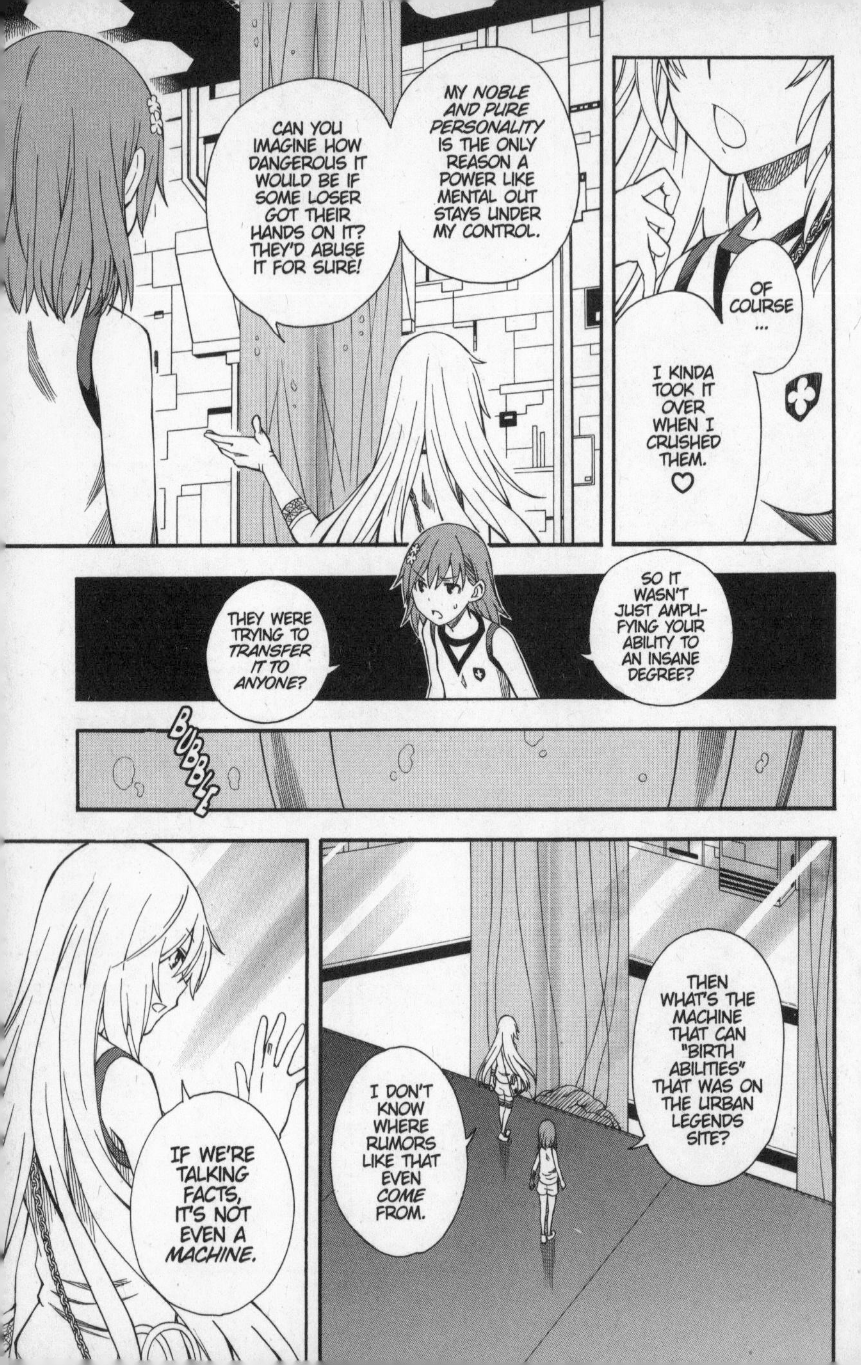
OF COURSE ...
I KINDA TOOK IT OVER WHEN I CRUSHED THEM. ♡
MY NOBLE AND PURE PERSONALITY IS THE ONLY REASON A POWER LIKE MENTAL OUT STAYS UNDER MY CONTROL.
CAN YOU IMAGINE HOW DANGEROUS IT WOULD BE IF SOME LOSER GOT THEIR HANDS ON IT? THEY'D ABUSE IT FOR SURE!
SO IT WASN'T JUST AMPLIFYING YOUR ABILITY TO AN INSANE DEGREE?
THEY WERE TRYING TO TRANSFER IT TO ANYONE?
BUBBLE
THEN WHAT'S THE MACHINE THAT CAN "BIRTH ABILITIES" THAT WAS ON THE URBAN LEGENDS SITE?
I DON'T KNOW WHERE RUMORS LIKE THAT EVEN COME FROM.
IF WE'RE TALKING FACTS, IT'S NOT EVEN A MACHINE.

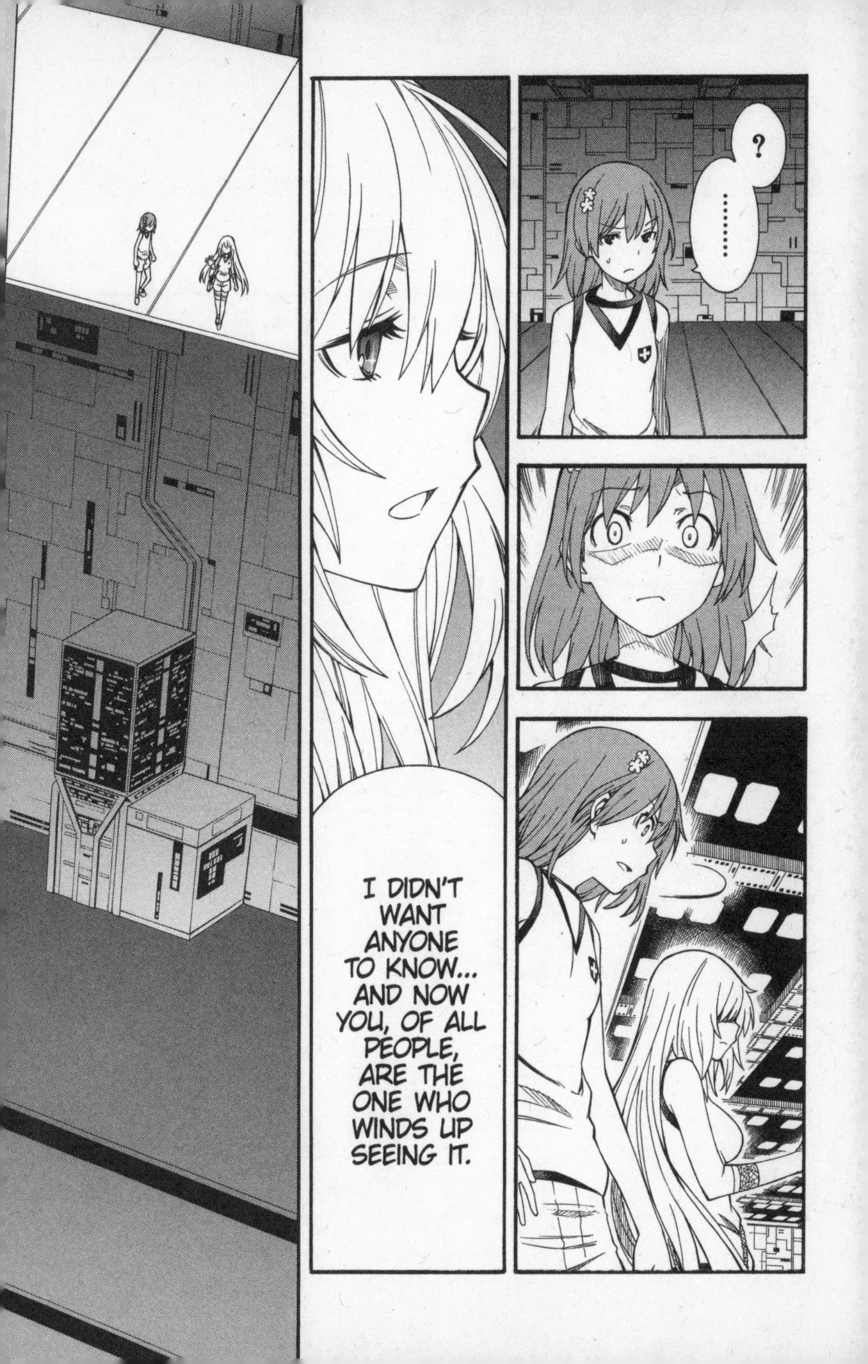
......
?
I DIDN'T WANT ANYONE TO KNOW... AND NOW YOU, OF ALL PEOPLE, ARE THE ONE WHO WINDS UP SEEING IT.

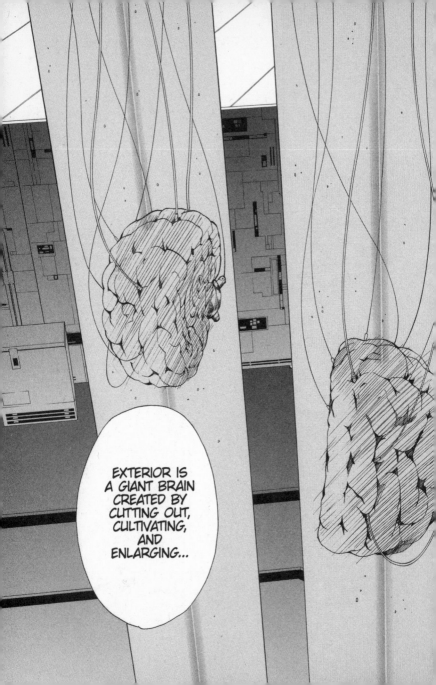

EXTERIOR IS
A GIANT BRAIN
CREATED BY
CUTTING OUT,
CULTIVATING,
AND
ENLARGING...

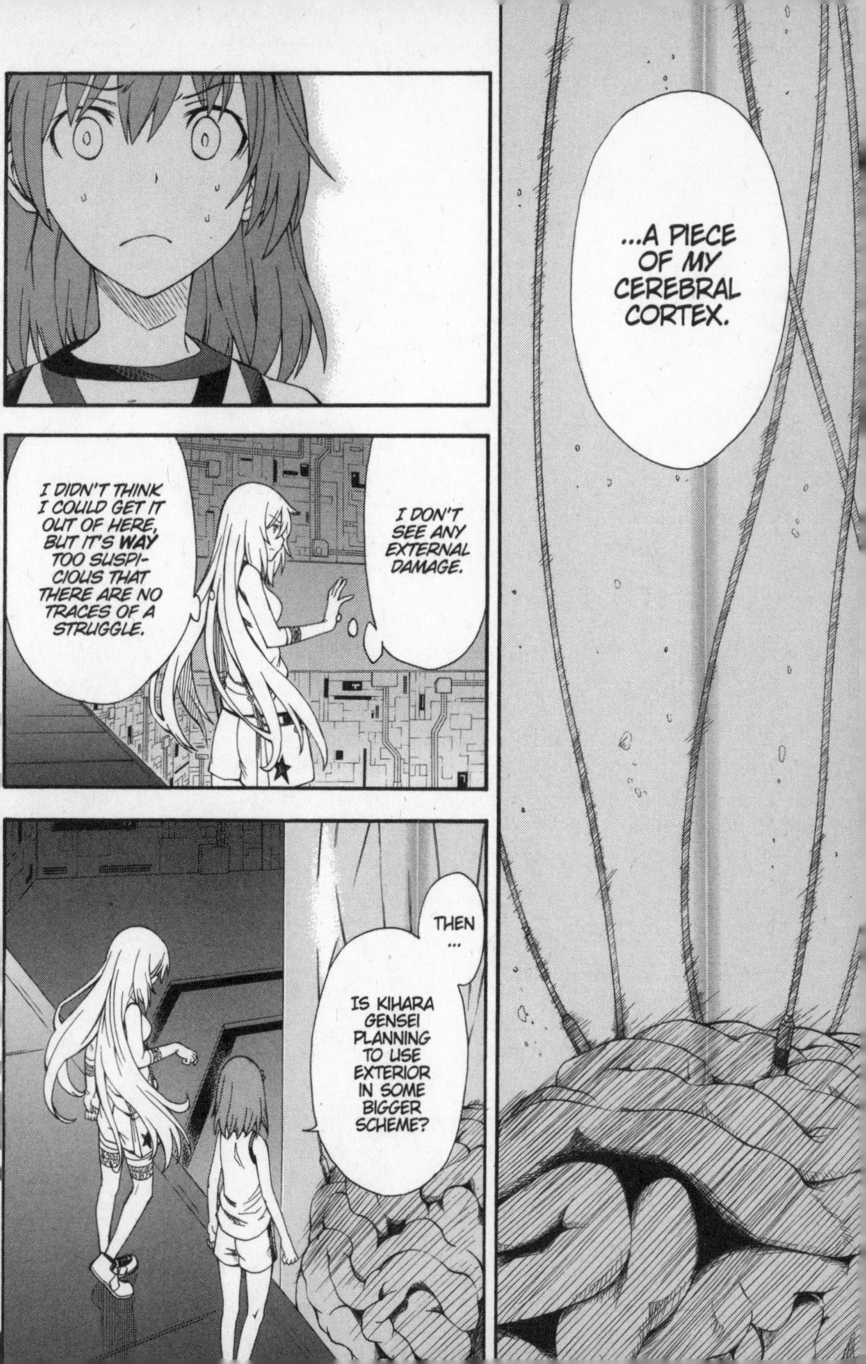
...A PIECE OF MY CEREBRAL CORTEX.
I DON'T SEE ANY EXTERNAL DAMAGE.
I DIDN'T THINK I COULD GET IT OUT OF HERE, BUT IT'S WAY TOO SUSPICIOUS THAT THERE ARE NO TRACES OF A STRUGGLE.
THEN ...
IS KIHARA GENSEI PLANNING TO USE EXTERIOR IN SOME BIGGER SCHEME?

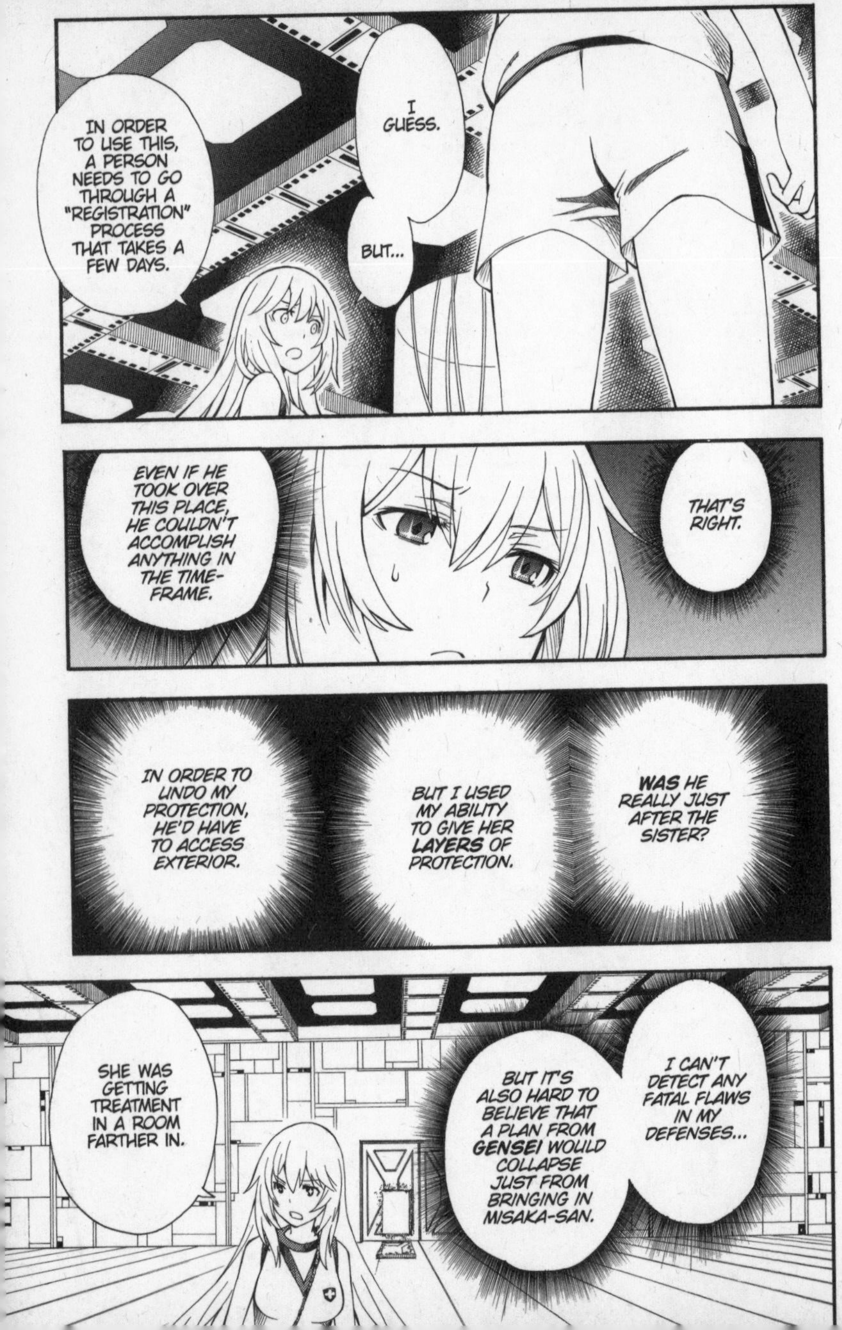
I GUESS.
BUT...
IN ORDER TO USE THIS, A PERSON NEEDS TO GO THROUGH A "REGISTRATION" PROCESS THAT TAKES A FEW DAYS.
THAT'S RIGHT.
EVEN IF HE TOOK OVER THIS PLACE, HE COULDN'T ACCOMPLISH ANYTHING IN THE TIME-FRAME.
WAS HE REALLY JUST AFTER THE SISTER?
BUT I USED MY ABILITY TO GIVE HER LAYERS OF PROTECTION.
IN ORDER TO UNDO MY PROTECTION, HE'D HAVE TO ACCESS EXTERIOR.
I CAN'T DETECT ANY FATAL FLAWS IN MY DEFENSES...
BUT IT'S ALSO HARD TO BELIEVE THAT A PLAN FROM GENSEI WOULD COLLAPSE JUST FROM BRINGING IN MISAKA-SAN.
SHE WAS GETTING TREATMENT IN A ROOM FARTHER IN.

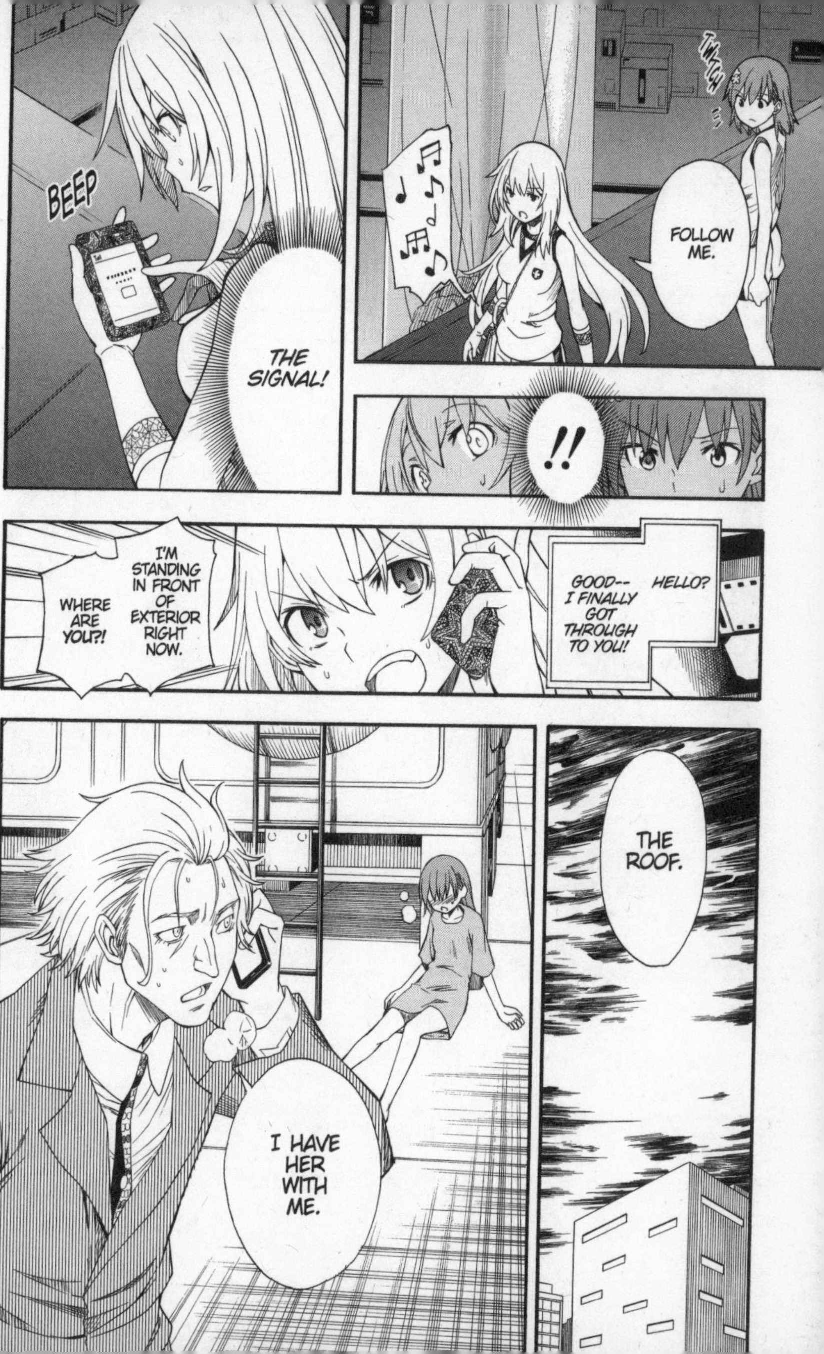
TWITCH
FOLLOW ME.
BEEP
THE SIGNAL!
!!
HELLO?
GOOD-- I FINALLY GOT THROUGH TO YOU!
I'M STANDING IN FRONT OF EXTERIOR RIGHT NOW.
WHERE ARE YOU?!
THE ROOF.
I HAVE HER WITH ME.

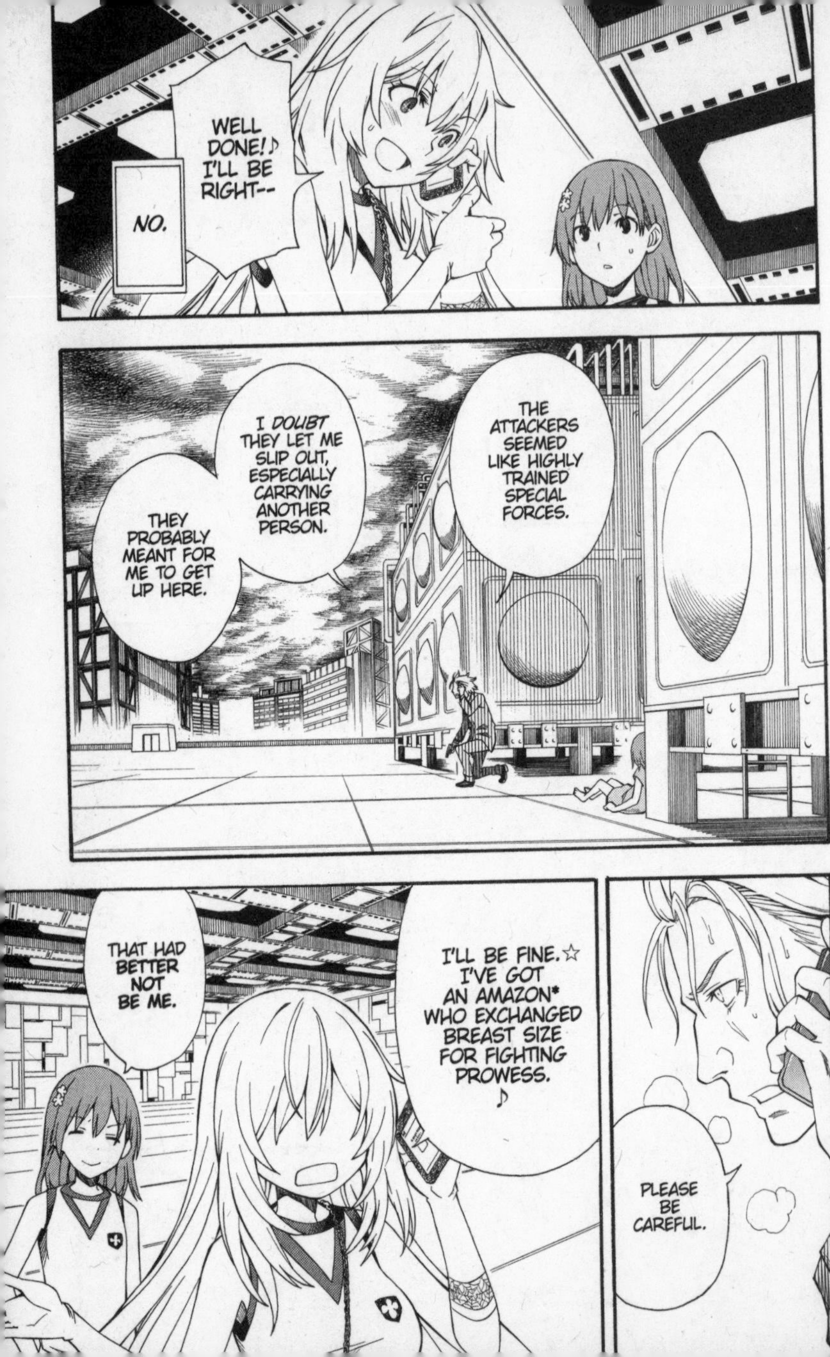
WELL DONE!♪ I'LL BE RIGHT--
NO.
THE ATTACKERS SEEMED LIKE HIGHLY TRAINED SPECIAL FORCES.
I DOUBT THEY LET ME SLIP OUT, ESPECIALLY CARRYING ANOTHER PERSON.
THEY PROBABLY MEANT FOR ME TO GET UP HERE.
PLEASE BE CAREFUL.
I'LL BE FINE.☆ I'VE GOT AN AMAZON* WHO EXCHANGED BREAST SIZE FOR FIGHTING PROWESS.♪
THAT HAD BETTER NOT BE ME.

*A tribe of warrior women from Greek mythology. It's said that in order to improve their archery, some Amazons cut off a breast.

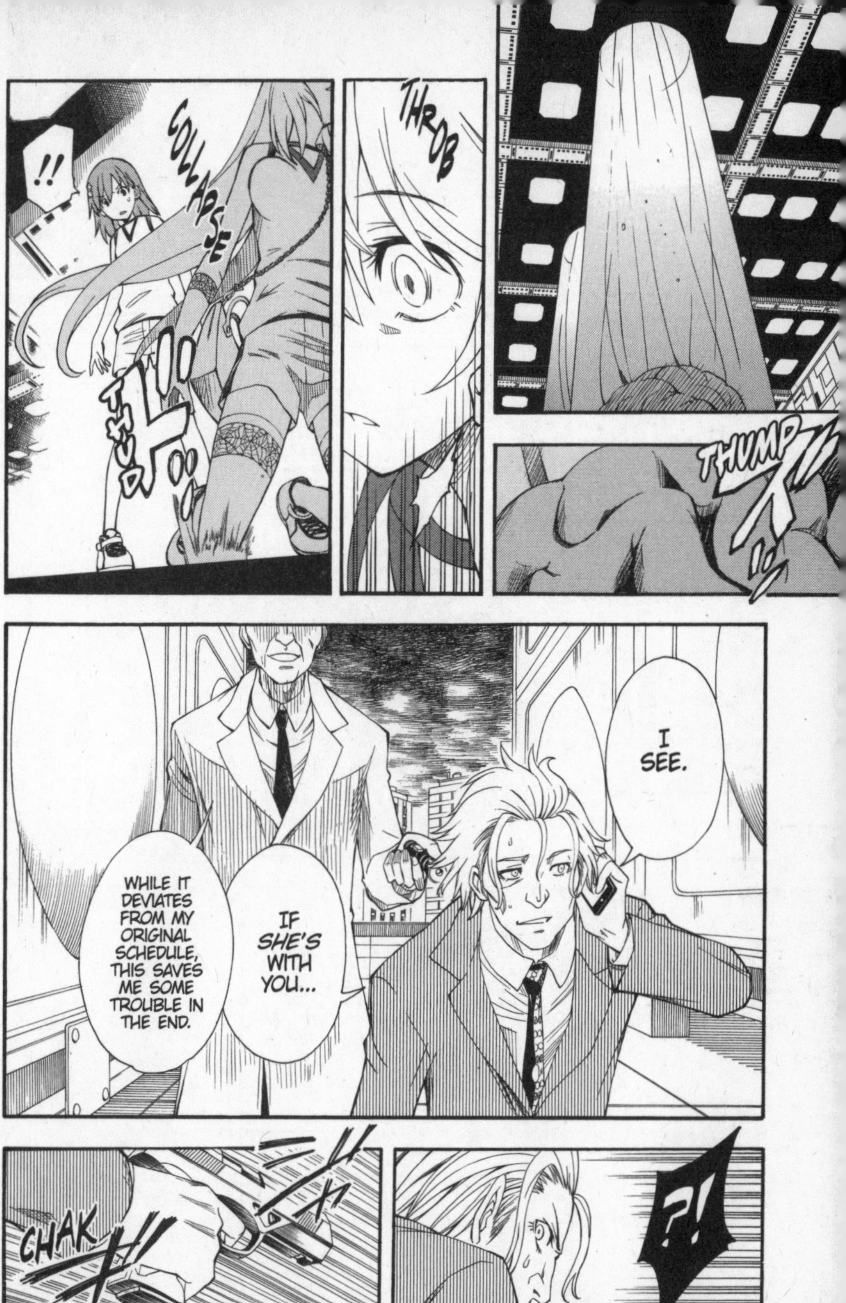
THUMP
THROB
COLLAPSE
!!
THUD
I SEE.
IF SHE'S WITH YOU...
WHILE IT DEVIATES FROM MY ORIGINAL SCHEDULE, THIS SAVES ME SOME TROUBLE IN THE END.
?!
CHAK

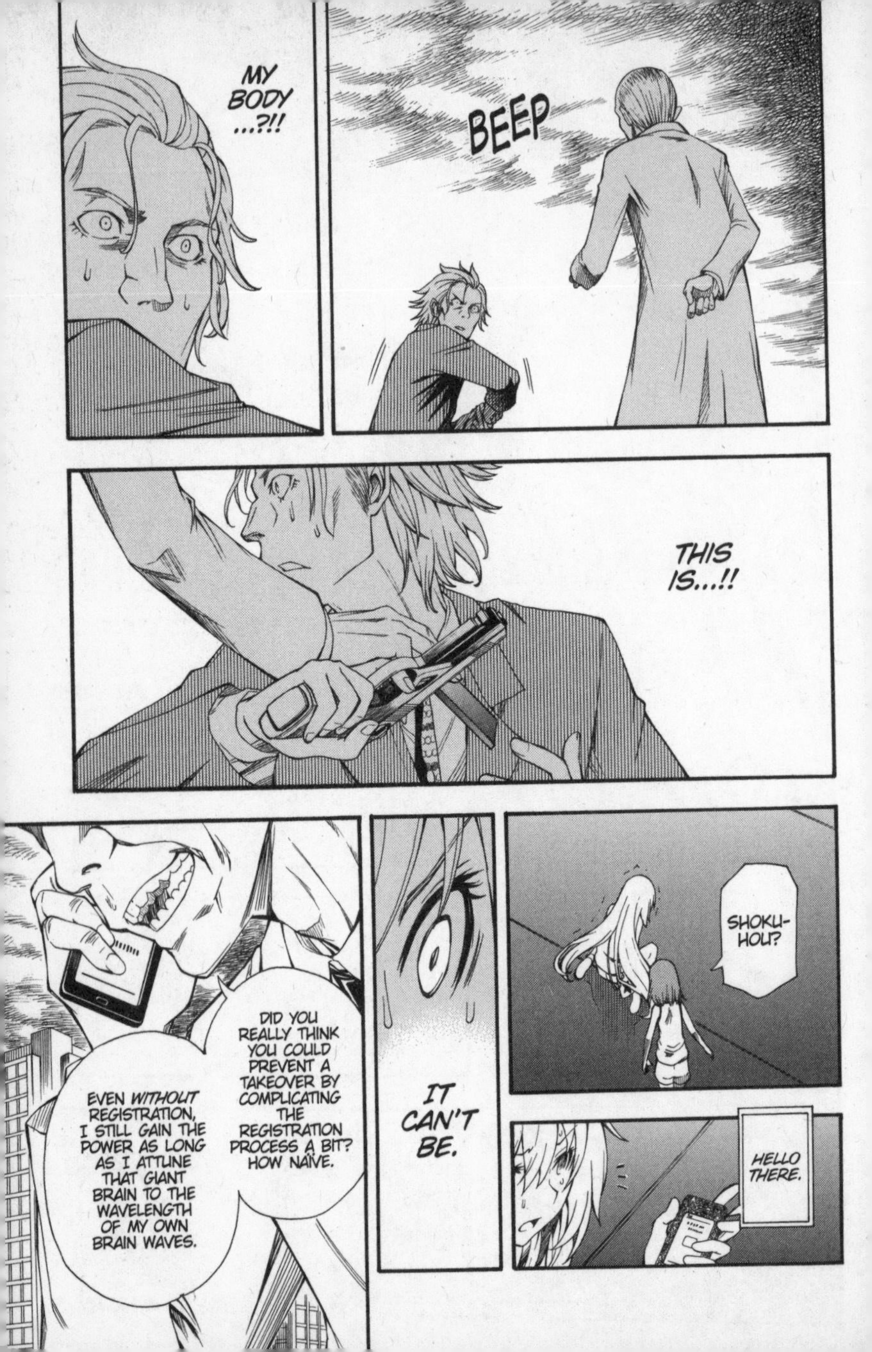
BEEP
MY BODY ...?!!
THIS IS...!!
SHOKU-HOU?
HELLO THERE.
IT CAN'T BE.
DID YOU REALLY THINK YOU COULD PREVENT A TAKEOVER BY COMPLICATING THE REGISTRATION PROCESS A BIT? HOW NAÏVE.
EVEN *WITHOUT* REGISTRATION, I STILL GAIN THE POWER AS LONG AS I ATTUNE THAT GIANT BRAIN TO THE WAVELENGTH OF MY OWN BRAIN WAVES.

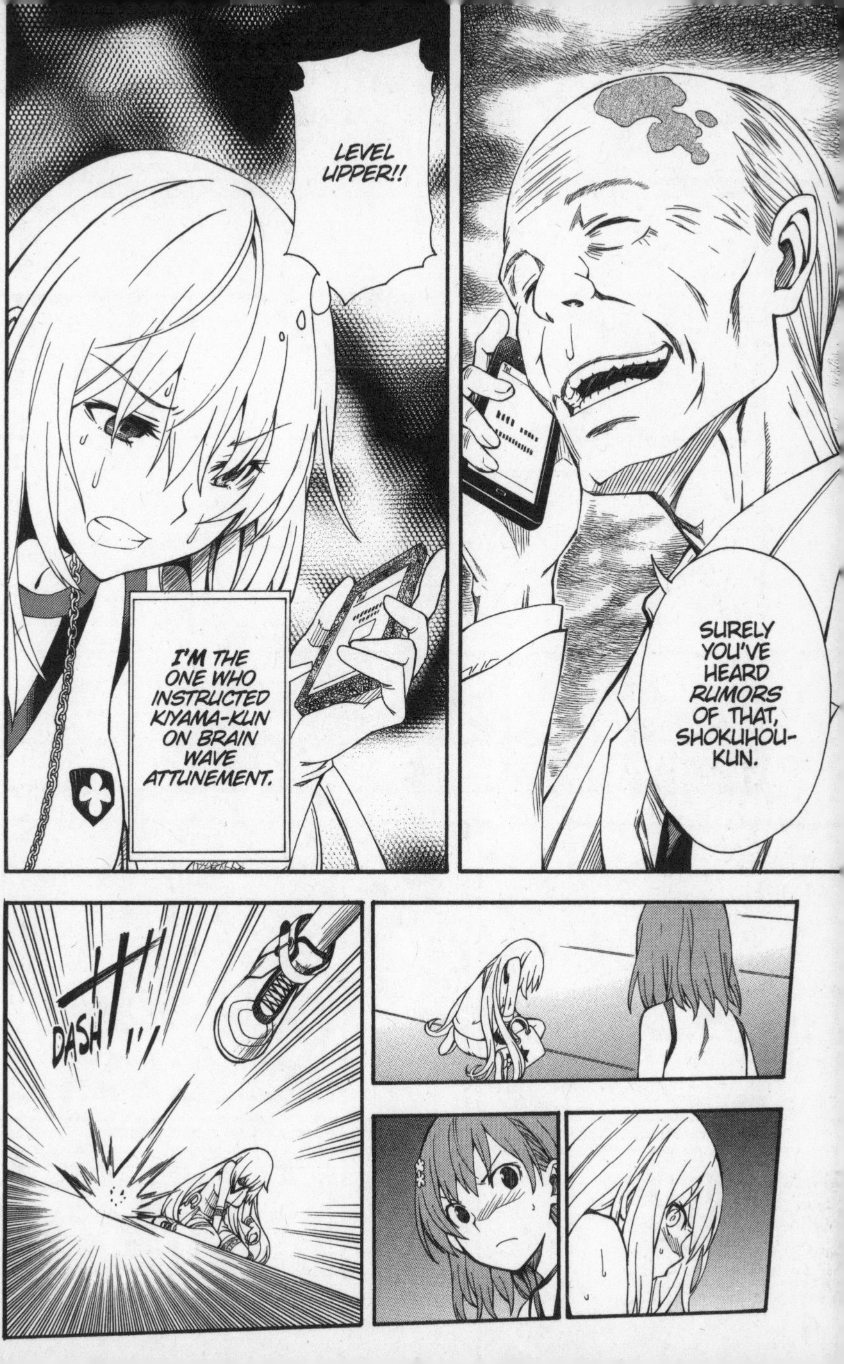
SURELY YOU'VE HEARD RUMORS OF THAT, SHOKUHOU-KUN.
LEVEL UPPER!!
I'M THE ONE WHO INSTRUCTED KIYAMA-KUN ON BRAIN WAVE ATTUNEMENT.
DASH

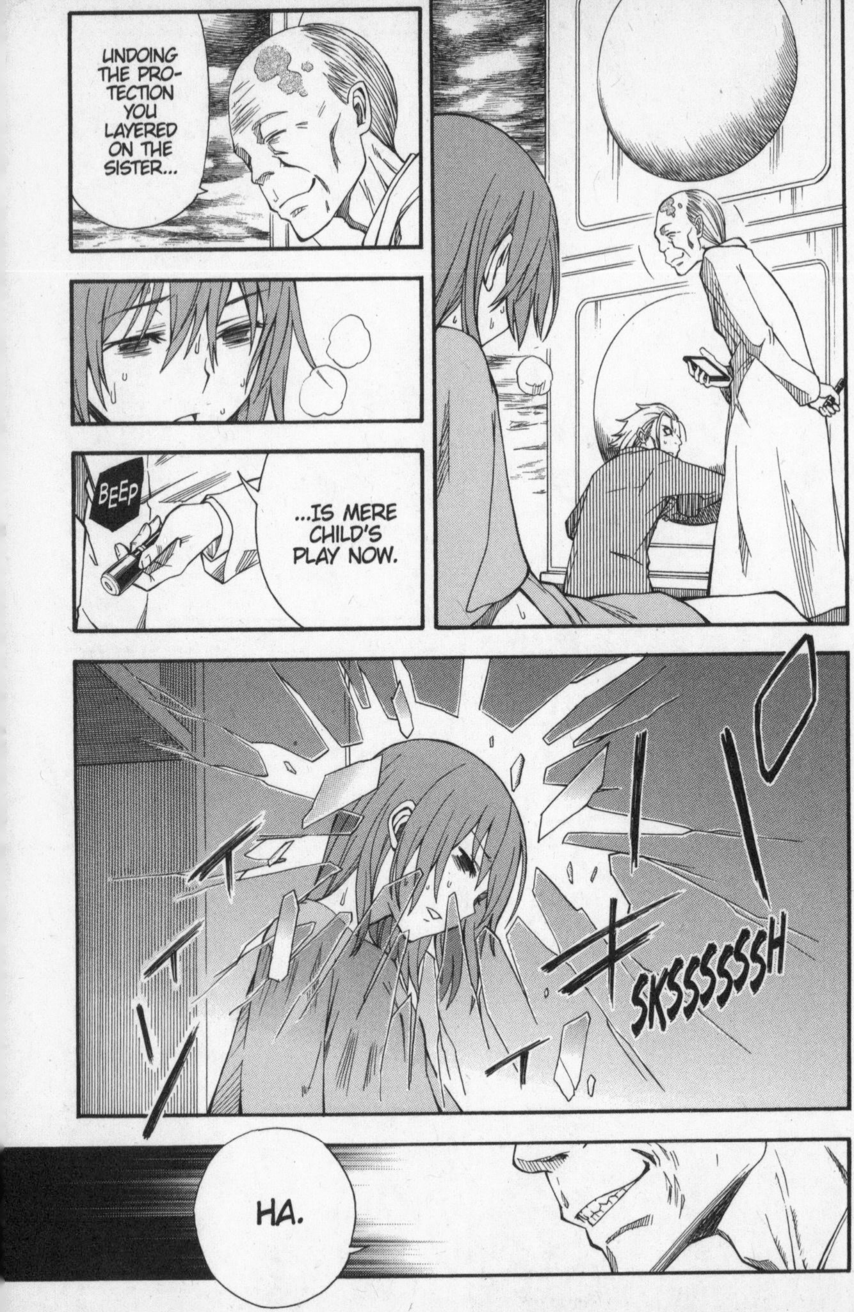
UNDOING THE PRO-TECTION YOU LAYERED ON THE SISTER...
BEEP
...IS MERE CHILD'S PLAY NOW.
SKSSSSSSH
HA.

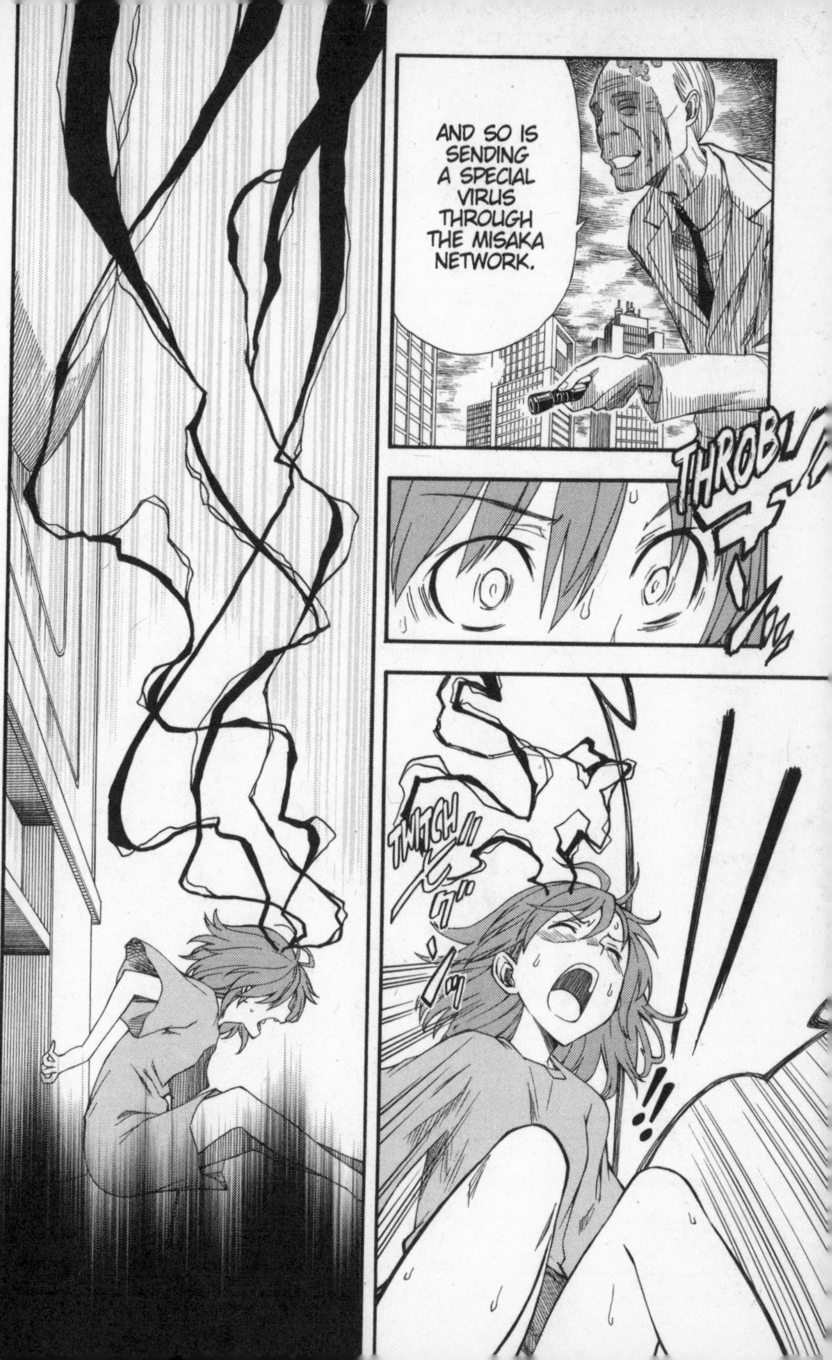
AND SO IS SENDING A SPECIAL VIRUS THROUGH THE MISAKA NETWORK.
THROB
TWITCH
!!

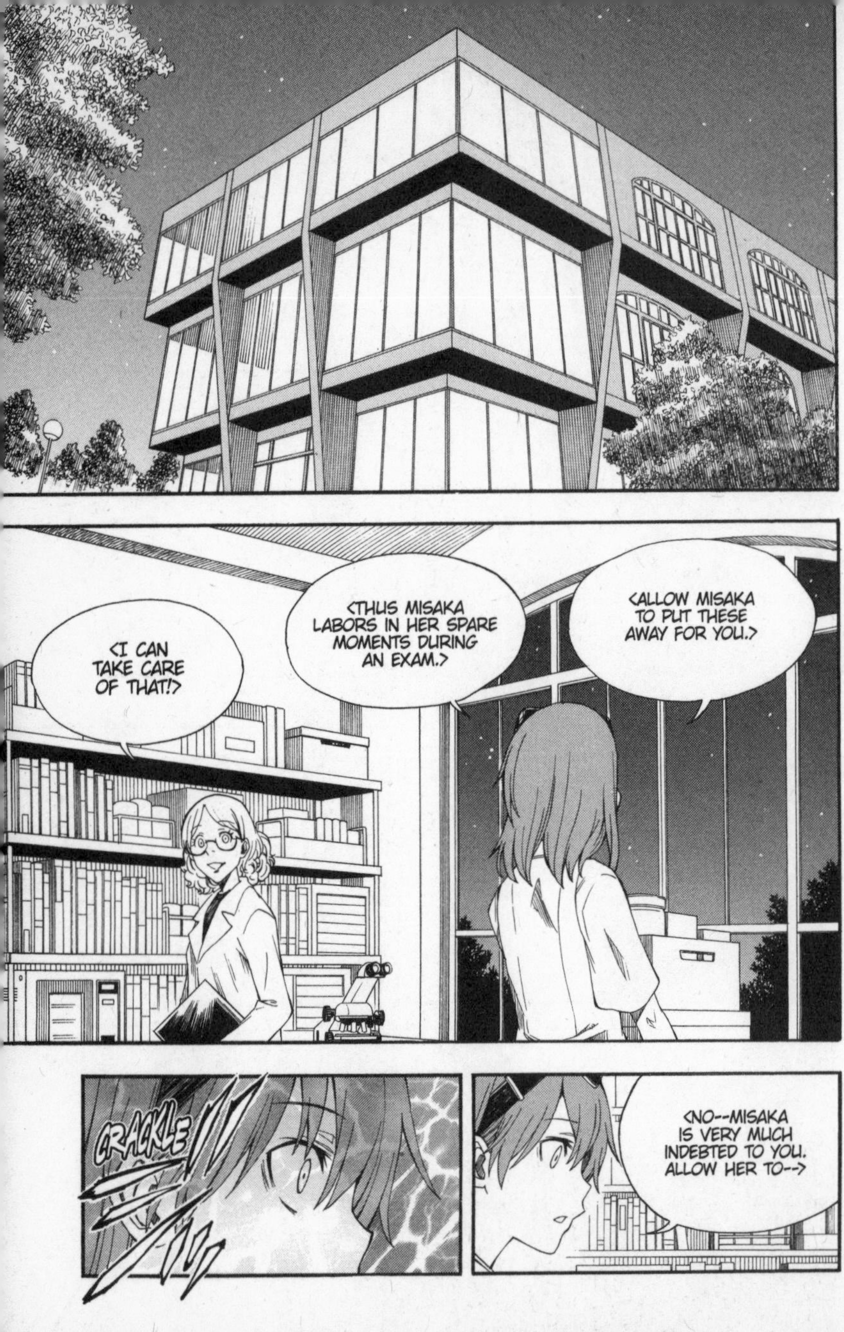
<ALLOW MISAKA TO PUT THESE AWAY FOR YOU.>
<THUS MISAKA LABORS IN HER SPARE MOMENTS DURING AN EXAM.>
<I CAN TAKE CARE OF THAT!>
<NO--MISAKA IS VERY MUCH INDEBTED TO YOU. ALLOW HER TO-->
CRACKLE

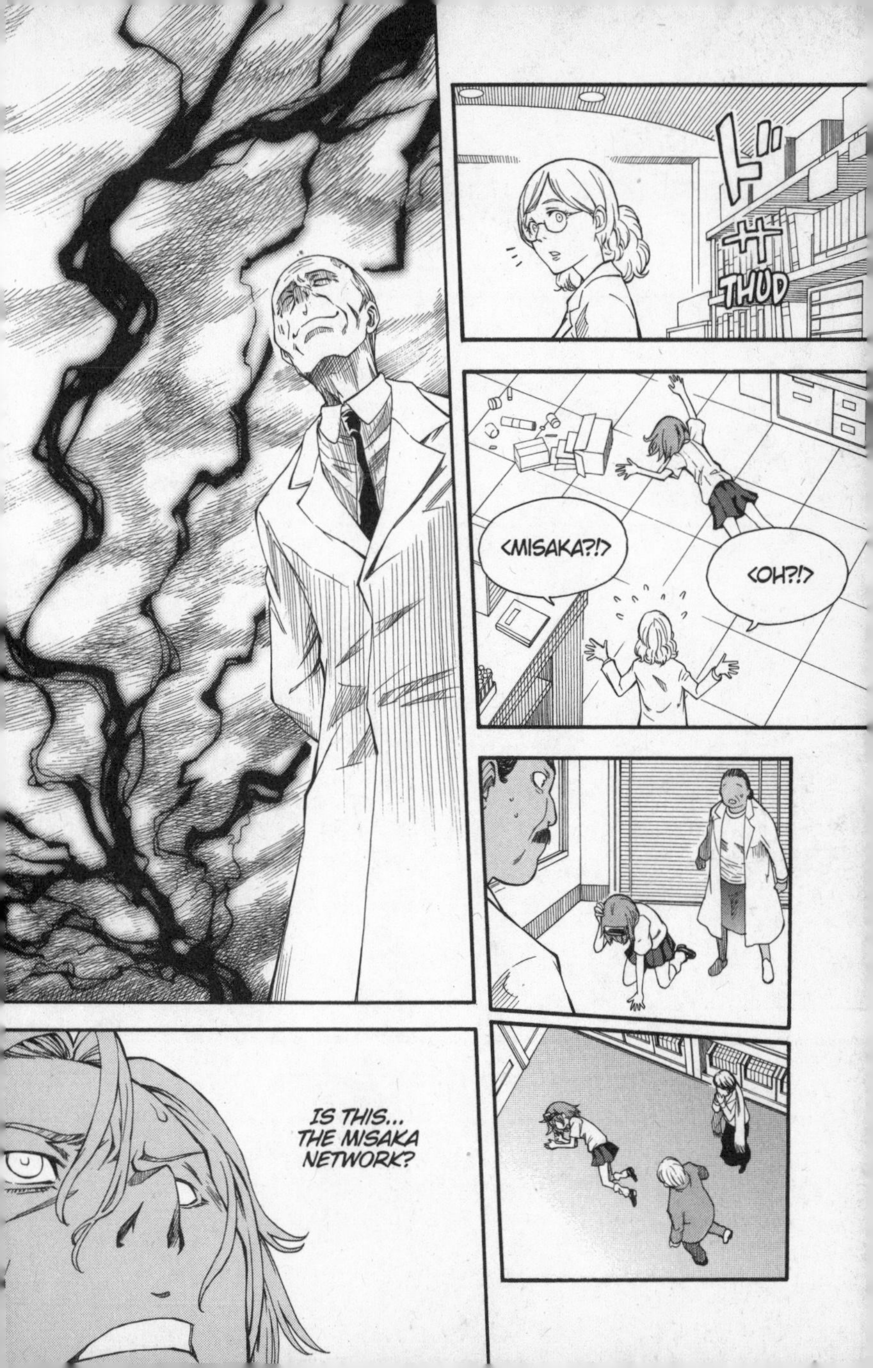
THUD
<MISAKA?!>
<OH?!>
IS THIS... THE MISAKA NETWORK?

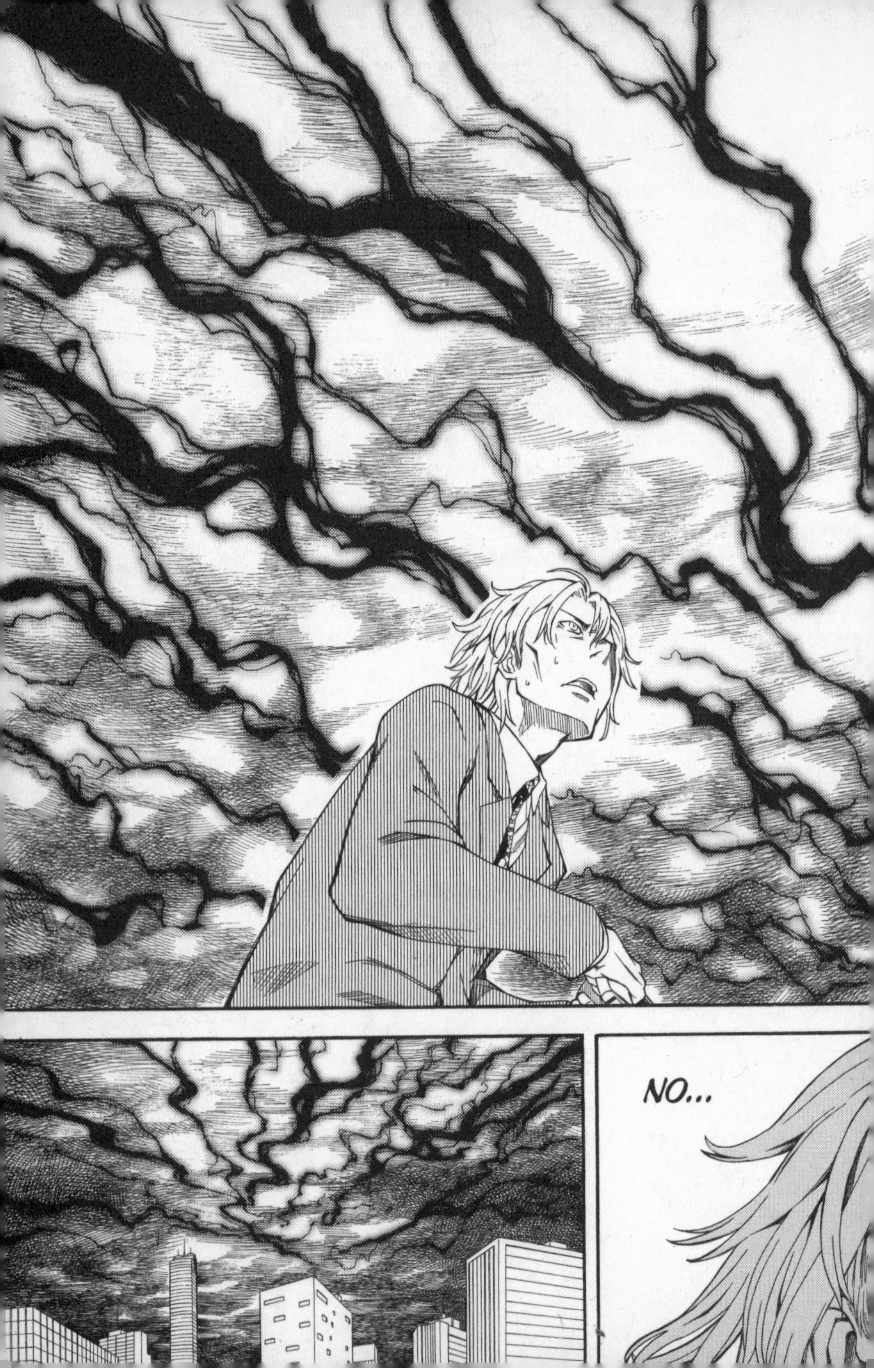
NO...

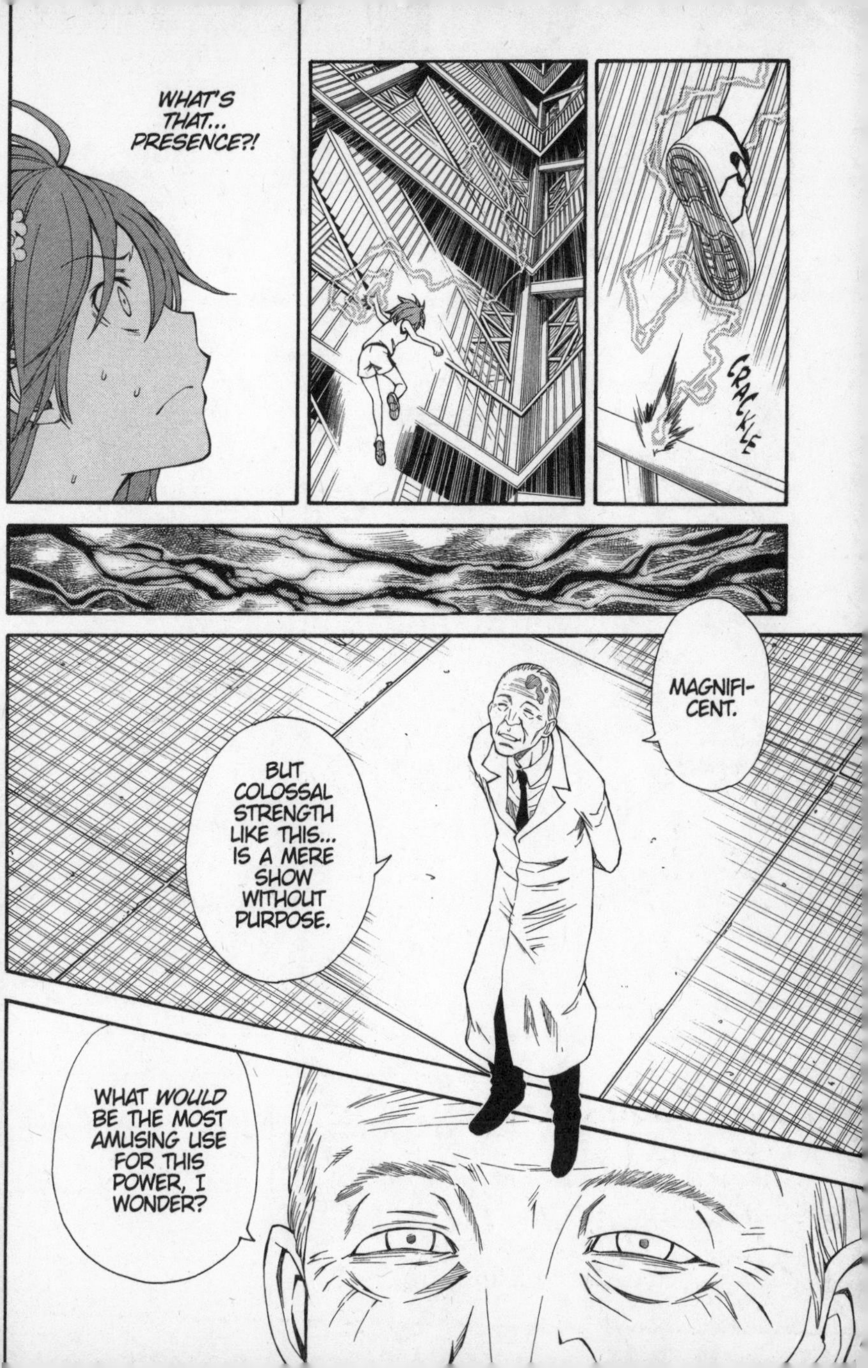
WHAT'S THAT... PRESENCE?!
CRACKLE
MAGNIFI-CENT.
BUT COLOSSAL STRENGTH LIKE THIS... IS A MERE SHOW WITHOUT PURPOSE.
WHAT WOULD BE THE MOST AMUSING USE FOR THIS POWER, I WONDER?

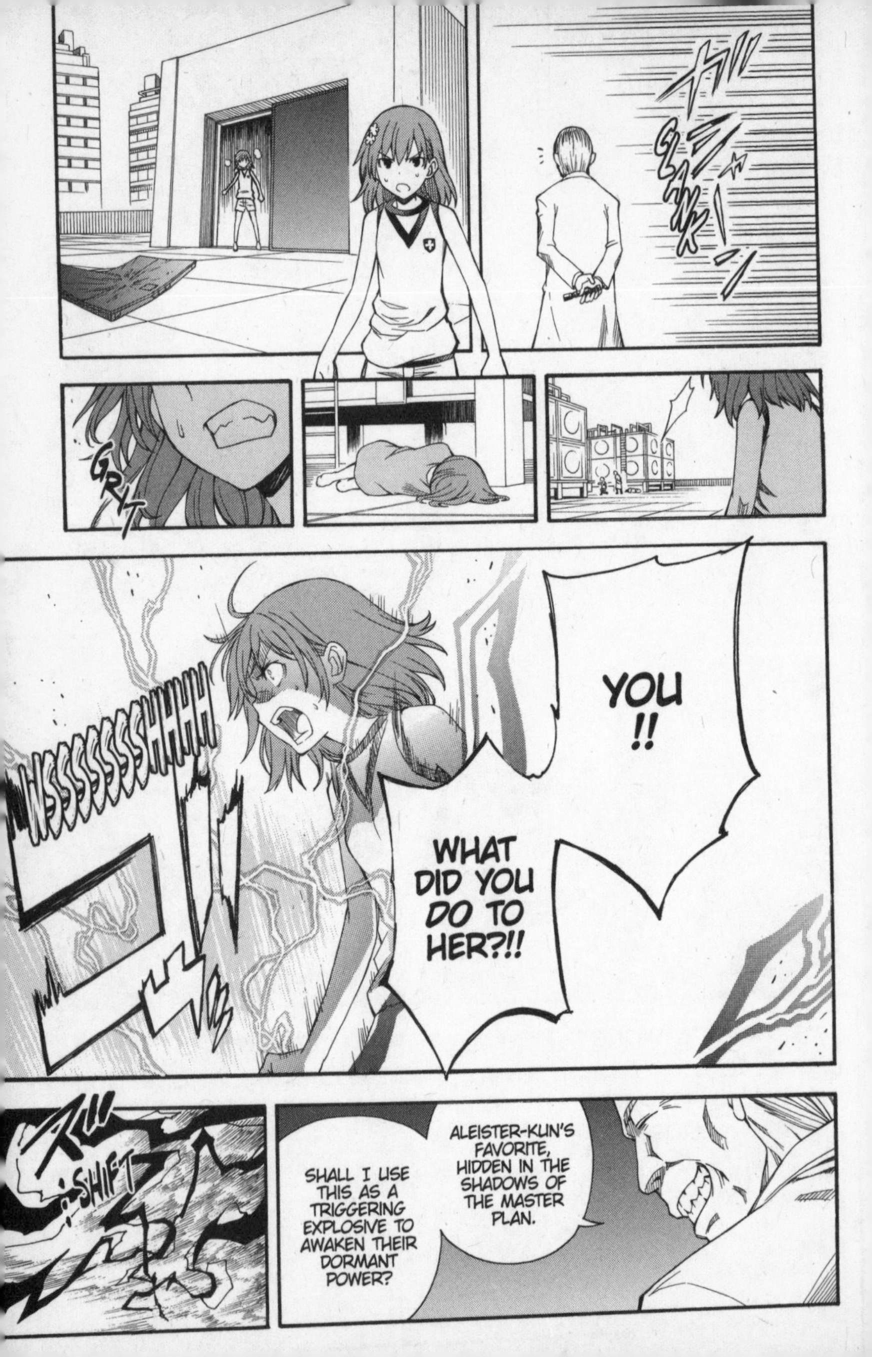
CLANK
GRIT
YOU!!
WHAT DID YOU DO TO HER?!!
WSSSSSSSSHHHH
ALEISTER-KUN'S FAVORITE, HIDDEN IN THE SHADOWS OF THE MASTER PLAN.
SHALL I USE THIS AS A TRIGGERING EXPLOSIVE TO AWAKEN THEIR DORMANT POWER?
SHIFT

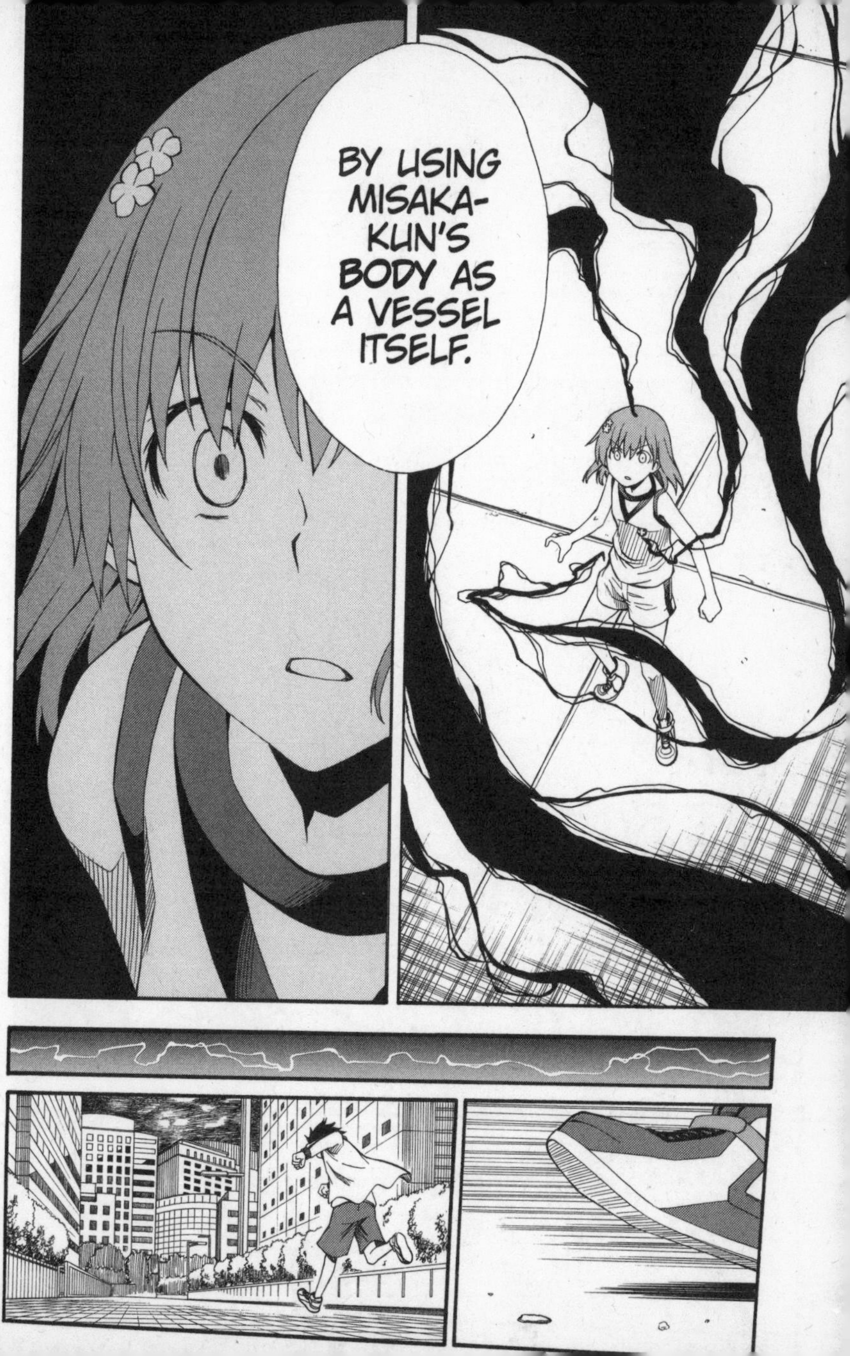
BY USING MISAKA-KUN'S BODY AS A VESSEL ITSELF.

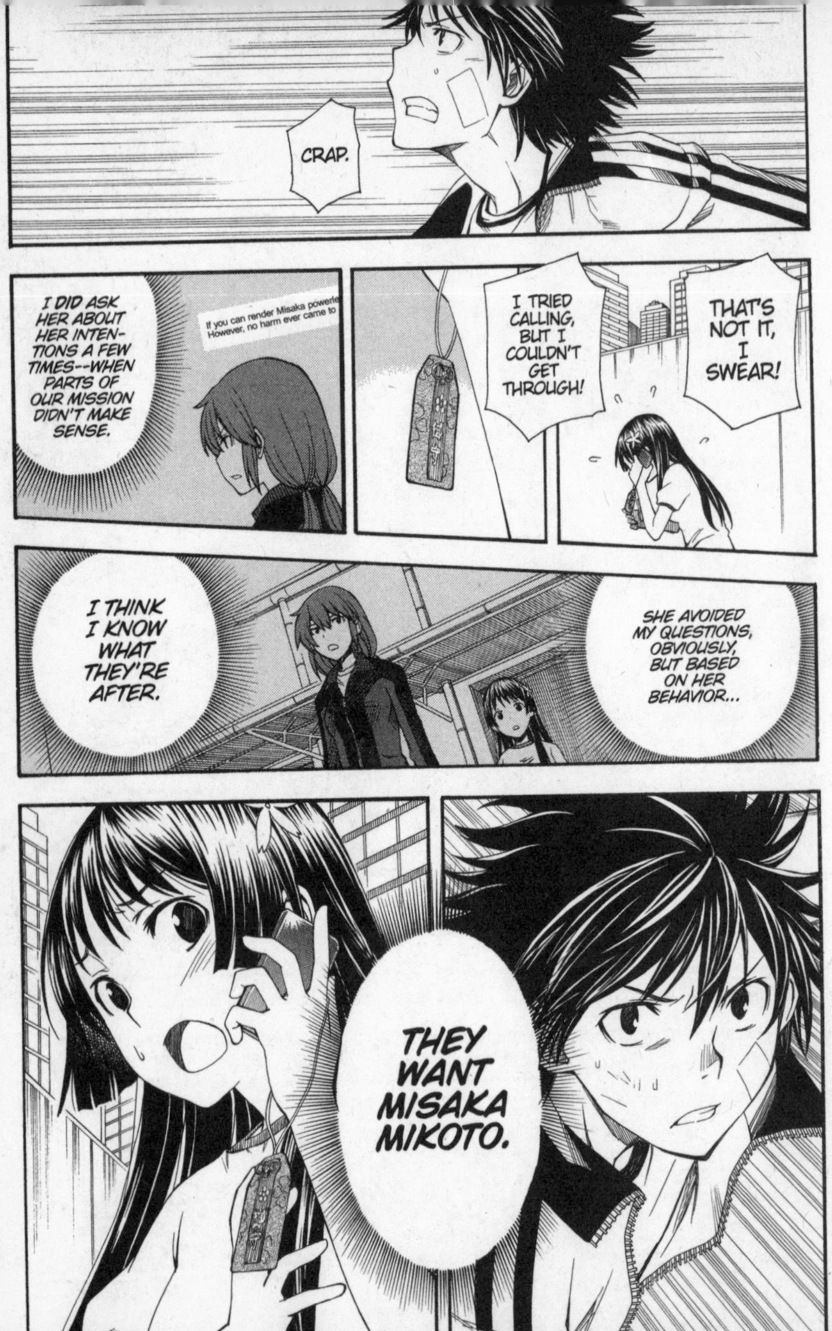

CRAP.
THAT'S NOT IT, I SWEAR!
I TRIED CALLING, BUT I COULDN'T GET THROUGH!
I DID ASK HER ABOUT HER INTENTIONS A FEW TIMES--WHEN PARTS OF OUR MISSION DIDN'T MAKE SENSE.
If you can render Misaka powerle
However, no harm ever came to
SHE AVOIDED MY QUESTIONS, OBVIOUSLY, BUT BASED ON HER BEHAVIOR...
I THINK I KNOW WHAT THEY'RE AFTER.
THEY WANT MISAKA MIKOTO.

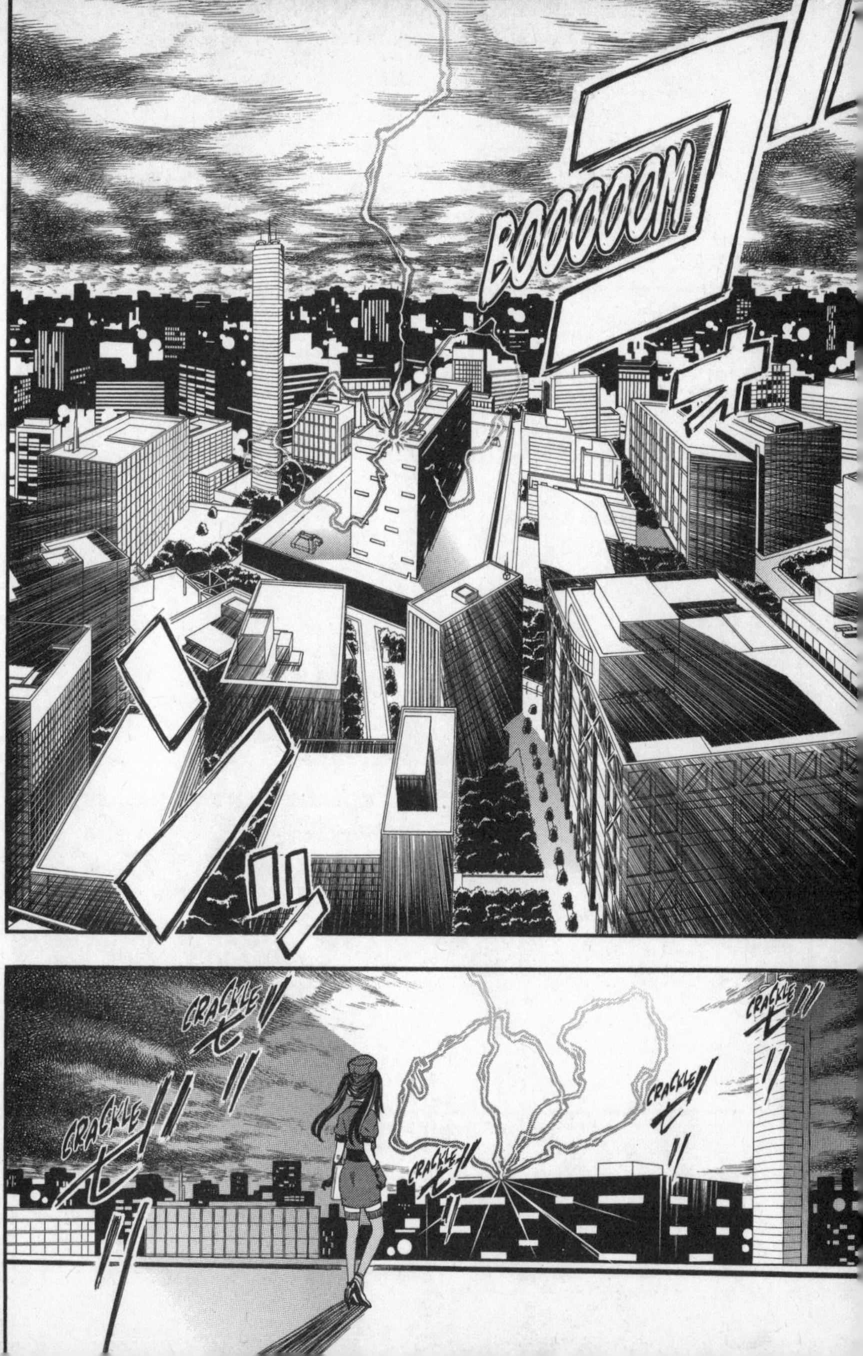
BOOOOOM
CRACKLE
CRACKLE
CRACKLE
CRACKLE
CRACKLE

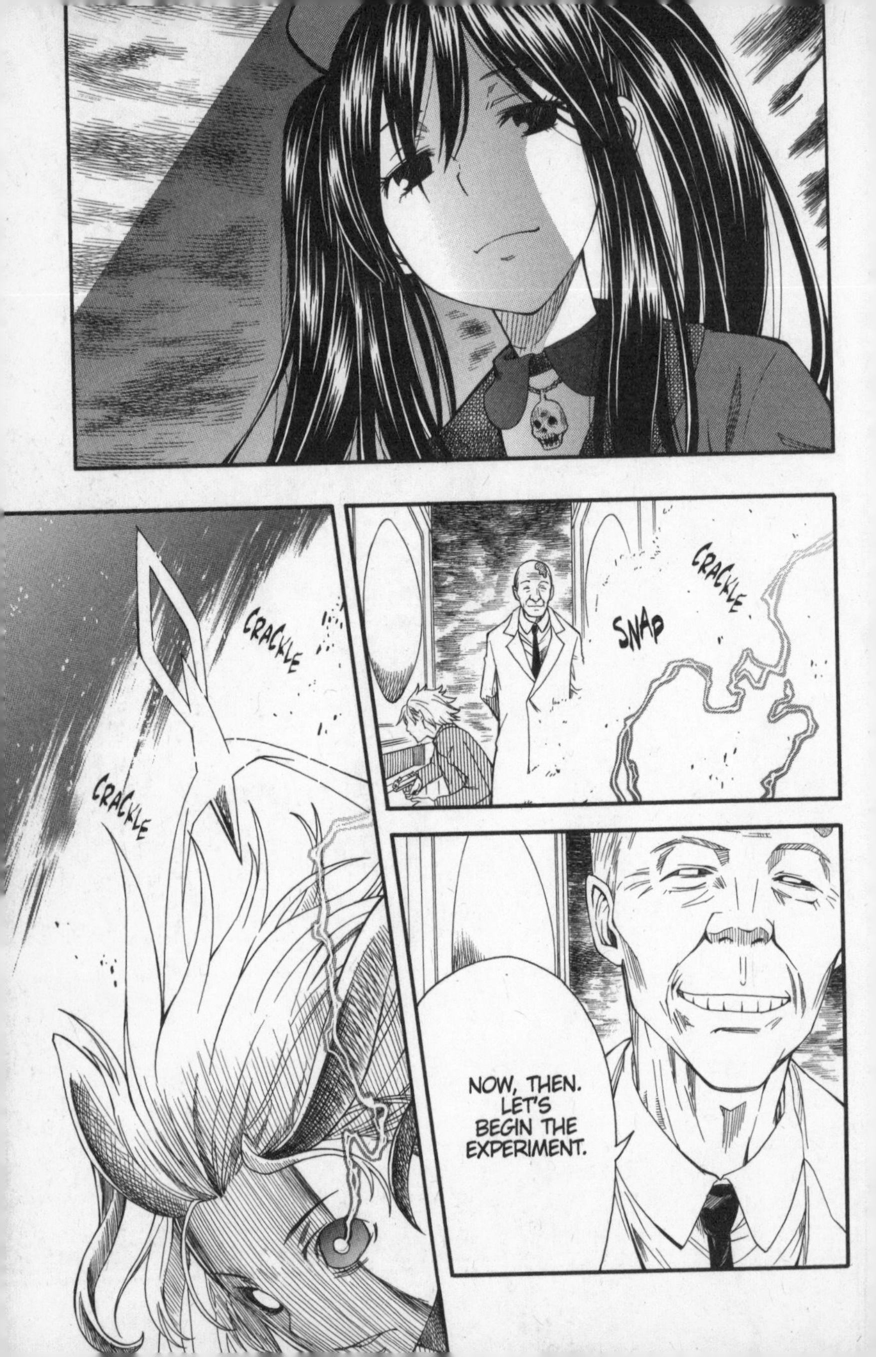
CRACKLE
SNAP
CRACKLE
CRACKLE
NOW, THEN. LET'S BEGIN THE EXPERIMENT.

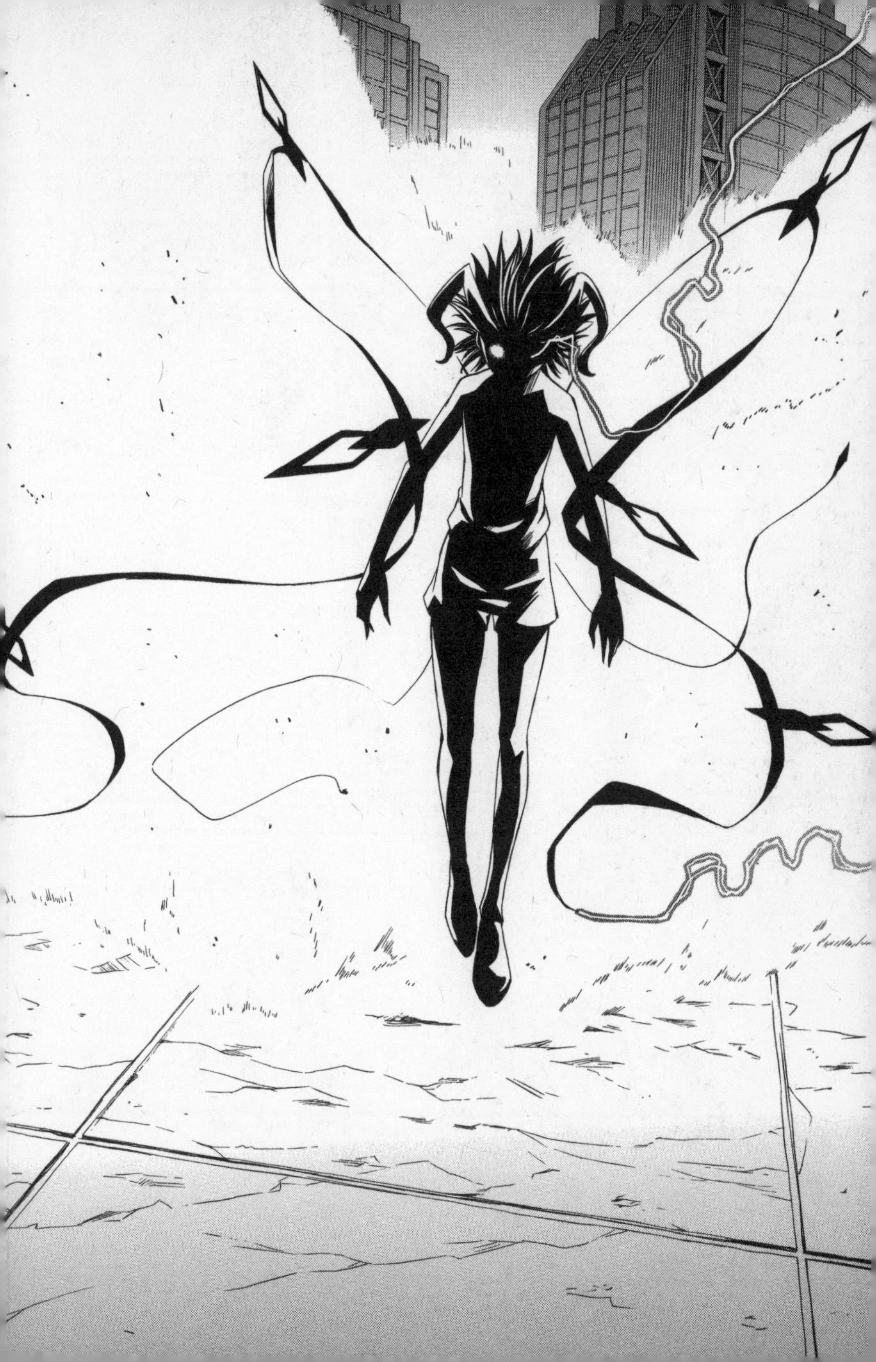

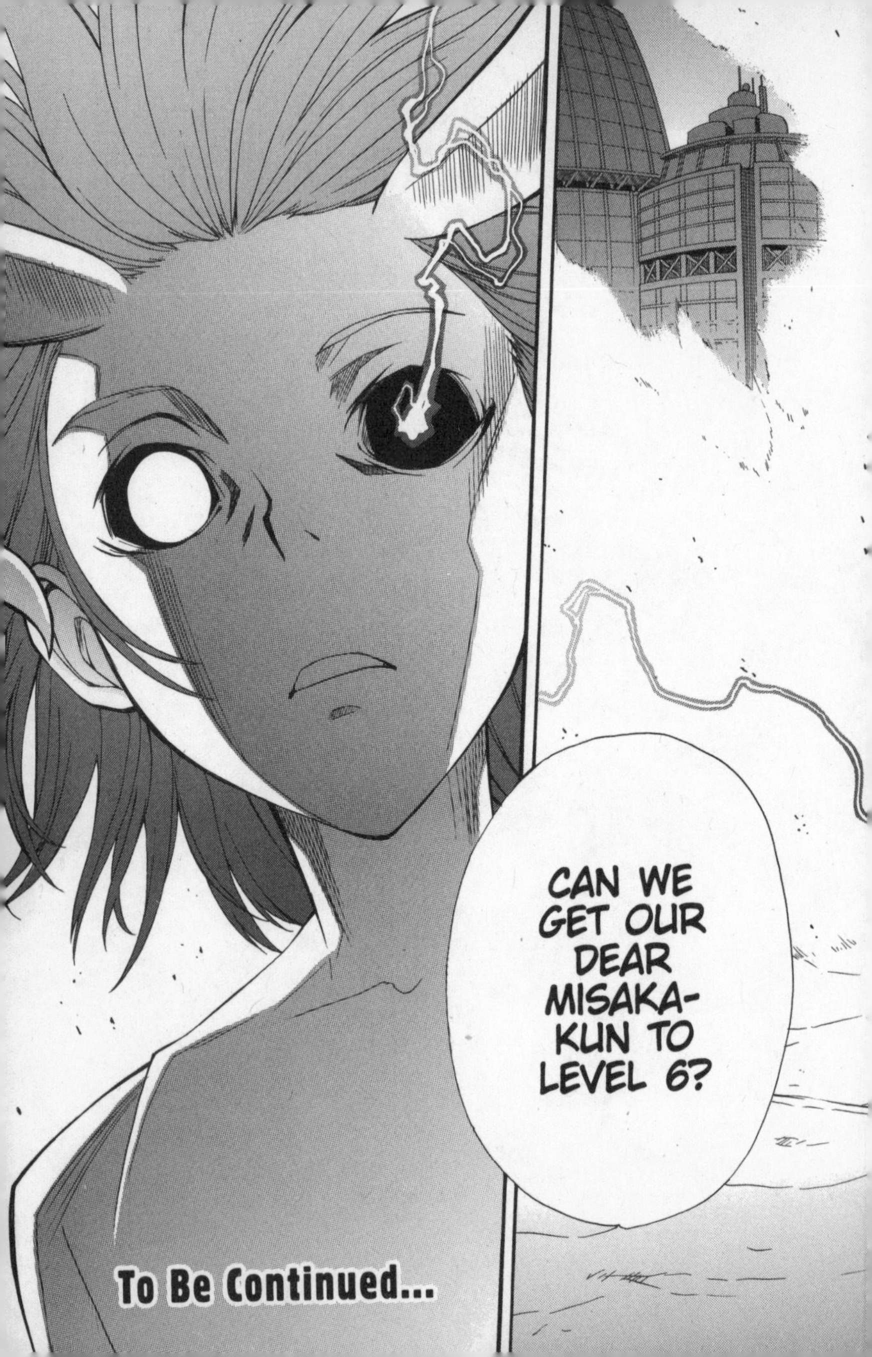
CAN WE GET OUR DEAR MISAKA-KUN TO LEVEL 6?
To Be Continued...

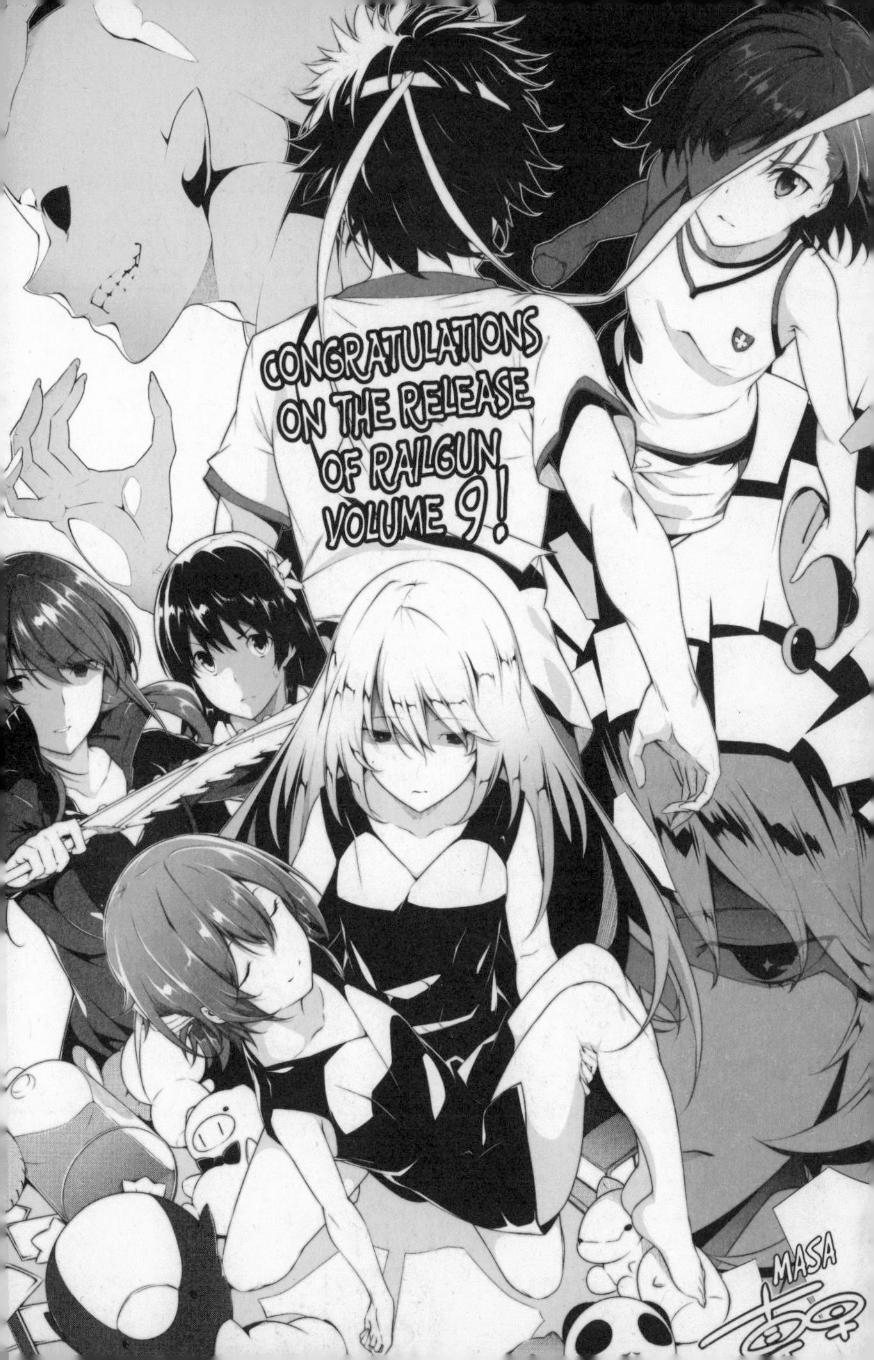
CONGRATULATIONS ON THE RELEASE OF RAILGUN VOLUME 9!
MASA

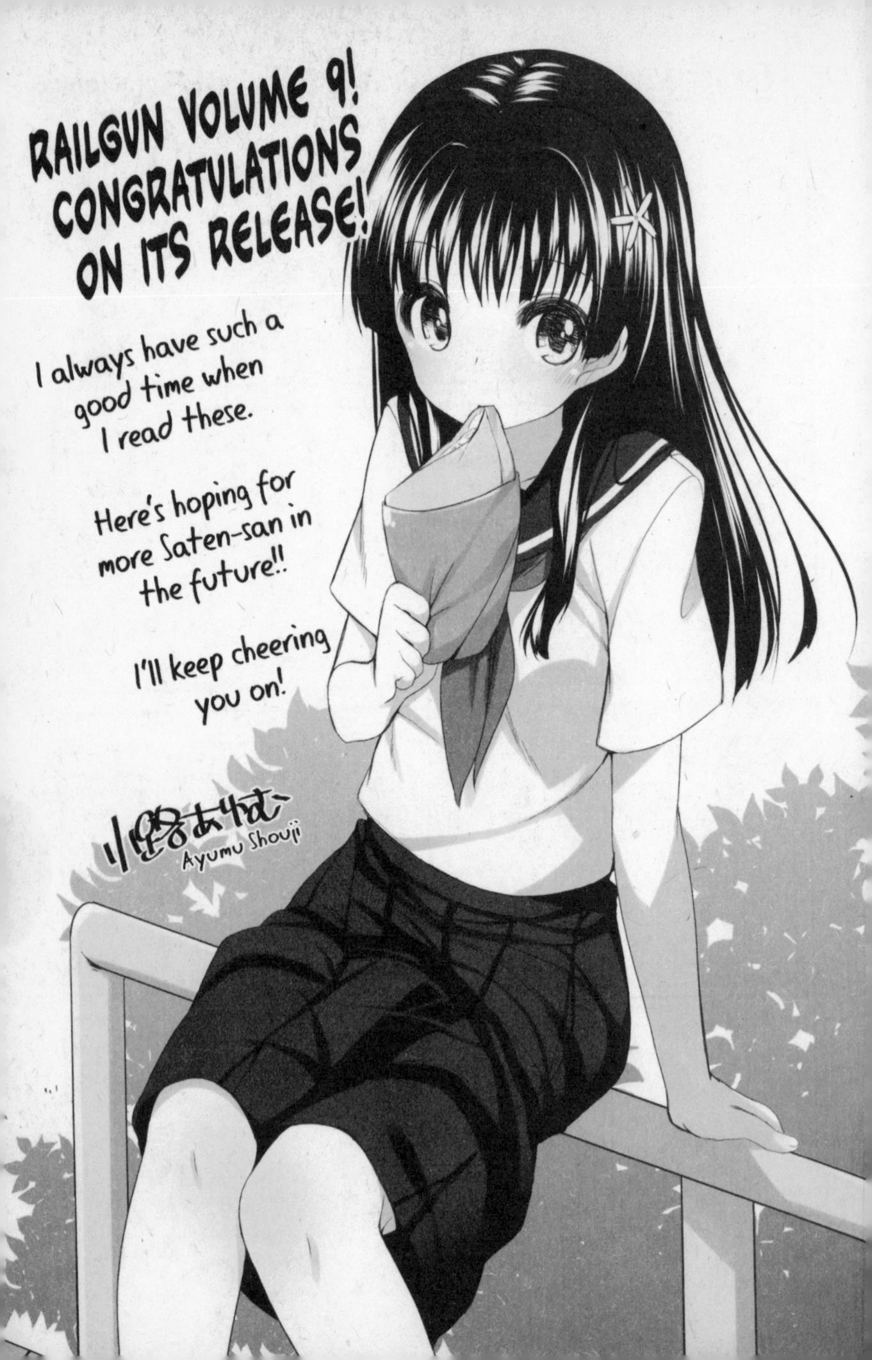
RAILGUN VOLUME 9! CONGRATULATIONS ON ITS RELEASE!
I always have such a good time when I read these.
Here's hoping for more Saten-san in the future!!
I'll keep cheering you on!
小路あゆむ
Ayumu Shouji

Don't Underestimate Such Things

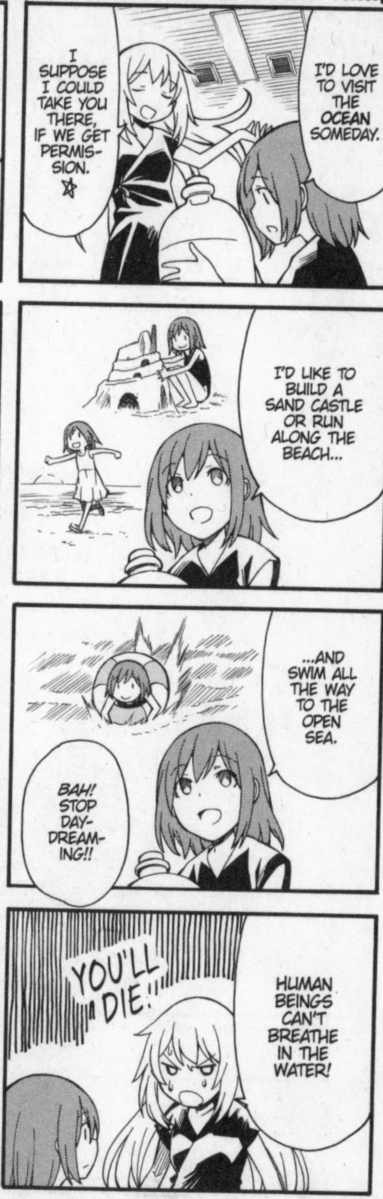
I'D LOVE TO VISIT THE OCEAN SOMEDAY.
I SUPPOSE I COULD TAKE YOU THERE, IF WE GET PERMISSION. ☆
I'D LIKE TO BUILD A SAND CASTLE OR RUN ALONG THE BEACH...
...AND SWIM ALL THE WAY TO THE OPEN SEA.
BAH! STOP DAY-DREAMING!!
HUMAN BEINGS CAN'T BREATHE IN THE WATER!
YOU'LL DIE!

I Got Some Special Training...

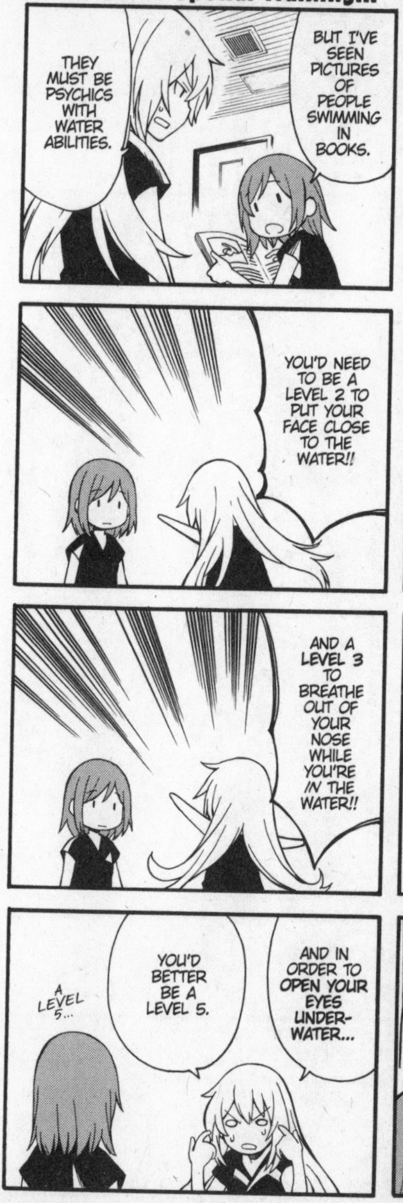
BUT I'VE SEEN PICTURES OF PEOPLE SWIMMING IN BOOKS.
THEY MUST BE PSYCHICS WITH WATER ABILITIES.
YOU'D NEED TO BE A LEVEL 2 TO PUT YOUR FACE CLOSE TO THE WATER!!
AND A LEVEL 3 TO BREATHE OUT OF YOUR NOSE WHILE YOU'RE *IN* THE WATER!!
AND IN ORDER TO OPEN YOUR EYES UNDER-WATER...
YOU'D BETTER BE A LEVEL 5.
A LEVEL 5...

A Level 5 Challenge

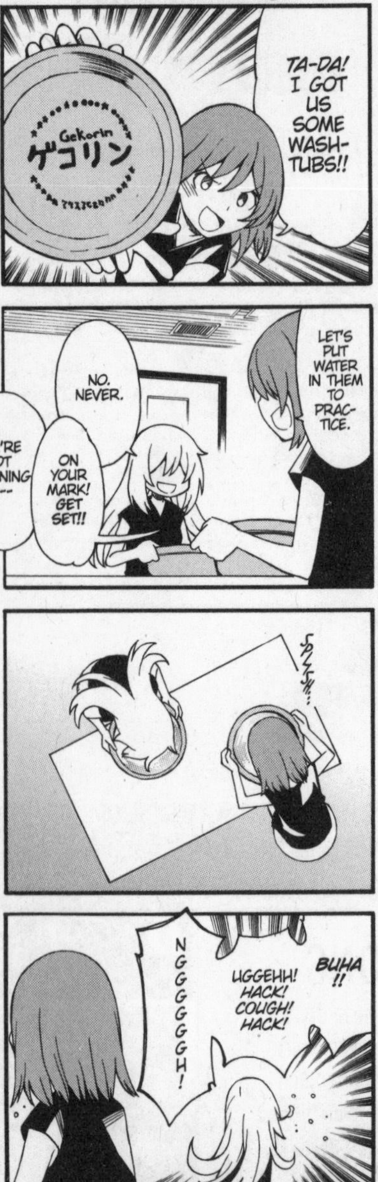
TA-DA! I GOT US SOME WASH-TUBS!!
Gekorin
ゲコリン
LET'S PUT WATER IN THEM TO PRAC-TICE.
NO. NEVER.
ON YOUR MARK! GET SET!!
YOU'RE NOT LISTENING TO--
SPLSSH...
NGGGGGGH!
BUHA!!
UGGEHH! HACK! COUGH! HACK!

Think Of The Targets

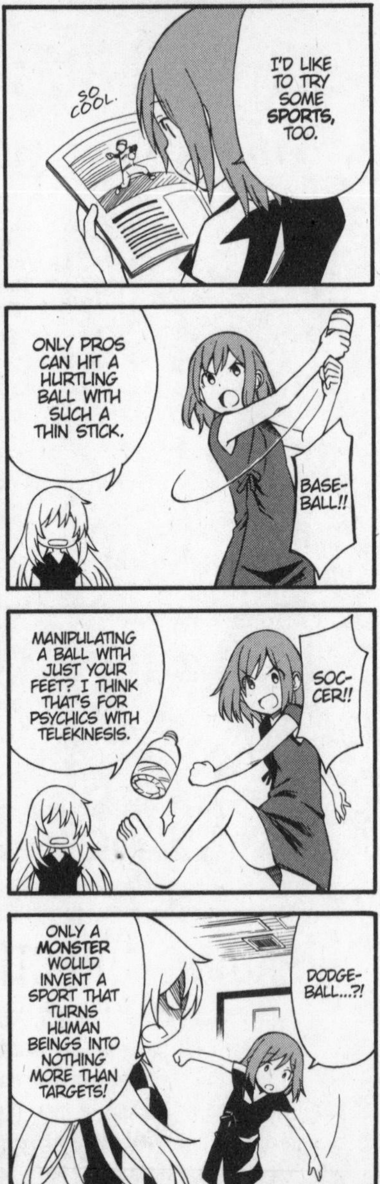
I'D LIKE TO TRY SOME SPORTS, TOO.
SO COOL.
BASE-BALL!!
ONLY PROS CAN HIT A HURTLING BALL WITH SUCH A THIN STICK.
SOC-CER!!
MANIPULATING A BALL WITH JUST YOUR FEET? I THINK THAT'S FOR PSYCHICS WITH TELEKINESIS.
DODGE-BALL...?!
ONLY A MONSTER WOULD INVENT A SPORT THAT TURNS HUMAN BEINGS INTO NOTHING MORE THAN TARGETS!

SEVEN SEAS ENTERTAINMENT PRESENTS

A Certain SCIENTIFIC Railgun

story by **KAZUMA KAMACHI** / art by **MOTOI FUYUKAWA** VOLUME 9

TRANSLATION
Nan Rymer

ADAPTATION
Maggie Danger

LETTERING
Roland Amago

LAYOUT
Bambi Eloriaga-Amago

COVER DESIGN
Nicky Lim

PROOFREADER
Shanti Whitesides
Janet Houck

MANAGING EDITOR
Adam Arnold

PUBLISHER
Jason DeAngelis

A CERTAIN SCIENTIFIC RAILGUN VOL. 9

Edited by ASCII MEDIA WORKS.
First published in Japan in 2013 by KADOKAWA CORPORATION.

ISBN: 978-1-937867-79-9

Printed in Canada

First Printing: April 2014

10 9 8 7 6 5 4 3 2 1

FOLLOW US ONLINE: ***www.gomanga.com***

READING D

This book reads from *righ*
If this is your first time r
reading from the top right
take it from there. If you g just follow the
numbered diagram here. It may seem backwards at
first, but you'll get the hang of it! Have fun!!

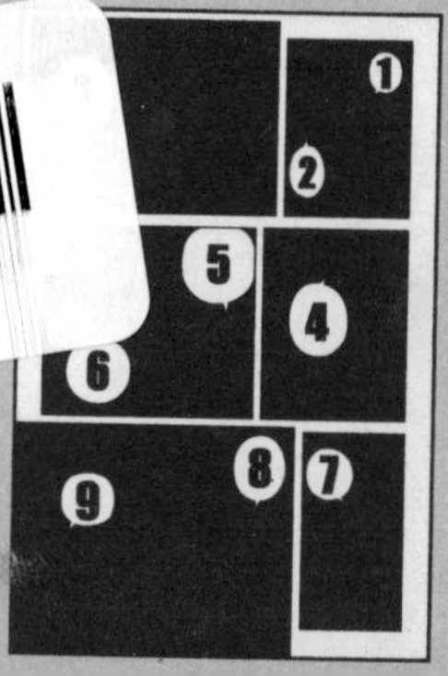
1
2
5
4
6
8
7
9